Anatomy of Inculturation

Transforming the Church in Africa

Laurenti Magesa

ORBIS BOOKS
Maryknoll, New York 10545

Founded in 1970, Orbis Books endeavors to publish works that enlighten the mind, nourish the spirit, and challenge the conscience. The publishing arm of the Maryknoll Fathers and Brothers, Orbis seeks to explore the global dimensions of the Christian faith and mission, to invite dialogue with diverse cultures and religious traditions, and to serve the cause of reconciliation and peace. The books published reflect the views of their authors and do not represent the official position of the Maryknoll Society. To learn more about Maryknoll and Orbis Books, please visit our website at www.maryknoll.org.

Library of Congress Cataloging-in-Publication Data

Magesa, Laurenti, 1946–
    Anatomy of inculturation : transforming the church in Africa / Laurenti Magesa.
        p. cm.
Includes bibliographical references and index.
    ISBN 1-57075-529-9 (pbk.)
    1. Christianity and culture—Africa.   2. Christianity—Africa.   I. Title.
    BR1360 .M34 2004
    261'.09676--dc22

                                                    2003023637

To the African Christian Churches
in the Diversity of Their Localities:

to Keep on Developing
in Faith, Hope, and Love

"Audi partem alteram"
("Hear the other side")
St. Augustine of Hippo
De Duabus Animabus, xiv, ii

Contents

Acknowledgments

Many people have contributed to making this book a reality. At the risk of overlooking others I must list some. Stephen N. Nyaga of Kenyatta University, Nairobi, Evaristi Magoti of the University of Dar es Salaam, and Agnes Nabbosa of Uganda Martyrs University, Kampala, assisted me with the research that forms the first part of this book. Each investigated how the Christian faith and religion have been received and are lived in their countries. They analyzed and compiled the data, and at various stages discussed it with me. I thank them for their dedication to the project and for the enlightenment they have brought to understanding the reality of inculturation in Kenya, Tanzania, and Uganda.

The research for this first part of the book benefited from a grant from the Central Mission Commissariat of the organization Adviescommissie Missionaire Activiteiten (AMA)-Africa Desk in the Netherlands. In particular I wish to thank in this regard Kees Ton, who facilitated the grant, thus making possible the groundwork for this study. The same organization also gave me a computer, which made the writing of this study much easier than it otherwise would have been. Ype Schaaf facilitated this request and I am also grateful to him.

Most of the writing was done during a three-year sabbatical period from pastoral ministry in Ingri-Bukama Parish, graciously granted by Bishop Justin Samba of the Diocese of Musoma, Tanzania. I thank the bishop for the leave to be away from the diocese for this purpose. I first discussed (and in some cases tested) many of the points that appear in Part Three with my parishioners at Ingri-Bukama. They had mixed reactions toward many of these ideas. This gave me insights into the intricate and complicated nature of the relationship obtained between popular and academic officials regarding inculturation. Most of all, it pushed me to reflect more on the dynamics of inculturation and to try to articulate it as clearly as I could for myself as much as for the churches in Africa. As far as the result is concerned, let me say with the author of the Second Book of Maccabees (15:38): "If it is well written and to the point, that is what I wanted; if it is poorly done and mediocre, that is the best I could do."

Most of the book was written while I was serving as associate pastor at the Church of the Immaculate Conception in Glenville, New York. I do not think I could have found a more congenial place to reflect and write. I thank Bishop Howard Hubbard of the Catholic Diocese of Albany and Father Edward Deimeke, Advocate for Priests, for receiving me into the diocese. I thank Father Thomas Connery for being a most gracious pastor and opening up his library for my use. Sections of Chapter 13 were first published in the Dutch missiological journal *Wereld et Zending*. I thank the editor for permission to include them here.

The Immaculate Conception community was most welcoming, an excellent example, in my view, of what a Christian community should be. Diane Bigos, Kathy Friscic, and Patricia Schorr, secretaries at the parish, were most helpful in every way, whenever I needed their help. Sister Betty Hunter, pastoral associate, introduced me to a new form of pastoral ministry with people in pain and suffering. Brian Farrell and Joe Frank of the maintenance staff and I became fast friends.

Let me mention a few special friends among the parishioners at Immaculate Conception. The families of Mr. and Mrs. Charles "Joe" Wilder, Mr. and Mrs. Trevor Schneider, Charles and Mary-Lou Moskov, Nancy A. Rochford, Teresa Kruszona, Joan Milovec, and Marguerite Lussier became everything from tennis partners, frequent dinner hosts, chauffeurs, and driving instructors. Both Mrs. Lussier and Mrs. Schneider read the first draft of the manuscript and made important suggestions for its improvement. Finally, I must thank Susan Perry, my editor at Orbis Books. As usual, she made possible the publication of this book in a remarkably short time.

Introduction

Some processes in the life of human beings, and in nature more generally, follow an innate and necessary course of evolution. How do various creatures adapt to the different kinds of environment that form their habitats? How do human beings as individuals and societies confront change and situate themselves in the ever-shifting natural and social situations that form their everyday existence? How do they cope with their changing physical and social surroundings from infancy to adulthood and through old age? When all is said and done, this happens within the "natural order" of creation, whether or not we are conscious of it.

It may be possible consciously and deliberately to control these processes of adaptation and acculturation to some degree; in fact, it is often necessary to do so in order to give individuals or societies a sense of direction and purpose in life or to safeguard nature. Of all creatures in existence, this is the special responsibility of human beings. The name we often give to the result of this deliberate intervention by human beings in the natural process of evolution is "development," that is to say, change shaped by men and women in certain directions. Genuine development is usually intended for the good of all of humanity and the cosmos, or a section of it.

However, human history has taught us that not all development is good or positive. In order for it to take place in a desirable and beneficial way, it is necessary, first of all, to appreciate the inevitability of the prior, "instinctive" process of evolution for all creatures—in one direction or another. As Christians we might even say that this innate movement is part of the divine plan of creation or, even more precisely, that it is part of the divine *creative* plan. As such, it must be neither completely nor permanently sidelined.

The Christian faith and its institutional expression—the church—are no exception to this rule. Since the beginning, they have gone through and continue to go through this natural evolution and, as various forces intervene, change takes place, for better or for worse. Whatever the case, in reference to the history of Christian mission the question is: What happens when the faith and the church are brought from one geographical and/or social situation to another? What happens when they are made to move across peoples and cultures? In other words, in their long history of evangelizing peoples, how have the Christian faith and church inserted themselves in different socio-cultural and economic-political situations?

The question is relevant beyond Christianity to other faiths too, both internally within each particular faith in different environments and externally as a faith and its institutions encounter other faiths and their institutions. These encounters always imply various degrees of transformation for all sides concerned, sometimes nearly imperceptible and at other times quite obvious. Christianity, an aggressively proselytizing movement, demands an immediate change in both perception and action as people are "converted," as they receive the "gospel" preached in their world. However, this change occurs in its own way and at its own pace, not necessarily in the way or at the pace desired by the evangelizers.

We must see this as a natural, continuous, and inevitable evolution in the reception of the faith, an evolution that cannot and must not be sidelined. Reception cannot occur except according to the perception of the receiver. It happened in this way at the beginning of Christianity; it happened in this way with each of us; it continues to happen in the same way in the African churches. It is part of God's creative plan, then as now. The vast majority of African Christians today, just like their counterparts in Jerusalem in 70 C.E. or in Rome in the fifth century, or anywhere or anytime, for that matter, simply live this process. They do not reflect upon it or articulate it in any logical manner.

This fact is now widely acknowledged and accepted *in theory* by many leaders in the Christian churches, and, indeed, in the last few decades it has not been relegated to the work of theologians or historians of Christianity alone, as was the case previously. Rather, it has been articulated in many different ways. In the last three decades or so, however, many observers of and participants in the African church scene—and here we have in mind particularly the Catholic Church—have been and are aware of ambivalent and almost contradictory reactions and attitudes toward this process of incarnation-inculturation among Christian church leaders. Some ignore the reality by pretending it does not exist, while others seem determined to wipe it away as an aberration!

Christians who promote the popular evolution of faith perception and life in Africa as an essentially valid, even if not perfect, appropriation of Christianity are a minority. They constitute primarily people who are academics and who are not in formal leadership positions in the churches. Moreover, some church leaders have been known to accuse them of heresy or treachery against the church. The situation is painful. It contradicts the divine creative plan for faith in Christ we have alluded to above. In this sense, as Gamaliel, "a teacher of the law, respected by all the people," warned almost two thousand years ago, it cannot succeed (see Acts 5:33–42). It also slows down the "enrooting" of the church in the African continent, causing the church and the faith to remain, as someone put it, a "potted plant," forever living in foreign soil. This belittles the dignity and self-respect of the African people as children of God.

This book intends to show how the process we refer to as the primary manifestation or "language" of the incarnation of Christianity is part and parcel of the Christian reality, how it has been with the church since the beginning, and indeed how it permeates the entire Judeo-Christian tradition. Understanding the process should be seen as a necessary step in the journey of understanding the church. This book wishes to emphasize the importance and necessity of consciously recognizing this process of church incarnation for Africa.

In a sense, the work is a sequel to my previous book, *African Religion: The Moral Traditions of Abundant Life* (Magesa 1997). In the preface to that book, which explored the religious traditions of the African peoples, I said that I had no intention at that stage of relating African religious values and insights to the Christian tradition. I wrote, "Where we go on from here in terms of 'critical correlation' of the two is another book" (p. xiv). In some ways, this is that book. It is my attempt to correlate critically the religiosity original to the African peoples with the Christian forms of spirituality they have received through the centuries, ever since the missionary movement introduced Christianity to the continent.

The book approaches this task in three parts. Part One traces the process of religious-cultural symbiosis—or we might term this "mutual enrichment" or "mutual illumination"—among different groups of people in three countries of eastern Africa: Kenya, Tanzania, and Uganda. What is the contemporary state of Christian faith reception in the region and, by extension, throughout the continent? This section offers some empirical facts about the process.

Part Two looks at the Bible and at subsequent developments within Christianity. The Bible also describes the reality of religious-cultural symbiosis, a process that is woven throughout the Old Testament as theological history. The Old Testament is essentially a story of a small band of people—a people who obviously knew much suffering through conquest by the surrounding tribes. Through the power of a remarkable spiritual determination to forge cohesion and carve a distinctive identity, they succeeded in liberating themselves. They experienced this power as the children of Yahweh, their only God, who was there almost exclusively for them and was personalized as such. They experienced God primarily through the lens of communal identity, so that whatever did not serve this goal was either eliminated from the story or made subservient to it. This is why it is proper to describe the Old Testament as a history "of sorts," because its ulterior motivation is obviously theological rather than historical.

At a different time, centuries later, in different circumstances and in slightly different ways, the Christian movement continued the process of incarnation. It continued to be realized and expressed in and through contemporary cultures, taking the life and message of Jesus Christ as the focal point. Some years after the death of Jesus, rational and systematic reflection began to explore the role of Jesus in the final destiny of humankind. As Christianity spread throughout the Roman Empire—which it did surprisingly fast—the reflection became even more intense and widespread; it developed in proportion to the increasing symbiosis between this new faith and the various cultures constituting the sprawling empire.

Part Three considers the future of the process or, rather, the process of the future of inculturation in Africa. What are some orientations in liturgy and in pastoral practice? If anything, the lesson here is that the church must learn to be flexible. It should not fear inculturation as an attack against the integrity of the faith.

This is only a start. In this study we have drawn much from what has already been achieved in various parts of Africa. In a certain sense it will always be only a beginning, although a very significant one, for Christians because such is the nature of the inculturation process; it is always in flux. This is because human beings, whom the church is called to serve, are always in flux in their environments. Change is always taking place. In a manner of speaking, a book on inculturation is "out of date" by the time it is printed. It remains useful only as a sign or rather a road map, pointing to where we have been and where we should go. This is the spirit with which I present this book to those interested in the development of the African churches.

Part One

THE CURRENT EXPERIENCE

Let the nobles come from Egypt;
   let Ethiopia extend its hands to God.
                    (Ps. 68:31)

From the Christian theological perspective, inculturation is understood to be the process whereby the faith already embodied in one culture encounters another culture. In this encounter, the faith becomes part and parcel of this new culture. It fuses with the new culture and simultaneously transforms it into a novel religious-cultural reality. In practical terms, this process involves the inter-action of mutual critique and affirmation. It entails acceptance or rejection of thought forms, symbolic and linguistic expressions and attitudes between the faith-cultures in question. This process is usually primarily instinctive and pop-ular, without much systematic planning and arrangement to it. But it can also be promoted and enhanced by institutional study and direction.

Previous studies of this process have been largely theoretical, rarely ben-efiting from evidence gathered from empirical research. They have relied mainly on intellectual imagination about how inculturation needs to pro-ceed and, to my mind, have not been grounded enough in the reality of how inculturation has been, and is, taking place in a given area. Here is where this book's approach is different. I wish first of all to lay out the phenome-nological foundations of the process that cross-cultural contact in Chris-tianity takes by making a case study of a concrete region. In other words, I want to describe, by way of existential examples, the forms of reception that the Christian faith has taken in Africa. How is it experienced and lived in practice among particular Christian communities there?

This procedure is, I believe, desirable and, at this point in time, necessary. This is because actual lived experience of belief is one of the aspects of reli-gion that usually precede any kind of sustained, rational reflection. Expressions of religious belief do not exist by themselves in isolation from a given human cultural environment; they begin existence in a community, and are always an aspect of a living community. As such, religious belief and its expressions are constantly nurtured by the community's language, sym-bols, attitudes towards life, and so on. In a word, they are cultivated by cul-ture. The same thing is true of Christianity, which entails the spiritual and practical expression of faith in Jesus Christ.

Consequently, a good analysis of the process of the lived experience of Christian belief anywhere, but especially in a new cultural environment, entails one necessary task. It requires a demonstrative description and articulation of the Christian faith experience in the life of the particular people as influenced by their political and economic conditions. It needs an examination of their existing religious, intellectual, and other conditions. In short, it calls for an understanding of their new—or renewed—vision of the spiritual, since this has now become their new religious culture (see Amaladoss 1995).

One thing must be made clear from the beginning in relation to the process of inculturation. It must always be borne in mind that, strictly speaking, Christian proclaimers of the gospel anywhere do not preach "the Gospel," or "the message of Christ," or "revelation," or whatever other expression may be used to explain this task. The gospel as proclaimed is not a disembodied reality, a pure emanation from God. It is essentially a cultural reality. What Christian missionaries do, rather, is to transmit to their listeners their own understanding of the gospel. They bequeath to their converts the interpretation of Christ's message as it has developed in their own communities. But these communities are formed by given circumstances through time. These in turn influence their interpretation of the message.

With regard to evangelization or evangelism, this is an understanding that is necessarily situated within the missionaries' original cultural experience. And, in order for missionaries to be understood by their hosts, especially people from a different culture, they must take into account key issues. These consist in at least some of the religious ideas and practices of the new culture. Depending on the strength and prominence of the host culture, this effort takes place either deliberately or unconsciously. In any case, it does take place. It is a necessary process of human communication.

No Christian mission, no gospel proclamation can happen, let alone succeed to any noticeable extent, without this interaction of human communication. In the process of communication, Rufus M. Jones has pointed out, many-sided "transformations," "adjustments," and even "compromises" imperceptibly take place at various levels for both parties. As a rule, the missionaries may not consciously realize that such changes are taking or have taken place. They may also refuse to recognize them. Nevertheless, "sooner or later," Jones asserts, "the new converts will be found to have a different outlook, atmosphere, interpretation, slant of thought and tinge of feeling, as well as an altered set of reactions and practices, from those of the person who first proclaimed the message to them" (Jones 1924:18). We might add that this is as inevitable in the case of the new converts as it was in the case of the missionaries themselves when they heard the Gospel the first time. The new converts, likewise, soon forget this fact once they in turn become evangelizers.

Jones is right. With regard to evangelization, "The habits of thought and action of a people—what we call 'the psychological climate,' or 'apperception mass'—together with their characteristic emotional tones, work powerfully, though silently, to alter and reshape whatever is transmitted." As the old philosophical adage has it, whatever is received is received according to the position of the receiver. It always involves a degree of risk, as Jones has noted, to impart new truths to a people "with its own peculiar habits of mind." Obviously, as he explains correctly, "some of the most vital features [of the message imparted] may be actually lost, while almost every aspect may be transformed. It [the message] will never be the 'same' after it has been assimilated and interpreted through a new group of minds" (Jones 1924:18).

Yet this is actually not such a great risk after all. It does not necessarily lead to peril. On the contrary, it is part of the normal process of intercultural communication. Without it there may be imposition but not communication. In Christian terms, imposition has no cultural roots; communication makes the message part of the culture.

The first part of this book intends to illustrate this fact. It consists of three studies. They are the result of recent research on the practice of Christianity in East Africa. They seek to show what Jones has described as people's reaction to the Gospel message, brought to them "dressed" in a different culture. How have they received it in the context of their spiritual, psychological and physical surroundings?

The research was conducted in Kenya, Tanzania and Uganda. I am convinced, however, that the process that the results indicate is paradigmatic for other regions of Africa and the world. At any rate, we will be able to see from these descriptions how people in this region have received Christianity not only theoretically, but above all how they have appropriated and actually practiced it. This section investigates religious habits of thought and action of East African Christians. How have they "incarnated" the Christian message? How have they made it part and parcel of their own human environment?

A remark attributed to one rather elderly Christian from West Africa illustrates what we are about here. Asked why the people in his area did not adhere strictly to the teachings given them by the missionary church officials, he smiled and replied, "We eat everything they give us, but we digest it in our own way." The "digestion" in the remark refers to the process of the appropriation of the faith. Food cannot be assimilated by the body without being digested; the Christian faith cannot be assimilated by people of a given culture unless it is digested by that culture. The process of assimilation in either case is particular because the body in the case of the individual and the environment in the case of a culture are particular.

How has the Christian faith been received and concretely lived by a given cultural entity? How have cultural groups appropriated and perceived it in relation to their own spirituality and practical expectations? This is, for the purposes of this book, the primary and basic sense of the process we have now come to generally refer to as "inculturation." The expression is perhaps rather static, and some have considered it somewhat pedantic. A few scholars have argued that it does not capture very well the meaning and intent of the dynamics of Christian cross-cultural communication. In the process of the debate, other scholars have suggested different terms and notions such as Africanization, Christianization, contextualization or inter-culturation to replace it. These concepts have failed to gain the wide-spread acceptance and currency that, for better or worse, the term incultur-ation has. For this reason, I have opted to retain the use of this more familiar expression, its shortcomings notwithstanding.

The description of actual, existing Christianity that is presented in this section will provide a basis for looking in the section that follows at the sweep of the history of Christianity on inculturation. That will be done in a more academic way that will hopefully help us to draw more general, reli-able and meaningful theoretical conclusions.

A NOTE ON THE RESEARCH PROCEDURE

The first three chapters of this book represent the conclusions of research conducted simultaneously in 2002 in Kenya, Tanzania, and Uganda to inquire about the state of inculturation—or African identity—of the Christian churches in these East African territories.

The aim of the survey was not primarily to test an hypothesis or to obtain specific, scientifically objective comparisons between the churches or Christian groups in these territories; it was rather to note and record sub-jective feelings and views on how, up to now, these churches have been able to attain an identity that the majority of Christians can, and perhaps do, identify as truly African.

Thus the research had a theological-pastoral purpose, and the question-naire administered for oral or written responses was designed with these objectives in mind:

- to evaluate the general understanding of "inculturation" among Christians;
- to assess the extent to which the official church facilitates inculturation;
- to learn to what degree the ordinary faithful are involved in inculturation;
- to uncover any constraints against inculturation;
- to note suitable strategies that may facilitate the process of inculturation.

In Kenya and Uganda 207 people were interviewed altogether and in Tanzania 80 people were individually interviewed. In Tanzania, 20 partici-pant observation sessions took place in churches and small Christian com-munities; of the 50 written questionnaires administered there, 15, or 30 percent were returned completed.

Whereas the main locations of the research in Kenya and Tanzania were the cities of Nairobi and Dar es Salaam respectively, in Uganda most of the research was undertaken in western and central Uganda rather than in the city of Kampala.

Researchers approached both church leaders and regular church-attend-ing Christians ranging from 12 to 80 years of age in the Roman Catholic Church (all three territories), the African Independent Pentecostal Church of Africa, and the Akorino Church (Kenya), the African Inland Church, Assemblies of God Church, Full Gospel Church of Christ, and the Marian Faith Healing Movement (Tanzania).

1

Inculturation in Kenya

Is It Happening?

RESEARCH PROCEDURE

The following represents the results of field research carried out among members of some Christian churches in Kenya—clergy and ordinary Christians. The respondents were selected from among members of the Catholic Church and the African Independent Pentecostal Church of Africa (AIPCA). The latter is one of the many African Instituted Churches (AIC) in the country. Views from some members of the mainly Kikuyu-dominated Akorino Church, many of whom belonged formerly to the AIPCA, were also sought and are included here. The population of respondents was multi-ethnic and composed of people living in both rural and urban areas. For each respondent who sought anonymity, only one name or a pseudonym is used.

The respondents represented three major categories of people:

(i) A Catholic bishop, priests, nuns and catechists, here referred to as church officials;
(ii) Catholic lay women, men and youth, often grouped together in this report as ordinary Christians; and
(iii) Officials and ordinary members of AIPCA.

Altogether we interviewed one hundred persons. We conducted face to face interviews with some, focus group discussions with others, while still others opted to respond to an administered questionnaire. During the interview sessions, the respondents reacted to issues covered in a prepared questionnaire. Some, however, spontaneously described their experience of different church ceremonies and rituals and their attitude toward various religious objects and symbols which accompany worship activities in their congregations.

Research for the material on Kenya was undertaken by Stephen N. Nyaga of the Department of Religious Studies of Kenyatta University, Nairobi, Kenya. The use of first-person pronouns reflects the observations of the researcher rather than myself. While I did not change the essential findings, I did adjust the language and style of the research report to give a consistency to the style of the book.

CONCEPTUALIZATIONS OF INCULTURATION
IN THE CATHOLIC CHURCH

All Catholic Church officials seemed to have the same perception of the meaning of the term inculturation as well as its process. Essentially, they understood inculturation as a programmatic endeavor, necessitated by the meeting of two (cultural) realities in time and space. They insisted that, for Catholic Christianity in Africa, inculturation implies integrating Christian doctrines with "useful" African traditional cultural values and a modern way of life. According to them, the goal of inculturation is to make Christianity a religion that is acceptable to all.

This group of respondents insisted repeatedly that inculturation means the effort to bring together "various aspects of our indigenous culture into the Christian context" so as to construct "a more authentic Christian life." Several of them referred to the Bible's place and role in the process. From their point of view, inculturation calls for the "fusion" of African cultures with biblical teaching, without sacrificing the basic values or principles of either.

Cultural awareness and pride, on the one hand, and Christianity's potential contribution to the growth of African culture, on the other, were cited almost equally as the reason or purpose of inculturation. So that African Christians may identify "deeply" with the Christian church and treat it as their own rather than as an alien institution, it ought to be rooted in the local cultures, taking into account the people's customs and ways of doing things, they said. Christianity shall in this way not only influence people's lives more, they thought, but it will also help to create understanding and harmony among the diverse African religious and cultural perspectives.

Is this happening? The responses here among the church officials were almost equally divided between Yes and No. Those who answered in the affirmative pointed to elements such as singing, dancing, the clapping of hands and the beating of drums in the liturgy as evidence of a new awareness toward accepting African customs in the church. They also noted that the shapes of some Christian symbols, such as crucifixes, altars and tabernacles, are taking on a more African cultural look, something which would have been impossible previously. For this new attitude, many pointed to the Second Vatican Council as the watershed between strict intolerance and a limited official acceptance of aspects of an African spirituality in the church.

This group of respondents saw further signs in which this, for them, positive move is evident in the church. They pointed out that there is increasing emphasis on chastity before marriage in Christian preaching as well as more and more involvement of parents and other elders in the marriage process of their children. What this means, they said, is that African values in these matters are seriously being taken into account by the church.

Another smaller group of officials, however, was of the opinion that inculturation was not taking place. They complained about the "foreign ways" in which Christianity is expressed in Africa. They especially cited as evidence of this "stagnation" what they saw as the Vatican offices' strong control over liturgical matters They felt that church leaders in Africa, and not Vatican officials, should be the ones to lead the process of the integration of the Christian faith into the local socio-religious realities. Considering that it is the local leaders who experience these realities on a daily basis, this group argued that local decision-making should be the normal way to proceed.

To most ordinary Roman Catholic Christians, inculturation as a concept proved to be too much of a technical term. Almost without exception, it was very difficult for them to define. Most of them asked for a translation or explanation of the term in their vernaculars. But even when equivalents such as *utamadunisho* in Kiswahili, or *Gutaura Kirikaniro kuringana na muturire wa gitene* (literally, "interpreting the biblical message in an African perspective") in Kikuyu were proposed, the problem of what the concept meant and implied in the life of the church remained substantially unresolved.

There was not much difference, however, between the understanding of inculturation by college- or university-educated youth—whether these were Catholic or not—and the responses of the church's officials. The only difference here was that in their responses the youth tended to emphasize much more than their elders, who are now in positions of responsibility in the churches, the aspect of cultural pride and identity. The young people saw in inculturation a way of advancing African cultural pride; they valued it much more than the priests, nuns and bishop interviewed. This is paradoxical because the youth are generally thought to be the group in Africa that is most affected by cultural globalization. To them the notion of African culture is usually thought to mean very little.

However, a young person questioned by us about this discrepancy noted that this may not be the case, or at least that the perception of the youth's alienation from cultural values should not be generalized. He exemplified the significance of African culture by referring to the view of love in the West, in the church, and in African culture. His reference to past ritual actions shows that he had studied them and been impressed by them because he clearly identifies himself with these processes. As he put it:

> The Christian concept of love is too abstract for most African Christians. We believed in love that is expressed in symbolic exchange of gifts, ritual visits and exchange of vows or agreements between the clan members of the betrothed before marriage. In this regard, marriage was a matter between relatives of the bride and the groom. After marriage the two groups were held responsible for the outcome [of the relationship] of the newly wedded couples. This has been watered down by the Christian concept of marriage, which is highly influenced by western, Euro-American values. Marriages are becoming more individualistic, secularist and hence the knot tied on the wedding day is loose and weak. No wonder divorce cases are prevalent.

Alex Kamwaria, a young Kikuyu man, offered a different, but theologically perhaps even more significant example of inculturation. According to him,

When we read or hear of the role of Jesus as the Redeemer, Healer and King, it reminds us of the role of traditional tribal seers and prophets, chiefs and kings who led the community in inter-tribal wars, healed diseases and led the people in overcoming calamities. These tribal healers, leaders, chiefs and kings were also believed to be the incarnation of God's redemptive powers.

Andrew Mutua, a young Kamba man, insisted that

The traditional Kamba concept of God is not different from the biblical one. In both contexts there is emphasis on one God, the Creator, who hates evil and rewards good deeds. He is loving and protective. But the teachings about the way to be on good terms with God are different: in Kikamba one has to strictly follow the traditions, beliefs and customs of our ancestors while in Christianity the Bible is the yardstick.

Andrew Mwaniki, at the time of our interview with him in October 2001, was a student at the Catholic University of Eastern Africa, Nairobi. He was glad, he said,

when the priests draw examples from Kikuyu and Meru traditions for practices such as sacrifices to cleanse evildoers or to appease community spirits and God (*Ngai, Murungu*). This can be compared to the biblical sacrifices of penitence—that is, the sacrificing of lambs [in the Old Testament] and the Eucharistic celebration [in the New]. In addition, our ancestors believed in offering sacrifices to God in times of adversities or disasters. Thus Christian faith came and strengthened the faith which they still had.

Mwaniki was representative of the general thinking of most of the youth. They generally thought that inculturation was taking place in the church in a limited way. On this they responded in almost the same way as the Catholic officials. Africanizing the accent of the liturgy, using songs which make the liturgy livelier and more enjoyable, they said, showed the church's appreciation of African-ness. Furthermore, they were convinced that reading the word of God in the vernacular and praying in the local languages was a step in the right direction away from the traditional Catholic practice of using foreign languages and styles of worship. Some young people pointed out that a good number of African traditional perceptions of the holy concur with Christian teachings on holiness.

As an example, several youth recalled that Christian belief in the sacredness of church buildings evoked for them how shrines were revered as God's dwelling places or even his manifestation in African spirituality. There was also a striking similarity in penitential hymns in both worship practices, they claimed. Nevertheless, for many of the youth, marriage arrangements, eucharistic celebrations, penitential rites, prayers and other rites and rituals should not be read from a book. Instead they should be improvised so as to be more related to the actual circumstances of the prayer and ritual.

A small group of young respondents expressed their conviction that inculturation was unnecessary. Both Africa and Christianity must change with the times. "Some of our traditions have become archaic," they said. "They have lost their relevance and applicability. So any effort at inculturation is an exercise in futility if it based on massive borrowing from indigenous African heritage of a bygone era."

UNDERSTANDING OF INCULTURATION IN THE AICS

The AIPCA officials were precise in their understanding of inculturation. Almost all of them said that it refers to "the integration of the Gospel into African culture." This integration, according to Archbishop Njeru Wambugu of the Organization of African Initiated Churches (OAIC) headquarters in Nairobi, must be done quite deliberately and consciously because the Christianity that came to Africa was already blended with European and American culture. He explained that a critical African reading of the Bible would show, for example, that some so-called "Christian names" have no theological basis. "This is why in many AICs indigenous African names are given prominence. In addition, elements of European and American culture not acceptable to Africans are rejected in these churches." An African-centered reading of the Bible, as Wambugu explained it, was one of the foundations of the AIPCA as well as other AICs. In the AIPCA, he said, worship practices included use of traditional singing and dancing styles, instruments and rhythms. The songs integrate both biblical and African moral and religious values.

The respondents made it clear that for most AICs inculturation involves understanding biblical teachings within the context of African culture. The Bible must be interpreted according to the people's own cultural experience. Modern institutions, like churches and schools, must be adapted to the customs, beliefs and social institutions of the particular group or people where they are situated. In the view of Macharia, a youth leader in the Akorino Church, "inculturation calls for the marriage of two cultures, to get the best from both." As far as the Christian religion and faith are concerned, this is the only way toward what he called "home-grown Christianity."

The AIPCA officials in general thought that it is easy to integrate biblical values with African religious perspectives. But this should be facilitated by pastors who are open-minded but who are at the same time ready to downplay all indigenous African values and customs that are not consistent with Christian teaching. High among the things to be rejected, the use of witchcraft and magic were consistently and frequently mentioned. On the other hand, the same pastors should be able to distinguish aspects of traditional Christianity or missionary teaching that have no bearing on the teachings of Jesus Christ. The aim, they said, is to eliminate as much as possible the alien cultural perspectives imposed on Africa in the name of Christian teaching.

The official stance of the AIPCA is that the purpose of inculturation is to bring people to see and understand the gospel in their own worldview, to make the Gospel part and parcel of their life. For example, among the Embu and Kikuyu, their God (*Ngai*) who was believed to rest on Mt. Kenya (Kirinyaga), would be seen as the same God who created the whole world and all peoples, and who sustains everything. Among the Maasai, the cow would be an important symbol used in Christian teaching, just as Jesus used the symbols of sheep and goats. From this perspective, a person without faith might be compared to "a lost cow."

Generally, however, the ordinary members of the AIPCA, like their Catholic counterparts, found it difficult to explain the term "inculturation" conceptually. They wondered why they needed to engage in such a process since their church was already African, as its name showed. Most AIPCA members argued that they had abandoned mainstream churches due to what they saw as the coercion inherent in these to follow "unrealistic" doctrines that were alien to their African heritage. Because the AIPCA was founded by Africans, the members interviewed believed that it was deeply African. To illustrate, some of them cited what they saw as the integration of tribal traditions in the church, particularly the use in the liturgy of local languages, African music and dances blended with biblical themes, and African musical instruments like drums, *kayamba* (rattles), horns, trumpets, jingles and shakers. The structure of the church itself, they said, was African. It was governed by councils of elders made up of people of specific age groups and marital status. They claimed that women share church responsibilities by participating in different social activities, cooking and catering services, singing and dancing, and undertaking light duties in maintaining church buildings and compounds.

In general their church is looked at as an instrument for helping the Kikuyu to maintain their culture. It gives them an identity. It is seen as working to protect Kikuyu religious perceptions, social values and customs against disintegration. It is helping the people attain independence from a colonial mentality and a socio-religious confusion caused "by white, western missionaries who taught that African religiosity was satanic, devilish, barbaric and primitive." It is helping to promote intercultural interaction in a balanced way, and therefore ensuring that no culture, Western Christianity or European culture included, was supplanting Kikuyu culture. For Akorino Christian youth this was seen as particularly important, "for they are undergoing strong influences coming outside of the Kikuyu cultural experience," as one church elder put it.

Still, there seems to be no theology consistent with practical pastoral behavior in the AICs. We can give some examples. Among the Embu and Kikuyu, these churches have largely adopted the people's common customs and emphasize their significance. For instance, the Akorino have maintained the practice of girls' circumcision, despite government disapproval, and accept the belief in powers of witchcraft and magic even as they discourage its use. In line with the cultural practices of these peoples, the AICs there encourage endogamy (restricted marriage within the same ethnic community). And the pastor is not at liberty to preside over a wedding where traditional agreements and the paying of bride wealth have not been finalized. The theological reasons for these practices have not been articulated.

In the AIPCA polygamy remains a common practice. It is strongly rooted there and has been accommodated since the early period when the church was taking shape in Kenya. The founders of the movement felt that missionary Christianity was too alien to African family values and societal structures and life. As some leaders argued during our interviews with them, polygamy has been accepted in the practice of the AICs because this form of marriage shows and demands responsibility. "An African man does not marry primarily for sex," they claimed. "He does so in order to have a big family so as to share happiness, labor and wealth with his children." In view of this, they said, polygamy was more acceptable and more favorable to Africans than monogamy.

According to the officials of the AIPCA, the spiritual and cultural teachings of the Old Testament largely concur with African spirituality and religiosity. They pointed out in several discussions that polygamous unions, for example, are acceptable in both cultures. Wambugu, Macharia and Kagai—all officials of the AIPCA—further explained that in the New Testament the issue of polygamy is elusive. Jesus did not preach against it, Wambugu exclaimed, "He was clever!" Wambugu added that St. Paul preached more against adultery and fornication, but his position on polygamy was not clearcut. Thus the branding of polygamy as sinful and unacceptable in Christianity was for Wambugu and others a Western, culturally conditioned ecclesiastical regulation. They did not see it as a biblical requirement.

The officials recognized in this regard that the decline of polygamy in the AIPCA was not based on church policies but on external factors, including economic constraints caused by the rising cost of living. The responses we received from AIPCA leaders suggested that church policy was generally that people who were already polygamous on joining the church were encouraged to stay together. Desertion of a husband by his wife, even after formal membership, was also an acceptable reason for polygamy, as was barrenness. Generally, though, polygamy after baptism was discouraged, especially among the young. The reason, as explained by AIPCA elders, was that polygamous practices today tend to encourage multiple divorces due to the loss of indigenous values that had regulated marriage stability. Still, according to Wambugu, divorce cases are very rare in the AIPCA and are strongly discouraged by all leaders.

A few AIPCA members, such as Ngari Waweru, favored a church wedding over the traditional form of marriage. They thought that marriage in the church bound the couple to the church laws and expectations as well as to customary values and customs. This ensured the stability of marriage. For Charles Kirwea, "A church wedding is a sign of piety, righteousness, commitment to the institution of marriage and associated vows and family values, and shows a readiness to be counseled by the pastor and church elders in case of difficulties."

PROCESS OF INCULTURATION

All the Roman Catholic officials seemed to agree that it was important for the Christian faith to be inculturated if it was to fulfill its goals in Africa. Sr. Ann Nasimiyu understood the process of inculturation as one that entails "inner transformation of the religious community [and] enhances contextualization of Christian teachings in their [believers' own] indigenous cultural context and worldview." According to her, other theologians refer to the same process as indigenization of Christianity. "But care must be taken to avoid encouraging ethno-theology which may create complex and intricate sub-divisions in the larger church," she warned.

Several Catholic officials mentioned that inculturation can be facilitated by introducing African rhythms and music in the church. This can happen through interreligious services and exchange of ideas with other religious communities about liturgical vestments, postures and signs. Churches, they suggested, could organize informal conversations and seminars to teach their members not to disregard totally their indigenous cultural values, particularly those relevant in worship. Nevertheless, they noted that the process is made difficult by many factors, one of which is tribalism within and between the churches. They also pointed out that there has been a lot of cultural erosion in Africa and most people have forgotten their own cultures. Many wondered aloud whether those individuals and groups initiating and implementing the process of inculturation today were qualified for the task. They noted, for instance, that in many places the program had been initiated by theologians, most of whom have, throughout their professional training, never come into contact with the real-life experiences of ordinary Christians in their contextual cultural heritage. According to Fr. Maina, this makes some of their proposals highly theoretical, without reference to reality.

Further, in the minds of many Catholic officials, the socio-political structures and cultural changes taking place in the world today make the process of inculturation delicate and complex. There is also the element of inflexibility: there are people who have the mentality that anything from African tradition is pagan and primitive. As Fr. Muchiri put it, such people feel that by inculturating doctrine and liturgy, we are going back to the dark ages. For her part, Sr. Mumbua noted that a lack of understanding of what it means to inculturate, the failure of the church to create the awareness of inculturation in its members, and the rigidity of church laws have also been great hindrances to inculturation.

To offset this situation, Fr. Nundwe recommended that agents of inculturation should be trained in theology and be familiar with the particular cultures they work in. According to him, whenever the church has to make an important decision, the local people should be given the first opportunity to suggest what to do. In the actual process of inculturation, however, cultural perspectives from one ethnic group should not be imposed on another. Substantially agreeing with this position, Fr. Guillaume suggested a method of interaction by dialogue: the knowledge of one people and their system of beliefs, customs and practices, he proposed, should openly enter into a dialogue with those of the others so that each people can learn to appreciate what the others have to offer.

Fr. Kamtembo observed as well that for sustainable inculturation to take place there has to be a continuous dialogue among all cultural communities. For this purpose, Fr. Kaweri recommended that the church should arrange seminars on inculturation for the laity, especially the youth, at the level of Small Christian Communities (SCCs). Inculturation materials should be written in local languages and the meaning and importance of inculturation should be explained before introducing any change to the people.

There is the need to promote respect for African cultural heritage and identity, to drop the Western mentality that leads to negative perceptions and mistreatment of African traditional religiosity and people. This was the view of Fr. Buimbo. There is a need, he emphasized, for everyone to open their eyes and look at African Traditional Religion (ATR) from a positive point of view. He further noted that a clear distinction should be made between Western culture and traditions on the one hand, and Christianity and the Gospel on the other. All Christians must be involved in the process of inculturation if it is to succeed. It is very important that those facilitating the process be knowledgeable in both cultural anthropology and church doctrine, he added.

Both officials and many ordinary members of the AIPCA were aware that some African religious customs were losing their force over the Kikuyu community and disappearing. They said that this was partly because of Christian influence. For example, Christianity had for a long time discouraged belief in the power of diviners, magic and sorcery. People who claimed to suffer from witchcraft were now prayed for instead of being exorcised by diviners. Blessing by elderly persons through spitting, and the practice of cursing by elder siblings or elders were also losing their vitality among Kikuyu Christians in AIPCA, they noted.

For the AIPCA, the process of inculturation means essentially people's participation in the affairs of the church—"all members, guided by the elders in their localities." Generally, for them, inculturation should as much as possible take the normal lifestyle of the local culture. The church leaders should guide their congregations into the Christian faith in such areas as customary marriage, practices of inheritance, blessings, curses and other aspects of religious and social life. One of them also added: "But they should draw on the wisdom of clan elders and all those familiar with (African) Kikuyu heritage."

WHAT AREAS NEED INCULTURATING?

Several areas were identified by all churches and groups as deserving particular attention in the inculturation process. Among them the most significant were the following:

The Language and "Mood" of Worship

Catholic Church officials had diverse views on the areas in Catholic life which they thought were in need of inculturation. The aspect that they referred to most was that of language: the language of worship in a given locality should be that of the predominant community. But they also insisted that every ethnic group should be allowed to integrate acceptable values, customs and beliefs into Catholic celebrations: for instance, traditional aspects of naming, marriage and burial ceremonies.

Concretely, many suggested that African customary marriage should be respected and recognized as sacred and hence acceptable as a sacrament for people who join the church when already married in the traditional customary rites. Traditional rites of passage should also be recognized, respected and dignified by being accompanied by appropriate Christian forms of singing, dancing and merrymaking. This would lead to these traditional and Christian elements of celebration being blended together. African rituals and ceremonies could, for instance, end with blessings from a priest, who would be accompanied by the elders and ritual leaders of the group. Prayers, songs, signs and symbols in the church should reflect the cultural richness of the locality. As one of the priests, Fr. Kamtembo, proposed,

> Let Christians know that their [the people's] physical environment is made up of God's creation, and that artifacts from the community are suitable for symbolic representation of the sacred. In their preaching, liturgical leaders should clearly emphasize that God has always been present among the community.

Overwhelming agreement among Catholic officials about inculturation concerned procedure. Before a final decision on any matter concerning inculturation is made, it was generally accepted, there should be widespread consultation, dialogue, and sharing within the laity and clergy, as well as between their groups, on what is to be inculturated and how to carry it out. All Christians should be involved in the process. Nevertheless the dialogue must be guided by the leadership of the church and informed by experts in theology and liturgy. To succeed in Catholic Christianity, this needs the support of the hierarchy. There should be no suspicion, coercion or reservation on any level concerning the extent to which Christianity should be Africanized or contextualized.

Liturgy

Most respondents among all groups of people interviewed said that the liturgy or worship services should be made livelier. In other words, the singing should be more cheerful and it should be accompanied by musical instruments, clapping and dancing. In the view of Githiru, the solemn, almost sad mood of most liturgies makes them resemble funerals. As he sees it, Bible readings in liturgies should be drawn from several books of scripture and people should be allowed room to pray in their own words instead of reciting prayers. According to Wanjugu, Njoroge and Mama Mwai, such prayer recitation can be so ritualistic that most people go through it without giving a thought to what they are saying.

Mama Mwai observed further that the rosary should be abandoned: she recites it all the time, she said, but does not receive the kind of spiritual satisfaction which she gets from her own "supplications" which address her immediate needs and experiences. For Owiny, the laying down of specific prayers for certain times, for example, morning prayers, evening and night prayers, prayers before and after meals and so on, denies Christians a chance to learn how to communicate with God using their own words and reflecting their own personal needs.

There are certain aspects of the liturgy that many respondents thought needed to be strengthened. These include penitential services, teaching on communal life, family life, social justice, forgiveness and reconciliation. The signs accompanying these services should be allowed more space. As Muchina argued, men should raise up their hands in prayer similar to the way that in Islam worshippers face Mecca. According to Ngari Waweru, waving hands in prayer gives strength to people and makes them feel that God will hear their prayers. It is also a sign of humility, Peninah thought. Mama Mwikali and Njoki were of the opinion that "people sing and dance to praise God in a joyous manner such that in heaven he can see that he has good people in the world." Muthoni observed that singing "makes God happy," therefore Christians should do it with all their heart. They should "imitate David who sang for the Lord until his clothes fell off. A person should never sing standing still if the spirit of God is in them," she added.

When receiving the Eucharist, people should kneel instead of stand, as a sign of respect for what the Eucharist signifies. For Kairu, "exaggerations," like crying and shouting in the church, especially among those in the new charismatic movements, should not be encouraged, and people should not be overburdened by frequent demands for financial contributions. Also to be discouraged should be the use of "Hellenistic terms and images" to refer to God, as well as "the unnecessary use of Latin."

AIPCA officials commented on the place of Mary and the saints in "some churches." *Which* churches was never made explicit, but most probably the reference was to the Roman Catholic Church. They observed that these "churches pay too much attention to Mary mother of Jesus," making it seem as though she is to be more revered than Jesus himself. It was claimed that in these churches, the saints are likewise sometimes exalted more than Jesus.

Many AIPCA members recommended that some African traditional symbols should be used by the church in celebrating certain rituals. Some of the examples given included anointing with oil (butter) and blood to purify and cleanse; blessing by water or (a coal of) fire to signify purity; incensing to cleanse; palm leaves and ashes to symbolize sorrow or penitence; sharing food to signify communion and unity; and praying while facing the altar "just as traditional people prayed facing a specific place."

Most respondents from all churches in the urban areas observed that English and Kiswahili are the main languages used in worship services because there are people from different language groups living together in the towns and cities. In the rural areas vernaculars are the most common languages of worship. Urban respondents observed that when praying as individuals, they use the language they feel most comfortable with, that is, English, Kiswahili or their mother tongue. But most of those from rural areas pointed out that they use only their mother tongues to pray, mostly because that is the only language they know and understand.

The body posture assumed in prayer and worship was considered a very important element by many respondents regardless of their church affiliation; they thought it reflected the psychological and spiritual attitude of the person praying. For most respondents kneeling is the best posture for prayer because, according to Wanjohi, "It is a sign of humility, respect, repentance, reconciliation and submission to a higher authority." Wanjohi argued that Jesus himself recommended the kneeling posture for prayer. In the view of Wanjiku, alternately kneeling and standing reduce monotony, increase concentration and create the mood conducive to prayer. Like Wanjiku, Mwamunye also thought that intermittently sitting, standing and kneeling help one to focus his or her attention on the sacred action in progress and to break any monotony. But, in the opinion of Mutua, one can assume any posture in prayer: "What is important is to remember that you are communicating with your Maker and need to be humble and respectful."

For many respondents, liturgy and worship were important because through them they received "spiritual nourishment, companionship, love, hope, comfort and internal peace." As Margaret Matheri put it, "God meets me there at my points of need, that is, when I am discouraged, sad, confused, hopeless and feeling low." Some respondents insisted that even their physical needs, such as food, clothes and shelter could be met in liturgy. The Eucharist was seen as bringing about the physical presence of Jesus in the assembly, and for many the final blessings enhanced God's presence in their life, far beyond the place of worship. As Kamoga explained, "Prayers of the faithful give me a chance to talk freely about my feelings to God. Communal confession erases the sense of guilt in approaching God's altar and opens me up for better communication with him."

What should be done about personal experiences that do not already have expression in the liturgy of a particular church or denomination? Owiny replied that they should be identified from among the faithful and incorporated in the liturgy without changing its meaning. Nyawir, however, thought that the only option was for the person or persons concerned to move to other churches where such practices are allowed. Philomena Mwaura's opinion was that church officials should be alert to people's needs as they prepare the liturgy and incorporate these needs into their preaching and other forms of admonition.

Generally, the youth from both urban and rural settings felt that Catholic liturgies were too boring, particularly the monotonous prayers "which involve recitation of 'contents' prepared many centuries ago. Prayers in the Catholic Church appear irrelevant to the contemporary needs of the congregation," as Esther Wanjiru put it. She said during one interview that she had once been a Catholic youth leader in Kiamumbi Girls Secondary School, but that she was thinking of joining any Pentecostal church or AIC where, as she claimed, "liturgies are less boring." According to Wanjiru, "the Catholic Church should borrow ideas from other Christian denominations which have been evolving with time to suit their congregations' needs and expectations. Church members would like to participate actively in liturgies. The youth are more badly hit by lack of this" in the Catholic Church.

Some of the youth addressed the issue of gender, saying that gender segregation in the church should be minimized by allowing women significant participation in worship activities and giving them roles in socio-religious leadership parallel to that of men. After all, they argued, women make up the largest part of any Christian congregation.

Concerning attire, most Catholic youth felt that priests in Africa should wear African forms of dress, particularly styles traditionally associated with ritual leaders, traditional priests and medicine persons in the regions and societies they operate. The congregation should also dress in respectable ways, according to the mores of the respective societies.

Disciplinary measures used in the Catholic Church, including the withholding of Holy Communion, appeared alien to the majority of our non-Catholic respondents. The argument was that such measures do not make much sense to the majority of Africans, who are accustomed to forms of discreet, not statutory, discipline, mystified into taboos. Since taboos guided traditional people's moral life more or less successfully, it was thought that they could be incorporated into Christianity for the same purpose. There was a general feeling from the respondents, perhaps flowing from this sense, that leadership in the church should be given to the elderly; youthful members of the congregation needed to recognize the resourcefulness of elders who were endowed with cultural and Christian knowledge.

Ancestors and Spirit Possession

There was a mixed reaction from the respondents concerning belief in the ancestors and in mystical ancestral power. While some acknowledged that they believed in them and in their power, others said they didn't. Njoroge pointed out that he relates to the ancestors by remembering them during prayers and by preserving and imitating the positive things they did while still in this world. For him, as for Alex Kamwaria, the ancestors are the dispensers of moral values in the community and their remembrance is assured through nominal reincarnation.

Nyawir observed that Africans relate to the ancestors through naming: "We tend to see them again in the physical features of the children who bear their names, which relate stories about their deeds and achievements." Andrew Mutua observed that he believed in the ancestors' prophecies. According to him, Matheri and Gathambo, in traditional communities "the religious leaders used to foresee some things which are actually happening now." Maina Kennedy and Cyprian Kavivya also noted that the ancestors are their forefathers and that without them they would never have come into existence. Said Kavivya, "I revere them because they are my grandparents, and many other people do so too."

Peter Kioko of the AIPCA was typical when he said about the ancestors,

> I do believe in their power because what they used to do and say is still done today. Disobeying those demands leads to curses: if one sells a piece of land inherited from the ancestors a curse befalls him and his family. They are our forefathers and mothers and thus we belong to the same extended family.

Can a person be possessed by the ancestors or other spirits? From the responses we received it was clear that the Catholic Church does not much value spirit possession as a gift among its members. Although some Catholics claim it, it is generally viewed by their church authorities as problematic.

The AIPCA faithful, however, when asked how their churches deal with the incidences of spirit possession, said that the church exercises no control over the members' spiritual experience. "These days spirit possession is prevalent even among the youth," as Nyooro Ndirangu put it. A few other leaders, John Mburu, for one, thought that spirit possession is an alien practice that "is being witnessed just today because some few years ago it wasn't there." He claimed that the people involved should be cautioned against causing confusion among the congregation because the church as a whole "can't bear it."

Suffering and Healing

Even though in general suffering was seen as something natural and part of human life, its sources were perceived to be of various kinds. The devil was mentioned by many respondents from all churches as the main source of suffering, the greatest enemy of humankind. He was depicted as rejoicing at human suffering. Fr. Kaweri and Sr. Patricia attributed to the devil environmental and natural calamities such as epidemics, famine, earthquakes, floods, and so on. Nevertheless, this was a minority view in the Catholic Church. Most Catholic officials argued that human beings bring suffering upon themselves on account of the evils they commit in society. Thus, from this point of view, suffering may be considered a form of punishment or penance for sin or wrongdoing.

A few ordinary Catholic respondents felt that suffering comes from God to test Christians' faith. When they do not give up because of it, it strengthens their relationship with God. It brings them closer to him, "because," as they kept repeating, "when one is suffering there is a tendency to remember God more." AIC members had similar views. Jane Wangari thought that in every kind of suffering God wants people to discover and learn new things about him and to deepen and strengthen their faith in and relationship to him. Maina Kennedy, on the other hand, saw suffering to be, as he put it, a bridge "to my God because, the Bible says, those who suffer for the sake of the Lord will not perish, but will inherit the Kingdom of God." For Andrew Mutua "we suffer when we fail to fulfill our ancestors' needs and expectations; suffering is a punishment from them."

Economic hardships also contribute to suffering, in the view of many respondents. According to Sammy Maina, without sufficient income, medical care, good food, housing and school fees, sustainable living becomes a problem and therefore a source of affliction. Other informants observed that it is not possible to explain suffering or its source because it is beyond rational human understanding. However, practically all respondents agreed that whenever there is suffering and pain of any kind, a healing process must be instituted. Often it may take the form of a ritual. In this case the source of the illness must first of all be identified. This is usually done mystically. Then follows an acknowledgement of sin or failure to a higher power on the part of the sinner and a willingness to ask for forgiveness, to pray to the mystical power and wait upon it to accomplish the healing process in the person's life.

Rituals of healing depend on specialists. In the Catholic Church, for example, the respondents explained that in the healing prayer leaders, usually the priests, place their hands on the sick person and invoke the power of God or Jesus to come down and heal him or her. However, the person being prayed for must have faith in the healing power of God for the healing to take effect, they said.

Healing rituals are more common in the AICs than in the Catholic Church. Although most AICs accept the use of modern (Western) medicines, school education and modern technology, the Akorino Church cautions other AICs against over-reliance on these things. The Akorino argue that the use of scientific medicine may betray lack of faith in the healing power of God through prayer. They prefer to use traditional herbal medicines alongside spiritual or faith healing. Archbishop Wambugu and Pastor Muriu of the AIPCA, however, held the middle road on this issue. They said they accept the use of modern science as well as traditional medicine for their followers "as long as they are not contrary to the Gospel."

Church Structure and Government

Many ordinary Roman Catholic respondents were not familiar with the meaning of the expression (or model) of the church "as people of God," and even those officials who were familiar with it explained it in different ways. According to Father Kamtembo, "It means acceptance of Christ as a redeemer and bedrock of the teachings which bind believers together, regardless of ethnicity or racial, social, economic or political backgrounds." For Kaweri, it meant that "God is continuously present in the community of his followers and has a personal relationship with every believer." For Maina, it implied that "Christ should be given a place in our culture, since he is the Savior, progenitor and determiner of people's destiny."

Does understanding the church as God's people have any relevance to the way in which the church is structured and governed? Most respondents implied that it does and linked the success of inculturation to the existence of dialogue in the church. They said that meaningful dialogue depends on what kind of governing structure the particular church had, but it also influences it. On whether dialogue was taking place in the church, there were differences of views. Many Catholic leaders agreed that dialogue is allowed, but only as long as it does not "undermine" established church policies or laws. These, they felt, were to be received from Rome and enforced by the bishops in all dioceses of the world. Other leaders argued that after Vatican II and the establishment of Small Christian Communities (SCCs), the church had opened wide the avenues of dialogue and people now may freely express their feelings, views, complaints and suggestions above the way pastoral services should be provided. There are also parish councils, many noted, whose views are usually relayed to the catechists and priests. These in turn can discuss them with the bishops. "There is a procedure to follow which is too long," Mwangi complained. "I have to start from the lowest leader, that is, the catechist, and then move up the ladder. So it is rather tedious and this discourages me."

Akwanalo observed that parishioners were free to make written and oral suggestions to the priest and catechist, but that it was up to the discretion of these leaders to consider and act on them. However, many respondents pointed out that priests, deacons and bishops often decide not to take the views or grievances of the general faithful into serious account. Therefore, whatever dialogue there is in the church is limited and largely controlled by the priests within their parishes.

Some respondents noted that they make their suggestions through leaders of small church groups, such as Young Christian Students (YCS), Christian Women Association (CWA), and Catholic Men Association (CMA), through church councils and committees or through suggestion boxes. Others observed that they do talk directly to the leaders, especially when their problem is personal. But a general sense of frustration lingers even then. Some individuals lamented that although they make their views known in this way, most of the time nothing is done. This is frustrating and makes them prefer silence. As Margaret Njeri put it, "I don't express my views any more; I don't know how to do it." And in the opinion of Githae, "Church doctrines are still too rigid. There is no freedom of expression." According to Nyawir, "In some churches, those who seek dialogue with their priests or bishops are regarded as dissidents, and end up being denied sacraments."

As a way to offset this situation, some respondents argued that the church should create permanent and known structures for dialogue between the leaders and the members whereby the members are given a chance to express their views freely. Depending on the outcome, the church would then know which pastoral practices to adopt and incorporate into its system and which to drop. This would promote harmony between church practices and people's feelings and actions. Nevertheless, it was agreed that the church has to be firm about her basic teaching: anything that might distort or imply cheap change should be rejected, even if it means losing some followers to other churches. The idea behind this was that accepting practices in a bid to attract members could cause a failure to safeguard the foundational teachings of the church.

It was generally clear from the responses that most educated Christians were convinced that it was only through dialogue that church officials could determine how the life of faith could be improved and inculturated. The general consensus was that for meaningful inculturation to take place, church officials should be aware of how ordinary Christians felt about liturgy and other aspects of the life of the church.

Most Catholics felt that changes in matters affecting the liturgy should begin from the bottom upwards, that is, that they should be initiated by ordinary Christians rather than by the bishops or Rome. As many of them saw it, in most congregations, issues relating to the liturgy are discussed in prayer groups (commonly called in Kikuyu *mwaki*) by the general faithful where priests and other leaders are not involved. Insensitivity to the laity's needs by the leaders, therefore, often leads to a sense of dissatisfaction and ultimately the defection from the Catholic Church. It may also cause for some people a situation akin to abdication from a committed Christian life.

There were a few dissenting voices that were against dialogue; these were not ready to accept completely the idea of dialogue in the church. Among the Catholics, they were concerned about the church's identity. According to them, Catholic identity is maintained by following time-honored regulations for liturgical practices as well as all other rituals. This implies observing the entire structure of church worship and government. Catholic doctrine must be conserved, they argued, if the Catholic Church is to avoid being influenced by "Protestants and other sects." Dialogue should consist only in the faithful in Small Christian Communities and other associations giving their views to church leaders and leaving the latter to make the decisions. Some elderly respondents even observed that feelings about liturgy are personal and should not even be discussed.

Just as in the Catholic Church, there is an established leadership chain in the AIPCA, from leaders of small congregations to pastors, bishops and an archbishop. But in the AIPCA, every congregation is led by a committee of twelve men and twelve women as well as by its pastors. Christian guilds like youth groups, choirs and men's and women's groups interact and deliberate on all matters touching the socio-economic and religious life of the church. These leaders are empowered to facilitate dialogue at every level. Nevertheless, any member of the congregation who appears knowledgeable, righteous and likable to many can be appointed to lead church services. The

AIPCA is therefore more open to dialogue than the Catholic Church and its structures most clearly provide for it. Here all issues are open to discussion, including the appointment or election of church leaders. This is perhaps why this church is usually perceived by outsiders to be "political" and full of "leadership wrangles."

The issues mentioned as relevant for discussion by members of the different churches were rather comprehensive. It was noted by some Catholic Church officials that in a few cases, matters in which dialogue sometimes took place included budget planning and participation in the various ministries of the church. Issues pertaining to ecumenism and interfaith dialogue were also sometimes discussed openly. Recently issues of contextualization, which involve integration of some cultural values and customs into Christian life and liturgy, have been given high priority in the dialogue agenda of various Catholic Church congregations.

In summary, most respondents across the board thought that the following activities should be open to dialogue in the church:

- Development projects—for example, building churches, schools, hospitals, water wells, and social amenities, as well as financial matters of the church;
- Appointments, demotions and reappointments of church leaders at all levels;
- Moral questions in society, such as sexual behavior, drug abuse, crime, respect for elders and mode of dress. (The wearing of trousers and miniskirts by women in places of worship and elsewhere was generally discouraged as immodest);
- The importance of traditional values, norms and customs which conform to Christian ethics;
- Parenting, that is, the best way for parents to ensure their children's moral development;
- Ways to resolve conflicts within the church;
- Issues of worship, liturgy, prayer, and preaching.

Church Law and Discipline

Most Catholic respondents agreed on the importance of having laws and regulations in the church. As Sr. Patricia put it, "Yes, I consider them [laws] to be good, as far as most of them provide guidelines in life. They are natural laws. Just like other organizations, the church needs laws for its wellbeing." In the church, according to Aazine, laws "follow the teachings of Jesus Christ who is the foundation of Christian faith." And according to the Roman Catholic bishop we interviewed, "A knowledge and understanding of church laws help officials in knowing how to conduct themselves in the presence of the laity, and how to interact with them in love, kindness and without conflict."

The respondents understood the purpose of laws in the church to be to guide and direct Christians in their relationship with God and fellow human beings. Since the majority of church laws are concerned with morality in the Christian's daily life, the respondents thought that they help to foster internal harmony and balance in the person's life as well as in his or her relationship with God and fellow human beings.

The laws and regulations most generally known by all Christians were the Ten Commandments. But other rules were also mentioned such as those which, in the Catholic Church, require tithing (or contributing to the church 10 percent of one's annual income), chastity (requiring that one abstains from sex before marriage), confessing one's sins at least once a year, receiving Holy Communion regularly, and so on. An Akorino youth leader, Timothy Macharia, asserted that being familiar with church laws makes it easy for church members to obey them and thus promote unity, peace, love and harmony between human beings and God, as also among human beings themselves.

In the AIPCA, church laws are passed on to the members through regular circulars published by church officials, through seminars organized at national and local levels, and through Bible studies offered during or after liturgy services. The AIPCA officials observed that it is very important to make all the members aware of the existing laws because failure to do so would be a great disservice to them. The same feeling was expressed by our Catholic respondents: "What is the use of laws and rules," Sr. Anna Njeri wondered, "if they are just written in books which members do not have access to?"

Mama Nguru and Ndirangu noted that in the AIPCA all laws are drawn from both the Bible and acceptable traditional values and customs. Accordingly, cohabitation, which most respondents said is very common today—50 percent according to Anne Wambui, or 20 to 25 percent according to Eric Mwangi—among people between 14 and 45 years of age, is proscribed. "In our church [the AIPCA]," Mama Mwikali confided, "the pastor is very strict on those who cohabit. Hence Christians in our church fear the consequences [of cohabitation] because a person can be excommunicated from the church [for it]." Cohabitation was said to be unheard of among the Akorino faithful. The church is very strict on all practices that would jeopardize its name and reputation, according to members Macharia and Muthoni.

Various factors that cause cohabitation were mentioned. Some AIPCA respondents claimed that cohabitation is on the increase today because society has become permissive to the point that people feel free to make their own decisions and act according to their own desires and wishes. Economic hardships and poverty are also factors in this matter, they said. They are forcing many people to opt for living together so that they can pool their resources and share a more decent life than they would have living alone, Margaret Matheri and Maina suggested. Some added that Western cultures and influence have had a great impact on people's view of marriage. In the view of Kamudiongo, the print and electronic media have combined to "demystify" the taboos and customs which restricted premarital and extramarital relations. For example, the electronic media exposes the youth to pornographic materials from the Western world, which are readily accessible in internet cafes in the major urban centers in Kenya.

In the view of one AIPCA member: "Unlike in traditional Africa where marriage was taken very seriously and involved the whole society, today people tend to feel that marriage is only for the couple involved. Thus marriage no longer bears the meaning attached to it traditionally." Church marriage laws and regulations have not been as effective in this matter as traditional institutions of initiation were. This was what Fr. Buimbo thought. For example, virginity as a virtue among unmarried youth in traditional Kenyan societies has almost disappeared, as have the rituals, rites and ceremonies that symbolized joy at, and appreciation for the guardians of, couples who married before indulging in sexual relations.

Osei explained that in his view, cohabitation acts as a form of trial marriage or testing period. People feel that they have to get to know each other before they commit themselves permanently to marriage. According to him, some people are not sure what to expect in marriage; they cohabit to "familiarize" themselves with what marriage means. Moreover, cohabitation is seen by some as a convenient way to avoid the "hassles" of church marriage which demand bride-wealth, wedding parties, and so on. A frequent complaint, voiced by Pastor Kioko, among others, is that girls' parents today tend to demand too much bride-wealth, which young men cannot afford to give. This forces young couples to live together, sometimes even without the parents' knowledge and consent.

Poverty among the unemployed (especially among girls and women), tends to make sexual promiscuity appear the only way of acquiring money for their needs. Youth who are suffering from an identity crisis often engage in pre-marital sexual relations because of peer pressure, so as to acquire a sense of belonging. Couples separated from one another for long periods because of work or other reasons also tend to engage in extra-marital sex. Most men respondents from the AIPCA argued that polygamy limited extra-marital sexual relations on the part of the men in circumstances such as these. They had little to say, however, about the wives of polygamous men, except that women were expected to be more faithful in marriage than men. Most women said that what they needed was a man to take care of them. They had little to say about their sexual needs in such situations. It seemed as if in the hierarchy of values it was given a low degree of importance.

Increase in marriage instability in the churches was also noted as a factor leading to cohabitation. Officials in rural and urban parishes observed that the divorce rate is very high. At least 30 percent of marriages now end up in divorce after fewer than ten years of marriage. Hence there are many single parents in search of sexual partners regardless of whether the latter are married or unmarried, young or old. It appears that single mothers generally tend to avoid long-term marital commitment and seek only short-term companionship for sexual gratification.

Consequently, the general feeling of our respondents was that abortion, proscribed by all the churches, was on the increase. Statistics are hard to obtain because, it was claimed, most abortions are clandestinely carried out. Sr. Margaret Mumbua, Njeri Ndirangu and Peris Muriuki all contended that the main factor behind incidences of abortion is the socio-cultural stigma associated with unwanted pregnancies in African societies. (An unwed mother is known in Kikuyu derogatively as *Gicokio*.) Another reason is the current economic constraints from the high cost of bringing up children.

WOMEN IN THE CHURCH

Most respondents appeared conscious of the changing role of women in contemporary society. Varied responses were given regarding the position and treatment of women in the churches. There was a general agreement that a higher number of women as compared to men attended church services. Nevertheless, according to Sr. Margaret Mumbua, the situation of women in the Catholic Church "is similar to that which is predominant in society: women hold very few leadership positions. They are not involved in decision making and are themselves still convinced that men are, and should always be, their leaders."

Respondents like Sr. Mumbua thought that this situation could be changed only at the family level. They argued that men should be sensitized to the equal status and role of women in the society, and should be ready to support them in their quest for recognition in the church. "We should not look at women's womanhood as incapacity to perform; rather men should give women a chance to prove themselves in different tasks," as Kamudiongo put it. For Fr. Muchiri, women should stop claiming "equality (sameness)" with men, but rather they should fight for "equity," that is, for mutual understanding between them and men. "They [women] should show that they can also perform in areas where they have been denied opportunities," he said. "They should promote their dignity as dignified beings and explore their gifts."

Against overwhelming opinions to the contrary, Fr. Kaweri, however, noted that there was no gender problem in the church: "There is increasing collaboration in ministry. For example, there are girls serving at the altar, women catechists, women eucharistic ministers, choir leaders, and so on. Nuns have been appointed as parish administrators as well as heads of institutions, such as schools and hospitals." So, according to Mukunga, "the situation is under control and most women are comfortable with things as they are."

CHURCH AND DEVELOPMENT

Should the church as an institution involve itself in development projects and in matters pertaining to politics? In the opinion of the majority of Catholic respondents, the church must be actively involved in lifting up not only the spiritual needs of Christians but also the social and physical needs of all "as the teaching of Jesus Christ demands." The responses indicated a view of Jesus tending toward this perception, that Jesus held a holistic view of life for all of humanity. Accordingly, Christians should follow the example of Christ, who cared for the physical, psychological and spiritual needs of his followers: the needy, the sick, the poor and the sinners. By proclaiming the good news of the kingdom of God, the church automatically enters the realm of development. It does not decide to do this on its own initiative; its message leads it there. It was pointed out several times that it is fortunate that the church started its mission in Africa with this in mind. It must continue to bear in mind that basic human needs must be met if an individual is to grow in spiritual health. Supporting economic development projects prepares the way for evangelism and for fostering Christian life among the people. This is the reason why the church is right to own and operate schools, health centers and vocational training stations.

Asserting that the church must participate fully in politics, some of the youth strongly supported the church's direct involvement in political issues. "Politics is about order in the house," said Joseph Githiru, "and the church is part of the house." But other Christian youth observed that such involvement should be very limited and regulated. The main role of the church, according to the latter group, should be restricted to the area of promoting social awareness or conscientization. "Church officials have a duty to help the voiceless, the oppressed and marginalized do things for themselves," they maintained.

This distinction was also made by many Catholic women: while some supported direct involvement of the church in politics, the majority argued that the church should concentrate its efforts on people's "spiritual concerns." The church, to them, should lead the "spiritual" and not the "political" struggle. Its duty is to guide leaders to think and work within the spirit of biblical teaching on justice. It should provide the moral guidance and pinpoint social evils in the society. In this way it will champion people's rights and fight against injustice and corruption, social marginalization, nepotism, tribalism and racism. It was particularly important for the women that Christians should see to it that the laws of the land take into account an ethical standard, especially in matters relating to sexuality, family planning and contraceptives, marriage and family life, as well as issues of abortion, divorce, inheritance, parenting, human rights, ownership of property, scientific innovations, war, and so on.

Although some AIPCA officials agreed that the church must be actively involved in politics, many were evasive and clearly did not want to discuss the question on the record. The lay members would not be interviewed without the consent of their pastors on this question. Their reasons are understandable. Besides its reputation for being "political," the AIPCA was formed by Africans who were opposed to missionary and colonial activities in Africa. According to Rev. Wambugu, the AIPCA evolved and developed in the 1920s in Kenya from members who were leaving the mainstream churches. They were protesting the interference in African culture by the colonialists and missionaries of the Anglican, Presbyterian and Roman Catholic Churches in parts of central, eastern and western Kenya.

The AIPCA founders argued, according to Wambugu, that the education given to Kenyans by these churches was meant to make them politically subservient to and economically dependent on the white people. Therefore, the British linked the AIPCA to the Mau Mau uprising against colonialism and the marginalizing of the African person. As some interviewed AIPCA officials put it, the colonialists and missionaries were unfamiliar with the African system of leadership. Therefore, they worked hard to break the social and political organization of Africa's societies by establishing chiefdoms over multi-ethnic regions. "Thus," in Wambugu's opinion, "began the wholesale degeneration of the African cultural heritage and the persistence of neo-colonialism in Kenya and the rest of Africa."

Wambugu explained that because of its activism, the AIPCA was widely criticized in the colonial and early post-colonial periods over its inclination toward "political issues" and its tendency, after independence, to align and re-align itself with different political leaders in the rural parts of Kenya. As a result the current leadership of the AIPCA tries to change this negative image of the church by evading direct confrontation with the government and refusing to take sides on political questions. AIPCA members are usually advised to let the leaders of the church make political decisions for the church.

The church, nevertheless, organizes informational seminars on matters of economic development. Like other churches it also owns schools and health facilities to promote the well-being of the public in different parts of the country. In conjunction with other AICs in Kenya, the AIPCA has established different socio-economic development programs. They include:

- Women's development groups, to educate and empower rural women concerning their rights;
- Ongoing campaigns against HIV/AIDS, other STDs and pre-marital and extra-marital sexual relations;
- Ongoing instructions on the relationship between gospel and culture, to enlighten people on the need to relate Christianity to their diverse cultural values;
- Construction of schools, hospitals and vocational training institutions, to promote holistic development.

UNITY IN DIVERSITY

Almost all respondents from all churches were of the view that unity in diversity among the Christians is both necessary and possible. Indeed, many argued that this has been manifested in varied ways throughout church history. The Christian church, they agreed, is composed of different peoples from varying races, nationalities and ethnicities. Yet all share a common belief in the Gospel of Jesus Christ, which unifies them spiritually. But the success of this depends on people's ability to open up and allow each culture to contextualize Christianity in a given place and time, with the Bible as the yardstick. This is the greatest challenge today for the Christian church all over the world. The church must realize and accept the fact that points of view developed and nurtured in one locality may not always be applicable to the universal church. The Christian concern should always be the core of the Gospel, the redemptive work of Jesus Christ.

For members of the AIPCA, the sole goal of the church of God is to proclaim the kingdom of God. This should not be seen as a threat to any other Christian denomination, any religion, or African traditional religious beliefs and practices. God's kingdom is the ultimate achievement of all humanity truly fulfilled. Therefore, conflict between the churches resulting from differences in doctrine or between leaders must not get in the way of this goal. As Kibet and Mutua felt, the basis of conflict is hatred, jealousy, stereotyping, prejudice and discrimination among Christians. What all Christians need, according to Pastor Mukunga, is to look beyond doctrine to their oneness in Christ. They need to reconcile with one another by showing respect for one another. Every leader must accept positive criticism that others find it necessary to make. All Christians and their leaders should learn to capitalize on issues of common interest that foster unity rather than the differences that divide them.

The respondents noted that among the many points of common interest that can foster unity is faith in God, creator, sustainer and progenitor of all things. This is one of the most powerful. But there are also the elements of belief in life after death, the shared concern of restoring moral values among African families, and the whole question of holistic development. Christians can cooperate in promoting justice, harmony, equality and honesty in society. They can also share places of worship as well as participate together in social activities and ceremonies such as weddings and funerals, and birth and naming celebrations.

Frs. Guillaume and Maina insisted that great flexibility should be allowed the local churches in this matter of cooperation among Christians. People should be allowed to apply their unique perceptions and authentic Christian reflection on Christian living in general and in the liturgy in particular. If slaughtering a bull and partaking of it by members of an SCC add value to their concept of a communitarian lifestyle, that should be allowed. If age is a strong factor in religious leadership, priests, pastors and catechists should allow the members of the church to elect from among their elders the persons to lead them in SCC or parish councils. In more specific terms, as the Catholic bishop insisted, there should be a lot of listening, sensitivity and readiness by church leaders to learn from the congregations, fellow clergy and theologians about the best way to proceed in ecumenical sharing.

Our respondents voiced a constant uncertainty about church unity given the diversity of African cultures. Although it was generally agreed that culture is necessary as the basis for fulfilling religious experiences at all levels of life, many respondents pointed out that Africa is divided into multiple ethnic groups of varying populations. These range from a few thousand members to millions. In Kenya, the Dorobos (the smallest sub-ethnic group in the country) consists of fewer than two thousand persons, while the Kikuyu (the largest ethnic group) has approximately six million people. Each of the forty-one or forty-two ethnic groups in Kenya possesses cultural values and practices which give it a religious perception peculiar to it. Should we therefore come up with over forty liturgical forms in Kenya? In the process of inculturation, should the cultural values of bigger ethnic groups like the Kikuyu, Luo, Luhya, Kamba and Kalenjin be emphasized at the expense of the smaller groups such as the Dorobo, Oromo, Samburu, Mbere, Taita and Pokomos? Must we not be conscious of the possibility of cultural change as we pursue the goal of inculturation? These are questions that did not receive adequate responses in the research.

UNDERSTANDING OF THE BIBLE

Generally, the Bible was accepted as the basic principle of all Christian teaching. For all our respondents, Christianity has the Bible as its sole guidebook and it is very important for all Christians to know how to read and study it. Through it, for most respondents, God makes Christians aware of what is expected of them. It is the authorized word of God, so that if a person actively follows its teaching, he or she is assured of a good life in this world and in the next.

Most AIPCA respondents observed that the Bible contains all that they need to know about God and their fellow human beings. A few, however, especially the educated youth, said that although the Bible is the inspired word of God, it does not contain everything. They argued that there is much one can learn from other sources, for example from African traditions. As Sammy Maina expressed it,

> Before Christianity was introduced in Africa, Africans used to live in harmony with their God because their traditions have a lot of guidance concerning their lives; there is no need to abandon our useful traditions just because we are Christians. Moreover, there are many elements in the Bible that are similar to African traditions.

These he identified as belief in one God, life after death, the power of prayer, and the existence of spiritual beings. They also contain the same proscriptions against killing, stealing and adultery and insist on the command to love one's parents and neighbors. These are characteristics of both traditions. Their message carries the same weight and relevance because it concerns the relationship between God and human beings. Both also challenge, encourage, correct, give direction, console, comfort, and strengthen.

Whereas many of the members of the AIPCA saw the Bible as exact history, telling of things that actually happened, and as prophecy in the sense of foretelling what would happen in the future, the Akorinos described the Bible as a measuring rod by which human beings should assess their daily lives concerning the extent to which they have accommodated themselves to and made relevant the word of God. There was general consensus in these two churches that all Christians must read and interpret the Bible for themselves, although the degree to which they can do so depends on each one's intelligence and maturity. (Women seemed to attribute this ability more to men than to themselves.)

For the AIPCA, the ability to interpret the Bible ultimately depends on the power of the Holy Spirit, who opens the believer's mind's eye, helps him or her to focus fully on the word of God so that he or she might come up with an authentic interpretation. This gift is given most of all to pastors. In the AIPCA pastors are seen as gifted people, with talents and wisdom that they use in interpreting the Bible. In this sense pastors are "extraordinary" people. Furthermore, they take a lot of time to study, meditate, pray, and fast over the Bible, and in so doing they are able to come up with the most authentic interpretation that will satisfy most of the spiritual needs of the congregation. The dedication and devotion of the pastors in serving their fellow Christians in their capacity as servants of Christ makes them the most appropriate interpreters of the Bible.

Most Catholics (approximately 75 percent) also felt that interpreting the Bible is a task for priests and catechists, sisters, seminarians, deacons, bishops and cardinals, as well as for other Christians who have a calling and are trained in the field. A few voiced the opinion that the village catechist was the best person to interpret the Bible because he is most in touch with the reality of his congregation and understands their daily needs and experiences better than the priest, who is seen rarely and is often perceived to be detached from reality.

AFRICAN THEOLOGY

Most officials in all the churches defined African theology as one that aims at contextualizing Christian scripture into the African's way of life, concentrating on the language, culture, traditions and customs of the locality. This is because, as Fr. Nundwe put it, there has been an excessive imposition on Africa of western Christian values at the expense of good African values. Most informants argued that missionary Christianity looked down upon African Religion, dismissing it as evil and its worship as pagan. "If inculturation means anything, it means the honest and serious attempt to make Christ and his message of salvation ever more understood by peoples of every culture, locality and time . . . ," Nundwe reasoned. "So, there is a need to study and appreciate the African values and incorporate them with Christianity. People should realize that not all African religiosity is pagan, evil, sinful or unacceptable." The two approaches need to stop focusing upon their differences and to appreciate and utilize more their similarities and unique practices.

Several educated Catholics were convinced that there is a lot that the church can learn and borrow theologically from African Religion. As they pointed out, in recent times there has been a lot of positive interaction between the two when the church began to appreciate African Religion as an integral part of African life which they cannot do away with. For example, African theology is looking at the times and ways of worship in African traditions, the importance attached to sacrifices and offerings and how this can be compared to the Eucharist, the importance and significance of supernatural beings, the importance attached to community life as opposed to individualism, and the importance of rites of passage. Where dialogue between mainline Christian churches and African Religion is difficult, it is seen to be largely due to the "pride" and "pre-meditated" agendas of some Christian officials. Sr. Anne Njeri and Fr. Muchiri, among others, voiced this view. They thought that there existed feelings of superiority among members of the Catholic Church and the AIPCA toward African Religion that stifle meaningful dialogue.

From the pastoral point of view, the issue of polygamy in traditional African culture was raised again and again. Many respondents said that on this question there is a need to respect the fundamental rights of every person without discrimination. According to Sammy Maina, for example, if the church is the family of God, all its members are the sons and daughters of God. Therefore, all should be treated with equal kindness. The church should try to make them aware of God's love for them regardless of the situation they find themselves in. If there is a way out of any spiritually compromising situation, the church should help those concerned to find it, but if for any reasons there is nothing that can rectify the situation, they can still be allowed to participate in church affairs to a certain extent. Although polygamists and the divorced should not participate in the Eucharist, Maina argued, they could be involved in other church activities in the SCCs, devotional groups, and parish councils.

2

Inculturation in Tanzania

Taking Popular Spirituality Seriously

INTRODUCTION

"But *Ndugu* [Sir]," said Osward Kayombo when I asked him what he thought about inculturation in the church, "*you* must be the one to tell me what inculturation is. I have never seen inculturation in the church. Besides, our culture contains so many things; I do not know what has to be inculturated and what does not." The respondent wanted *me* to tell him what inculturation means, what the church is doing about it, and point out those elements in our culture that are relevant for inculturation.

He was touching on a general problem that has affected the process of inculturation in Tanzania. While a good number of theologians now accept that inculturation is a task for all the faithful (for example, see Waliggo et al. 1986), official church leaders see the process as a scientific task which they have to teach, guide and protect. Because of the tight grip the leaders of the church have over the process, ordinary Christians have learned to distrust their own views on the matter, and rely on what the leaders of the church say. Like Kayombo, they have learned to be passive recipients of church teachings and not active participants and agents of change in their own church.

Yet official control seems superficial. As I found out during the research, lay people in the church have their own way of responding to the Gospel and the challenges of everyday life that is different from what the church leaders teach. The uncertainty of Kayombo regarding the cultural elements that should or should not be inculturated is rooted in the difference between what the church teaches and what he himself actually lives. How can this tension be resolved? How can the widespread uncertainties about the cul-

Research for the material on Tanzania was undertaken by Evaristi Magoti of the Department of Philosophy, University of Dar es Salaam, Dar es Salaam, Tanzania. The use of first-person pronouns reflects the observations of the researcher rather than myself. While I did not change the essential findings, I did adjust the language and style of the research report to give a consistency to the style of the book. In addition, the reader will note some repetition of observations from the Kenya and Uganda research reports since challenges facing the churches in the East African countries of Kenya, Tanzania, and Uganda are often similar.

tural-religious (i.e., Christian) responses to various life situations be eradicated so that people can begin to have confidence and faith in what they do as Christians? What weight should be accorded to the responses of the ordinary Christians in the process of inculturation? Indeed, what does inculturation mean?

CONCEPTUALIZATIONS OF INCULTURATION

Local Definitions

In Swahili, the lingua franca of Tanzania, the word inculturation is translated as *utamadunisho*. The prefix "u" refers to a situation or a condition of being or acting. *Tamaduni* often denotes the nature, the seed, the origin, and even the essence of a culture. In ordinary Swahili, the word simply refers to a culture. The suffix *sho* turns the noun *tamaduni* into a verb or an act. Thus *utamadunisho* literally refers to the condition of making culture. It denotes the process or act of making something alien (foreign) part and parcel of a particular culture. It has the connotation of adaptation, integration and indigenization.

Closely related to *utamadunisho* is a term which many church leaders I interviewed referred to as *umwilisho*. Like in the term *utamadunisho*, the verb *umwilisho*, derived as it is from the noun *mwili* (body), signifies the condition and the process by which something immaterial acquires a material body that can make it accessible to the senses, and thus become an object of sense experience. My respondents noted that the term refers to the event of God taking on the human condition and becoming one like us in all things except sin. It is the incarnation, which is translated in Swahili as *umwilisho*.

Church Leaders' Responses

Many church leaders in Tanzania were familiar with both terms—*utamadunisho* and *umwilisho*—and often used them interchangeably. "Our culture," said Sr. Veronika Joseph, "has to take flesh . . . in Christian life. That is why for me, *utamadunisho ni sawa na umwilisho na umwilisho ni sawa na utamadunisho*" (inculturation is incarnation and incarnation is inculturation). The implication of this is that up to now African culture has been like something that has had no flesh in the church.

To some respondents in this category, however, the term *utamadunisho* did not convey the real theological meaning of inculturation. According to Fr. Kaombe, a third-year sociology student at the University of Dar es Salaam, "The [Swahili] term was coined at the time when the word adaptation was in vogue. No other word for the notion existed when the concept of inculturation was introduced." In other words, the Swahili term does not reflect the shift in the debate over the appropriate conception of the process of inculturation. As a result it has retained an old connotation of adaptation that is no longer adequate in describing the concept of inculturation. Yet it is now in common use in church circles and the meaning attached to it varies considerably. While for some it means bringing to life African culture (as for Sr. Joseph), for Fr. Kaombe it means the "complete assimilation of the Christian faith into the lives of people." As he put it,

> Christ is our Savior. He is the one who came to show us the way of becoming fully human. Those who claim to be his followers have no alternative but to follow the way he pointed out. The disciples of Christ are called to make his way their way, so that they may have life to the full.

To church leaders in general in Tanzania, inculturation is primarily about living the message of Christ or the Gospel. The auxiliary bishop of the Dar es Salaam Archdiocese, Methodius Kilaini, understands inculturation as "a process by which the word of God enters the peoples' lives so that they practice it in their everyday life." This understanding was echoed by the leaders of the Catholic Women Organization of Tanzania. According to its chairperson, Mama Luena, inculturation must be seen as the process whereby the church becomes truly understandable and its teachings livable by assimilating "the customs and the traditions of the place where it is."

All descriptions of inculturation by the leadership infer a relationship between the Christian faith and culture. Where the word "culture" is not mentioned, reference is made to "people and their lives," another way of alluding to culture. Another common feature of the descriptions that surfaced concerned the purpose or ultimate aim of inculturation. Many Catholic respondents across the board conceived this notion in terms of a better understanding of the faith, making the Christian message relevant in the modern world, enabling the church to be truly local, that is truly African, and making the Christian faith livelier. Other understandings made reference to the dignity of the African person, freedom or liberation, and development as purposes of the process.

Among the leaders of the African Initiated Churches, such as the Full Gospel Church of Christ, the African Pentecostal Church, and the African Independent Church, inculturation did not appear to be a systematic theological subject. In the words of G. Mulisa, a pastor in one of the AICs in Dar es Salaam:

> We did not have a council or a synod to tell us how to live our faith. We did not even have a meeting about the meaning of *utamadunisho* and its implications for our life and faith. We do not have meetings to discuss whether what we do is *utamadunisho* or not. You see, *ndugu*, our church is not like your church [the Catholic Church]. We freed ourselves from the domination of whites and our founders tried to find other ways to relate to the spiritual resources of our indigenous traditions, and that is what our spiritual workers are doing. So if you ask me about the meaning of *utamadunisho*, I may mislead you. But I suppose it is a way of being that it enriched by our heritage.

This places into sharp relief the different approaches to the question of inculturation. The Catholic approach involves wide intellectual discussion culminating in a decision by higher church authorities. In other churches they "just do it," as Mulisa, above, put it. In practice, however, the AICs' approach virtually depends on a charismatic leader who discerns the spiritual needs of the people and determines what to do. Both approaches have the same concern in the end: they seek to make Christianity an indigenous faith.

Ordinary Christians' Responses

With most ordinary Christians, inculturation means the use of specific cultural elements in specific areas of Christian life. For instance, when asked to describe *utamadunisho*, they named elements like drums, singing, ululation (*vigelegele*), and use of proverbs in liturgy and moral teaching. This was particularly the case in rural areas where the term was generally understood to mean the incorporation of good traditional customs into the liturgy. According to Mama Imma Kapinga, the good customs are "ululation and the use of rattles and drums, sitting when the gospel is proclaimed, using locally made liturgical vestments, and respect for the Bible."

At Mkuranga Parish, people also highlighted a "respect for the ancestors, healing, community solidarity, respect for the elders, hospitality, rites of initiation, naming ceremonies and singing" as elements of inculturation. However, the respondents were sharply divided over the handling of some elements of traditional customs, such as divination, charms to protect oneself from evil, witchcraft, spirit possession, polygamy, and magic. Young respondents in particular were vehemently opposed to these elements. The more adult members of the congregation were very cautious, arguing that these elements were not in themselves bad or evil and that it is some practitioners who were distorting their value for selfish reasons. For instance, according to Gaspar Materu,

> Some witches are good but others are bad. The good ones do not lie, antagonize or create hatred between people in the community. And if you have a problem to which they have no solution, they tell you the truth. The bad ones pretend to know everything. Thus they cheat their patients and in the end [gain] no good results. All they are interested in is money.

Disagreement was also visible in the area of morality. Inculturation in this area meant to some the use of the good customs in the church. According to many ordinary respondents, there are two criteria for moral discernment: an element's existence in tradition and its efficacy. An element is considered good and worthy of being incorporated into the church if it exists in tradition or if it was practiced by the ancestors and its practice produced the desired results, that is, if it was efficacious. This seemed to be the core of Teoford Komba's intervention in the debate about polygamy at Mkuranga Parish when he said:

My grandfather had seven wives and all of them had children. They did not abandon him or run away because they loved him. With them he created a big family which became the clan of the Kombas. Without that my father would never have been born and I would probably not be here today.

With this statement he was underlining the morality of polygamy.

In urban areas, ordinary Christian respondents tended to define the concept of inculturation rather academically. Their understanding was not essentially different from that of church leaders, namely, they saw it as the process of making Christianity an indigenous religion. Urban members of the Pentecostal churches, however, emphasized as essential to inculturation the African heritage of singing, dancing, spirit possession, healing, trust and respect for elders and the Bible, and prayers for protection from evil. These were mentioned as good customs that have shaped the character and spirituality of their churches.

PROCESS AND PRAXIS OF INCULTURATION

The Official Process: Liturgical Mediation of Inculturation

If for many church officials inculturation is about making the Gospel part and parcel of the people's lives, the question is, How do they anticipate going about it? What is actually being done to make sure that the Gospel is "deeply rooted" into people's lives?

The official response to this question was given by Bishop Kilaini. Because of his position in the church and the significance of what he said, I quote his words at length:

The first and the basic effort of inculturation is the Small Christian Communities [SCCs]. They are the basis of inculturation. They help the Gospel to be part and parcel of people's lives. They help the people to find ways to live together in peace, love and justice. In a sense, SCCs are the extended family, that is, the clan where people know each other well.

The second effort of inculturation is the language. Here in Tanzania we are very lucky to have an indigenous common language in Swahili. With this language, people are able to express their faith in a language they know well. And in the SCCs, inculturation is expressed in the liturgy. Liturgy is one of the expressions of inculturation. For inculturation does not necessarily mean living in the old traditional ways. Inculturation is not the digging out of the old ways and making them relevant in the present context. Rather it is about what people feel comfortable with at a given moment in history.

For instance, songs used in secular environment are also used in the liturgy. So on the one hand, we have the secular *twanga pepeta* [a contemporary popular local dance rhythm in Tanzania], and the religious *twanga pepeta* on the other. That is how people feel comfortable to express themselves, and it is only normal that the people's way of expressing themselves should find a place in the liturgy of the church. This is particularly true for the liturgy of the church, especially the Eucharistic celebration. People appreciate much better the descent of Christ if it is expressed in the language they understand.

   Another effort at inculturation is in the organization or structure of the church. We have in every parish now parish councils. This means that the leadership base of the church has been broadened. We have participatory leadership, so that the laity may have a say in baptisms, development projects and marriages. The lay people in the SCCs decide who should be baptized or marry in the church and who should not. They are also involved in development projects, for they are ones who decide the kind of projects they want in their cells and in their parishes.

The significance of Bishop Kilaini's views lies in the fact that although he does not tell us exactly how inculturation happens in Tanzania, he nevertheless spells out the activities that help the church there be truly local by making the Gospel part of the peoples' lives.

In addition to the initiatives pointed out by the bishop, other Catholic respondents mentioned as evidence of inculturation several more things that have taken place in the Catholic Church. The position of the altar and the celebrant facing the people were mentioned by Sr. Pauline. Another nun, Sr. Cecilia Boniphas, listed as further examples such things as the availability of prayer books (e.g., the missal, the breviary) and the Bible in Swahili, the establishment of local religious congregations of nuns in almost every diocese, the formation of the local clergy and other leaders of the local church. Sr. Maria Theodosia added to these the use of drums, *manyanga* (rattles or shakers), and *vigelegele* (ululation) during the liturgy, the opportunity for the faithful to wish one another peace during Mass, the reception of Holy Communion under both species, and the reception of Holy Communion in the hands. Ndomba mentioned further initiatives involving the naming of children at baptism with indigeneous names, lay people acting as extraordinary ministers of the Eucharist, their greater role in Christian funeral and marriage arrangements, and the use of locally made clothes as liturgical vestments.

Many educated respondents recalled that, although Swahili has always been a common language in Tanzania, spoken and understood by most people in the country, the Catholic Church did not use it as a liturgical language even after it had been declared a national language after independence. The church continued to use Latin in all of its major acts of worship. Father Mogela, a senior lecturer in the department of political science and public administration at the University of Dar es Salaam, recalled how he used to serve the Mass in Latin: "I was an altar boy for a long time and I remember serving Mass in Latin. I still remember the prayers we recited. But then I did not know what we were saying, and after Mass we could not use the language anywhere else."

According to Bishop Kilaini, Catholic youth choirs have played a big role in introducing new ideas in music. "They are the most inventive group and offer their services freely," he remarked. The bishop noted that it is this group which has "set aside" the "secular words" from the rhythm of the *twanga pepeta* and replaced them with "religious words." A similar process took place with hi-pop music, according to the parish priest of Changombe parish, Fr. Andreas Komba. As he put it, "Pop music is fashionable in the parish. Young people have simply substituted the secular words with religious words and they are making an impact. Their songs have an important message to everyone in the community and they are liked very much." He adds, "You cannot forbid them [the youth] from using it [this kind of music]. They [the songs] are so good that even if the parish forbade them, people would keep on listening to them. . . ."

Reference to Vatican II in Catholicism

How did these changes come about? What necessitated the birth of the SCCs, the use of the vernacular and secular music, and participatory leadership?

For the Catholic respondents, it was the Second Vatican Council that officially initiated the process. Referring to the Council's documents, the director of the lay apostolate in the country Fr. Vitus Sichalwe spoke for many leaders when he said:

> The tension between what people live and what they experienced in our liturgies was resolved to a large extent during the Second Vatican Council, when the Council Fathers promulgated the Constitution on the Sacred Liturgy. While maintaining the use of Latin in the Latin rite, article 36 (2) of the Constitution makes the following exception: "But since the use of the mother tongue, whether in the Mass, the administration of the sacraments, or other parts of the liturgy, may frequently be of great advantage to the people, the limits of its employment may be extended. This extension will apply in the first place to the readings and directives, and to some of the prayers and chants, according to the regulations on this matter. . . . The power to decide whether and to what extent the vernacular language is to be used, was given to the competent ecclesiastical authority, who according to article 22 of the constitution, is the Apostolic See and the bishop of a diocese concerned, or in some cases, the territorial body of bishops. No other person, not even a priest, may add, remove, or change anything in the liturgy on his own authority."

The Council ended in 1965, but it was only in 1968 that Swahili was first used in public worship in Tanzania. This was an expression of inculturation.

With regard to the role of the laity Fr. Sichalwe again read from Vatican II's Decree on the Apostolate of the Laity:

The laity should accustom themselves to working in the parish in close union with their priests, bringing to the church community their own and the world's problems as well as questions concerning human salvation, all of which should be examined and resolved by common deliberation. As far as possible, the laity ought to collaborate energetically in every apostolic and missionary undertaking sponsored by their local parish. They should constantly foster a feeling of their own diocese, of which the parish is a kind of cell, and be ever ready at their bishop's invitation to participate in diocesan projects.

Small Christian Communities (SCCs)

Conceived in the late 1970's by the Association of Member Episcopal Conferences in Eastern Africa (AMECEA), SCCs were meant to be cells where the Christian faith would be intensely lived and shared. They were in fact seen as the ecclesiastical extension of the African extended family or clan. It was a very ambitious pastoral plan and one that still characterizes the thinking of the Tanzanian church today. But like all other official church initiatives for inculturation, the SCCs are usually made to follow specific procedures laid down by the leaders of the church.

Maseke, the leader of St. Brigitha SCC in St. Anthony of Padua Parish, Dar es Salaam, explained the structure of its meetings. The gatherings begin with a prayer or hymn. Then follows the recitation of the rosary. After that a text from scripture is read. (Since they meet on Sunday evenings, they read one of the readings for the appropriate Sunday.) They repeat the reading several times until the members of the community understand it. After that, the chairperson (often referred to in Swahili as *Mtumishi wa Neno la Mungu*, minister of God's word) invites the members to remain silent and meditate on the scripture just read. This is followed by a moment of sharing ideas from the reading. If there is no response from any member of the gathering, the scripture passage is re-read and more time is given for sharing. This is followed by prayers of petition (*sala za maombi*), a collection, and a concluding prayer by the chairperson.

Ndomba recalls participating in leadership seminars of the SCCs which took about two weeks and involved all the catechists and elected leaders of SCCs:

We were taught how to initiate the SCCs, how to run them, and how to make them effective. When I came back from the seminar, we started sharing responsibilities in the community. Although I am no longer a community leader, our community is one of the best in our area. Apart from having *Mtumishi wa Neno la Mungu* (the chairperson of the community), we also have *Mtumishi wa Malezi* (caretaker of children and the youth), *Mtumishi/Mlezi wa Ndoa* (marriage counselor), *Mtumishi wa Ujirani Mwema* (person responsible for acts of charity), *Mtumishi wa Ushauri Mwema* (counselor), *Mtumishi wa Uchumi* (treasurer of the group), and *Mtumishi wa Watumishi* (servant of the servants in the community).

One of the most commonly used books in SCCs is entitled *Mwongozo wa Jumuia Ndogondogo za Kikristu*, published in 1978 by the Benedictine Father Ndanda-Peramiho. According to several respondents, this book is a must in every community. This was confirmed by my own visits to several SCCs. I observed that the pattern of conducting these meetings is the same in both rural and urban communities. In some communities, even the concerns are the same—an indication that the book is widely read and consulted by many SCC leaders.

ETHICAL DIMENSIONS OF OFFICIAL INCULTURATION

Almost all the elements mentioned by my respondents related in one way or the other to communal acts of worship. Liturgy was for many of them the cultural mediation of inculturation. But what role does inculturation have in the moral life of the Christian?

All church officials interviewed knew the laws of the church and the specific area of conduct where they applied. The opinion of most was that church laws help Christians to live a better Christian life. Other respondents, however, were more nuanced in their responses. Fr. Sichalwe, for example, was not sure whether the law of monogamy has helped people in this sense, considering the damage it did to the traditional customs of polygamous marriage. He was also not sure whether an unjustly divorced person should be prohibited to remarry.

Generally, the responses by church officials to questions of sexuality were similar and seemed to leave no room for contextualization. For instance, they unambiguously condemned premarital sexual relationships. On this issue, most of them recommended Fr. Lukaville's book, *Kumbukumbu za Semina ya Ndoa*, as a tool for instructors in seminaries. In some parishes, the church's teachings on sexuality are passed on to the young people during the period leading to confirmation. In short, there were no exceptions allowed to the rules of the church on sexuality. When I discussed the problem of polygamy, divorce and remarriage with Bishop Kilaini, he said, "These are big issues. The SCCs help to resolve some of the practical problems, but Christ was very categorical that there should neither be divorce and polygamy nor remarriage after divorce."

Baptism in the Catholic Church requires that catechumens must first of all be instructed, examined and certified. In some cases, converts have to wait for as long as four years before receiving baptism, as Valentine Mbai claimed. During this time, the candidates for baptism are being investigated to assess their moral character. According to Neema Lazaro and Rose Komba, this also means ensuring that they have rejected aspects of African culture that the church finds unacceptable, such as polygamy, performing ancestral rituals or seeking ritual protection against witchcraft. As a result of these controls, Neema Lazaro told me, almost half of the candidates for baptism who went through the process with her were not accepted for the sacrament.

With reference to illness and medicine, most church officials were against the use of condoms as a prophylactic against HIV-AIDS. They argued that condoms were not reliable and that their use encouraged sexual promiscuity—fornication, prostitution and adultery. Legalizing the use of condoms was a breach of the Sixth Commandment, they said, and that, as Bishop Kilaini put it, "is unacceptable to the church." Most respondents made reference to the slogan by Radio Tumaini, the official voice of the Archdiocese of Dar es Salaam, which encourages people to say "No" to sexual activities outside of marriage and asks them to be faithful to one sexual partner in marriage. Hagamu, the co-coordinator of the organization Pro-Life in Tanzania, singled out Youth Alive, a young people's organization against HIV-AIDS, as a step in the right direction.

The creation of peace and justice commissions in each parish was considered by Catholic Church officials to be a proper response to the inequities that prevail in society. In Yombo Parish, for example, the commission has the duty of making Christians aware of their rights as human persons. It runs seminars about women's rights in relation to the new land laws, and campaigns against child labor, female genital mutilation, and corruption, as Kania Musuri and Margret Rose informed me. In Manzese Parish, the commission concerns itself with the problem of street children and has been instrumental in establishing a center for them known as Jua Kali Centre. Apart from providing them with basic needs, they also teach them trades like carpentry and sewing, according to Chuwa Marian, Kipenye William, and Jacquiline Kapile.

Many of the leaders of the churches complained that there was too much foreign influence among the people coming through the means of mass communication. "Unfortunately," lamented Bishop Kilaini, "it is the worst of this [influence] which comes first and which has influence here. Through her own means of communication, Radio Tumaini (Archdiocese of Dar es Salaam), Radio Ukweli (Diocese of Morogoro), Radio Maria (Diocese of Njombe), to mention only a few, the church is helping people to retain their culture. In the future," the bishop hoped, "the church should have its own television station and network." Thus, the church seems to be responding to the challenges of modern technology in the field of mass communication by using similar means. This is an approach that analysts like the Latin American Diego Irarrázaval have called "hyper-inculturation."

There is a striking contrast here between the Catholic Church and the independent churches. The Apostolic Church of Christ, for example, does not have a written code of moral conduct. According to Haikael Mshana, the Bible is their only moral guide. They argue that strictly followed, God's law in the Bible is sufficient to create a world of justice, peace and love. For the Assemblies of God Church, it is blasphemy to have another law beside that given by God. Gregory Ntibani, Rosemary Makene, and Honorina Msoka, members of the Assemblies of God Church were all categorical that the introduction of any other law is simply an attempt by modern society to undermine the supremacy of God. As such, they had

problems with civil laws which legalize abortion, divorce, alcohol, cigarettes, condoms, or prostitution.

Most of these AICs do not have the structures and material affluence of
the Catholic Church. They do not even have organized and systematic catechetical programs. Their evangelization methods depend almost entirely on
what Sophia Kessu described as "personal encounter" with a "saved"
Christian. Instead of people going to them, the members of the church go to
the people wherever they are. They visit homes, offices, markets, shops, and
meet people on the streets and talk to them about the salvation that Christ
offers. They distribute leaflets and ask people to read them. As C. K. Sallu
told me, this service is called HUMANN or *Huduma ya Uinjilisti na Maombi
ya Nyumba kwa Nyumba*. When they meet people in their homes, they pray
with or for them about any problem they may have. Unique to this service
is that the religious affiliation of a person is not a factor: anyone whatever,
regardless of whether he or she is a Muslim, Catholic, or Protestant, is
approached and invited to pray with the evangelists. Elihaika Kessi insisted
that this service is open to everyone, sinner or upright. However, the Bible
is central and is often quoted to justify any moral position the church takes.

As ways of evangelization, the AICs also conduct public rallies, meetings,
and Gospel crusades in the open air in public parks. The aim is usually to
pray for the healing of the sick by charismatic leaders. But the rallies usually begin with speeches on a biblical text that has a moral message on social
issues. Not infrequently, criticism is made of the mainline churches for their
conduct.

At a healing session of the Revolutionary Church of Christ that I attended
in Sabasaba, Mbagala, Dar es Salaam, on November 10, 2002, the minister
began with the following call:

> Rise up, dear fellow soldiers. The revolution has begun: away with
> wasting time playing religious. Let the dead stay in bed. Let the Babylon
> babbles who intoxicate the mind and corrupt the heart with their hyp-
> ocritical poison continue to sink deep in the stink. We must rise up,
> shake off our religious grave clothes and put on the whole armor of
> God. We must become one with the fiery sword of the Word. . . . We
> must go to war.

Less militant groups do not use such language; they simply announce what is
going to happen, that is, the healing of the sick members of the community.

Perhaps the most specific catechesis for these churches is given during the
liturgy, when the minister comments at length on a selected biblical text. The
minister does not stick to one biblical text, however, but keeps on referring
to other texts in the Bible that he deems to have a similar message. Delivery
is often punctuated by phrases from the congregation like "Praise the Lord,"
"Amen," and "Alleluia." As Daniel Lukas explained to me, the style of delivery—particularly the strong and loud voice—is intended to reinforce the
grave moral message. And by their "Amens" and "Alleluias" the congrega-

tion signals their consent to what the minister is saying. Sometimes the moral message is reinforced by curses. Valentine Mbai, a member of a Pentecostal church, recalled to me how the minister threatened with incurable diseases those members in his congregation who had fetishes and juju: "May incurable diseases meet those who have fetishes in their homes. All must adore the true God in Jesus Christ and you must serve him alone. He is the only protector of our lives and everything you have."

Membership in the Apostolic Church of Christ, an AIC, is open to everyone who wants to join. As Baraka Mrehe explained it, "People come to us because they want to be saved. They want to change their sinful life and live a life of holiness. If they accept Christ and believe in him we baptize them." This rather liberal view of rituals helps to give the church a distinctively African content. Not only does it link ritual with purity and protection but, in the view of Haikael Mshana, it also makes baptism the sign of entry into a theocratic community that is free from domination and moral prejudice. By refraining from subjugating their converts to rigorous moral scrutiny, and acting as both judge and jury of the moral disposition of the converts, these churches seem to have established themselves as a haven for people who have experienced rejection and alienation, but who are genuinely seeking God in spite of, or even perhaps because of, the complex life situations in which they find themselves.

This does not mean that the AICs I investigated are indiscriminate in their membership, however. They can be very rigorous in certain aspects. For example, they consider most secular realities to be permeated by sin, so they try to create an enclave of their own with a very strong community ethic based on the Bible. Bernard Henry, a minister in the Apostolic Church in Mtoni kwa Aziz Ali, explained this in the following words:

> The Bible is the word of God. It is the word of God that is meant to lead us who are saved. It is the same word which is supposed to lead people in society in general, not the other way around. But people no longer listen to the word of God. They have erected their own idols in the form of money and power. We cannot let people perish. Those who accept to be led by the word of God [are welcome in our church and] will be saved.

These churches' understanding of the Bible leads them to a literal application of it to everyday realities. Thus their members are not allowed to drink alcohol, smoke cigarettes, or eat certain kinds of fish or meat because they interpret the Bible to proscribe these things. Like the leaders of the mainline churches, they, too, deplore pre-marital sex, abortion, the use of condoms, and all artificial methods of family planning. They condemn witchcraft, polygamy, homosexuality, and corruption. The civil authority obscures the authority of God, they claim, and as such many do not gladly accept it. There is a great mistrust of modern medicine among them because, as they see it, "it is only God who can cure illness."

CHALLENGES AND PROBLEMS

According to Bishop Kilaini,

> The biggest challenge [to the Catholic Church] comes from the Pentecostal Churches which have captured the typical African feelings of joy and practical inspiration in life. New movements within the Catholic Church, such as the Catholic Charismatic Movement, have responded very well to this challenge of the Pentecostals, but this Catholic response, usually called *Uamsho* [Catholic Awakening or Revival], must be careful not go to the extremes. The Church [by which the bishop here was referring to the leaders] is trying to control Catholic Charismatics, so that they do not resemble the Pentecostals. Pentecostals value practical inspiration and the communitarian aspect of togetherness. These are good elements, but the Church wants to make sure that it does not become merely a sentimental church.

Many participants in *Uamsho*, however, did not share the bishop's worry. They did not think that the leaders of the church understood them. As Domitila Gisbelt and Josephine Israel, for example, saw it, what the church leaders call sentimentalism is in fact the manifestation of the Holy Spirit, the consequence of being "taken over" by the spirit of God. As Faraja Samson claimed for himself:

> In everyday situations I am not a sentimental person. That only happens during prayer with my fellow charismatics, and it is seldom that I have control over it. The leaders of the Church should try to understand us and give us the freedom to express ourselves in prayer. After all this is not our doing. It is God's spirit working in us.

To this, Fr. Muba, the rector of the cathedral church in Dar es Salaam, responded:

> The problem of *Wanauamsho* [Catholic Revivalists] is that they think they are more of Christians and closer to God than anyone else in the church. They want to be a church within a church. They do not listen to the leaders of the church because the leaders are not charismatic, and they want to do everything the way they like, without taking into consideration that the church has leaders who are responsible for the welfare of all Christians.

But Salva Kapinga retorts against such accusations:

> We rarely consider ourselves as the holy ones of God. Nor do we think that everyone else is a sinner. We have great respect for our priests and

other leaders of the church. The real problem is that we have different ways of praying, of expressing ourselves to God, and we believe that through prayer God can heal people and help them in their problems. I think that this is not what is acceptable to some of our church leaders.

Closely related to this debate is the tension between the *Wanamaombi* (The Marian Faith Healing Ministry) of Fr. Felician Nkwera and the Catholic Church in Tanzania. Nkwera is an ordained Catholic priest who claims that the Blessed Virgin Mother appeared to him and ordered him to conduct a faith healing ministry throughout Tanzania. After conducting this ministry for some time without hindrance from—and often with the active support of—many of the country's bishops, he was forbidden by the hierarchy to do so in the late 1980s. Nkwera did not heed this interdict, citing as reason the prior authority of God's calling over men's.

Referring to this conflict, Bishop Kilaini said that "the tension between 'Nkwera'" (the bishop does not recognize him as a priest since his excommunication several years ago) "and the bishops is cultural. Nkwera has embraced too much cultural elements in his movement that put him at the risk of 'doctrinal errors.'" However, Sr. Maria Goreti Kente, a senior lecturer in the Department of Political Science and Public Administration at the University of Dar es Salaam, and a close associate of Nkwera and *Wanamaombi*, insists that the problem between them is not so much cultural as it is about the bishops' need for power and control. Explaining, she says:

> We [*Wanamaombi*] are Catholics and have never become anything else. Moreover, we do not do anything that you do not find also done in the Catholic Church anywhere in the world. Our devotion to Mother Mary is not unique to us. Reception of the Holy Eucharist while kneeling and on the tongue is an option in practice in many churches in our country. So, where is the problem? There is no problem there. The real problem is that the leaders of the church cannot bear differences and alternative ways of doing things in the church. For them, differences mean opposition, and if you do not comply with what they want, you become a rebel and a heretic. That is why, according to me, the problem does not involve culture but power.

Reacting to this and similar issues, some members from the Pentecostal Church did not think that the Catholic Church in Tanzania was independent enough to make bold decisions about the life and faith of its followers here. This, Elikana Zuberi said, is because everything the Catholic Church does must be confirmed and authorized in the Vatican. There were echoes of this from within the Catholic Church itself. Fr. Gerald Dereckson, parish priest at Makuburi Parish sought the answer in the three "selfs." "A truly local mature church," he stressed, "must be self-propagating, self-supporting and self-ministering." Explaining what he saw to be at the root of the problem, he said, "In Tanzania we [in the Catholic Church] may be self-propagating and even self-ministering, but we are not self-supporting. This deprives us of the freedom to decide and implement our decisions."

All respondents admitted that a crisis in morality, especially in Christian morality, exists. Again they listed the high rates of abortion, especially in urban areas, rampant corruption among civil servants, unstable marriages that end in divorce, adultery, and pre-marital sex as examples. They also mentioned "irresponsible parenthood," a situation that causes young mothers to throw away babies and forces other children to end up in the streets as street children, drug abuse and drug trafficking, the sexual abuse of minors, and homosexuality as additional reasons for the crisis. Finally, lack of respect for the elders, the oppression of women and prostitution, child labor, the growing gap between the rich and the poor, and the spread of HIV/AIDS were also seen as symptoms of the moral crisis.

According to Kayombo, all this is happening even among Catholics, because

> people are not learning religion during infancy. People have no training in their faith. They just listen but their faith is not very deep. This is because the churches do not teach the faith very well. Priests themselves are not encouraged to study the faith in depth, so they do not explain it very well to the faithful. And another reason is that people are not close to the Bible; they do not study it.

But not every respondent shared the explanation of Kayombo for the moral crisis. On the contrary, some respondents blamed the official church for its method of evangelization which, they said, did not encourage Christian decision making. They complained that the question and answer format of the catechism still used in some parishes during the period of training before baptism merely encourages learning by rote. It is naïve to think that the whole content of Christian teaching can be summarized and codified in some standardized way that is universally valid at all times, they argued. This way of learning, Fr. Komba said, does not prepare people to face the challenges of life that are often not as clear, and the answers to which are not as precise as the catechism presents them.

Sr. Theodosia, who teaches religious education in secondary schools in Dar es Salaam, complained further that catechetical literature has for a long time now not been updated

> There is a need for updated material at all levels of catechesis, beginning with religious education syllabuses in primary schools, adult catechumenate programs, adult Christian formation, marriage preparation and renewal, and so on. Otherwise it is very difficult to make an impact on the moral consciousness of people today.

Sr. Sophia, however, pointed out that this cannot be the whole reason, nor can it solve the problem because many ordinary Christians in Tanzania are illiterate. Even if religious literature were available, they could not use it. This necessitates the current catechetical method of learning by rote.

Reference has already been made to the SCCs as a source and expression of inculturation. During a recent (2002) AMECEA meeting held in Dar es Salaam, the bishops made a point by visiting some of the communities in the city. In their final communiqué they asked "the pastoral agents in the region to revitalize SCCs, which often encourage people to live as members of the family of God." However, the communities I visited in Dar es Salaam and its suburbs, and in whose liturgies I took part, were in a sorry state. The participants were mainly children and elderly women who could neither read nor write. The leaders of all of these communities, though, were invariably from among the few men attending, who also assumed the responsibility of interpreting the scripture readings. The constant complaint concerned the absence of men and young people from these meetings. Why, then, have SCCs not been the success story the bishops wanted and want them to be?

According to Bishop Kilaini, "These communities are still new, and they are not inventive enough." But Fr. Dereckson saw a theological implication in their situation. In his view, even in their present form the SCCs may be seen as communities of the poor, namely, the children and women. They are a living testimony and a constant reminder that the true church of the God of Jesus is the church of this "remnant." If they become mass movements, he argued, they may lose their "prophetic witness."

Some respondents complained, however, that most of the present activities of the SCCs in the archdiocese are designed to serve parish administrative purposes. In the community of St. Agatha, for instance, they held four collections at one sitting: the first collection was for the extension of the parish church, the second was for thanksgiving, the third for the diocese, and the fourth was for seminarians! There was also discussion about who should or should not be baptized, married or confirmed. The leaders had to submit a list of all members of the community to the parish priest, register new members, and arrange details for the visit of the parish priest to the community. At the end of the meeting everyone was tired and many stayed away from the following meeting because of this.

Sr. Jane explained that

> the communities show this failure not because people do not like them, but because they were imposed from above and remain too much under the control of the leaders of the church. They have lost the typical African spirit of community not because the members have lost it but because there is no room for it in the current set up.

The community of St. Josephine Bhakita, which she was instrumental in founding, she noted, was doing very well, and people were happy because

> we discussed how to solve real problems that faced them in the community. But then when I got transferred, everything collapsed. Now they have only children and aged women. What can they do? How can

the very people [i.e., children and aged women] who are supposed to be helped by the community now build an active community? We are in an impossible situation.

The absence of an ecumenical spirit was mentioned by some respondents as one of the biggest obstacles to forming genuine Christian communities. Massawe, for instance, wondered whether the SCCs deserve to be called "Christian" given that they are all made up of Catholics alone. Some Catholic respondents thought that the occasional ecumenical services usually organized after Easter in these communities were not enough. In their view, more effort must be made for Catholics to meet with other denominations often so that a relationship can be established not only with the Christian churches but also with African Traditional Religion. Any effort in that direction was encouraged by Bishop Kilaini. He wished to "clarify" with regard to African Traditional Religion, however, that it "is not an organized religion, although it is in all of us and is part and parcel of our lives." This means that there can be no formal relationship with African Traditional Religion as there can be with other Christian denominations. "But we cannot afford to ignore it. It is the starting point for our evangelization and the source of our concept of community and solidarity in the church," the bishop insisted.

CONSTRUCTIVE IMAGINATION: PRAXIS OF INCULTURATION AMONG ORDINARY CHRISTIANS

Worship/Liturgy

Liturgy in the Catholic Church recognizes and celebrates only seven major moments of grace. These moments correspond to the seven sacraments of the church. But these in Africa do not seem to embrace the whole of life. As some respondents pointed out, there are certain aspects of life that are not addressed by the seven sacraments. For example, according to Hagamu, the reality of people's struggle for survival is not explicitly addressed by the liturgies of the sacraments and the church in general. By this he was referring to the effort to attain the normal daily human needs, such as food, shelter, clothes, and everything that contributes to a decent human life.

Ndomba made a similar remark. He was concerned about ancestral worship and divination. The absence of an explicit liturgy on ancestral worship was for him a big omission, as was the lack of an explicit liturgy of healing and protection from evil. At the moment, this is done in Dar es Salaam by *Wanauamsho* (charismatic revivalists) but, as Celestine Kasele explained it,

The church should know that [healing] is a need for everyone. Just as the Eucharistic celebration involves every Catholic, so also the liturgy of healing and protection from evil should include everyone who is

Catholic. In the prayers of the Church, there are words that ask for God's protection. There is even the sacrament of reconciliation, which is also a sacrament of healing. So perhaps the problem is not so much their absence as in the way they are celebrated and the place they occupy in the whole scheme of the church's priorities.

Not readily experiencing this emphasis on healing in the church, people resort to their traditional culture. I will recount here an incident in which I was personally involved. It concerns Ndomba who, as we have already noted, was a staunch Catholic and a retired catechist. After the death of his wife several years ago, he got married to another woman who was younger than he. Their marriage was blessed in the church but problems began to crop up soon afterwards, dismantling the peace and the joy of the family.

Sharing the situation of his marriage, Ndomba told me that he was having dreams about his deceased wife. She was appearing to him in dreams, discontent with his new wife. As things at home were not going well, he concluded that this was his late wife's doing. He loved her and did not want to do anything to upset her. He also loved his new wife and could not contemplate leaving her. First, it was too early in the new marriage, and second and perhaps more important, a divorce would have destroyed almost fifty years of his moral integrity and good reputation as a teacher in the church. After consulting the older members of his SCC, he decided to perform a sacrifice *(tambiko)* for his late wife in accordance with the traditions of the Wangoni, his ethnic group. (It is significant to note that he did consult the priests at his parish.) In the absence of a liturgy that specifically addresses ancestral concerns, Ndomba resorted to the most natural way of meeting the challenge that was facing him. He opted to offer a sacrifice to appease his late wife.

This is how the sacrifice was performed. Ndomba's neighbors, friends, relatives (from his side and his late wife's), and members of the SCC were invited to his house. The function began at 5 A.M. Ndomba invited the guests to sit on the ground. (There were many chairs belonging to the community there but they were deliberately not used that morning because it is taboo to sit on a chair during this kind of sacrifice.) A woman in her late sixties known as Mama Kagusa presided over the ritual. She was a member of the community, but not a leader. She started off by what can be described as the rite of calling *(okumutogonya)*. She called out loudly the names of the deceased woman, the tribe she belonged to, her clan, and her own family (that is, her husband and her own children, dead and alive). That was followed by the rite of identification *(okwitogonya)*. Here she identified herself to the dead person and to the community there present. She mentioned her names, her tribe, her clan, family, and the kind of relationship she had with the deceased (a kind of recalling of past shared events, experiences and moments that brought them close during life).

Then came the words that defined the function and the purpose of our gathering there in the family home of the deceased. Mama Kagusa intoned:

We are here because of you and your family. If you are not the one causing these misfortunes, we ask you to intervene and save your family. If you are the one causing these misfortunes, we are here to tell you that you are not forgotten. Your husband had to marry in order to have someone to help him take care of the family. He did not do it out of malice, nor has he forgotten you. He takes care of the children the way you wanted them to be taken care of, and his new wife is not a bad person. You certainly know her. [Here she mentioned the new wife's name, the names of her parents, her ethnic group, clan, and place where she lived]. All of us gathered here this morning still have good and fond memories of you. If there is something wrong that we have done or anything we have not done for you, we ask your forgiveness and protection from bad things. Be with your family and guide them in everything they do. (Translated by Ndomba from Kingoni to Kiswahili.)

Then she went on to mention the names of each member of the family, beginning with the husband, the oldest child, down to the last born, asking protection, peace, love and progress for each of them. Mama Kagusa was not reading from a book. She didn't have a Bible, a prayer book or a written script at hand for her invocations. Throughout the function, there was no reference to the name of Jesus. This was a rite for the ancestors and so it remained. The community sat in complete silence.

This verbal prayer was at first discursive, then it changed to argumentative. The final part was mainly petitions for peace and harmony in the family. After the prayer, there followed expressions of thanksgiving. People sat in any way they felt comfortable: some looked directly at Mama Kagusa as if in wonder, surprise, and admiration, while others had their heads bowed down as if expressing regret, sadness, or shame.

There was no spoken response from the community during the ritual; there was only deep silence. Even as she concluded, there was no word to indicate that the prayer was over. There was neither "Amen," "Praise the Lord," nor "Alleluia" or anything like "We ask this in the name of Jesus our Lord." Nothing. Everything seemed to depend on natural, spontaneous reaction and behavior. It gave me the impression that prayers can never be ended and that the functions or activities following them were part and parcel of the prayers themselves. I sensed a certain perception in the group that a conclusion at that juncture may have separated the verbal prayer from other activities that were to follow, thus giving the impression that they were not part of the prayers to the ancestors.

After finishing the prayer, Mama Kagusa sat down. The younger members of the community and family began serving food and drinks. At this time people started singing and dancing to the rhythm of drums. Again, there was no special choir, no special dancers. There was no meeting to select hymns or a hymn book from which songs would be sung. In fact the singing and dancing were initiated by one man, who suddenly intoned a song and everyone joined in spontaneously. Suddenly, the sad faces changed into joyous ones as everyone sang and danced. It was a marvel to behold. We danced in circles, early in the morning, men and women together, holding hands as the drums scintillatingly articulated the joy of unity between the living and the dead. The songs were simple refrains that allowed everyone to join in.

Body language in the form of dancing, singing, holding hands and standing expressed thanksgiving, joy, and happiness at what had just taken place. But this language was also accompanied by symbols: the dancing was done in circles and the dancers were holding hands. A circle among the *Wangoni* may represent the world but it may also represent the cycle of human life. Holding hands may be a symbol of solidarity and unity but it may also be an expression of the fact that we are all involved in a life cycle with our ancestors. These messages were passed on instinctively, making an impression on those present.

Most of the food and drinks were prepared the night before, except the *ugali* (stiff porridge) and the chickens. Ideally, a goat would have been slaughtered for the occasion, but because of financial constraints, Ndomba was only able to afford chickens. These were well cooked but were eaten without salt. Part of the food was thrown onto the ground. We were also not supposed to collect the bones or any part of the food that fell to the ground during the eating. Whatever portion of food happened to fall to the ground was for the ancestors. Besides water, the drink consisted of a mild homemade brew from fermented corn and millet. People left at their own time, each wishing Ndomba and his family a good and peaceful life. The event took place in 2000. Ndomba, a confidante of mine, has never complained of the problem since. The family is at peace and very much united.

The incident is not unique to Ndomba's family. There are many rituals of this nature taking place in Christian families in Dar es Salaam that address different problems of life. Christians who revert to traditional ways do not seem to feel guilty about it. Apparently, they do not believe that they are offending God. They keep on going to the church, receiving the sacraments and fulfilling their church obligations as usual, as Ndomba continued to do after his sacrifice. They perceive themselves to be as good Christians as anyone.

Illness and Medicine

Witchcraft exerts considerable influence among Tanzanian Christians in spite of their faith. Even the most devout Christians, such as Mama Mage Boniphas, find it difficult to resist the attraction of the witch doctors. Born in a Catholic family and being very close to her young sister who is a Catholic nun, Mama Boniphas got married to a Catholic in a church ceremony. After a couple of years of marriage she got divorced. Taking her only child with her, she left Moshi, her home area, to settle in Dar es Salaam. Her former husband also moved to Dar es Salaam, with another woman. The problem that tortures her conscience, she said, is not that she divorced but that she did not find someone else to marry her. "Men talk to me and sometimes I go out with them, but after that no one comes back to me. They never come back. So I do not know what is wrong with me," she lamented.

For more than ten years Mama Boniphas did not find a partner. She consulted her sister, the nun, who advised her to persevere in prayer with the hope that God would send someone with whom she could enter into marriage. She joined the choir at Mwananyamala Parish and became a member of *Uamsho*. There were friends who advised her to consult a witch doctor, but she refused saying she would rather die without a husband than go to a witch doctor. But after ten years of life alone, the situation became unbearable. She thought about what her friends were telling her, that she had *nuksi* (a spell in her body that repelled men), and finally decided to visit a witch doctor. There she was told that the *nuksi* had been sent to her by her husband's current wife who did not want the two to get back together again. She had sent the spell to make her unpleasant to all the men she met. She was given a powder to bathe with so as to remove the spell and make her body "clean" again and attractive to men. At the time of my interview with her, she was a very happy person and full of hope. Later, her sister, the nun, told me that she was seeing someone.

Lucy Agostine had her first baby by caesarian section before being divorced. She lives alone with her child, now about twelve years old. But since her delivery she has never felt well. She always feels pain in her stomach. She visited all kinds of medical doctors with no success. The pain subsides for a time only to reappear accompanied by high fevers and vomiting. Eventually her brother brought her to Dar es Salaam where she could get close medical attention. Suspecting HIV/AIDS, he took her to the hospital where she was examined. The results were negative. X-rays did not reveal anything either. There was nothing that the doctors could do apart from giving her painkillers. In despair and with the help of some of her friends, she too decided to see a witch doctor.

The witch doctor told her that the trouble with her was evil spirits. To remove them, he instructed her to give him a goat or ten thousand Tanzanian shillings. She paid the money. The healing session took place in the evening at the house of the witch doctor. She recalled to me how she was covered by a white bed sheet with a tray of medicine burning slowly inside it. The man uttered some words and she lost energy and fell completely to the ground. From then on she did not remember what happened. She only knows that she woke up in the morning feeling much better than she had ever felt before. Lucy is a Catholic and a devoted member of the church. She does not think that it was bad for her to go to the witch doctor. On the contrary, she believes that the man saved her life.

Sexual Ethics

Almost all respondents considered sex before marriage inappropriate and wrong. All of them admitted that young people engage in it, but they did not approve of it not only because of the fear of AIDS, they said, but also because it went against the spirit of traditional cultural values. Some respondents thought that there was nothing that could be done about it. Others, such as Eric Mbambati, however, struggle to put their children—especially the girls—into boarding schools, hoping that they might get good moral training there and have less time to get involved in sexual liaisons.

While admitting that education is important for their children, and that they do in fact struggle to make sure that their children have a good education, other respondents did not consider any school situation the proper place for children to learn sexual mores. Martin Lutoke saw the school environment as contributing heavily to the "destruction" of the young people's morals. "They teach them sex education," he complained, "and by the time a child is through with the class, she or he knows everything about it and is eager to try it out. Most girls end up pregnant."

Some ordinary Christians, attentive to what is happening in society, have restricted their children from pornographic programs on television, reading suggestive tabloid newspapers, and listening to radio stations that broadcast pornographic material. One of the alternatives for such parents has been to encourage their children to join Pentecostal churches, where there is a strong community ethic, a clear and straightforward message against sexual activity, and the promise "to be saved." As Joan Ndumbati put it, "The Pentecostals teach people to refrain from all evil activities, especially sexual activities, and when you come to think of it, it is perhaps better to let your child be saved in these churches rather than perish so young."

In suburban and rural areas, however, most parents have almost given up enforcing traditional sexual mores before marriage. They seem to accept as inevitable the responsibility of bringing up their children's children born out of wedlock. This is not new in many traditions around Dar es Salaam; grandparents have always brought up their grandchildren. But with the financial constraints now affecting everyone, grandparents are finding it more and more difficult to play the role they used to. But even then, respondents such as Mulisa Andrew and Fatuma Rhodes thought that it was better "to suffer for the children of one's children than to let them be aborted or thrown into dustbins at birth." Ronjino Kayage agreed:

> If this kind of care [for babies born out of wedlock] is not found in our extended families and especially among grandparents, the community will not be able to bear the number of abortions that will occur each day, let alone the number of newly born babies that will be thrown in dustbins or toiletpits at birth. Many young mothers too will die seeking [unsafe] abortions.

Marriage is the institution within which sexual activities are allowed and even encouraged in African societies. But how do people understand the institution of marriage? For many ordinary Christians, marriage implies a shared life between a man and a woman (*maisha ya pamoja kati ya mke na mume*). This shared life is understood to be a community affair involving, besides the man and the woman in question, also the extended families on both sides of the union. According to Joseph Tindo, the chairperson of Kibena Hospital Village, Njombe, marriage was formerly pre-arranged by the parents; they decided who was to marry whom. In and through sharing their lives together, the spouses eventually sealed the alliance between them and, through them, between the two extended families. The two groups became relatives in fact.

Pre-arranged marriages however, are now very rare. Even in the rural areas visited, respondents admitted that the practice is no longer popular. In Njombe and Songea, where the population is 98 percent Catholic, respondents could not recall one recent case of pre-arranged marriage. According to Joseph Mgao, Christianity has contributed to the death of the practice. But this does not mean that parents are no longer involved in the process of their children's marriages. They can and sometimes do propose a partner to their children when they think it is time for them to marry. "We may identify the son of so-and-so to a girl or the daughter of so-and-so to a boy. But the final decision now belongs to the children themselves," Eric Kitine told me.

Faustine Mwendwa, a teacher at Kibena Primary School argued, however, that parents no longer have any significant role in the marriage arrangements of their children. According to him, "By the time the issue reaches the parents, a boy or a girl has already found a partner for him or herself, and the presentation of the issue to the parents is only a formality. Whether the parents accept or refuse his or her choice, it now makes very little difference." In the view of Weston Luttumo, once the children are in love and want to live together, it is not prudent for the parents to prevent them. Given the many cases of real and attempted suicide when parents intervened negatively, parents have learned to let children have their way in this matter. The task of the parents now, he says, is merely to pay the bride-wealth and bestow blessings on the marriages of their children.

In some cases, parents no longer even pay the bride-wealth. Given the economic hardship in many families, sometimes the boy pays the bride-wealth out of his own resources. This is often the case if the boy has a job and financial resources that his parents do not have. In the view of Yona Mhavilwa, even in such cases it is the boy's parents who have to present the dowry to the girl's relatives. The prospective bridegroom is not allowed to do so himself. He in fact rarely meets his in-laws. He must avoid them as much as possible. Even with the social changes taking place in traditional society, the community dimension is still very important in marriage.

Over and above their traditional practices, Christians are obliged by church law to marry in church. Catholic respondents were unanimous in their observation that young people are not fulfilling this obligation. In the view of Kelvin Nchimbi, a local government leader of Undera Village, Mbinga, Songea, marriages of young people in church today are few and far between. The lack of "fresh marriages," as they are called, was also confirmed by Jordan Komba, a catechist in Mbinga Parish, who lamented that in the previous year (2001), they had only twenty marriages between young couples. The remaining three hundred and fifty were between elderly couples.

The main reason given for this decline was the fear of a long-term commitment among the youth. This does not mean that Christians are not getting married in church; they do so only at a much later date in life. "Many Christians today," Jordan Komba explained, "contract marriage in old age, when they have already stayed together for a long time and have had several children." Church leaders in urban parishes also made the same observation. In Mbagala Parish, for example, such "delayed" marriages are on the rise. According to Fr. Balenge, the assistant priest at Mbagala, a total of three hundred marriages were contracted in the parish in 2001. Dubbed *ndoa poa*, or cheap marriages, they usually do not require all the ceremonial trappings traditionally associated with youthful church marriages. They do not require much expense. Most Catholic respondents in rural and urban areas noted that *ndoa poa* was a popular form of marriage; it constituted the highest number of marriages in the Catholic Church today.

Besides being financially "affordable," another reason for their popularity is that they take place at a stage in life when couples are "cool," that is, when they have known each other for a considerable length of time: the heat of their youth has subsided, ideals have been realistically confronted, and life rationally accepted. These are the marriages that last because the couples have already come to terms with the realities of life and are at that moment "settled," according to Manyama Fabian.

Lasting they may be, but it seems that extra-marital sex is not unknown among them. A good number of respondents admitted that married couples have sexual affairs outside marriage before and even after their church marriage. Hagamu, whose pro-life movement brings him in contact with many couples, surmised that, conservatively, between 40 and 60 percent of Christian married couples have sex outside of marriage at one time or another during their life. In urban areas like Dar es Salaam, Mwanza, Mbeya, Arusha, Moshi, Iringa and Songea, the percentage may be as high as 70 or 80 percent, he said. In rural areas, his estimate was between 30 and 40 percent.

Explanations vary as to why there is such a high rate of sexual infidelity in monogamous marriages. According to Ndumbaro James, women in urban areas are exposed to lifestyles that lure them to aspire to a standard of living that their husbands cannot afford. So they commit adultery in the hope of obtaining the money to afford the things they want. In the view of Manyama, there is also the factor of sexual boredom, the monotony caused by sexual intimacy with the same partner. Hagamu agreed with these reasons, but he also thought that the problem was much more culturally rooted. Traditional ethos, he argued, did not encourage the kind of fidelity that Christianity demands from its followers. He cited as illustration the traditions of many of the ethnic groups along the Indian Ocean coast.

For example, he said, among the Zaramo and Dengereko, a girl is taught during initiation not to count on only one man for her security in life. A girl is told in figurative language to have three cooking stones (*mafiga matatu*).

These corresponds to the three men she should have in her life in order "to be secure." The first stone is her actual husband; the girl is taught to consider him as the father of her children and the general caretaker of her welfare. He is the legal husband. But given her many needs, one man cannot satisfy them all. Thus she is told that she will need a second man ("the second stone") whose task it is to provide services that are not catered to, or not sufficiently so, by her husband. But to be really secure, a girl is told to have a third man ("the third stone"). He is sometimes referred to as "reserve man." Just in case one of the two previous ones falters, she must have another man at hand to call upon to supply these needs. In reality these are sexual partners that she meets for sexual liaisons at different occasions during her marriage.

The same is true for a boy or a man. He is traditionally entitled to several wives (or even mistresses), and this is known by his wife-to-be. The existence of this tradition was confirmed to me also by the anti-HIV/AIDS campaigner Adela Mvula. Herself a senior nurse for a very long time, she complained that the war against HIV/AIDS was doomed to failure because of the tradition of the "three stones" so prevalent in this part of the country. In spite of every warning, even from government and church leaders, the custom is being passed on to young people unabated.

Respondents generally admitted the occurrence of divorce. The most common estimate from the rural respondents was that 20 percent of all marriages end in divorce while in urban areas it was between 30 and 40 percent. Among the women interviewed, the main reason for divorce was sexual dissatisfaction. Magdalena Mkoka claimed, "If a woman cannot be sexually satisfied, it is very difficult to sustain a marriage. This is true also for men; if a woman cannot satisfy her husband sexually, it is very likely that the marriage will end up in divorce." Some respondents pointed out that domestic violence is also a cause of marriage failure. But the most prevalent cause cited was barrenness. When a woman, for one reason or another, cannot bear children, divorce is almost automatically the outcome, in the view of Festo Lupogo. And according to John Mkoba, unemployment in urban areas has deprived couples of the means of survival and that has put many marriages to the test. Some marriages have survived but many have collapsed on account of poverty.

Some respondents were of the opinion that the problem of divorce was to a very large extent the consequence of the structure of monogamy. This was the view of Alex Kapinga, among others, who thought that there was a very close relationship between monogamy and divorce. Comparing Islam (which encourages, or at least allows polygamy) and Christianity (which forbids it), Kapinga noted that the problem of divorce was much more acute in marriages enforced by Christianity. He pointed out the example of HIV/AIDS. In his view, the disease is much more prevalent among Christians than among Moslems who may have, by religious sanction, many wives. He contended that monogamous Christians tend to be more unfaithful in their marriages than polygamous Moslems.

CONCLUDING REMARKS

Considering the above responses we need to inquire about their significance for inculturation: What do people's experiences tell us about the process? Data collected from ordinary Catholics seem to suggest that they are aware of what the church teaches and proclaims. They are also aware of what is required from them in terms of moral living. But what is proclaimed by the church is not necessarily what they practice. This is particularly true in the areas of liturgy and morality. Based on these findings, it seems to me that the church's prohibition of witchcraft, for example, has not prevented even the most devout of Catholics from reverting to it in times of need. Equally the case is the church's condemnation of ancestral veneration: although it is prohibited, ordinary Catholics still practice it when certain occasions in their life demand it.

Not much guilt seems to be associated with going to a witch doctor, performing ritual services to the ancestors, having extramarital affairs, or divorcing and remarrying. Paradoxically, although many Catholics thus fall short of the requirements of their church, they consider themselves committed Christians. The guiding principle for many of them seems to lie in the usefulness of any of these behaviors: if a practice is effective in dealing with the negative elements of a particular situation, they will do it. In this study, the principle that whatever is effective in promoting "happiness" is good comes out clearly in the example of sex before marriage. Neither the Christian churches nor secular society has been able to control it. At one time Catholic Church officials refused to baptize children begotten outside Catholic wedlock as a way of curbing the practice. However, the policy only served to increase the rate of abortions and abandonment of babies. The popular practice of grandparents accepting to bring up their grandchildren begotten outside marriage helped both to protect and save lives.

When analyzing the responses I received on inculturation, I get a picture of it as a process rich and fundamental for the life of the church. From this analysis it seems clear that inculturation is not nearly the adoption of certain cultural elements into Christianity or the integration of certain cultural elements into the liturgy. It does not even appear to be the fusion of certain foreign elements with the culture of a people. What these findings suggest to me is that inculturation is a prism through which the whole personal and communal life can be understood, including one's relationship to church laws and practice. If we imagine that this prism is permanently fixed onto our eyes, then we cannot escape the perspectives that it brings. This means that our culture (the prism) always brings with it to life's experiences a certain way of understanding, and therefore of thinking and behaving. I realize that this has its own limitations, and the research has indicated some of them. Nevertheless, it gives inculturation profound meaning: it makes it a way of life inspired by the spirit of God. Inculturation in this way becomes a people's daily response to the realities of life.

3

Inculturation in Uganda

Appreciating New Ways of Being Church

INTRODUCTION

This report represents the final analysis of data obtained from fieldwork research on inculturation in Uganda. The majority of the respondents in my research were women from both rural and urban areas of the country. The data was analyzed with the following objectives in mind:

- To find out what ordinary Christians and church leaders in Uganda understand by "inculturation";
- To assess the extent to which inculturation is facilitated at various levels there;
- To indicate how far the mass of the Christian faithful are involved in the process;
- To identify and explain major constraints against effective inculturation; and
- To recommend suitable strategies which facilitate inculturation and the identity and maturation of the African church.

SCOPE OF RESEARCH

The research was mainly carried out in the western and central parts of Uganda, but some individuals from the urban areas of the northern and eastern parts of the country were interviewed as well. At Uganda Martyrs University in central Uganda, the interviewees were mainly church officials who have had extensive pastoral experience in rural areas all over the country. Most of them were priests, nuns, and brothers and were very cooperative when I interviewed them on the issue of inculturation.

Research for the material on Uganda was undertaken by Agnes Nabossa of the Department of Religious Studies, Uganda Martyrs University, in Kampala, Uganda. The use of first-person pronouns reflects the observations of the researcher rather than myself. While I did not change the essential findings, I did adjust the language and style of the research report to give a consistency to the style of the book. In addition, the reader will note some repetition of observations from the Kenya research report. Challenges facing the churches in the East African countries of Kenya, Tanzania, and Uganda are often similar.

Altogether I interviewed a total of 107 people, either individually or in groups, ranging in age from 15 to 80 years. All of them were Catholics. They included 5 priests, 4 brothers, 13 nuns, 5 catechists, 5 chairpersons of parish councils, and 75 ordinary lay persons. Of the total number, 24 were male and 83 female. One interesting group I interviewed in central Uganda is known as "The Marian Movement of Priests" (MMP). They were over 60 in number, but only 42 of them stayed with me to the end of the conversation and actively participated in the discussion, which took over two hours.

Moreover, in the western part of Uganda, I visited individual Christians at home and at work in the villages of Katojo, Ngara, and Nyakakoni in Mbarara District. There I also talked to different groups of people in the Charismatic Renewal Movement. In Katojo village, I spoke with a congregation of over 50 people who had come for the Sunday service. The catechist allowed me to use the time usually allotted for the homily for the conversation, which I taped on audio cassette.

UNDERSTANDING OF INCULTURATION

The data indicate that people had various ideas about what the term "inculturation" means and implies for the pastoral activity of the church. The definitions most mentioned included:

- The process of rooting Christianity into a culture;
- Celebrating our liturgies in an African way;
- Integrating our cultural elements into Christian worship;
- Evangelizing Africa in an African way;
- Immersing the Christian faith in the local culture.

Although a large number of respondents could not initially explain the meaning of the term "inculturation," almost all were able to carry on a conversation about it with relative ease when I explained what the research was all about. This implies that although the theological term as such may be unfamiliar, the experience and the reality it stands for are not.

Inculturation was in most cases linked with the liturgy among both church officials and the laity. However, some of the parishioners of Mitala Maria Parish went a little deeper in explaining the notion. For example, Mary Nantege explained inculturation as *"Okulaba nti edini essa amakanda mu mpisa zaffe ezekinnassi"* (To see to it that religion is rooted in our cultures). Another parishioner said that inculturation is *"okulaba nti ediini wamu namayisa gaffe byona biba kyekimu"* (to make sure that religion and our customs are one). It seems that at this parish there was a priest who made a conscious effort to explain and integrate the people's cultural values and practices with Christianity, so that the process was no longer strange in the general consciousness of the people.

But only a few places and people appear to have had this opportunity. Many respondents lamented the fact that they had had no opportunity to learn from anyone what inculturation was all about. Placeda Kamanyiro, a catechist, thought that if catechists were made more aware of this issue and its importance for the church, if they were sensitized about its demands and implications through courses, they could be some of the best catalysts of inculturation. According to her:

> Very few courses on how to go about our evangelizing work are offered to us. Trained catechists are also very few. In fact, the conference in which I first heard about the term inculturation was attended only by people who could sponsor themselves, which, of course, meant that there were very few participants. Some parish priests do not even care to inform us about courses taking place, let alone organizing some.

On the same issue, Emmanuella Adokwun, a religious sister, said that some parishes are too poor even to feed their parish priests and so planning courses for catechists was a luxury for them. They could not afford it.

Two young priests who defined inculturation from the liturgical perspective indicated that inculturation was not well explained even in formation houses. Although there was the need for inculturation, they thought that the training given in seminaries for priests and in formation houses for nuns did not give them enough content on the subject. This, they said, is eventually reflected in the pastoral agents themselves as well as the people they serve. For this reason, lay people find it difficult to make the transition from what the missionaries taught them—that the church acts in the same way throughout the world—to what is being taught now concerning the cultural implications of teaching and living the Christian faith.

I observed in many locations I visited that some old people find that what they are told now is inculturation can be the very things they were previously forbidden to do. As Veneranda Kamurago complained, "*Kwonka manya eby'obyomu diini yeitu nabyo nibibuzabuza. Nibatugira ngu tukore ebi bagaruka bagira ngu tukore ebi*" (Things in our religion do confuse us so. They [the church officials] tell us to do one thing today and then again tell us do to a different thing tomorrow). She thought that this might explain why many sects like the Movement for the Restoration of the Ten Commandments break away from the Catholic Church. (This group was led by Credonia Mwerinde and Joseph Kibwetere who defected from the Catholic Church and claimed to be Marian visionaries. In March 2000 they were believed to have caused the death of many of their followers by burning them in a locked church at Kanungu.)

Within the charismatic renewal groups, spontaneous prayers, vigorous gesticulating, loud singing and shouting are seen as forms of inculturation. But this does not seem to be universally appreciated. Butagasa, whose wife is a member of the movement, told me angrily:

> What this new religion is bringing to our families is unheard of. My wife leaves me in bed before 5:00 A.M. and goes to the village chapel

for prayers. Often she leaves home for more than a week to join others for what they call seminars. She is married to the movement: I cannot say anything.

But Sr. Adokwun thought that a more aggressive method must be used to effect inculturation. According to her, the church can adopt some of the rituals used in crowning kings in Buganda and Ankore, for example, in the liturgy of the feast of Christ the King. Fr. Peter Kanyandago, a professor at Uganda Martyrs University (UMU) held a similar idea, insisting, "The whole structure in the church should be inculturated." He found it "unfortunate to practice and emphasize inculturation only in the liturgies."

Scholastic Kobusingye and Juliet Atuhairwe, both students at UMU, commented about the dress code. They wonder why priests have to buy and wear those foreign robes. For me, they should simply put on a *kanzu* [a long, usually white robe worn by men] when in Buganda, and keep on changing according to what people wear in a particular area. Nuns also should dress like other women. This will bring them near to us because they'll look more like us.

FACILITATING INCULTURATION

Is inculturation taking place? According to three catechists I interviewed, inculturation is happening, but at a very slow pace. This is because it was, in their view, not sufficiently promoted by the priests. They listed some of the obstacles to inculturation as:

- The parish priests do not care to sensitize their people to it;
- It is expensive;
- Some church leaders are very rigid in their ways;
- It goes against the way Christianity was introduced;
- Many leaders either do not know or ignore the culture of the people;
- The people themselves are indifferent.

Rigidity of church leaders was cited most often as the chief reason for the sluggish pace of the inculturation process. Placeda Kamanyiro, the woman catechist, had not forgotten the time when a missionary who could hardly speak Runyankore, the local language, insisted on reading the Gospel on Christmas Eve. She had offered to do it but the visiting priest asked if there was a male catechist around. On being told that there was not, the priest said then that he would do it himself. Kamanyiro commented, "*Egyo ntekateka eri omu Baseserdooti baitu tekubaasa kwikiriza edini kwijura gye omubantu*" (This way of [shortsighted] thinking among our priests cannot enable religion to be rooted in our cultures). Daniel Tibamanya, a retired catechist, thought that the bishops and priests should make it a point of encouraging inculturation in the parishes. Then it would be easier for the catechists to emphasize and promote it.

Sr. Kankya, an elderly sister from the Congregation of Immaculate Heart of Mary Reparatrix, emphasized this same thing, saying:

> The leaders are the ones who taught the people that all that is in African Religion is bad. So I think they should be the ones again to say that what we used to teach you was not right and that there is need to revisit culture and let religion be part of it, giving examples of how the two religions can promote goodness!

A respondent from Ggoli parish, Kampala Archdiocese, told me how surprised he was when their parish priest, a missionary, once forbade them to dance a Kiganda dance during Mass, claiming it was obscene. The priest interpreted the local dance in this way because the Baganda execute some dance movements which to the uninitiated eye might appear sexually suggestive, but in fact are not. If inculturation was not happening, he said, it was because of attitudes like this from the higher leaders of the church.

On the question of who the agents of inculturation should be and what areas needed it, I interviewed a group of five women, members of the charismatic group of Katojo sub-parish, Mbarara archdiocese. They responded in order of importance in this way:

Who are the agents of inculturation?

- Priests and catechists;
- Those people who are trained in the process of inculturation;
- All of us.

What areas of Christian life should be inculturated?

- Liturgy;
- Preaching;
- All ceremonies: marriage, burial, baptisms, and so on.

The main reason given by the five women as to why priests and catechists should be the principal agents of inculturation was the knowledge they are supposed to have about it because of their training. Although Geraldine Nalunkuma, the group's leader, thought that all of us should be involved in the process of inculturation, the group itself was of the view that priests and catechists had to have a greater role to play in it. They observed, moreover, that when they as laypeople get involved in it they meet with general resistance and misunderstanding. One of them remarked:

> Many people think that we are spoiling the Catholic faith. In fact, some people do not even want to listen to us. We are associated with the followers of Kibwetere and Credonia [see above] who brought about the Kanungu saga. Some see the dancing in praise to the Lord [that we do] as evil. They say we are diverting the Catholic Church and its believers to "our sect"! I think priests and catechists should take the lead to correct this misinterpretation and misrepresentation.

Her implication was that people listen more to the officials of the church than to anyone else. Across Uganda now, any change in the liturgy from the usual practice is associated with the mushrooming sects that are rife in Uganda. Thus many Christians can hardly stand the way some members of the charismatic groups pray.

THE PURPOSE OF INCULTURATION

For most church leaders interviewed the purpose of inculturation consisted mainly of the following four points:

- It enables Christianity to be localized;
- It helps people to understand the Christian faith more fully;
- It helps people to live their faith more integrally as Africans;
- It facilitates the spread of Christianity in Africa.

Most respondents found it easy to name some areas in their lives that they feel are already integrated with Christianity. The examples of ceremonies like marriage, burial, and birth came up often.

In central Uganda, for example, it is now a requirement for the *ssenga* (paternal aunt) and the *mukko* (brother-in-law) to give their consent as a precondition for the priest to proceed with the blessing of the marriage, as was done in traditional society. The two witnesses are now recognized by the church as creating a sort of bridge between Christianity and culture. Dorothy, a member of the parish council of Nkozi Parish, confirmed this when she said:

No marriage can be blessed when the people from both sides of the couple's families are not in full consent. The *mukko* and the *ssenga* must therefore be present at the rituals that take place in preparation for marriage and at the marriage itself. The two play an important role in making sure that the marriage is valid in the eyes of the church and tradition.

Burial in central and western Uganda involves many ceremonies and rituals, including the ritual of installing the heir. All relatives are supposed to gather for the occasion. Husbands, wives, and children who have been misbehaving are reprimanded and reconciled there. During the ceremony, people eat and drink because the deceased has been made "alive" in the heir.

This takes place during Mass and so is integrated in the liturgy. Namusisi, a primary school teacher, said that she felt relieved and happy that this was so:

At least the church is now actively involved in the celebration of the last funeral rites. These rituals and celebrations are now done within the celebration of the Holy Eucharist and both groups [Christians and traditionalists] have accepted it. This is good because formerly it was a problem for us. One could not combine such important family celebrations with those of the church.

Nevertheless, a few respondents considered these traditions to be evil and devilish and said that they could not attend them. Mrs. Kato, a born-again Christian, for example, told a story about what once happened to her when members of the clan chose her to be the heir of her deceased mother. She said that she would feel her hands go stiff whenever she would think of joining them with those of relatives in the village, as the ceremony required. She consequently decided not to join the celebrations.

Concerning the birth of twins, Mrs. Kiwanuka, an elderly lady at Nkozi hospital and a mother of twins, said that when she had her babies, her family simply behaved "in a European way. We just took the children to the church for baptism. When we came back, we served a meal, and that was that" (*Ffe ebyaffe twabiyisa kizungu. Abaana twabatwala mu eklezia nebabatiza, bye twada awaka netugabula abantu*). But in many cases still, according to her, after baptism the parents of twins visit traditional healers for protection rituals. It is believed that the twins can "burn" (cause a skin disease to) family members when these rituals are not performed.

My respondents were in general quite happy about many of the symbols used in celebrating the sacraments and other Christian rituals: Water, they said, is used for blessing among the Baganda and Banyankore just as it is in the Catholic Church. Similarly, fire is a sign of survival after death among these two ethnic groups just as it is the symbol of resurrection in Christianity.

AFRICAN THEOLOGY, CHURCH AS A FAMILY, AND DIALOGUE

How familiar is African theology? Are African theologians known? Very few respondents were in any way familiar with either African theology or the names of African theologians. At the university and among the church officials, African theology was described as understanding or knowledge of God "in an African way." Only eleven people among the thirty-two interviewed on this issue could mention the name of an African theologian.

The Church as Family of God was understood and explained in terms of the oneness, unity, and relationships that are expected to exist in any family. Just like an ordinary family where there are parents and children, the respondents said, the church is made up of the faithful as children. According to John Chris Kigyezo,

> The church is a spiritual home. Meeting a Catholic in a bus, for instance, I feel more comfortable and at home with him than when I meet a Muslim. This means that there is a kind of togetherness with the people of the same religion. In Uganda, this bond is at times very strong and has unfortunately been misused by politicians, breeding hatred among different religions.

On dialogue, Sr. Bonny Tumusiime did not see much of it happening in a meaningful way. As she saw it:

Dialogue in the church occurs only when the church officials, for example the parish priests, are planning to carry out a project that needs money or other types of services rendered by the rest of the Christians. Even then, the dialogue tends to be a kind of monologue whereby the church official spells out what is to be done and he/she cannot be opposed.

Sr. Adokwun agreed. She saw "dialogue" in the church to be mainly concerned with money. Talking from her experience of southern Sudan, she remarked with considerable emotion: "There is little dialogue in our Catholic Church. . . . There is a tendency on the part of the church leaders to impose their wishes upon the rest." Fr. Kanyandago was of the same opinion. He thought it

unfortunate that dialogue takes place only when church leaders want to do something practical, for example, building or organizing for a visitor—that is, when they want money. However, in the area pertaining to the administration of the church, or even its doctrine, there is little dialogue; the tendency there is for Church leaders to dictate solutions to the people.

However, both he and Fr. Lucian saw much room for dialogue in the church. They regretted that chances for it were neither exploited nor used well. As Fr. Kanyandago, a theologian and canon lawyer, summarized it, "There is plenty of room for dialogue in the church, but unfortunately, this advantage is often not taken up. I know that dialogue is foreseen in the doctrine and laws of the church, but this does not happen sufficiently in practice."

Mr. Steven Bazirake, an experienced university administrator, did not see it in exactly the same way:

Room for dialogue in our Catholic Church is very limited. What there is is mainly monologue. Church leaders rarely listen; they rather enjoy giving directives and the faithful are expected to implement them. Our leadership in the Catholic Church is very slow at adopting new changes, less so when the initiatives are made by ordinary Christians.

Bazirake went on to recommend that the church must open its doors more widely so that as many faithful as possible may get involved in shaping its future.

Fr. Edward Ndakire, a student at UMU, blamed the lack of dialogue in the church on the problems that can come about because of it. For instance, he said, in the Protestant churches where dialogue is allowed, there is division; the Catholic Church fears division. So although the church knows that there should be dialogue, it is trying to avoid it for that reason.

Sr. Immaculate, also a student at UMU, pointed out that "Christians do not even know that they have a right to dialogue." A number of respondents confirmed this view, since, when asked about it they appeared unconcerned, as if dialogue was not called for, or as if they had no right to it as members of the church.

CHURCH UNITY AND DEVELOPMENT

To most of my respondents, diversity of cultures and languages in Uganda posed no problem for the unity of the church. They were convinced that differences of languages and cultures did not mean that the people could not work together for their own development. Geraldine Kabanda expressed this view in a very simple way when she said: "With Christianity, we [of different languages and cultures] have come closer together; we now believe in one God. We should be able to resolve our religious differences and strive after things that unify us."

Fr. Herman Nsubuga, serving as a missionary priest in Rwanda, gave the family as the best example that shows the possibility of unity in diversity, when he said:

> For me, unity does not necessarily mean physical unity. The politicians use unity to meet their goals, and in the church it is used to define the Trinitarian God. The family is a good example of unity in our daily life. Wife and husband live together in unity although they are different individuals with different backgrounds. Their unity is expressed in the way they organize family life, as, for example, when they plan together family economic strategies, save together for the future, and so on. If [church] people were able to work together for human dignity and freedom, for instance, in this way, then it would be easy to have unity in the church despite our differences. In all this, there must be some kind of a common goal and interest. A reciprocal relationship is basic. . . .

The question of the church's involvement in politics and development programs gave no clear-cut answer. A good number of the respondents thought that the church should be involved in these things while as many others thought that this would disrupt the work of the church and the reputation of the church leaders. Clare Ssozi thought that church leaders could be involved in politics, but not directly. "Its [the church's] main work should be to guide people in morals," she said, "and because of their commitment to spiritual leadership and to avoid misunderstandings about this, I think priests should keep their distance from politics." In the opinion of Leolyn Twikirize, for the church to involve itself in politics means diverting its leaders from their duty of spreading the gospel.

Miss Kyokuhirwa, however, saw things differently. According to her, "If our church leaders were to really join politics fully, Uganda would be a more peaceful and developed country." With a serious demeanor she continued:

> You see, the Catholic Church has many educated people, but most of them are church leaders and, at the same time, they are not fully useful to their people. Can you imagine that when the President [of

Uganda] chose Sr. Magoba to join the Electoral Commission her Congregation "caught fire" [i.e., was up in arms against it]? Our capable people remain uninvolved in politics and development issues because they have to obey the orders of the church. Meanwhile, society suffers.

Similarly, Eric Twesigye, a secondary school teacher, argues that politics is part of life. "Man [sic] is a political animal, so there is no way the members [of the church] can avoid engaging in politics." He thought it a good thing that one Rev. Kabushanga was a member of parliament. Sr. Bonny Kyaligonza agreed. "People say that the church should not get involved in what has been classified as profane [but deal only with the sacred]. In real life, however, the two must influence each other because the people you see in politics are the same people you see in church." Fr. Peter Kanyandago also thought that the church should be involved, "provided its involvement promotes justice and is for the common good." He continued:

The moment you get responsibility as an administrator to manage a group of people, that is politics. Politics for me is not a matter of standing up to ask for votes; rather it is management of society where we try to see how power should be used to promote justice and solidarity. [Thus,] as soon as we do this [even] in the church, we are in politics.

In a conversation about this issue with John Ahimbisibwe, Miss Kyokuhirwa angrily said, "The church is more than a hundred years old in Uganda, but some people still go about without food. Is it not a shame that many Christian families do not have toilets?" She argued that people cannot be divided in spiritual, economical, political aspects: "A person is made of all that."

THE LITURGY

What areas should be strengthened in the liturgy or what aspects should be left out? In summary the following are the main areas which most of the respondents thought ought to be strengthened: spontaneity and more activity; more involvement of the congregation; good and interactive preaching; and more Bible reading. Elements to be rejected included favoritism and monotonous prayers (and, for Protestants, statues and confessionals).

For Evelyn Ayot, an employee at Uganda Martyrs University, the congregation should be more involved in the liturgy:

Worshippers get bored in our churches mainly because they are not helped to participate meaningfully in the worship. They are given the impression that they are there because they have to be there. There is need for the church leaders to allow people to be more spontaneous. For example, people should be able to ask questions of the presider, more especially in areas of the liturgy which they do not understand.

Alphonse Nyambare, a Seventh Day Adventist who was once a Catholic, had this to say on the monotony of prayer:

> In the Catholic Church, we were taught a certain way of worship, so that when one worships in a different way, people say that it is not the right way. One is made to pray in the same way our forefathers did when Christianity was being introduced here. They use the same words, phrases and posture; a person is never given an opportunity to express her or himself.

Jane Mbabazi suggested, "When preaching, the church leaders should use the discussion method. In this way the believers would be able to express their own views and stop just being passive listeners."

Edward Lumasi spoke with annoyance about what he called the discrimination of church leaders in favor of the rich in places of worship. He insisted that in the church "there should be no division of people on economic grounds." He gave the example of people who were poor and the priest refused to go and bury them. Florence Mukamuhabwa also experienced the same thing when her grandmother died. Her father asked the priest to say a Mass for her, but the parish priest excused himself, saying he could not do it. However, he later agreed to say Mass when her rich uncle asked him to. Fr. Kanyandago noted something similar with some priests in the sacrament of matrimony: "The parish priest may organize the church choir to sing at a rich person's wedding, but when the couple is poor, the marriage is quiet, or sometimes takes place in the sacristy!"

Regarding the liturgy as a whole, Bazirake was of the view that Mass should not take a long time. "Doing too many things during Mass tires the people out; they do not learn anything." To exemplify his complaint, he gave the example of a eucharistic celebration he attended where a priest preached for more than forty-five minutes, and conducted baptisms, and confirmations. Concluded Bazirake, "We do not go church to see all these things happening; we go looking for something for spiritual nourishment for our lives."

INSTRUMENTS AND SYMBOLS

Almost all respondents mentioned musical instruments as one of the main and important elements in worship. The traditional musical instruments most frequently mentioned were drums, shakers, rattles, and xylophones. Daniel Tibamanya, an elderly man, said that singing while drumming helps him to enjoy prayer. "Music is much better now [with traditional instruments], many songs and praises have become more meaningful," he said. He also expressed his joy that "our languages" are used. "I understand English but I feel closer to the Mass when I pray in Runyankore." The use of musical instruments in liturgy was seen to signify joy, praise, honor and respect.

Dominic Kaawa, commenting on the food offerings that are usually brought by Christians on what is known in Uganda as "Harvest Sunday," said, "One feels one has really offered something to his or her creator [on such occasions]. You know, in paying homage to your creator in this way, you show respect and gratefulness."

Sharing was seen as an important value. Matilda Nnabbuto, a member of the Legion of Mary, said that giving some of what we have to the poor is a liturgical experience; it mirrors Holy Communion. For Ayot, the joy and sadness we experience in life must manifest themselves in the liturgy if it is to be a successful one.

I happened to visit Nyakakoni Village when some Christians were planning to build a shelter for two old ladies. When I asked why they were doing this, they related their action to worship, saying that "outside the church building" this is what liturgy demanded of them. In most cases, respondents readily quoted from the prophets and the New Testament to confirm this. The passages most frequently referred to seemed to have been Micah 6:8 and 1 John 4:20.

MORALITY

Most respondents said that there is a decline in morals at all levels of society today. Incest was cited as an example. It is not uncommon these days, several people said, to hear instances of a father having sexual relations with his daughter. Sr. Christine Akech was very concerned about what she said was the increasing occurrence of premarital and extra-marital sexual activities in her home area. She argued that this was because there was no longer control of parents over their children. She cited an example of her nieces who, unlike the time she grew up, "do not live under strict orders from their parents." As she saw it, "Today children have too much freedom, resulting in their doing dangerous and destructive things to themselves and society."

Cohabitation was blamed on the many stages one has to go through before getting married. For many young people, as one respondent expressed it, "There is no way one can avoid cohabitation; in the first place, the rules of the church are too many." Several respondents claimed that this leads young people to resort to what is known in Uganda as the "short route" to having a partner. On this Anne Kyakuhaire said "We are living in a 'throw away' age. So, the attractive thing with cohabitation for young people is that when you get tired of each other, each one goes his or her way." No expectations or demands are made of the partnership. According to Ayot, "Some couples stay together in this way as if to say: 'Let us try it out and see if it works.' There is no long-term commitment in such unions. But there can be no stable marriage without commitment."

Because of cohabitation and casual sexual relations, the respondents generally agreed that there are many abortions. The reasons mentioned were embarrassment, fear of parents, the desire to continue with studies, or just the wish to "stay in shape." They said that church officials try to discourage it by preaching against it, but their success is very limited when one considers the number of women undergoing abortions.

The youth had divergent views and attitudes toward the HIV/AIDS pandemic. For example, while Margaret Nalubega thought that AIDS was "terrible," and that she was sure "everybody is trying very hard to avoid it," Joyce Namusoke was not so sure. "Up to now it is not clear, but I think many youths are getting used to this killer disease," she said. "They seem to be taking it for granted." The same opinion was echoed by Clare Ssozi who said:

Today we take AIDS like any other disease. We are past being shocked on hearing that so and so is infected with HIV. It is no longer as it used to be; in fact, the youth have now made the whole situation part of life. They say, everyone is going to die some day and so it does not matter how you die.

THE BIBLE

Regarding the Bible, many respondents said that they find the Bible very helpful but that not everything in one's life is addressed by it. Asked, "How is the Bible important to you?" the three most frequent answers were:

- It is a source for me to learn from the experience of others;
- It helps me to live my life holistically;
- It contains important guidelines for a person's life.

Many saw similarities between the message of the Bible and their own traditions in the Bible's insistence on the value of human life, its promotion of love and justice, respect for parents and the elders in general, and respect for women.

Concerning how the Bible is used in the church, several respondents could not avoid some historical memory. Fr. Lucian Arinaitwe was concerned that

some people still think that the God taught by missionaries as the biblical God is not the same God worshipped by Africans. The missionary God is taken to be superior to that of traditional Africa and therefore talking about God in connection with African rituals puts many off. In fact a parish priest who is very charismatic [seeing the biblical God in African rituals] can be seen as a problem by his parishioners.

He thought that this was unfortunate. Agreeing, Fr. Kanyandago noted that the gap between the missionary Christian and the traditional African concepts of God will take long to bridge because Christianity came not only as a faith, but also as part of a culture which was presented as superior to the indigenous one:

I believe that missionaries brought us a religion and an image of God which I insist on calling western and missionary because we were evangelized by people from the West. The danger is in the risk of confusing their culture with Christian values. Many of the values and religious images they think are Christian are in fact simply Western. But they tended to suppress African religiosity.

But what can be done to bridge this gap? Br. Aloysius Byaruhanga, a university lecturer, said: "I think it needs dialogue between the different cultures." Sr. Tumusiime and Fr. Edward Ndarike suggested also that it is important for people in the modern world to try to know and appreciate other people's cultures so as to bring them together. However, Sr. Gudelia Ndebiika was convinced that the process of bridging the gap between African culture and missionary Christianity might not be successful since, in her words, "it is hard to deal with them [the Africans] on a religious level because they think you do not understand or know their affairs." Fr. Arinaitwe held a similar view and said that bridging the gap would remain difficult unless serious research is done. "The gap can only be bridged by critically making surveys and research to get some important concepts [from African Religion] that can be used in our [Christian] faith."

Fr. Herman Nsubuga gave an example of how this is done in Rwanda:

Among the Rwandese, the cultural naming ceremony is always done on the eighth day after birth, when the woman is brought out of seclusion. Formerly considered a pagan ritual, today the naming ritual begins with Mass at the home of the couple. Every person present gives a name to the young one and from these, two names are selected for the child.

RECOMMENDATIONS AND OBSERVATIONS

There is a need for African theologians to be more publicly visible and their work more widely disseminated and known. In Uganda, the majority of the nuns and priests I approached during the research did not know what African theology is and therefore could not name a single African theologian. It is high time theologians started to go to the people, holding meetings with them, and listening to them, instead of gathering in meetings in towns like Nairobi or Kampala. Writing books is all right, but African theologians should try to find other means of direct contact through which their ideas can reach down to the ordinary people.

Throughout the research, I observed that people were not clear about whether or not there is dialogue in the church. Although many answered "yes" to the question about whether they thought there was dialogue in the church, they could hardly explain why or even point out where dialogue was happening or where it was needed. In the Catholic Church, many Christians seem more to be spectators than participants in their church. Church officials need to have dialogue with their people because it is through dialogue that the laity will understand the needs of their church and assist in meeting them.

Concerning the family, some of the urgent areas to be addressed by the church include cohabitation and premarital sex. Both of them are common among the youth so that they are taken as a normal way of life. In institutes of higher learning, cohabitation and pre-marital sex are rampant. A remedy to this situation can perhaps be found in the family itself. In their pastoral activities, church officials must stress the necessity for parents to educate their children on family values.

My survey indicated that extra-marital sex is practiced more by men than by women. I estimated that out of every five married men three engage in it, and out of five married women, one sleeps with men other than her husband. The type of "polygamy" that is taking place now is completely different from the earlier, traditional one. Today, rather than having his wives in one recognizable homestead, men have mistresses in different locations, most of them in trading centers. Most of the time, these women do not know one another, again unlike in the past. Christian communities should try to bring these people close to them, dialogue with them, and counsel them by bringing the ideal of the traditional marriage commitment to their consciousness. Most of all they must be treated with understanding and love. Judging them as sinners can be disheartening. This can serve only to make them more rigid.

The church must also revisit some of its rules. For example, cohabitation may not be completely the responsibility of the individuals concerned. The church and society do play an indirect part in the situation. Many young people would like to have their marriages blessed in church, but going through the many prescribed and often expensive stages discourages them. For example, the tradition of making two feasts—one for the traditional and another for the church ceremony—drains the financial resources of the couples-to-be. Why, then, should the church not bless the traditional ceremony and make it the official rite of marriage?

Let the Catholic Church in particular learn from the other Christian churches about how to minister in Africa. This can help it to devise a means for going about the process of inculturation with ease.

4

Where Are We?

Learning from the Data

After presenting the research data on the three East African countries in the foregoing pages, I would like in this chapter to try to summarize some of the main ideas and insights they provide. Although these insights as such are already contained there, I still think that bringing them together here in one chapter will make the picture of what is taking place at present in the East African (and by inference in the wider African) church and its implications clearer as far as the process of inculturation is concerned.

I wanted the research to paint for us a realistic picture—not merely an imaginary one—of the church in East Africa, and how the faith is expressed and lived there; what the church is now rather than what anyone wishes it could or should be or must once have been. After about a century and a half of evangelization this task is necessary, and in fact more detailed research on the issue needs to be carried out from time to time. A realistic picture of the state of the church can be drawn only by looking at what is happening in popular belief and practice at the present time. For the time being, the important question is: What form or forms is the relationship between the missionary Christian church and its understanding of the gospel on the one hand and African culture and religiosity on the other taking in the experience of Christians here? What is happening?

THE PRACTICE OF THE FAITH

Looking at the data of the research, it is easy to see that there is a pattern in all denominations and at all social levels of Christian adherents. Simply put, the pattern takes the forms of affirmation and repudiation, with the latter (repudiation or rejection) determining the unique shape of inculturation, or the face of the emerging church, more than the former (affirmation). Aspects of church doctrine and practice that are accepted by African Christians from missionary Christianity are usually taken for granted; little fuss in terms of discussion or clamor for change is made about them. Even among the inarticulate gatherings of Christians everywhere, this is the case: people go about worshiping one God and basically affirming Jesus as Lord. This is partly because these elements already exist in the traditional religiosity, or can be easily identified there, and partly because they are the very definition of Christianity.

With a few of the African Initiated Churches, as Stephen Nyaga found among the Akorino in Kenya, the affirmation goes to the extreme in some pastoral respects. Sometimes God is thought to be so powerfully and immediately present in human affairs among the Akorino as to dispense with any need for human intervention. In the case of illness, for example, the use of medicine is often for the Akorino almost a sign of a lack of faith in God. For them God's power and authority over evil is carried to its utmost theological and practical expression. Although there are only a few AICs holding positions such as this, it is an example of how seriously God and God's power to act in the world are held in African Christian religiosity.

Perhaps one of the most interesting and intriguing points we can infer from the research in all three countries is the hiatus that exists between what, for lack of a better term, I will call the "unconscious" or instinctive behavior of the general Christian population on the one hand, and the conscious, cognitive performance among them on the other. This gap shows up in popular action at different times. Faith orientations differ among Christians between taking instinctive personal initiatives in applying the faith, or acting according to official rules in concrete circumstances. In critical issues, such as illness, the understanding of marriage and its procedures, or the relationship with the ancestors and spirits, the pattern of unease between the two orientations (in the same individuals) seems universal in African Christianity. From the research it became clear that people usually take instinctive personal or communal initiatives in addressing an issue at hand, and may tackle a problem in ways that may not be sanctioned by the church, or even by the people concerned when they are themselves rationally confronted. Cognitively, they may profess to know and wish to act differently about the same issues.

For example, most Catholics will admit to knowing that polygamy is unacceptable by the church. Confronted with childlessness, however, many of them—both men and women—will instinctively opt for plural unions as the answer to the situation. And this is not limited to Catholics only. At present it is the case in all churches, to the extent that some AICs from all three countries accept it as a normal, legal form of marriage. The AIPCA in Kenya accepts it within certain limits. In the Catholic Church, where it is strictly prohibited, it constitutes one of the most perplexing and intractable pastoral problems. The question is: Is polygamy wrong? Whereas the general Catholic population would answer the question positively when they are thinking in legal terms (cognitively), they would act differently (instinctively) when the question happens to present itself to them as a practical moral issue involving the need for having children to assure their ancestral survival.

There is also the case of those Christians who call upon their ancestors, mentally or ritually, to intervene in certain difficult circumstances. Where it is proscribed, Christians were reluctant to admit that they occasionally did so, but the research revealed it to be a practice widespread across the Christian spectrum. These, and many other similar instances, have been referred to as "dual religious consciousness" (see Magesa 1997:4–14), but perhaps the term "consciousness" is inadequate in this context because one of the orientations here is more instinctive than conscious. I would today rather characterize it as a dual religious "instinct," personality or spirituality.

Evaristi Magoti relates an incident about Ndomba, the "retired catechist" and "staunch Catholic" in Dar es Salaam, Tanzania. To pacify his deceased wife whom he thought was troubling him in dreams because of his marriage to another woman, Ndomba thought there was nothing wrong in offering a sacrifice, despite the fact that this is forbidden as idolatry in Catholic doctrine, and Ndomba must have known and taught this many times during his career as a catechist. Many of those who attended and participated in the sacrificial meal were Catholics. What has moral priority here between the official teaching of the church and the spiritual requirements of African religiosity? Ndomba and his family and friends did not offer this sacrifice as "pagans"; they did it in the context of their Christian faith, although the legal aspect of it may have been at the time subconscious.

When in such circumstances the legal aspect is brought up, then there is in many cases psychological ambivalence and suffering: it is a case of doing good from the African spiritual point of view by breaking the law of missionary Christianity. Now, even within the boundaries of missionary Christianity itself, this should not have been an occasion for a crisis of conscience. Curing a man with a withered hand on the Sabbath, Jesus seems to be saying in the Gospels that sometimes this is permissible (Mt. 12:9–14, Mk. 3:1–6, Lk. 6:6–11; see also Mt. 12;1–8, Mk. 2:23–28, Lk. 6:1–5): for him there is no question but that goodness overcomes the law. But the crisis of conscience for African Christians, as for the Pharisees of the New Testament, is in the fact that the law has been made paramount and absolute as a measure of spirituality. It is most difficult for the majority to consciously escape from this kind of psychological bind.

- There is a lot of psychological and spiritual ambivalence in the practice of the Christian faith in Africa in relation to African cultural-religious practices.

WORSHIP/LITURGY

Because it is the center of Christian participation in the life of the churches, worship or the liturgy is where most changes are most clearly visible, and desire for change most frequently expressed by the Christian faithful at all levels. The AICs seem to be among the churches that have achieved a degree of success in indigenizing forms of worship, accepting such change internally and radically, and not being self-conscious about it. There may be several reasons for this but two are most significant.

The AICs that have emerged as truly African initiatives, that is, not breakaways from the older missionary churches, have not been saddled from the beginning by the forms of worship and proscription of the latter. They were free from the start to construct the forms of worship that they wanted and that were suitable for their own circumstances. Since most of these churches originated as tribal churches, and many of them remain as such, they adopted and adapted the tribal cultural ways of worship. As such it has not been difficult for the faithful there to understand these forms and to structure their worship according to them without feeling in the least awkward, or requiring of them to adjust mentally and emotionally in any major way. Their spaces of worship, if not in the open air, reflect this.

The churches that have broken away from the missionary established churches did so in reaction against the older churches' teaching on certain issues as well as a protest against the latter's forms of worship. In the research from Kenya this is obvious: the lack of emphasis on healing and exorcism being the element most often cited. So here a deliberate effort is made to make the liturgy responsive to the mental and emotional outlook of the African people.

In the mainline churches, this kind of movement in the liturgy is also clearly desired by the majority of Christians in all three East African countries. It can be seen in the charismatic movement groups which Agnes Nabbosa encountered in Uganda as well as Fr. Felician Nkwera's *Wanamaombi* in Tanzania, members of which group Magoti interviewed. The complaint that mainline churches' worship services are "boring" and do not touch the heart of the African person is a constant in all three findings. The students at UMU noted this to Nabbosa in no uncertain terms.

The problem, in philosophical-social terms, has been described by liturgist Elochukwu E. Uzukwu as being the question of the understanding of the person, and the practical influence of this understanding in liturgy (1987:61–74). In the mainline churches, as Uzukwu explains, the notion of person is, in spite of Vatican II, still predominantly Greco-Roman, emphasizing "incommunicability of the subsistent being as characteristic principle of individuation": the person is a unity in itself and autonomous. The axis is, as it were, personal sovereignty and emotional containment. With this outlook as supreme, shared emotions and actions are not essential to the liturgy. One may even say that the less sharing the better.

In the African worldview, on the contrary, the main characteristic of the human person is not individuation but relatedness: the "person" is a project, and for it to flower into the "human"—which is its goal—it has to relate to other persons in order to form a community. So what does this mean for the celebration of the liturgy, if, indeed, the liturgy consists of the expression of the person, the self? As Uzukwu shows with an example of a reconciliation ritual among the Igbo of Nigeria, "Sharing, communion [in all senses of the words] constitutes *the* value, to define and shape personality." The point, as he says, is the creation and re-creation of community by sharing life through "living-in-the-world-relatedness." When people like the students at UMU complain that worship services in the mainline churches are "boring," this is what instinctively they miss.

- In general, there is not as yet an adequate level of participation by all the faithful in the Christian worship of the mainline churches that African sensibilities would ordinarily demand.

HEALING AND DELIVERANCE

If the instinctive cultural impulse of most Africans leads to the belief that being community or in community is healthy, then it also implies that any lack of community harmony is "dis-ease." Specifically, lack of physical health is often understood to be symptomatic of a lack of spiritual, emotional or moral health; it is physically and spiritually harmful to the society and the individuals concerned. The research in all three countries reveals that healing is a high priority in African religiosity, and that the AICs have best captured this. It also shows that this is also one of the emphases of groups in the mainline churches, such as the charismatic movement and other groups in the Catholic Church.

Although some of the AICs, the Akorino, for example, would like to rely solely on divine intervention for physical cures and, from my own pastoral experience, I know that sometimes this desire may lead to community disruption (witch-hunting) rather than integration, the need for healing remains an important aspect of African Christian religiosity that permeates all levels of society. Magoti speaks of SCCs in the archdiocese of Dar es Salaam being "in a sorry state" because very few adults attend the gatherings. One of the reasons for this is that in these meetings people miss the healing experience, physically and socially. One of the tasks that members of SCCs do everywhere is to help those in need, certainly a healing activity highly resonant with African family values and expectations. But even then the symbols of inner healing, the "living-in-the-world-relatedness" used in these gatherings are weak. This is partly because participation in these activities is often presented in individualistic terms and not as a communal responsibility that brings harmony to the community by "an act of charity" that is ultimately meant to benefit the participant.

The research shows that belief in spiritual powers remains an integral aspect of African religiosity even within the boundaries of Christianity. The ancestors are seen by African Christians to be such powers. But there are also evil and simply "neutral" powers. When ancestors make their presence known in one way or another, the way to deal with them is by pacification through sacrifices and offerings. When evil or neutral powers do so—Catechist Ndomba's wife appearing to him in dreams was as a neutral power—sacrifices and offerings may also be performed. But in this latter case the purpose is not pacification but deliverance. This goes on quietly but frequently in all Christian churches in the East African region, and as Ndomba's case shows, Christians do not seem to be scandalized by it; they look at it as the normal way of acting under the circumstances.

Nowhere during the research was scripture cited directly to illustrate the interplay between prayer and inner healing and deliverance. However, although we may perhaps be anticipating ourselves in the flow of the argument of this book, let me quote a passage from the Wisdom of Sirach or Ecclesiaticus (38:9–15) from the second-century B.C.E. which seems to cover this ground from the African Christian perspective:

> My son, when you are ill, delay not,
>   but pray to God who will heal you:
> Flee wickedness; let your hands be just,
>   cleanse your heart of every sin;
> Offer your sweet smelling oblation and petition,
>   a rich offering according to your means.
> Then give the doctor his place
>   lest he leave; for you need him too.
> There are times that give him an advantage,
>   and he too beseeches God
> That his diagnosis may be correct
>   and his treatment bring about a cure.
> He who is a sinner toward his Maker
>   will be defiant toward the doctor.

- Absence in some churches of rituals that emphasize healing from physical illness and deliverance from unwelcome spiritual powers does not attract many Africans emotionally to their worship services.

SYMBOLS, LEADERSHIP STRUCTURES AND GENDER ISSUES

Generally, people were very pleased with the use of local languages and symbols in the church. Musical instruments were some of the most visible things people would like used in church: they helped them to be much more engaged in prayer, they said. Not much was said with regard to this subject about, for example, the shape of spaces of worship or church buildings, the type of matter used in the celebration of the sacraments (e.g., bread and wine for the Eucharist, what kind of oil for anointing, the symbols for matrimonial union or reconciliation, or the manner of baptism, namely, full immersion or symbolic washing by the pouring of water on the forehead), or other signs of unity, communion and community prominently used in the region. But this is probably because the research did not ask questions to that effect.

Most of the AICs do not think twice about using whatever symbols and materials the local culture uses in ritual or expression of religious sentiments and values. They place great importance on religious dress: robes resembling those of ancient Israel, headpieces, crosses or crucifixes, and rods, as well as the specifically African symbols of authority and power, such as flywhisks and walking sticks. AICs that have their origin in the mainline churches usually retain symbols of authority found in the original churches—the books, the garments and, at least in one case, that of the Legio Maria, even the language of worship, namely, Latin.

For the smaller churches, membership is a family and neighborhood affair; and even when they expand, they remain structured according to this model as far as leadership is concerned. Conversion into membership of these churches may occur in the usual way where an individual or family seeks admission, but most often they are open to anyone who would care to join their worship services. Any such person is considered a member, at least for the time he or she is there in the assembly. Rarely are formal membership rosters kept. Deliverance from severe misfortunes such as sickness and spirit possession wrought by a member of a given church is often a very strong motive for an individual to join it.

Unlike the mainline churches, leadership positions in the AICs were until recently not awarded through long training but on the traditional basis of chronological and social elderhood, or through some sign of divine choice. This remains largely the case, although with more and more literate people joining or initiating churches, there are signs in a few of them that the situation is slowly changing. As a rule, however, longevity of life and influence in society on account of personal behavior and/or wealth put a person in good stead for becoming a church leader. Another consideration for leadership, especially for women, is the size of their family and how well they manage it. These characteristics are usually not consciously considered in the leadership selection process, but they are assumed as normative both by the church members in general and by the individuals considering themselves eligible for such positions.

As I have just mentioned, a readily acceptable sign for leadership in these churches is personal charisma indicated in claims of privilege of apparitions of a spiritual nature, dreams, divination, prophecy, power of exorcism, and so on. In Uganda, Ms. Credonia Mwerinde, whom Nabbosa mentions, was able to build up her Movement for the Restoration of the Ten Commandments of God because she claimed to have seen apparitions and to have been commissioned for what she was doing by the Blessed Virgin Mary. In Tanzania, as Magoti observed, the leader of the *Wanamaombi*, Fr. Felician Nkwera, claims a similar mandate for his ministry of faith healing.

As more and more women members of the mainline churches become educated, the claim for women to enjoy full rights and responsibilities in their respective churches is being articulated more often and louder than just a few years ago. Religious sisters and other young university trained women, especially in both Kenya and Uganda, made this quite clear. Catechist Placeda Kamanyiro in Uganda described the slowness of the mainline churches to accept women in leadership positions and as equal participants in the churches' rituals as a "rigidity" that hinders the progress of inculturation.

- The use of local symbols in liturgies is as a rule welcomed and makes the celebrations meaningful to the people and more participatory. There is little dialogue in the mainline churches on many important issues of the life of the church. Generally women do not have much voice in these churches. In the AICs, however, although the participation of women in leadership positions is not complete, it is much more widespread and influences the decision-making processes.

THE BIBLE

That the Bible forms the basis of Christian belief and of its interpretation there seems to be no doubt among all the churches, but the weight attached to it seems to vary between social classes and its interpretation varies among churches. Whereas Christians without formal education take the Bible as the sole source of the "will of God" for humanity, many university-educated youth see in African traditions also a source of God's self-revelation. And whereas most AICs understand the Bible literally as historical truth, the mainline churches tend to bring a more sophisticated approach to it, not undervaluing it, but not considering it as factual history either.

This is to say that the biblical theology of the mainline churches is more elaborate. But this is not to say necessarily that it is more "contextual." For, although the biblical interpretation of the AICs may be extremely literal, it is much more allegorical, substituting more directly Africa and her experience for that of biblical Israel. Consequently, in a sense, it helps to promote the religious identity and dignity of the adherents of these churches when they see themselves as the "new Israel." At any rate, one thing is clearly apparent: compared to the mainline churches, the AICs possess a much more positive outlook on African cultural values.

The laypeople in all the churches were almost universally agreed that the task of interpreting the Bible belongs to the officials, those who have had the training, have the time, and are endowed with the inspiration to do so by the Holy Spirit.

- Perhaps because of the predominance of illiteracy in Christian congregations in Africa, the Bible is not yet a "people's book"; generally its interpretation is relegated to the leaders.

ECUMENISM

Interreligious dialogue and ecumenism present an ambiguous situation in the East African churches. Apart from the criticism against the mainline churches that Magoti heard in public rallies held by some AICs (apparently Pentecostal revivalists) in Dar es Salaam, the research by Nyaga in Kenya and Nabbosa in Uganda shows that interreligious dialogue and ecumenism were viewed favorably by those interviewed on this issue. This was especially the case with ecumenism or relations between Christians. Because Christians share the same Bible and the same fundamental belief in Jesus Christ, the general argument went, they can understand one another even if they are separated. There is no need to fight. In Uganda, the sentiment was summed up by the suggestion that ecumenism is best expressed by "working together," and in Kenya the sentiment was that we should "look beyond doctrines" to the core values of the Christian message.

However, apart from the mainline churches in which an attempt is made now and then to have some kind of dialogue with Islam—a major presence in this region—such consideration seems out of the question as far as the AICs are concerned. And even criticism or condemnation of other Christian churches that Magoti, for example, reports, is strange because it runs against the spirit of African traditional religiosity in this matter. Traditional religiosity was as a rule very tolerant of other beliefs and faiths, as long as these did not disrupt the unity of the community. "There is only one God" was the operative phrase when a member of a family, for example, opted to join a certain religious community. It did not cause any dissention or friction in the family. But this spirit is slowly disappearing from the scene.

- The desire for Christian unity may be real, but it is vague, and the mechanisms to advance toward it are undefined.

THEOLOGY

The only thing that is surprising here is the lack of familiarity with African theology on the part of the mainline church leaders. Their clergy spend a considerable number of years in the academic study of philosophy, theology and church history. One would have expected that they would keep up with developments in these fields after ordination. In Uganda, Nabbosa found that this was clearly not the case, and this seems to apply more or less to the other areas of the region as well.

Most leaders of the vast majority of AICs are not as academically trained as their counterparts in the mainline churches. Some of them are even illiterate but, as we have seen, have been able to reach leadership positions because of personal charisma. The churches themselves do not have a system of theology from which they operate, except on an ad hoc basis—the leaders construct an oral theology from a foundational idea as the church develops and grows. It is therefore not surprising that they would not be aware of developments in academic theology. Their main concern is morality, liturgy, and church life rather than a consistent body of teachings, and this is determined from situation to situation.

This raises the question in East Africa of the relationship between African theology and inculturation. It would seem that the success of a theology imposed from above, as in the case of the formation of SCCs, is not unequivocal. People accept it because of the traditional respect they have for authority, but how deep are its roots? Perhaps this gives prominence in the process of inculturation to a "theology" from below, a largely intuitive appropriation and application of the faith by the faithful to their lived environment.

- As an academic activity, African theology is something that is not yet as well known and as influential as it should be either among the general faithful or the majority of the leaders in the churches. African and Africanist theologians need to find ways to address this situation.

Part Two

THE EXPERIENCE AT THE BEGINNING

The first part of this study was an attempt to draw a picture of the factual reality of inculturation among representative groups of the African faithful, taking East Africa as a case study. What is actually happening? One question that we must now try to address is why this process takes the course it has taken in East Africa and, by extension, throughout the continent. In other words, what are the general internal dynamics of inculturation at work whenever and wherever church and faith meet culture?

To help us in this task we need to look at other moments of Christian history. If I may use a biological analogy, we need to dissect the beast somewhat and explore the different parts of its anatomy so as to understand its nature. How did the Christian movement develop, particularly during the formative years of its existence in its birthplace and the surrounding areas? How did it develop in its formative years in Africa? Is there a difference between the processes as they have taken shape in Africa and elsewhere? Is this difference, if indeed there is one, essential so as to qualify as erroneous the contemporary orientation of the process in Africa? Or is what is developing in Africa only a different and, given the circumstances, necessary representation of the same original Christian spirit?

What this implies—and the implications will become clearer as we proceed—is that inculturation as a process is not something new. It is not something that has been discovered by and is relevant only to Africa. Inculturation is innate to Christianity everywhere, and was part and parcel of the phenomenon since its inception and wherever it went. Much earlier, it was also part and parcel of the foundations of Christianity in the Hebrew scriptures, what Christians refer to as the Old Testament. All of this leads to the conclusion—which we might as well make now—that the kind of Christian spirituality people will have in a given community, at a certain place, and during a certain time is necessarily a consequence of inculturation. It is the result of the faith becoming localized and hopefully more fully assimilated by the people concerned. To use a time-honored definition of theology, it is the result of "faith seeking understanding" through the medium of culture, the only medium that can make the understanding of faith possible.

But the assimilation process between faith tradition and concrete situation, this dynamic of faith-culture interaction or dialectic leading to understanding, produces results that are not one-dimensional. The process of inculturation in general takes what we can call, for want of a better expression, a dual activity. It involves assimilation on the one hand and transformation on the other. Just as the food and drink that a person takes become part of his or her physical system, and transform the body in any number of different ways, so also the dynamics of inculturation. The food and drink seem to disappear in the human body, but they are there in the body in a radically different form. And even though the body may now seem to be the same, it is necessarily transformed. Not only is bodily life nourished and sustained by food and drink, but with time the body is actually changed, often beyond easy recognition. Similarly in the church: as the Christian church and faith encounter new cultures they transform them even as they themselves are transformed, sometimes in very radical ways.

In Part One of this book, we have had glimpses of the mutual influences and mutations of both church and culture. Thus, as a result of the work of Christian evangelization, the East African Christian faith and church on the one hand, and the East African cultures on the other, are no longer the same today as they were, say, fifty years ago—one hundred years after the arrival of Christian missionaries there. (See Baur 1994:224–287 for the history of the evangelization movement in Kenya, Uganda, and Tanzania, and pp. 288–502 for a survey of the transformations throughout the continent. See also Walls 2002:85–135 on the same issue.) But neither did the Hebrew people remain unchanged in their faith and culture throughout their long transition, which the Old Testament tries to interpret. They were transformed from a wandering group of polytheistic nomads, easy prey to empires looking for slaves, to a comparatively well organized, ardently monotheistic people with a central government (on this see, for example, Legrand 2000 and Blenkinsopp 1992). The same is of course true of early, medieval and contemporary Christianity. But we need to illustrate these claims with some concrete examples. This is the task to which I now turn, beginning with the Old Testament.

5

Old Testament Foundations

Scholars of the Old Testament (for instance, see Maher 1982) have shown that the Hebrews were always in contact with cultures and religious traditions other than their own, and that they borrowed liberally from them; this even before they came to understand themselves fully as "Israel," Yahweh's privileged nation. For example, from Egypt they borrowed and modified for their own social and religious purposes some fundamental Egyptian cultural-religious ideas. The most venerable Israelitic institutions, such as the Temple and the king's court during the time of David and Solomon, are of Egyptian inspiration. The customs of the Canaanites as well provided more than just the raw material for the concept of the covenant between Yahweh and Israel.

Moreover, Mosaic Law (the *Torah*, meaning "guidance," "instruction," or "teaching") is in many ways similar to the Assyrian, Babylonian, Sumerian and Hittite law codes, all of which predate it. And although the prophets of Israel were very sensitive about mixing any characteristics of foreign gods, such as the Canaanite god Baal, into their faith in Yahweh, the Yahwist religion of Israel could not escape it entirely. When they settled down (between 1250 and 1130 B.C.E.) and came into more intimate contact with the religions of their neighbors, they intuitively incorporated some of the latter's elements into the image of Yahweh. What is significant and original in these developments is that despite this massive borrowing the Israelites were not content to put Yahweh and the Canaanite god Baal side by side as equals. In the end, Yahweh superseded Baal and all the other gods in the communal belief of the nation. So, for Israel, Yahweh became the only God.

But the point must nevertheless be made that throughout the Old Testament Israel's God is depicted as a "jealous" God. What does this suggest? Obviously, it points to the situation that although other gods were not acceptable in Israel's image of God, they were understood to exist, at least in the popular mentality. Thus the first commandment Moses receives for the people from Yahweh relates to this understanding of multiple gods. Yahweh has to command the people: "You shall not have other gods besides me. You shall not carve idols for yourselves in the shape of anything in the sky above or on the earth below or in the waters beneath the earth; you shall not bow down before them or worship them. For I, the Lord, your God, am a jealous God" (Ex. 20:3–5). Israel will be blessed if it adheres to this injunction; it will be punished if it does not.

Therefore, although monotheism is the central tenet of the Yahwist religion—"Hear, O Israel: Yahweh is our God, Yahweh is One" (Deut. 6:4), as the

Shema phrases it—it is a culmination of a historical-cultural process. In popular pious perceptions, it is usually connected to God's covenant with Moses—easily the most towering figure in Israel's history—as if it happened at one moment in this history, a single event. In actual fact, it represents the end result of a long development of cultural-religious contact between Israel and its environs in terms of Israel's adoption and rejection of some "foreign" notions of God.

R. J. Zwi Werblowsky is quite right when he observes that, although the conception of God in Israel was "universalist" at the time many of the books of the Old Testament were being redacted, it left much leeway for divergent beliefs and practices in matters of worship. "In fact," as he correctly notes adducing Micah 4:5, "Israel alone was required to serve this one God in absolute fidelity, whilst the gentiles were not to be held punishable for their idolatry" (in Zaehner 1997:8).

ISRAEL AND THE NATIONS

The perception of Yahweh as one and alone, the only God, in the Old Testament is predicated firmly on his acts in the concrete experience of the people. That is why monotheism grew in clarity as the history of Israel developed. In hindsight, the history of the nation made it increasingly clear in the people's consciousness that it was Yahweh who saved them from slavery in Egypt, and that it was Yahweh who worked miracles for the people to make them into a "great nation." What this meant was that Yahweh was stronger and more majestic than all other gods. Consequently, the preface to God's covenant with Israel, which firmly shaped Israel's image of God, is: "I, the Lord, am your God, *who brought you out of the land of Egypt, that place of slavery*" (Ex. 20:2). This is the centerpiece of what the Hebrew Bible refers to as the Law and the Prophets.

The Israelite conception of Yahweh, described as he "who brought you out of the land of Egypt, that place of slavery," arises out of a human-divine concern for love and justice among human beings as a society. It is a concern shown throughout the entire Hebrew Bible, but most explicitly in the legal content of the entire Pentateuch. It is also very clear in the emphasis on social justice of the prophetic books, properly so called. Of course, in practically all of the books of the Old Testament, this concern is somewhat limited to Israel itself.

This is not strange. All early human civilizations were limited and limiting in this way: the band or the tribe constituted the people over and above all others. In Africa there are still stark examples of this. Indeed, present civilizations are not themselves far removed from such limitations: the idea of nation-states with their currently growing jingoistic exclusivism is nothing but a replica on a larger scale and in modern clothing of this "tribalism."

Israelite monotheism, born of the experience of being liberated from the suffering of slavery, "gave weight to their consciousness of being different from the inhabitants of the valleys and the cities. They were the people of

Yahweh and had no kings 'like the other nations,'" namely, the neighboring Canaanites, Moabites, Philistines and so on (Boff/Pixley 1989:23). "In those days," as the redactor of Judges declares, "there was no king in Israel" (Jg. 21:25); only Yahweh was king. But then we encounter another very significant development in Israel's history of political and cultural accommodation with the surrounding peoples. The transition from a nomadic to a sedentary style of life, sheer growth in numbers and the consequent danger of anarchy forced the community to think better of this extreme form of democracy. The lack of a central political power to unite and galvanize the population in the face of war and other kinds of danger was making life almost unliveable.

In 1 Samuel we read that the transition from charismatic-theocratic leadership to institutionalized kingship came about by the insistence of "all the elders" among the people. They came "in a body" to Samuel at Ramah and said to him, "Now that you are old, and your sons do not follow your example, appoint a king over us, *as other nations have*, to judge us." This decision was the conclusion of a drama that evolved over a period of a century or more of constant borrowing of political, military and economic ideas and practices from neighboring tribes. In the beginning these borrowings went fundamentally against the community's initial convictions about what it thought itself to be; but, in spite of all that, many of them finally won the day and were incorporated into the religious consciousness and practices of the people.

The monarchy in Israel was a radical departure from the initial and literal conviction that Yahweh alone was king, and there had to be a price to be paid for this "rejection," one which would be high in comparison with their former freedom. Still, the benefits of having a king eventually seemed to the people to outweigh any negative impact. The people insisted, "There must be a king over us. We too must be like other nations, with a king to rule us and to lead us in warfare and to fight our battles" (1 Sam. 8:19–20).

Here we have an ingenious example of a religious-spiritual way of explaining what must be seen as a normal and inevitable sociological development, similar to what happens all over the world and throughout human history. The experience of the cultural disintegration of Africa mirrors the experience of Israel almost point by point. During colonialism, the imitation by some Africans of Western culture was subtle, and only a minority desired to be like "the other nations," the colonizers. The majority of the population was still too insular to be impacted by the ways of life of their colonial masters. Not so shortly after independence in the 1960s and 1970s, when the continent opened itself up to the influences of economic and cultural globalization, it was not individuals but the whole body politic of the various African nations which now constantly cried out to its leaders, "Let us be like the other nations," invariably meaning the Western world.

Let us consider yet another Old Testament example, relating to the creation accounts in Genesis. What was the purpose of these accounts?

Michael P. Gallagher offers a plausible explanation that, again, underlines the role neighboring cultures played—even if in a negative sense—in the development of Israelite religious culture. As he points out: "Scripture scholars now widely accept that the creation accounts in Genesis were shaped to counter Babylonian myths of origin during the period of the Exile. In other words those great narratives are early examples of dialogue between faith and culture." The Babylonian influence thus takes place by way of negation. "As against the Babylonian stories of conflict and chaos," Gallagher continues, "Genesis shows God serenely and freely creating as a gift to humanity, and indeed portrays God as an artist rejoicing in the sheer goodness of the finished work" (1998:105–106).

CHANGE AND GROWTH THROUGH PRAXIS AND EXPERIENCE

The fact that the reflections on creation in the Bible arose out of Israel's experience of communal suffering in exile, a sense of liberation from it, and a renewed consciousness of national cohesion is extremely significant. By this experience, Israel's religious conscience reappears in much sharper relief. Perhaps, Israel reflects, it was not such a good thing to copy wholesale other peoples' ways of doing things after all. Perhaps we have given away far too much of our identity as a people than we ought to have done. Perhaps it is time to reconsider the importance of our heritage. May it not be that the experience we are undergoing is the result of our infidelity to ourselves as a people and to the God we believe in? These are the kind of questions that Israel must have been struggling with during the Babylonian exile, as is made clear in the prophetic literature. Israel is radically transformed by the exilic experience as it tries to address these questions.

If we may now begin to look at Africa in this light, we must say that these are equally the kind of questions that the "prophets" of Africa have been struggling with for some time now in both the socio-political and the religious arenas. Ever since the struggle for political independence began, the founding fathers of the various African nations, the politicians, were driven to provide answers to them. They are certainly the questions that in the Christian religious arena African theologians, theologies and processes such as that of inculturation and African initiated Christian movements are trying to address. They similarly arise out of the various social, political, economic, psychological and spiritual exiles that Africa has historically experienced (such as the slave trade and colonialism) and continues to experience (in the form, for example, of globalization and absolute poverty). Reflections on and activities against these situations are agents of popular awareness. They are making people stop and say: Wait a minute; let us reconsider. Perhaps we are heading the wrong way in terms of our identities as a people!

With reference to the Bible, Gallagher (1998:105–106) rightly interprets the Genesis creation accounts as texts meant, in the end, to testify to Yahweh's fidelity to Israel and, through Israel, to the world. Old Testament redactors could not have drawn out completely and clearly the implications of their work for a faith-culture dialectic. But, as Gallagher argues, "Creation theology, in this light, is the basis for the long adventure of human culture—

symbolized in the mandate to human beings to grow and rule the earth or in the act of naming all the animals (Gen. 1:28; 2:20). . . . Thus there is a biblical foundation for seeing culture as *the* human response to God's continuing creative gift, as cooperation through responsibility with the Creator in the whole complex challenge of history—becoming 'fellow-workers with God' (1 Cor. 3:9)."

Similarly, there is a solid basis in looking at the current process of cultural-historical re-evaluation in Africa as the interpretation of and faith-response to God's continuing self-revelation in the African historical experience. The process of this re-evaluation for the recapturing of the essential values of African culture amounts to the effort to name the African reality in terms that Africans can own and understand. This is an act through which God creates reality with the African people.

If we are honest about the evidence, we can observe that many of the Old Testament writings are not an attempt to understand Israel in terms of an ahistorical, preconceived idea of God. Rather, they are primarily an attempt to explain God's work, or to form an idea of God in terms of Israel's actual historical experience. These writings are trying to answer the implicit question: Who and what is God for us in the particular experience of our own history? If our God has made us what we are now, how and why has he? The answers to these sorts of questions can be gained in no other way than by examining a history in which God, as universal Creator, is intimately involved. Different peoples will see this God and describe the God they see in a variety of ways according to their situations.

In ancient times, historical events were generally written down and interpreted much later in time than they actually took place. These interpretations benefit literally from hindsight. And added to them we can in almost every case detect a few elements of nationalism, and at times even chauvinism and jingoism. In the case of Israel, these characteristics are evident in demonstrative claims by Yahweh to the people, such as: "This is how you shall know that a living god is in your midst [that is, on your side], who will absolutely certainly drive before you Canaanites, Hittites, Hivites, Perizzites, Girgashites, Amorites, and Jebushites" (Josh. 3:10); and in commands such as: "All the peoples that the Lord your God delivers to you you are to exterminate, showing them no mercy" (Deut. 7:16). One cannot but wear an understanding smile when encountering passages such as 1 Kings 3:10–12, where God promises that King Solomon will be the wisest king on earth *for all time*. One knows it is nationalistic hyperbole.

These and other Old Testament passages lead to one inevitable conclusion, that events in the history of Israel have conditioned or, in some places, even created the image of God in the Hebrew Bible. The depiction of God as an extremely jealous, exclusive and brutal god arises from a desire to maintain Israel's identity among the nations. In the face of what the leaders of the time see as the danger of too indiscriminate an imitation of foreign attitudes and their encroachment on Israel's long-held and proven values, this is deemed necessary.

Think about it: don't we do the same today for our national heroes as Israel did for King David and Solomon? We inculcate their memory, especially in the minds of the young, as the greatest people on earth, past, present and future. For a few people, this may be only a calculated pedagogical tool, but for the majority, with the passage of time the assertion becomes an article of faith.

In much of the wisdom literature, dependence upon God alone was the only thing that could save the nation of Israel from annihilation. Dependence on the great nations of the day, for example Ethiopia and Egypt, would ultimately come to nothing. They were not dependable. This is the message of the Pentateuch and the wisdom books. The God who emerges from the prophetic literature is not much different. He is a powerful, yet just and holy God who loves his own people and is ready to forgive their transgressions if they repent and take refuge in him by living wisely. What he demands of the people in return is an integrity similar to his own, which they must show by means of cultic purity and responsible living. This image of the divine was essentially assumed many centuries later in Christian belief.

DIVINE INSPIRATION IN THE OLD TESTAMENT

There is no place for cynicism in any of these developments in the Old Testament. Explaining them as fundamentally "normal" processes is certainly not meant to impugn the inspired character of the Hebrew scriptures. It is, at any rate, not warranted to say that God was not behind the Old Testament texts, or that ultimately God was not their "author," provided we understand correctly the meaning of these claims (see Comfort 1992:35–6). The development of the faith of Israel warns us that the Old Testament is religious literature with a theological message as sophisticated as can ever be found in any other religious literary product. It must be perceived in that context if we are not to distort its essential theological import.

Take the example of the story of the flood. What is basic in it? According to Harland (1996:1), the story brings forth a profound theological and sociological lesson. It "sets out Israel's understanding of the worth of human life, and the prohibition of murder. In the aftermath of the flood, the command not to kill is given special prominence (Gen. 9:5–6). The story places the question of the value of human life in a suggestive light."

With reference to Africa, we might reflect similarly on issues of human dignity and worth in the context of the struggle for the abolition of the slave trade and slavery; in the context of the struggle for independence in the various countries of the continent; in the context of the struggle against HIV/AIDS; in the context of the struggle for democracy and respect for human rights, and so on. It may at present be too close to some of these experiences for any myths to develop and become established around them. But it may also be an example of the poverty of corporate imagination in Africa that myths, or even epic myths, have not developed about the heroism of the African personality during the older and devastating experience of slave trade, arguably one of the most humiliating and destructive, but also potentially most instructive period of the continent's history.

One is immediately reminded of the story of Joseph and his brothers (Gen. 37ff.), how he identified himself to them in Egypt as the one they had sold into slavery, and how they were remorseful for this offence. An aspect of the story of African slavery that is rarely admitted in Africa is how Africans themselves deliberately captured and sold, or were tricked into selling their subjects, brothers, sisters and children into slavery. For the sake of purifying this memory, this fact needs to be recognized, and they need to ask pardon of their brothers and sisters in the Diaspora for this offence.

But it is perhaps up to the Africans in Diaspora to set in motion this process of purifying the history of slavery by demanding this recognition and apology from their brothers and sisters in Africa in a spirit of communion and fellowship. They are certainly entitled to say: "I am your brother Joseph, whom you once sold [into slavery]. But now do not be distressed for having sold me. . ." (Gen. 45:4–5). Joseph in the Genesis story believed that it was by God's design that his brothers sold him so that later he might save the whole tribe from starvation. Africans on the continent cannot presume to say how their brothers and sisters might interpret their unfortunate history and respond to them, but it may well be that the event can also be interpreted as being able to contribute to the economic "salvation" of Africa, especially in today's globalization.

Throughout its history Israel recognized the hand of God and interpreted significant events accordingly. This is the deepest meaning and significance of divine inspiration. It is certainly not impossible for African-Americans to see divine action in their long struggle for racial emancipation. In a way, they have already done so, particularly in their religious songs and in the work of such figures as Martin Luther King, Jr. In Africa itself, the movement for independence, for all its flaws, and those who spearheaded it must begin to be seen also in a religious light, eschewing the unhelpful separation between the "political" and "religious" spheres that is foreign and inimical to the meaning of divine inspiration in human history and people's lives.

The Old Testament exemplifies two sources of divine inspiration. Whereas the main concern of the Pentateuch and the historical books is to paint a picture of God deduced from his mighty actions on behalf of Israel, the approach is slightly different in the wisdom literature. With the latter, ordinary human wisdom garnered from the experience of daily life provides the resource for morality and a portrait of the divine. In other words, while the Pentateuch depicts the drama of the life of Israel from a vertical perspective, with God making his will known to the people "directly" through a few chosen representatives (something that happens again in the prophetic literature), wisdom literature is in general horizontal, more humanistic. Whereas in the Pentateuch what has been called the covenant motif dominates, wisdom is concerned with the question of how people, everyone, can know God from the ordinary relationships they enjoy with other people and the whole of creation and how, in doing so, they can lead an ordered, ethical life. The sages of Israel's wisdom literature were, as Dianne Bergant (1982:17) writes, "students of human experience." The Old Testament sees no problem accepting this also as divine inspiration.

THE HEBREW BIBLE, HISTORY AND MYTH

She kept asking if the stories were true.
I kept asking her if it mattered.
We finally gave up.
She was looking for a place to stand
& I wanted a place to fly.

(Andreas 1993: no page; italics added)

We now need to touch very briefly on the intricate relationship between history and myth and myth and history, and between fact and interpretation of fact. We will consider first the role these play in the theological construction of the Hebrew Bible, and then briefly in the African situation.

Paul Ricoeur (1967:5) says something that is now commonplace about the relationship between history and myth, but which perhaps needs recalling. Ricoeur has explained profoundly in several of his works that myth, in contexts such as that of the Old Testament, should not be understood in the sense of "a false explanation by means of images and fables, but a traditional narration which relates to events that happened at the beginning of time."

The purpose of myth, Ricoeur explains, is to provide "grounds for the ritual actions of men today and in a general manner, establishing all forms of action and thought by which man understands himself and his world." In these myths, "at the beginning of time" implies a degree of definitiveness and exclusivity. It implies the beginning of time as we, the members of this particular society, know it. It relates to "us" as opposed to "them." Karlheinz Ohle (in Bühlmann 1982:181) calls this a form of "ethnocentrism" and acknowledges that it "is a basic structure of human behavior." "Without the foreign there would be no domestic. Without what is strange, there would be no 'one's own.' . . . Social problems arising out of a mutual strangeness remain constitutive of a society's integration. They cannot be removed, they can merely be eased."

There seems to be no way out of this ethnocentric tendency for human societies. "Long before nations like Israel and Greece began to write history as a way of explaining the present by reference to causes in the past," van Seters (1999:115) argues "they had their myths to account for origins." John Dominic Crossan (1998:60–68) also observes that myth-making is part of the process of constructing any human society's cultural identity. A nation without national myths in the above sense stands built on shaky grounds, as Elochukwu E. Uzukwu (see 1997:84–219) confirms.

The contemporary pursuit of rational truth in history or theology, devoid of all mythical foundations—if indeed this were possible—runs the danger of impoverishing national identity by depriving it of intuitive, creative truth. In myth, historical fact can easily become non-fact and non-fact (or fiction) fact for the purpose of supplying meaning to the self-perception of a given society. Such were the dynamics of the national, cultural and religious construction and development of Israel as we find them recorded in the Hebrew scriptures. They are the same as those of any other national construction and cohesion.

It seems necessary to repeat here that we are not implying that the redactors of the Hebrew Bible deliberately falsified their accounts of events. On the contrary, what we mean to point out are normal psychological processes in the field of faith, belief and religion (as well as in all forms of secular religion in our own day). Sometimes "memory does not remember," as Crossan has said. This helps to justify a desired belief or practice. At other times memory is "selective" for the same reason. Finally, memory amplifies or diminishes evidence to achieve a certain effect. Even in rational processes of thought, any one or a combination of these elements may be present, but much more so in intuition.

There are many examples of myths from the African context. The obvious ones are the ethnic or tribal myths of creation that almost every African ethnic group has to explain their origins and development as distinct tribes. But there are also legends of individual heroes who are recalled as having performed something special for society. These individuals are invariably painted as thoroughly good, generous, strong—almost flawless. In Africa, as in the Old Testament, supreme characteristics of influence in myths and legends are not reserved for human beings alone. Other members of creation in the inanimate and animate worlds are very much part and parcel of myths, now properly called fables.

Let us take another, slightly different example in the Catholic Church. For a long time there has existed the belief in Catholic Christianity that the strength of local and universal manifestations of the church can be enhanced by the presence of known role models, called saints. The point to emphasize is that, even given the usually long process of ascertaining the virtue of the candidate to blessedness or sainthood, in the end making saints in the church is like creating heroes in society. It is a social-psychological-emotional act, conferring onto the saints or heroes an almost inviolable status and making them role models for everyone.

The process is an exercise in selective or "mythical" memory. Memory may not remember all the details concerning the historical life and achievements of a given saint or hero, but it does not need to. It is the task of "forgetful memory" to supply these details as well as any missing links. That is why theological imagination needs to be fertile, drawing from existing myths and legends, and, literally, reconstructing the "image" of the saint or hero it desires to "canonize" for the purpose of guidance, edification, or warning. This constitutes the "stabilizing role" of imagination in society. In its absence a people's socio-cultural system may collapse.

The Old Testament has reached us by a long process of "selection, translation and interpretation," as Jesse Mugambi (see Getui/Holter/Zinkuratire 2001:13) observes, "guided by a wide variety of ideological and theological considerations embedded in the texts but not directly accessible to the reader." (The same thing, as we shall presently see, holds for the New Testament.) The Old Testament cannot be properly understood unless and until it is contextualized in this way and situated historically in the Mediterranean and northern African environment within which it arose. This will facilitate its proper interpretation in and pastoral application to Africa.

To look at the historical development of almost any aspect of the theology of the Old Testament is to unearth an array of influences and interests that shaped it over a period of centuries. We have given examples relating to the development of monotheism and kingship, and also said something about ritual. But we could have considered further the development of central Israelite institutions such as the priesthood and prophecy; of religious themes such as justice and the love of one's neighbor; of ethical ideas such as the meaning of good and evil; and even of symbolism, such as the significance of body parts such as hair and skin. As is and has been the case among human beings everywhere, geography, demography, politics and economics all play a role in shaping the development of religious belief. It is up to each group of people to make what they can of such a confluence of influences in terms of their religious view of life in the world. This was the case for Israel as well.

For our purposes, it has been sufficient to note that in the Old Testament we see how Israel in many different ways molded the disparate myths, fables, traditions, and histories they formulated and encountered into a "narrative" or "history" of the "Chosen People" of God—Israel itself—beginning with the very origin of the human race and the world. Once the purpose of the narratives was established and accepted, that is, to show the greatness of the God of Israel over all others and his goodness to his people of choice, nothing else mattered much. Discrepancies, contradictions, or even absurdities could be tolerated and indeed understood in the light of this purpose. For Israel itself, but even for modern readers of these theological narratives, it is futile to try to explain or justify them apart from this goal.

Given the events that influenced these narratives, the student of the Old Testament has to concede that there must have been a certain arbitrariness in how the authors and editors chose to arrange them in terms of which points to emphasize, which to simply mention, and which to eliminate altogether. This "arbitrariness" is what constitutes the creative role of the human authors under divine inspiration. It is similarly what should evoke for Africa the divine presence in its own traditions and history.

Nothing is left out *a priori* in the Old Testament in this process of "evocation"; similarly in Africa all reality must be taken as a genuine subject from which to "read" and interpret the economy of salvation. History itself, culture, and the confluence of cultures that have taken place in Africa, struggles against social, political, and economic subjugation, diseases and epidemics—

all are raw material for theological reflection. In terms of Christianity, one major theme for critical theological thought suggests itself: how, in the encounter between the Old Testament and African religiosity, do the two realities confirm and critique each other, and how may the values each espouses be seen as revealing the divine mystery to humanity?

AFRICA AND THE OLD TESTAMENT

What, then, does it involve to interpret the Old Testament with the development and rootedness of Christianity in Africa as the primary aim? Two elements necessitate this question. The first is the fact that the Old Testament forms part and parcel of the sacred writings which Christians all over the world hold to be foundational to their faith because they are revealed. The New Testament is based upon the Old Testament and acts as a "fulfillment." For this reason, the Old Testament cannot be eliminated in Christian consciousness from the totality of the economy of God's self-revelation to the world.

Second and practically speaking, on account of the similarity in symbols, metaphors and rituals described in the Old Testament and those found in African religiosity, there seems to be a natural affinity between the Hebrew scriptures and African religiosity, to which African Christian believers seem to be attracted and drawn. Many—perhaps the majority—of the AICs exemplify this intuitive preference, which in these churches goes to the extent of not only including the word "Israel" in their nomenclature, but also replicating many Old Testament rituals (such as mandatory circumcision) and symbols (such as dress) in their religious vision and practice. For these, if for no other reasons, it becomes important to understand how Africa and the Old Testament do or might interact.

To elaborate this interaction, let me turn to some useful sources. A fairly representative group of African and Africanist scholars have tried to address the question of how to understand the Old Testament in the African situation in essays compiled in a book called *Interpreting the Old Testament in Africa* (Getui/Holter/Zinkuratire 2001). The work is ongoing, but in what follows I outline the major pertinent points of their insights and offer some critical remarks about the endeavor.

To begin with, Knut Holter (see Getui/Holter/Zinkuratire 2001:27–39) adduces convincing evidence that Old Testament scholarship is not lacking in Africa: there currently exist, he notes, many studies in the form of dissertations, monographs and articles by Africans on the Old Testament and its relationship to Africa. Holter reminds us that bibliographies of this scholarship have been compiled and are available in a variety of sources. Although some of these studies have been written from a Western perspective, given the heavily Western training of their authors, Holter nevertheless asserts that an impressive number take the African religious context seriously into account in their biblical theology and exegesis. He categorizes these studies into four approaches to the Bible: thematic, institutional, contextual, and interactional.

The thematic approach's main concern seems to consist in the attempt to find Africa in the Old Testament. In other words, which texts refer to places in Africa and, consequently, what light do these "African" texts shed on such places as Nubia or Cush, Ethiopia, Egypt, Put or Libya, Ophir, or Sheba—historically and metaphorically—on the relationship between the African peoples and Israel? Further, how many of these texts help to stimulate the Christian religious identity of the contemporary African reader of (or listener to) the Old Testament? Can African cultural experiences be a help in interpreting the Old Testament because of this?

While it would be unwise to dismiss the concerns of this "thematic" scholarship, one must say, nevertheless, that it tends to be too literalistic, comparative and piecemeal. Its fruits too are bound to be limited. On the one hand, looking only for concrete references to Africa in the Old Testament, as this approach tends to do, may cause us to miss its larger and perhaps more important message to Africa. On the other hand, in comparing only selected aspects of the Old Testament to African religiosity, it may miss the larger contribution of African religiosity to the interpretation of the Old Testament. At any rate, the thematic approach cannot be very productive in the long run since, when it exhausts reflecting on the few direct references to Africa present in the Old Testament, then what? The approach seems to lead to a dead end. Still, in spite of all this, it is necessary to acknowledge that the pride this approach has helped to stimulate in African Christians has been considerable, and is legitimate.

To what extent has this pride been able to spread and how deep is it? Here we touch on another level of the problematic African scholars address. They note that, almost by definition, the study of the Old Testament in Africa has been "institutional," that is, it has come from academic institutions. Perhaps this could not be helped where biblical translation is concerned. It is not accurate, however, to assert the same thing in the case of the process of interpretation or "hermeneutics." Old Testament hermeneutics, besides academic study, can also benefit from popular inspiration and interpretation, if this is taken seriously into account by the scholars. Then what Holter describes as the thematic approach can be very rewarding in terms of the awareness of the role African wisdom can play in understanding the Bible.

As an example, Sammy Githuku illustrates briefly how the taboo on counting in Africa may be useful in understanding 2 Samuel 24:10. In this biblical account, we are told that David "regretted" having counted the people and considered his action a sin before God because, in his case, as among the Kikuyu or Kipsigis of Kenya, God alone is true totality. Counting by a human to establish a total may therefore be an expression of pride (see Getui/Holter/Zinkuratire 2001:113–18). This cannot be interpreted as a complete ban against counting in contemporary Africa, but as Madipoane Masenya shows, in this case by use of the proverbs, the two worlds—that of the Old Testament and Africa—can be used to explain each other (Getui/Holter/Zinkuratire 2001:133–46).

The point of all of this is to insist that the institutional, "privatized" approach to biblical hermeneutics in Africa needs to interact on an ongoing basis with "popular" hermeneutics in order to appreciate in the African environment the meaning of covenanting, the importance of naming, the significance of work, and so on. In general, African and Africanist Old Testament scholars are generally agreed that Old Testament interpretation would gain in depth if it were approached from an African mental, religious, and cultural framework (see Kinoti/Waliggo 1997:25–39).Victor Zinkuratire notes further that there are as well some linguistic correspondences between Hebrew and the Bantu languages that should not be ignored (Getui/Holter/ Zinkuratire 2001:217–26).

Holter correctly observes that despite the existence of serious scholarly work, there is in Africa a serious lack of forums for scholars to share their insights. Only a few theses and dissertations get published. Moreover, there are not many specialized periodicals in Africa on Old Testament studies that would make the dissemination of such ideas widely possible. Added to this is the shortage of academic guilds and conferences which, on account of lack of financial resources, make opportunities for scholars to meet and exchange insights few and far between. As a result, most biblical research and findings are not able to influence the larger Christian community by seeping down to more popular forums, such as popular publications and the mass media.

This somehow entails also the problem of "context," which the contextual approach to Old Testament studies in Africa raises. It is the problem of the "publics" of interpretation, as David W. Tracy (1981) has called them. Between the religious and secular contexts in one dimension, the popular and professional in another, and the local and global in a third there is always tension. How can these contexts or publics be related in Old Testament studies in Africa and with what results? Finally, how are they themselves internally and structurally related?

What is crucial in the study of the Bible in Africa is that in interpreting it, scholarship needs to have a base from which to do so if the results are to be beneficial to all levels and aspects of African Christian life. We need to have, as Jonker (in Getui/Holter/Zinkuratire 2001:78) puts it, an African hermeneutic, which implies "a stance or disposition according to which, and in the service of which, a whole variety of exegetical methods and tools are used." Accordingly, an African hermeneutic would use all the methods of biblical interpretation and criticism in existence or yet to be proposed, but with the controlling stance or disposition of promoting the identity and dignity of Africa in mind.

An African hermeneutic would not only emphasize the identity of Africa, but would also enrich itself by considering the diversity of all approaches to biblical interpretation, both from within Africa itself and from outside. This is what Jonker characterizes as the communal approach, and proposes it for biblical studies in Africa. "A 'communal' approach," he writes, "provides the opportunity of discovering how the hermeneutical and exegetical contributions from our own contexts enrich [and, I would add, are enriched by] the (what one would call) communion of biblical interpretation" (Getui/ Holter/Zinkuratire 2001:79).

It opens up "the possibility of a discourse on . . . interpretations" while assisting "African scholarship to focus its research energy and resources on those areas where an African contribution is very much needed." These areas include sensitivity to the "context of interpretation," the various "historical contexts within which biblical texts have been interpreted in the past," the "role [and input] of the reader in biblical interpretation," "the world-behind-the-[biblical]-texts," knowledge of the dynamics of oral literature, called "orature" in African academia, and the "use of proverbs (and other poetic-stylistic techniques) and story-telling" (see Getui/Holter/Zinkuratire 2001:80–4). Looking at the New Testament critically, one can say that in its relationship with the Old Testament it developed taking all of these areas into account.

6

Christianity in History

Early Beginnings

There have been numerous attempts over the last two centuries to reconstruct the whole life of Jesus into some kind of factual, objective biography. The main purpose has been to seek to distinguish between the "historical Jesus," or Jesus as he actually lived as a man, and the "Christ of faith," or Jesus as he came to be depicted and venerated as God's son, and indeed as God, by his followers after his death. This became an issue because of what some biblical scholars came to see as an unhistorical portrait of Jesus drawn by the New Testament writers. Their study led them to the conclusion that the picture of Jesus that is portrayed principally in the New Testament as well as in other non-canonical but, for the Christian tradition, important writings of the first six centuries is controversial. Did this tradition represent the real, human Jesus as he walked on this earth, or was it intended for purposes of belief? This was the central question.

JESUS IN HISTORICAL CHRISTIANITY

From the very beginning, this issue was a source of controversy, and caused fractures within the church itself. A vast literature, of which the New Testament forms a part, developed as a result, constituting attempts to explain the different and often antagonistic points of view and convictions about who Jesus was and what his teaching was about. The most serious of these controversies, especially from mid-second century onward, had to do with the most central aspects of belief in him.

Because of the claim that Jesus was God, there emerged at the very start of the Christian movement many philosophies and theologies on the nature of God, the nature of Jesus himself, and the Christian understanding of the human person and of salvation. All of them are rich resources for understanding the processes of the maturation in the understanding and appropriation of Jesus and the faith. Although in their thinking about Jesus all early Christians shared the conviction about Jesus' centrality (they all professed him to be the Messiah), they disagreed about his essential characteristics as well as about the interpretation of his teachings. With reference to his nature as God and man, for example, some tended to stress his humanity over and above his divinity. Others did the opposite: they emphasized his divinity over and above his humanity.

In this as in many other issues, there was a tug of war and a competition for people's minds and hearts. The individuals and groups whose ideas did not carry the day on either side were soon called "heretics" (literally, holders of divergent philosophies). The fact that the attacks and counter-attacks among the different camps were so frequent and bitter at the beginning of Christianity was partly because there was as yet no official teaching, no central doctrine. But, rather ironically, it was as a result of these struggles that a more specific teaching on various issues emerged. Similarly, it was as a consequence of the affirmation of "defined" doctrine that heresy was pinpointed. Heresy was therefore essentially a condition of doctrine. The reverse was also true: doctrine was essentially a condition of heresy.

Rufus Jones (1924:12–13) explains the dynamics of orthodoxy and heresy then and now very well. As he has put it, there can be no heresy "until certain truths have been accepted as sacred and have won a group of adherents who believe them to be both true and essential to life and salvation." He goes on to say that true heresy is at least as strong in conviction as orthodoxy; it is not merely doubt, skepticism or infidelity. "Heresy proclaims something to be true and important. It announces a way. It asserts a fiery positive. It has the emphasis of infallibility no less than orthodoxy has. The point of importance is that it challenges the ideas of orthodoxy and insists that something else is more true and closer to the eternal nature of things."

The heretics' "gift" to the church or, in other words, the church's "debt" to them, to use Jones's expression, lies in the fact that they forced the Christian communities as a whole to think. Their intellectual leaders were aided in articulating their convictions mostly by the Hellenistic philosophies of the time. They engaged passionately in explaining the fundamental issues of the faith and so propelled the formulation of decisions or doctrines that were relevant to theological understanding of Jesus and his teaching at the time.

Because of the foundational character of what came to be accepted as the orthodox position, its decisions made at this time are highly esteemed by the church everywhere and have deeply influenced it since. Nevertheless, these decisions of antiquity, at least in their expression, cannot be seen as the final solutions to all issues of faith in an absolutist or static sense. First of all, because they are a result of an earlier process of understanding and appropriating the faith, they themselves require new analysis, renewed understanding, and re-appropriation. They need "to be interpreted or translated into present day language and made understandable to the modern mind," as Brox (1996:150) notes. "For they were formulated by men of late antiquity who thought in Greek, and whose world of questions, thought and language is not directly that of present-day Christians. . . . [Therefore, they] can be assimilated only through historical and theological explanations, through laborious reconstructions and intermediaries."

What this means is that, in the material sense, in their formulation, language, and symbols not all early doctrines are infallible criteria of the faith's orthodoxy for every age, in every place, and for everyone (Jones 1924:24). Their lasting importance as standards of Christian orthodoxy is rather to be found in what they are trying to point to. In a fundamental sense they all pose a question for the Christian of every age, namely: What is the reality and purpose of the life, teaching, and death of Jesus Christ, the meaning of the Christ event?

The fact that the controversies on the nature of Jesus Christ and the other issues related to it were not as prominent in the history of Christianity after the seventh century as they had been in the previous centuries was therefore largely because doctrine had been formulated and established. In more concrete terms, we may note that the earlier heresies had been subdued, sometimes ruthlessly, by ecclesiastical and imperial powers, especially during the years following the first quarter of the fourth century. Thus, for the Great Eastern Schism in the twelfth century and the Protestant Reformation in the sixteenth, the contentious questions had less to do with the understanding of "the essentials for salvation." They had much more to do with the "experience" or "application" in day-to-day life of these essentials.

We have noted that scholarship on christology is immense. More and more today, scholars are again showing interest in finding out the real beginnings and historical activity of the Christian movement through the ages. One important question they are asking is: Does the practical image or "biography" of Jesus presented in early Christian traditions, the result of the heretical and apologetic perceptions and controversies and their later doctrinal developments, fit our view of him?

Overall, the supposition this time, while not totally different from the discussions in the earlier history of Christianity, bears a different slant. Now the fundamental premise seems to be that some understanding of the historical life of Jesus as a man might help to make his message clearer. Some scholars are arguing now that such an understanding is necessary in order to apply Jesus' teaching more effectively and successfully in the radically diverse circumstances we now have. The goal is to avoid imposing on them too much of the language, symbols and value system of another age because these are realities that they may be unable to understand or assimilate. In addition, there is a danger of doing unnecessary violence to cultures and identities that are very different in many ways from those that existed when the teaching of the church on Jesus was being formed and formulated.

Critically reviewing the current research on the Jesus of history, however, one must agree with those scholars who argue that, despite the important light that the Jesus-of-history studies shed on the issue, it is not possible to have a dispassionate, objective biography of the man Jesus, his "authorized biography," as it were. This is because his personal characteristics as a man cannot be definitively known from the evidence at hand. Apart from only certain basic indisputable facts supplied by history, everything else is speculation.

But if we cannot know much for certain about the Jesus of history, we know a lot about the Christ of faith. It is this aspect of him that most evidence has been concerned with preserving. The Christ of faith is the content of the canonical writings of the New Testament; he is also the subject of nearly all of the early Christian literature on both sides of the early doctrinal divide—the heretics and the apologists alike. Moreover, the Christ of faith—and how to act as his disciples—is the concern of the writings of the Fathers of the church, the ecumenical councils, and regional synods throughout the two-thousand-year history of Christianity. Similarly, it is also mostly the subject of the writings of the thousands of theologians throughout the world from early on up to the present day. What has really been at stake throughout this spiritual-intellectual journey is twofold: not only to get to the truth of what Jesus and Christianity mean for different peoples and epochs, but also to show how this meaning might be made effective in the lives of different communities at different times.

What does this history show? It leads to one basic conclusion: since the death of Jesus and his immediate apostles, peoples and communities have encountered Jesus not directly, but on the horizon of a story, a narrative, a teaching, a calling for belief. Each Christian community in every epoch has perceptibly or imperceptibly struggled to own this teaching, this belief. Each people in their specific socio-historical location have attempted to make it meaningful and effective for them. The history of Christianity shows that this struggle is intrinsic to it. It also shows something else that is crucially important, that the temptation has perennially been present for each group to make its particular understanding of Jesus Christ universally applicable. From the very beginning, yielding to this temptation by certain Christian communities in the church has again and again been a source of friction among Christians.

APPROPRIATING THE FAITH IN NEW TESTAMENT TIMES

The death of the apostles brought to the fore perhaps the most important question most of the New Testament writings had to struggle with. As Raymond Brown (1984:13) puts it: How were the different Christian communities to believe and behave "when the last apostolic witness disappeared from the scene, and the church could no longer depend on the testimony of those who said, 'I saw'?" Brown provides an account of how this developed in the various churches the apostles founded, to which the New Testament writings are testimony. Each of these sub-apostolic books in the New Testament, he offers, is a result of a situated process of appropriating faith in Jesus in a particular situation. Each community, each church, faced by ongoing and/or new problems, had to try to find answers to them.

Most of the questions were down-to-earth. They were practical and ethical: What relationship should the Christian community have with the Jews who, in most part, were hostile to it? What should the Christian attitude be toward the Judaizers, those among Christians who advocated strict adherence to the Law of Moses for all converts, even non-Jewish ones? How should the church be organized? How should the saving work of Jesus Christ be understood and portrayed, and what form should the contemporary

Christian's belief take? Obviously every particular community answered these and other questions in different ways. And with the absence of the apostles, there was a lack of firsthand witnesses and consequently of authority to enforce a given position, as especially Paul had done earlier. To whom then should the community turn to verify the truth or authenticity of their positions?

Because different Christian communities traced their origin to the different apostles, it was to its founder that each community appealed for its own orthodoxy. Whether its position on a particular issue closely resembled the particular apostle's position or was quite independent from it, when the name of the apostle was invoked and affixed to the document it often became sufficient proof and criterion for the correctness of belief it expressed. This procedure had strengths and weaknesses. On the one hand, it preserved the teaching and witness-value of the particular apostle. On the other hand, however, it was also possible to put words into the apostle's mouth and affix his signature. Some of the extant non-canonical writings of this period are an example of this. But the point is that the sub-apostolic communities felt at liberty—or perhaps more accurately saw the necessity—to answer questions of faith-practice and church order soon after their apostolic founders had died.

A major philosophical-theological problem these communities faced was—once again—what to make of the person of Jesus. Was he divine or human? Was he pre-existent or created? This seems to have been the question that most vexed the thinking of the communities from which the New Testament literature arose. For the orthodox, synagogue-attending Jews, among whom the Christian communities initially lived, there was only one God, Yahweh: "The Lord our God is one." As we have seen, this was the most basic statement of the Hebrew scriptures. Therefore to posit, however remotely, another God besides Yahweh, as the Christians did in Jesus, was the worst blasphemy. How, then, could the Christians defend the divinity of Jesus as Messiah, something that was central to their faith?

The Johannine Christian communities and the Gospel and epistles emanating from them may be cited as a good case. They polemically emphasized Jesus' divinity in the face of Jewish objections. As Brown explains, "The entire presentation [of the writings attributed to John] protects Jesus from whatever could be a challenge to divinity." It does not say much about his humanity because that was never in dispute, Brown (1984:105–6 and 1979:69) argues.

As a result of different locations, needs and questions, there is, however, neither a consistent christology nor ecclesiology in the sub-apostolic New Testament writings. Each community had different situations to face, because of their different geographical, sociological, economic and theological realities. To provide a uniform answer to these realities was neither possible at a time when means of communication were very primitive, nor would it have been desirable. Faith in Jesus could in fact not have survived if such had been attempted because both Jews and non-Jews would have probably rejected it. Instead, diversity triumphed. Despite the different theological opinions and pastoral responses, the various Christian communities did not, however, break unity and communion or *koinonia* between them. By firmly professing faith in Jesus as Lord in the best way they knew how, holding on to the tradition of a given apostle, they possessed a communion of essential belief among them. In this sense their diversity was an aid, and not a hindrance, to their unity and oneness, and they were seen by non-Christians as such.

The necessity of diversity is further implied in the Letter to the Hebrews. The author or editor of this letter tells the members of this largely Hellenistic-Jewish Christian community that, having accepted the basic principles of the Christian religion, they must go ahead and build a firm house, a vibrant living faith. This writer makes it very clear by the vocabulary he uses that such a faith is one that is expressive of their own and their community's commitment to Jesus Christ in the context of their own environment and religious heritage as Jews. He is anxious to assure his addressees that such is the challenge facing true Jewish Christianity.

The authentic letters of Paul, just like the Letter to the Hebrews, remind the Pauline communities to grow in maturity in the faith where they are. In each one of them, Paul deals at some point with specific issues facing the particular community to which the letter is addressed and either commends the community for the position it has taken or takes them to task if he sees it to be wrong.

But it is Luke who perhaps most clearly shows his own "bias" in his theological methodology. In the two books he is certain to have compiled, namely, the Gospel according to St. Luke and the Acts of the Apostles, he puts his writing into context. Addressing his friend Theophilus (Lk. 1:1–4), Luke explains that he is by no means the first person to attempt to write the story of Jesus. Nevertheless, he thinks his attempt is important. In other words, Luke is saying to his friend: "What I am going to give you is a different view on the same subject." In the process he gives us a glimpse of the variety of Christian lifestyles and expressions of belief in Jesus.

The same insight can be found in other New Testament writings besides the Lukan corpus. There also, we encounter many varieties of christologies, ecclesiologies, and even ethical outlooks.

The Gospel writers interpreted all relevant events in the life and death of Jesus as acts of God in order to suit the expectations, needs and catechetical conditions for their intended audiences. Theirs was the genius of shaping the developments of opinions of faith and belief through interpretation, controversy, promotion and suppression of ideas so as to realize the ultimate vision. They employed literary license and believed that they enjoyed God's guiding hand, and they did. But just as clearly, geographical, cultural, theological and even economic and political influences also played a role in the development and maturity of the various New Testament texts. They are factors that are behind the different interpretations of events in Jesus' life. The writers and editors of these texts betray them.

AFRICA AND THE NEW TESTAMENT

Much of what was said earlier about the relationship between Africa and the Old Testament applies equally well to any discussion about Africa and the New Testament. But some points need to be repeated in specific application to the New Testament, if only for the sake of clarity and emphasis. The New Testament as well as the Old must be interpreted in the context and language of African culture and religiosity to be truly "appropriated" by African Christians as foundations of an authentic, home-grown African Christianity.

I shall discuss below the contribution of Africa to the intellectual and doctrinal self-identity of church during the patristic era, shortly after the time of the New Testament. For the moment, it might be useful to look at the same issue with reference to the New Testament itself. What, as Benjamim A. Ntreh (Getui/Maluleke/Ukpong 2001:68–82) asks, was Africa's contribution to the inception of Christianity, of which the New Testament writings are the cornerstones?

Ntreh notes a conspicuous reluctance among New Testament writers/editors to acknowledge Africa's place and role, not only in the beginnings and survival of Israel as a nation, but in the historical success of the work of Jesus and Christianity itself. Whenever this role is admitted, he explains, it is rather grudging and its full implications are not spelled out. Ntreh argues that the fact that Africa is mentioned at all makes it all the more likely that the role it played in this development was considerable. The influence Africa brought to bear to the formative events of Christianity was perhaps more significant than immediately meets the eye. Had it not been so, it would probably have been ignored altogether.

The New Testament carries over from the Old a predominant feeling of antipathy against Egypt. Egypt as the place of suffering is contrasted with the "Promised Land," a place of freedom, full of milk and honey. The two are generally shown to be antithetical, not only sociologically but also ethically. Egypt becomes a metaphor for moral decadence and depravity. And, in Ntreh's estimation, general biblical scholarship has reinforced this view.

However, from an African theological perspective, the exodus story cannot be limited to this negative view. Without in the least falsifying the message of the Bible, it must also be seen in the context of very positive antecedents in the formation of Israel as a nation. We cannot lose sight of Egypt's initial hospitality to Joseph, Jacob's son by Rachel, and eventually to Jacob's entire family and still claim to be doing justice to the scriptural message in its entirety. The theological implications of this story alone, which begins in the book of Genesis, are immense. We can easily infer from the biblical account that had it not been for Egypt, Jacob and his sons would have perished from hunger, and there would have been no Israel as a nation. Egypt is thus, in Ntreh's phrase, a place of "security and protection" for

Israel. In a real sense, God uses Egypt as an essential agent in his plan of salvation, without which it would have been impossible for this history to have taken off.

From the theological point of view, what the biblical story is admitting by locating the beginnings of Israel's growth in Egypt is that Israel and Egypt (and the world) are inextricably tied together. Even the epic narrating, which constitutes the whole of Exodus, is a way of confirming the same thing. This fact is very closely connected to events in the New Testament and to Christianity as a whole.

There is, of course, no way of knowing whether or not the flight of the Holy Family into Egypt, which the Matthean tradition mentions briefly in 2:13–15, was a factual, historical event. Whatever the case may be, the principal point of the story is theological. It is remarkable, isn't it, that just as God used Egypt to mark the beginnings of national identity for his people Israel, God used Egypt to keep alive the roots of the new dispensation in the infant Jesus. Had not Jesus been taken by his parents into Egypt at God's behest, he would have been killed as an infant by Herod.

God therefore calls both ancient Israel under the leadership of Moses and the foundation of the new Israel in the person of Jesus "out of Egypt," as Matthew writes, alluding to the prophet Hosea 11:1. Egypt becomes for Jesus, and therefore for Christianity, a place of security and protection. This is an important role, which deserves study and elaboration.

Ntreh refers to the synoptic Gospels' mention of Simon the Cyrenian whom the accounts say was "made," "pressed" or "compelled" to carry Jesus' cross and follow "behind" him, as Luke (23:26) puts it (see also Mt. 27:32, Mk. 15:21). There is debate about many elements of this story—for example, whether Simon was a Jew living in Cyrene (modern Tripoli in Libya). In any case, this incident in the gospels is extremely important theologically. Here is an African, by birth or habitat, depicted as the example of the true disciple who carries the cross and follows after Jesus, something which Jesus repeatedly emphasized in his teaching.

Ntreh (Getui/Maluleke/Ukpong 2001:80) finds it remarkable that "it was this Cyrenian who, presumably, had not heard of the exhortation Jesus gave to his disciples to 'carry their cross' who came to his help." Simon "made it possible for Jesus to get his cross to the mount of crucifixion so that Jesus could then die on the cross" for the world's salvation. But he is astonished at how, in spite of all of this, biblical scholarship could have largely failed to recognize in Simon Africa's contribution to "making it possible for Jesus to fulfil his mission." We can also understand Andrew Walls's assertion that Christianity in Africa cannot accurately be looked at merely as "a colonial leftover"; it was here from its very beginnings, and certainly before it reached many other parts of the world.

One important implication of this which Walls (2002:91) makes clear is that Christianity as it develops in Africa cannot be relegated to the margins of true Christian identity. Specifically, "African Christian thought belongs in the Christian mainstream; and African theology should not be satisfied with a place that reduces it to solving local difficulties."

INTERPRETING THE NEW TESTAMENT IN AFRICA

The general neglect of modern biblical scholarship to recognize Africa's presence in, or contribution to, the formation of the New Testament can be attributed to many causes. But among African New Testament scholars, the reason is mostly because in their study and interpretation they have not asked the right questions. Where critical questions are absent, no fundamentally new reading of the texts will emerge which critiques and enriches these other readings.

Gerald O. West (in Getui/Maluleke/Ukpong 2001:86–87) speaks of several paradigms that have been widely used in biblical interpretation; namely, the professional (or almost exclusively academic), comparative, inculturation, and liberation paradigms. They are not necessarily mutually exclusive, he says, and need to be brought together for the task in Africa, although what paradigm is emphasized will depend on who the interpreter is, what the occasion is, and what the situation is that is being addressed.

The liberation paradigm is of crucial importance in interpreting the New Testament in Africa. I would call it the problem-oriented or "functional" method. It brings with it two major implications. As West advises, one of the tasks for African New Testament scholars involves making explicit not only the "ideologies" inherent in the New Testament itself, but also unmasking how it has often been used as an ideological instrument. This is functional hermeneutics' first task. Second, this "unmasking" is helped, as West (Getui/Maluleke/Ukpong 2001:84) again rightly observes, by attending to African popular readings of the scriptures. We need to investigate how African Christians have "at a deeper level negotiated and transacted with . . . and partially appropriated the Bible—by relativising it, resisting it, and modifying it with uncanny creativity."

Functional hermeneutics is analogous to functional christology; it takes full account of Jesus' incarnation event. When we talk about functional christology we focus less on what Jesus was "in himself" and more on his saving activity; less on ontology and more on soteriology. Similarly, functional hermeneutics in Africa would concentrate on what West has characterized as the "transaction" or "encounter" between the New Testament and the totality of the African environment. This is the process of recovering or discovering the New Testament's essential message from and in the African environment. We would then allow the very same message to transform the environment anew while at the same time enriching the other paradigms.

Let me illustrate the workings of this (liberation) paradigm by adducing the example of the African ancestors. Kwame Bediako in his book *Christianity in Africa* subtitles the chapter discussing this encounter, "Will [the African] Ancestors Survive?" He has in mind the negative onslaught which missionary Christianity brought to bear against this element of African religiosity, an onslaught which was based on a "misconception" of the significance of this religious category for both African spirituality—from which it cannot be disposed without damaging the African personality (Bediako 1995:216)—and New Testament spirituality for which it also appears to be pivotal. The question for functional hermeneutics is how to recover the presence of the New Testament sense of spiritual existence in the African ancestral existence so that African Christians can appropriate ancestral spirituality as the new (Christian) circumstances now demand.

Ancestors in Africa are the "principle" or "source" of personal, family and community life. What happens to living humanity and the universe in general flows through the ancestors from God and back to God. Life—in both its positive and negative aspects—cannot therefore be conceived apart from the ancestors. Jesus Christ is not contradicted by this principle of ancestorship in Christian theology, but rather is vividly expressed in and by the category. As an ancestor, the Christian vocation toward life in God cannot be conceived apart from Jesus.

As the Christ, the Anointed One of God and Savior, Jesus is the principle of life in the world. When the Gospel of John says that he is the Way, the Truth and the Life, this is what he means. Whoever wants to travel the way of good and God must somehow accept and put into effect the traditions and customs he, as the founding ancestor, has established and which his community has received (see Jn. 14:6). These comprise faith, hope and charity, as well as taboos that must not be broken if the community and the individuals comprising it are to fare well (1 Cor. 13:13).

African christology might express it this way: Jesus Christ is the Proto-Ancestor or Ancestor par excellence "by virtue of his incarnation, death, resurrection and ascension into the realm of spirit-power" (Bediako 1995:217). Thus the Christ-event's ultimate purpose is to confer the fullest possible life on humanity, the world and everything in it (Jn. 10:10). Insofar as they serve this purpose, the other functional depictions of Jesus in African theology as Chief, Master of Initiation, or Healer are deeply incorporated in the depiction of Jesus as Ancestor.

Volker Küster (2001:63–64) presents in summary form François Kabasele's reasons for rediscovering the function of Jesus as Ancestor in African christology as follows:

- *Jesus Christ is the ancestor because he mediates life.*
- *Jesus Christ is the ancestor because he is present among the living.*
- *Jesus Christ, the ancestor, is at the same time the eldest.*
- *Jesus Christ is the ancestor because he is the mediator between God and human beings and within human community* (italics in original).

Of course, no one is advocating a process of simplistic equivalence between Jesus and the ancestors. We realize that the theologian will have to use his or her analogical imagination and qualify many aspects of ancestral activity (because essentially human) as falling short of Jesus' ancestral activity (because divine). What is being suggested is rather the dynamic interaction between them where the activity of the one (Jesus) is realized in the conceptual and practical idiom of the other (African ancestral spirituality and religiosity). This is the kind of New Testament hermeneutics which will enhance the understanding of Jesus Christ in Africa (see also Goergen 2001).

7

Fine-tuning Structures and Doctrine

The Patristic Period

There is perhaps no period in the entire two-thousand-year history of Christianity as fertile and as rich in doctrinal development and the "adjustment" of the faith to concrete situations after the death of Jesus' apostles as the patristic era. It lasted for roughly six centuries, from the beginning of the second century with Sts. Clement of Rome and Ignatius of Antioch to the middle of the eighth century with the death of Bede the Venerable in 735 in the Latin-speaking western part of the Roman Empire and that of John Damascene in 749 in the Greek-speaking East.

The literary genre at this time becomes distinctly different from that of the sub-apostolic period, when the writings contained in the New Testament were compiled. Various influential individual Christians began to write documents under their own names and on their own authority. Even though a few pseudo-letters exist, they can today be easily distinguished as inauthentic with a high degree of certainty.

The patristic era was marked by almost continuous doctrinal and pastoral controversies. We will discuss a sample of these controversies to show how the process of insertion of the faith into culture by mutual influence was acting itself out. This is indispensable for understanding the anatomy of inculturation. This is the period which, apart from the Bible itself, is seminal for all subsequent theological thinking and for the organization of the church.

The two elements of this development that will concern us here are (a) the rise of a clear structure of the church, culminating in the institution of monarchical leadership, with the bishop of Rome eventually emerging as supreme; and (b) the establishment of certain doctrinal positions against which other contrary positions appear to be, and are formally declared definitively heretical.

DEVELOPMENT OF CHURCH STRUCTURE

To be able to appreciate fully the radical nature of the transition that took place in the organization and government of the Christian communities in little more than sixty years between 95 and 150 C.E., we must quickly review the organization of the communities in the sub- or immediate post-apostolic period. The overwhelming evidence from the New Testament is that the communities during this period were autonomously organized, each with its own form of government and ministries (for example, see Brown 1984, Bernier 1992:31–51). At this time, social status and moral authority (usually on the basis of age) were perhaps more important in keeping order in the community than any formal function anyone might have held. At any rate, functions, such as presiding at the eucharistic table, were also normally based on seniority of age, and were shared or revolving. Thus presbyters, literally elders and heads of households who had proven themselves in good moral standing and wisdom, were cited as "overseers" of community order.

Towards the end of the century, some of the presbyters, as Bernier (1992:49) writes, "eventually became bishops or deacons, positions that had more definite responsibilities," such as managing community finances and teaching. This is clear especially in the pastorals. But apart from the communion that existed between and among the communities, particularly those tracing their origin to a common apostle, there was not as yet trans- or supra-community authority. There is no evidence in the whole of the New Testament that, for example, the Twelve were ever "rulers," "presbyters" or, to use an anachronistic designation for this period, "bishops" of any church.

Bernier notes that as far as we know, the Twelve "made no efforts to replace themselves" as such or in church leadership, as Clement of Rome would soon afterwards rather hyperbolically claim. Because of this, these communities were faced with a real problem. Bernier (1992:48) is right: "The second generation [of Christians], faced with the problem of survival, had to determine who could function authoritatively in the community and how to remain faithful to the faith they had received." Again, "Different churches answered this in different ways." This is why it is a telling development in the beginning of the patristic period when the (First) Letter of Clement to the church of Corinth (c. 96/98 C.E.) already suggests that presbyters as governors of the church are a necessary element of church order, determined not only by the apostles but by Christ and God himself.

Clement, intent on restoring church order at Corinth, takes the extraordinary step of identifying the presbyters with bishops and assigning them a specific cultic ministry in the community. Therefore, rebellion against them, something which had apparently taken place at Corinth, became the equivalent to rebellion against God. "Our sin," he warns the rebels, "will not be small if we eject from the *episcopate* those who blamelessly and holily have offered its Sacrifices" (Jurgens 1970:11, emphasis added).

Subsequent patristic writings, but especially those of Ignatius of Antioch and Hermas amplified this line. Whereas, for example, Clement seems to say that there were several bishops in one community, as at Corinth, Ignatius posits only one, and argues that without a bishop present no eucharistic celebration is valid. He likens the bishop to Christ, or indeed Christ to the bishop, saying that Christ is the "unseen bishop" of every church. In his letter to the Smyrnaeans (c. 110 C.E.) he spells out his position about the bishop very clearly when he orders them to "not do anything of concern to the Church without the bishop. Let that be considered a valid Eucharist which is [only] celebrated by the bishop or by one whom he appoints. . . ."

Ignatius continues to assert that it is not permitted "without the bishop either to baptize or to celebrate the agape; but whatever he [the bishop] approves, this too is pleasing to God, so that whatever is done will be secure and valid" (Jurgens 1970:25). Furthermore, whereas formerly there was no sharp distinction made between bishop, presbyter and deacon, Ignatius makes one when he writes in the same letter, "You must follow the bishop as Jesus Christ follows the Father, and the presbyter as you would the Apostles. Reverence the deacons as you would the command of God" (Jurgens 1970:25). Ignatius thus opens the door for the later development of distinctive offices in the church.

From the literature surrounding and following Ignatius, it seems that the development of the institution of monarchical bishops at the expense of the position of other ministries in the church became irreversible. Why did this radical transition take place?

There were several reasons. The major one was sociological, and pertained both to the internal and external form of the church at the time. Others were psychological and economic. But by the first quarter of the fourth century, the dominant and determinative reason for consolidating the type of organization based on a monarchical bishop as a central figure had become decidedly political.

As the church grew in numbers, it could no longer afford the kind of structure, most common in the Johannine communities, but present also in much of the New Testament churches, where discipline depended solely on the work of the Holy Spirit in the community, on charisms. The ministries of seers and prophets, each claiming direct instruction from God for the church, especially threatened to lead the churches into confusion. And as a uniform doctrine was now developing regarding who Jesus was and what he did, and what exactly his legacy was to the church through the apostles (as is already evident in the pastoral), the church could no longer afford the luxury of doctrinal "anarchy" that charismatic leadership seems to bring.

The similarity with the transition from charismatic to royal leadership in the Old Testament cannot be missed. The need for a central authority in the churches was everywhere felt, and the most charismatic, or intellectually strongest, or socially most influential person from among the presbyters seemed to be the most obvious choice to bring coherence and order. Given the gravity of the need for unity within the communities and even between them, it did not take too long for such persons to assume exclusively many of the powers which had previously been shared among many, and thereby to become hierarchical and monarchical. Instead of several bishops and presbyters in one community, we now have a single bishop without whom even the celebration of the Eucharist is "not valid" (as Ignatius instructs the Smyrnaeans), and who is now instead of the deacons charged with the responsibility for the finances of the community.

The Eucharist or thanksgiving meal had always been a central part of the Christian communities. Previously celebrated in different homes as family gatherings, the number of converts soon outgrew the practicality of such a tradition. There was the need to have one central place in which the faithful could congregate and celebrate this *agape* or love meal. But even if such a place could be found, who among the presbyters would guide the celebration? A concrete symbol of eucharistic unity was needed, and it was easily found in the emerging charismatic and powerful figure, the bishop.

It was the bishop, too, who could most easily symbolize the unity between one community and another because of the relationship, association, or friendship he might have with his counterparts. He might send material help to bishops whose communities were in need, but more importantly he might stand in agreement with them on doctrinal issues. As doctrinal uniformity grew and became prized by the leaders, this latter eventually became the most important characteristic of an authentic bishop, and cause to spell his greatness and survival as leader, or his failure and fall as a heretic. This scenario was to play itself out again and again until the end of the patristic period.

Doctrinal agreement by the Christian communities was fundamental because of the emerging and rising waves of contrary theo-philosophies (particularly Greek), general anti-Christian sentiment, and distrust, disdain and persecution of Christians by the agents of the empire. Persecution prompted a huge output of apologetic literature from many of the major monarchical bishops, many of whom were, of course, martyred. The structural "triumph" of Christianity came only at the beginning of the fourth century when Constantine the Great took control of the empire.

During the time of persecution and intolerance, the Christian communities needed strong central rallying points for encouragement and perseverance against apostasy. The bishops in general provided such points. Psychologically, many Christian communities felt the need, indeed the pressure, to distinguish themselves from Judaism, not only in teaching but also in organization. Although Christian organization continued to retain much that was Jewish in character, they wanted to show quite clearly that they were not merely a continuation of Judaism. They were the "fulfillment of the age," the community or *ekklesia* (those called out) of the promised Messiah, before and after whom there is no other. Again, the figure of the bishop seemed to provide a reference point for this difference.

Useful as this was, it was also paradoxical. The development of the monarchical bishop in the Christian communities of the second century never distinguished him sufficiently—in function, at least—from the Jewish high priest. In fact, the Letter to the Hebrews attempts to apply the characteristics of the high priest retroactively to Jesus himself, perhaps—even then—to justify theologically the development of the office of bishop as high priest, and as representative of Jesus Christ *the* "High Priest." But we cannot assert this with absolute certainty.

Very practical needs and exigencies determined the development and eventual institutionalization of the monarchical episcopacy during the period of the early Fathers. Nevertheless, not all communities took kindly to this centralization of power and ministry. The writings of Clement and all subsequent patristic literature defending the position of the bishop attest, by their aggressive insistence on the importance of this figure, to the resistance against it. Clement notes the rebellion against the presbyters (then incipient bishops) at Corinth, and Ignatius, writing to Smyrna, uses very strong language and vivid images to defend the authority of the bishop, the presbyters, and the deacons. Ignatius does not speak about the existence of bishops in Rome when he was writing, which suggests that the communities there were still led by presbyters. The literary evidence we have leads to the conclusion that there was no monarchical bishop in Rome until the middle of the second century.

STRUGGLES ABOUT DOCTRINE

Setting the institution of bishop over and above the ministries of presbyters, prophets and other forms of ministerial leadership, and finally replacing them completely in the early church was, in the final analysis, a struggle for correct doctrine, mainly about God, Jesus, and Mary. How should we understand God? Who, precisely, is Jesus? What is the place of Mary, the mother of Jesus, in the Christian scheme of things?

We have seen how these were already elements underlying the New Testament writings and producing not only different images of Jesus, but also different conceptions and organizations of the Christian communities. Shortly afterward, these differences led to the issue of authority in the church: Who has the right to determine what Christians should or should not believe about these matters? The numerous philosophies abroad purporting to answer these and similar questions were causing even more confusion as the church grew and expanded in different regions. Clearly, amid all of this jungle of ideas, positions, teachings and even "revelations," some firm doctrinal clarifications for the wider church were needed. The bishops and, starting with Constantine, the emperors, played a leading role in this development.

Different philosophies and theological movements, old and new, had a big influence in the process of formulating doctrine in the early church. To begin with, philosophy, just like the Law, was taken by some Fathers to be an aspect of divine disclosure. The Greek philosophies of Plato, Aristotle and Zeno were especially significant, and were taken very seriously, whether positively or negatively. They were to shape the Christian understanding of God, the church and human relationships in a profound way.

Obviously, all of the existing philosophical views could not co-exist each in its entirety in the Christian community. So they were a source of numerous controversies. Consequently, Marcion rejected the God of the Old Testament as cruel compared to the good and loving God of Jesus. In reaction, the orthodox wing affirmed even more strongly the authenticity of the canon of scripture, especially the New Testament, whose main content became generally agreed upon by 200 C.E.

I would like to review very briefly some significant events in the fourth century, a period when Christianity was enjoying religious hegemony in the empire. Arguably, it constitutes one of the greatest, if not the greatest, periods in the history of Christianity in terms of its impact on the shape of the church and the content of its teaching for succeeding centuries and for the contemporary church.

Among others, two pivotal councils stand out: Nicaea (325) and Constantinople (381).

The Council of Nicaea has been called the first truly ecumenical (in the sense of general or worldwide) council or synod, gathering together about three hundred bishops. The immediate issue was the theological problem represented by Arius, but the more fundamental and long-range issue—at least for the emperor—was the question of imperial power and unity, an issue which was decidedly political (Kee 1982). To get a clear picture, it is necessary to explain why the theological opinions of Arius were seen to be a threat to the unity of the empire and the power of the emperor. Only then can we understand why Emperor Constantine and his successors decided to deal with this "threat" with an ingenious combination of Machiavellian political wile and arm-twisting in the guise of religious fervor.

Arius sought to define the precise relationship between God the Father and the Son, but he was accused by his enemies of teaching that there was a time when the Son did not exist. The eternity of God the Son was the most important issue in the whole Arian controversy.

Arius' ideas were popular in Alexandria. Consequently, Bishop Alexander of that city, meeting in council with a group of bishops from Libya and Egypt, excommunicated him. Arius fled to Palestine where he obtained the ear and protection of two important and influential bishops, namely, Eusebius of Caesarea, the well-known scholar and author of the history of the early church, and Eusebius of Nicomedia, who wielded considerable influence in Constantine's household. They exonerated Arius of any heresy and Arius returned to Alexandria. Immediately riots broke out in the city between Arius' and Bishop Alexander's camps.

Unwilling to let this chaos spread, Constantine intervened. The empire did not then have any organizational network to keep order. Constantine was shrewd enough to perceive the church to be well organized for this purpose. All he had to do was to give it the power to do so. He himself had little understanding of the theological niceties of the Arian controversy and, it has been suggested, he could not care less. The fact that he did not receive baptism until the very final days of his life is perhaps a testimony that he did not care much about the Christian faith either: throughout his lifetime he had continued to pay homage to the Unconquered Sun (*Sol Invictus*) as a god. The main purpose for his intervention was therefore clearly political. He called the Council of Nicaea to deal with the Arian question in 325 C.E. to establish his own grip over his fractious empire.

At Nicaea, the Arian position was officially condemned, and the foundations of what would later be known as the Nicene Creed were laid. In the acts of the council, God the Son was pronounced to be "of the substance of the Father . . . true God of true God, begotten not made, consubstantial with the Father." Constantine wanted it this way. He wanted to preserve the unity of the empire by preserving that of the church, and this is why many of the nearly three hundred bishops who attended voted the way they voted, against Arius. There were a few bishops who resisted this statement because of the ambiguity in its wording and refused to sign it. But to achieve his political aim, Constantine exiled all of them.

Still, the Council of Nicaea did not succeed in putting an end to the Arian issue, so that many people on both sides of the divide continued to suffer persecution and death for their convictions. While Bishop Eusebius of Nicomedia figures prominently in the controversy as dissenting from the Nicene position, Athanasius, who was made bishop of Alexandria shortly after the council, became one of its staunchest supporters. Other prominent figures in favor of Nicaea, although at different levels of intensity, included Sts. Hilary, Ambrose, Basil, Gregory of Nanzianzus, and Gregory of Nyssa.

Not even all the emperors following Constantine agreed: some supported Arianism while others upheld the Nicene position. The theological situation and the political status of the church thus shifted, depending upon who was emperor. This state of affairs continued until Emperor Theodosius I (378–395) proclaimed Christianity to be the state religion throughout the empire and claimed virtually for himself alone the authority to determine Christian orthodoxy. It was Theodosius who in 381 summoned the bishops to Constantinople to deal further with the Arian situation, which was still simmering in many parts of the empire.

At Constantinople political strategies and arm twisting also played a role. All known Arian bishops were excluded from the assembly to assure unanimity of outcome. The trinitarian principles established at Nicaea were accepted and amplified into the Nicene Creed or, more accurately, the Nicene-Constantinopolitan Creed.

The point of this discussion is to provide a sense of how a vital doctrine of the Christian faith, the doctrine of the nature of Christ in relation to the Trinity, developed and was finally conclusively explained. It took a long and circuitous way to arrive at Constantinople and the oneness of nature between God the Son and God the Father. In the course of this development, fortunes changed often: orthodoxy was frequently considered to be heterodoxy and vice versa. Theological corners were cut and political concerns played at least as much a role as theology (Hall 1991:121–72). Above all, the faith and convictions of individuals in the church and secular philosophies were necessary instruments in this development.

THE AFRICAN CONTRIBUTION

Those familiar with the early history of Christianity will easily appreciate the contribution of Africa in the formation of church structures and the formulation of doctrine during the patristic period. But it has for so long been sidelined and often distorted in many descriptions, even by church accounts themselves. For example, John Baur (1994:21) in his otherwise admirable account of African Christianity writes that among modern Egyptian Christians, "A *spurious* tradition goes as far as pointing out the palm tree which Our Lady embraced during childbirth. Other legends affirm that the Holy Family spent some time in the mountains of Ethiopia.—Do not these traditions, *naïve as they are*, reveal the conviction that Christianity existed early in Africa and that deep in their hearts Africans are truly Christians?" (italics added).

If we were to look for "spurious" and "naïve" traditions in the sense that Baur appears to imply here, we would find them aplenty in the corpus of writings we call sacred scripture. But they are not necessarily so. For Africa, as Baur himself notes accurately, they underline "the conviction that deep in their hearts Africans are truly Christians." They have their place in the spirituality of African Christianity.

Let us in this section make more explicit Africa's contribution to early Christian theological and structural development through the activities of two prestigious African institutions of the late second and third centuries. The catechetical school of Alexandria, the workplace of Clement of Alexandria and Origen, and the theological school of Carthage, the workplace of Tertullian and Cyprian, have a legitimate claim to honor in the annals of Christian thought. The significance of these institutions and their intellectual output lies in their success in marrying the message of Christianity to the prevailing cultural circumstances of each region. The effects of the effort have survived in the church to our day.

The Alexandrian School

The overriding concern of the Alexandrian school was to create a bridge between the message of the gospel of Christ and the Greek philosophy and Hellenistic culture flourishing there. Scholarship at Alexandria was characterized by the speculative method of theological investigation into revelation. This gave rise to the allegorical method of interpreting scripture. Clement saw no conflict between faith and reason and argued that reason must be at the service of faith. As Neill and Schmandt (1957:58) have correctly noted, the pedagogical approach to theology that takes philosophy as its handmaid—an approach amplified and perfected by St. Thomas Aquinas nine centuries later—must be traced back to Clement's work. Through Thomas the influence of Clement lives on, especially in Catholic theological education.

Origen succeeded Clement as master of the catechetical school, and of all the Christian scholars of the first five hundred years of the church, he must be counted the most impressively creative in theological production, with the only possible exception of St. Augustine of Hippo. Jurgens (1970:189–90) sees Origen as "the greatest scholar of Christian antiquity," and describes his work *The Fundamentals of Christian Doctrine* in superlative terms as a "theological monument of absolutely epic proportions." He notes that St. Jerome and Bishop Epiphanius of Salamis, Cyprus, both fiercely anti-Origenists, admit that he wrote thousands of books.

Following in the footsteps of Clement, his predecessor at Alexandria and possibly his teacher, Origen was concerned to "find in Jesus Christ a fulfillment of the best in Greek culture" (Hall 1991:239). His unwavering commitment to the project of harmonizing the two consumed him and influenced all his theological work as well as his translations and interpretation of scripture. The Greek philosophical notion of the primacy of reason led him to posit as key to all his theological thinking the pre-existence and purity of the "spiritual principle," the mind or the *logos*, represented in the human person by reason. He took this as the basis for interpreting the relationship of God to humanity, the divine and human natures in the person of Christ, and the internal relationship of the Holy Trinity itself.

This approach rendered much of Origen's work suspiciously heretical to many of his enemies in the years after his death because it was interpreted (almost like Arius' position) to subordinate Jesus Christ to the Father and the Holy Spirit to the Son. His work was maligned as a consequence, particularly in the West. Many of his books had by then been tampered with and some destroyed. Much of the condemnation of his work was based on hearsay and corrupted manuscripts. At any rate, through their integration of Hellenistic philosophy, culture and the Gospel, Origen's, Clement's, and the Egyptian-Alexandrian influence on the universal church is perpetual. The explanation of the idea of Christian martyrdom in the writings of Origen is one example (Heisey 2000).

The Carthaginian School

Much the same thing can be said about Carthage and its shining lights, Tertullian and St. Cyprian. The Carthaginians' approach to the Christian faith was pragmatic, representing perhaps much more closely the African mentality. Faithfulness to the tradition of the apostolic churches was for Tertullian the linchpin of theological thinking. His famous saying, "What does Athens have to do with Jerusalem?" reflected his disdain of Greek philosophy as a tool of theology.

As far as theological thinking and writing is concerned, Tertullian was a pioneer in introducing into Latin theological discussion such concepts and notions as "trinity," "consubstantial," "nature," and "person." These are concepts and notions that we now take for granted in the doctrine of God. Always the theological rigorist and moral ascetic, Tertullian was attracted to these characteristics through Montanism, a heresy which forbade second marriages to widows, practically denied the church the power to forgive sin, especially apostasy, and inculcated in its followers the desire to embrace martyrdom. Tertullian himself affirmed, "The blood of martyrs is a seed [of the Church]," a conviction which he embraced to the very end of his life.

Cyprian was bishop of Carthage from 248 to 258, when he was beheaded. He administered the diocese more by correspondence than by physical presence. For most of his time as bishop he remained in hiding from the persecutions of Decius and Valerian. He had troubled relationships with some of the clergy and laity in his diocese. Later he also fell out of favor with Pope Stephen I over the question of readmitting apostates into the church and the validity of baptism by heretics and schismatics. Contrary to the pope, Cyprian favored the former if performed according to regulations by the clergy, and he rejected the latter. The questions he posed and addressed on these issues and the answers he proposed still constitute part of Christian teaching.

In one of his most significant documents, *On the Unity of the Catholic Church*, Cyprian reflected on the relationship between the local and the universal church. What is the authority of the bishop in his see in relation to the bishop of Rome? Two authentic versions of this document have survived. In the version written in 251, Cyprian defends the primacy of the bishop of Rome, probably because he enjoyed a cordial relationship with Pope Cornelius. About the primacy of Peter, he asks: "If someone does not hold fast to this *unity of Peter*, can he imagine that he still holds the faith? If he deserts the chair of Peter upon whom the Church was built, can he still be confident that he is in the Church?" In the second version, however, he seems to have changed positions. Possibly because of his sour relationship with Pope Stephen, Cornelius' successor, there is here no mention of Petrine primacy. Instead, he lays stress on the authority of each bishop in his own diocese: "If anyone does not hold fast to the *unity of the Church*, can he imagine that he still holds the faith? . . . The episcopate is one, of which each bishop holds his part within the undivided structure" (Jurgens 1970:220–21, italics added).

How relevant and pertinent these questions and answers are for our own times can be seen in the organization of the Eastern Church since the eleventh century, that of the various Christian churches since the Protestant Reformation, and in the discussion of the documents of the Second Vatican Council in the Catholic Church, particularly the Decree on the Pastoral Office of Bishops in the Church, *Christus Dominus*. Following the Council in 1966 another relevant document, called *Ecclesiae Sanctae*, was issued spelling out the norms for implementing *Christus Dominus*. But more recently, the discussion sparked by Pope John Paul II's 1995 encyclical letter *Ut Unum Sint* about the ecumenical role of the Petrine ministry today shows even more clearly the genius that Cyprian was, and the contribution he bequeathed to the church on this question.

8

The Age In-Between

Philosophers and Reformers

We have seen examples of the theological outlook and Christian living that characterized the life and ministry of the sub-apostolic and patristic church periods. We should recall that the same processes occurred in different situations in the development of Old Testament theology. Similar modifications, changes and even merging of positions and opinions took place there before the establishment of what was considered the accepted or, to use a later term, "orthodox" position. But in either case, controversy did not usually end immediately with the establishment of orthodox opinion; often it continued, forcing orthodoxy to define, redefine, refine and defend itself more and more acutely.

Since the patristic age, the same processes have marked the development of the worldwide church in all of its aspects. As illustrations of what happened in what I call "the age in-between"—the period between the Fathers and the modern and contemporary era—let us reflect here briefly on the influence on subsequent theology by St. Thomas Aquinas in the thirteenth century and the Enlightenment in Europe in the seventeenth.

THOMAS AQUINAS, SCHOLASTICISM AND THE ENLIGHTENMENT

Apart from St. Augustine of Hippo, who died in 430, there is perhaps no other personality who has influenced the theology of the church—and certainly the Catholic Church—as much as the Dominican friar Thomas Aquinas, especially through the theological methodology he proposed.

Working toward the end of the scholastic period, Aquinas was the first major philosopher in the Christian world to consciously and deliberately use Aristotelian and, to a lesser extent, Platonic philosophy and logic as a way of approaching the totality of the Christian doctrine. In his writings, he emphasized that reason can and must illuminate Christian faith. Similarly he held that, in the divine plan, nature and grace are not contradictory but work together in the human person's journey toward God. Aquinas arranged his arguments in such a systematic way that he remains unrivalled. That is why even though the influence of scholasticism in theology had waned by the sixteenth century, Aquinas' endured. Pope Leo XIII's 1879 encyclical, *Aeterni Patris*, declared Aquinas's work to be an expression of the true teaching of the Catholic Church, a position the Catholic Church maintained to the middle of the twentieth century. De-emphasized for about two decades after 1965, with the fervor of plural philosophical and theological approaches that Vatican II unleashed—existentialism, humanism, phenomenology, process theology, liberation theology, African theology, and so on—Thomistic philosophy and theology with their emphasis on logic or "rational thought" as the main motivator, are once again, through official pressure, gaining a resurgence in the educational system of the African Catholic Church.

Though not directly, the thinking of Thomas Aquinas can be considered a precursor of the Enlightenment, an intellectual movement in eighteenth-century Europe which had its roots in England, with authors such as John Locke, but which spread also to France and then to the rest of Europe.

Isn't there an essential "religion" of all humankind—based on reason alone—beyond that which faith orientations make for themselves? Isn't there an essential "reasonable" ethic that might apply to all humanity to the exclusion of any other ethic based on faith in a god? These are the philosophical, religious, and social questions that occupied the thinkers of the Enlightenment.

Enlightenment philosophers carried the work of the scholastic philosophers and theologians to its extreme conclusion. Whereas the scholastics had made use of reason within the bounds of religion, and specifically the Christian faith, the Enlightenment scholars used reason to ridicule or refute the claims of faith and Christianity in particular. The universal, essential religion or ethic represented by the latitudinarianism of the Englishman John Locke, for example, aimed to downplay the importance of institutional Christianity in favor of an ethic arising from the sentiment or feeling and reason which all human beings possess, a type of natural religion. To Locke, the good was what felt pleasurable and religion was what seemed reasonable.

With Voltaire's biting sarcasm against Christian belief and the church, and Denis Diderot's wide-ranging and enormous *Encyclopédie* project, the Enlightenment reached its apex in France. Although for these French thinkers God did indeed exist, he did not interfere in the running of the world; the world ran according to its own logic and natural laws, a deistic proposition. Jesus was, in their view, not the Son of God; the supreme good for an individual and for humanity as a whole was rational knowledge: the "proper study of mankind is man," according to Alexander Pope (Porter 2001).

In the evolution of Christian thought, the Enlightenment is an interesting period in two ways. First, it forced the church to rethink its relationship with the state. Since the days of Emperors Constantine and Theodosius I, the church had enjoyed a high degree of hegemony in society, and generally its leaders—the pope, bishops, and clergy in general—had enjoyed special material and social privileges. In some regions, such as in France and Germany, where the Enlightenment became most influential, the church and state were closely associated. One served almost as a department of the other. The Enlightenment started the movement to disassociate the two institutions. It reached its apex with the French Revolution and gained its clearest expression in the American Constitution, which spelled out the separation of church and state.

Second, the Enlightenment occasioned deeper reflection within the Catholic Church concerning the relationship between the local national churches and Rome. This reflection was much more profound than that occasioned by the Reformation. In the eighteenth century, discussion was most vibrant among the Febronianists in Germany and Austria. Instead of according supremacy in the church to the pope, they attributed it to general councils of national synods of bishops. According to them, the bishops as successors of the apostles were not necessarily subject to the bishop of Rome, who was seen as one among equals. The Febronianists insisted that bishops held authority in their own right.

This independence of the bishops from Rome was supported by the important bishops of Cologne, Mainz, and Trèves in their statement the "Punctuation of Ems." It foreshadowed the discussion that started again in the last century with theologians such as Hans Küng, and is going on now as an open tension between Rome and national episcopal conferences throughout the world.

ECUMENISM AND INTERRELIGIOUS DIALOGUE

One important theological change that took place in the church in the second half of the last century deserves special attention because of its radical nature and potential consequences. I am referring to the question of ecumenism, the ecumenical movement, and interreligious dialogue. Although the unity of all humanity under Christ is the motivation and fundamental meaning of the church as it is understood to have been intended by Christ, contemporary ecumenism and interreligious dialogue alter the theological underpinnings of this vision. The ecumenical movement has changed the perceptions, landscape, and the actual practice of Christianity on an issue which has been in existence for almost a thousand years.

The distinctiveness of Israel in the Old Testament consisted in considering itself the chosen people of God. Therefore, it was not like "the other nations." As understood by Israel only Yahweh was God; all other "gods" were no gods. The cult of Yahweh was alone the true cult; everything else was idolatry. These assertions were made despite Israel's massive borrowing from the neighboring tribes both of characteristic descriptions of Yahweh and the practices of the Yahwistic cult. Human sacrifice may have been proscribed in Israel early in its history, as the story of Abraham and Isaac (Gen. 22:1–19) is possibly intended to indicate, but animal sacrifice was an integral part of the worship of Yahweh in Israel well into the Common Era.

In the Old Testament theology of election there are intimations, in the wisdom and prophetic literature, that Yahweh is indeed God of all peoples, and that divine election extends to the whole of the human race. Election and divine favor were, however, predominantly restricted to Israel by contemporary commentators, so that their universal application was not made as clear as it perhaps could have been. The early church took over the theological image of Israel's election and applied it to itself; it felt and often described itself as the "New Israel," the "New People of God," the *Qahal*

Yawheh of the New Dispensation brought about by Christ. In doing so, it also, of course, took over the theological elements of exclusiveness and exclusion that had characterized the notion in the Old Testament. This appears in the New Testament, too, despite a distant awareness, appearing in some places (for example, Mk. 7:27–29, Mt. 3:9, Gal. 3:27–29, and Acts 10), that the application and efficacy of the salvation wrought by Jesus Christ are universal.

From the beginning Christians and the church thus considered themselves an exclusive entity in terms of salvation. In the Catholic Church, this was traditionally expressed in the maxim *"Extra Ecclesiam nulla salus"*—there is no salvation outside the church. It was thought necessary to belong physically to the institutional church as the way (and not only the *ordinary* way) to gain salvation. Some Catholic theologians may now try to explain this assertion away by various qualifications, but the maxim's original and intended meaning was explained officially as recently as 1943 by Pope Pius XII in his encyclical *Mystici Corporis Christi*, on the church as the Mystical Body of Christ.

Not to belong to the Catholic Church, Pope Pius affirmed in the encyclical, was to be insecure of divine salvation. Consequently, all non-Catholics ought to "enter catholic unity . . . and joined with us in the one organism of the Body of Jesus Christ, hasten together to the one Head in the fellowship of most glorious love." The pope concluded that the Catholic Church is the true home of all people, so that "with open arms we await them not as strangers but as those who are coming to their own father's home." Sixteen years previously, his predecessor, Pope Pius XI, had declared even more forcefully, "There is only one way in which the unity of Christians may be fostered, and that is by promoting the return to the one true Church of those who are separated from it; for from that one true Church they had unhappily fallen away" (Hastings 1991:113).

Nevertheless, internally within Catholicism itself on the one hand, and within Protestantism on the other, there were nagging questions which led to deep soul-searching about the meaning of the unity of the church and the salvation of Christ. How are Christians in different places to live out their commitment to Christ? How is the church in different regions to be constituted as church? Are only those who profess explicit belief in Christ to be saved? How about the eternal "fate" of millions and millions of people who either do not know Christ or have decided to follow their own religions?

In the sub-apostolic period onward some of these questions were answered through an unrehearsed practical application of what we call now the principle of unity in diversity. The different local churches adhered to different theologies and held different practices, but maintained unity with one another, expressed principally in the belief that Jesus Christ is Lord. This diversity eventually caused problems: beginning in the second century, some interpretations of belief in Jesus were rejected as heresy. But, again, in the midst of all of these differences and controversies the principle was unquestioned:

belonging to the Christian church (always, of course, implying one's own as the orthodox branch) was essential for salvation.

It was nothing less than theologically and ecclesiologically revolutionary for Vatican II to orientate the Catholic Church toward a path of ecumenism and interreligious dialogue. To be sure, not all the documents of the Council are completely free from the former "exclusivist" spirit, but the general orientation of the Council was not only to accept Protestant communions as "churches," but—something even more remarkable—to acknowledge the potential for truth and salvation in non-Christian religions.

When the Protestant churches started the ecumenical movement in Edinburgh in 1910 through the formation of the Faith and Order and Life and Work Commissions, the Catholic Church, because of its conviction that true unity meant that all other Christian communions had to join it, looked askance. In 1948 in Amsterdam the two commissions joined to form the World Council of Churches for the purpose of fostering Christian unity. The Catholic Church still did not join the World Council. Up to now, it has elected not to be a full formal member but to have only observer status. However, the Secretariat (now Pontifical Council) for Promoting Christian Unity, established in 1960 by Pope John XXIII, and the Secretariat for Non-Christians (now Council for Inter-Religious Dialogue), established in 1964 by Pope Paul VI, were responsible for a new, more positive tone in ecumenical and interreligious relations in the Catholic Church (see Hastings 1991:182–84).

In contrast to an earlier official stance, which seemed to suggest that in matters religious "error has no rights," the documents of the Vatican Council that were influenced by these offices moved the church not only to tolerance but to a remarkably positive attitude. It now recognized that other Christian churches can be "a means of salvation" (*Unitatis Redintegratio*, n. 3). Even more remarkable, the church recognized that choosing one's own religion in conscience, and being allowed to practice it within the boundaries of legitimate law is a matter of fundamental human dignity (*Dignitatis Humanae*, nn. 1–8).

The United Nations Declaration of Human Rights had already established this in 1948. In recent years, however, there has emerged some reaction against this opening up of the Catholic Church to other Christian communions and other faiths. The reaction has taken the form of censoring theologians who advocate this spirit. There have also been documents addressed to the Catholic Church worldwide, such as the declaration *Dominus Iesus* from the Congregation for the Doctrine of the Faith (see text and critical reviews in Pope/Hefling 2002) trying to turn back the clock.

THE AFRICAN SITUATION

Walls (2002:92) argues that the missionary movement in Africa south of the Sahara was an unintended result of Portuguese imperial ambitions. Unable to control by force the vast territories they acquired, or wanted to acquire, there developed "a body of people whose task was to commend, convince, illustrate, and persuade, but who were unable to coerce." These were the missionaries—first Portuguese, but soon followed by other similarly motivated Europeans. But the work of the administrator and missionary at this time complemented one another. To take the example of the Portuguese, "Where there was a Portuguese presence there was a church presence, and the church was, by agreement, under the supervision of the king of Portugal."

Circumstances were difficult for African converts to Christianity. Their participation in any kind of church was extremely limited. The discussion in European theological circles about whether Africans possessed a human soul and therefore could be validly baptized into the church was finally settled in favor of baptizing them, but many prejudices still remained. Africans were not deemed fit for ministry, particularly ordination to the priesthood. According to Walls, this helped to assure the eventual disappearance of Christian missionary activity and Christianity itself from the region for the next three centuries.

This is not to say that Africa did not make its mark on the Christianity established during this phase of missionary endeavor. Catholicism in the Soyo kingdom of the Congo is one of the best known examples. Recent studies show that, despite all the missionary constraints, there developed here "a genuinely African church growing in depth of understanding, and rethinking African institutions in Christian terms" (Walls 2002:93; see also Quinn 2002:15–17). Furthermore, the Soyo kingdom was conscious about its identity in religious matters. It "was no Portuguese puppet." As Walls (2002:93) informs us, "It preferred non-Portuguese missionaries and insisted on trading with the Dutch (from the Portuguese point of view both interloping rivals and Protestant heretics)." Such independence of spirit is all the more remarkable considering that it was a time when the trade in slaves was taking place.

The centuries of the trade in slaves, in which the church was at different times a willing or unwitting participant, remains one of the saddest—if not, indeed, the saddest—periods of African history. Through the slave trade, African humanity was diminished in the eyes of the traders and of the Africans themselves. Treated for a long time as property, African people's confidence in their own humanity and ability to shape their own lives was eroded, even though, by an amazing inner resilience, it was not crushed. By and large Christian missionaries and the church of Europe at best tolerated, and at worst facilitated or blessed this situation. They rarely spoke out against it because of their close association with those engaged in this commerce.

The colonial movement replaced slavery in Africa. Formally legitimized by the European powers at the Berlin Conference of 1885, it continued the psychological and cultural (to say nothing of economic) erosion of the African continent. And Christian missionaries continued to be an ambiguous party to this situation. Many supported it broadly in the name of Christian civilization, and collaborated with the colonial rulers. A few prophetic figures in the missionary movement, however, saw colonialism—as some previously had seen slavery—for what it was, an affront to human dignity and rights and, as much as they could given the circumstances, acted against it.

A few missionaries played an important role in helping not only to sustain the resilience of the African spirit against their oppression under colonialism, but also to restore the credibility of the Christian religion among Africans. They are the ones who, in practice, proved for many perceptive and initially skeptical Africans that there was indeed a difference between the colonial governments and the church; between the European colonizer interested merely in power and wealth and the missionaries who, though often compromised by their collaboration with the colonizer, had something precious and life-giving in the Gospel to offer to Africa.

In the twentieth century, several other examples of similar humane and farsighted missionary leaders can be identified. But the most forceful impetus for reclaiming African dignity and identity came from secular quarters, the founding politicians of African independence. The success of the movement for African political independence began in the late 1950s—in Ghana in 1957—and culminated in the 1960s for the vast majority of countries.

The contribution of the churches in this movement, though often indirect, can nonetheless never be easily ignored. Many of the new African leaders had been educated in mission schools, and in many cases the Bible was an inspiration to them and their activities. It is an open secret too that some missionaries encouraged some of them in the struggle for independence, to the annoyance of the colonials. That some of these leaders later rejected the Christian faith as an "ideology" for the discrimination, oppression and exploitation of Africa was more a reaction against the church as a whole, which was slow to embrace the changes. It was also a result of the Cold War, then at its peak, between the "Communist" ideology of the East and the "capitalist" ideology of the West. Desiring to distance themselves from the Western world, they generally appeared to be moving closer to the East and its atheism. But, misguided and definitely harmful though some of the policies consequent on this shift may have been with regard to their methods, many of these leaders' motivation was obviously to establish the dignity of Africa.

Independence, when it came, affected the Christian churches on a wide range of issues: in their administration, pastoral approaches and theologies, though not without resistance from many quarters. As one can tell by the slow pace of inculturation in the various areas of the administrative and pastoral life in many of the churches at the official level, resistance to change has not been completely overcome.

Structurally, the creation of an African hierarchy began in earnest shortly after independence. The church, it would seem, could not stand the embarrassment of maintaining a foreign hierarchy in the church alongside a local civil authority. To do so would have been to risk the accusation—which many politicians were already making—of being either a relic or a servant of colonialism. But the creation of a local hierarchy and a local clergy and religious could not but change both the face and the spirit of the church. Even though thoroughly trained in Western Christian religiosity, aspects of these native officials' African religiosity inevitably showed in their lifestyle and teaching. These were instinctively picked up by the laity, silently and unconsciously augmenting their own instinctive perception and application of the faith in their life.

Admittedly, in Catholic Christianity, Africa's role and influence during the Second Vatican Council were very limited. Of the 2,625 bishops attending the Council, only 311 were from Africa, and of these only six were indigenous Africans. Patrick Kalilombe (see Hastings 1991:310–11) is therefore right in arguing that the questions that determined the direction of the Council hardly related to African concerns. Yet, in facilitating their coming together, the Council made it possible for the hierarchy from Africa to meet and identify their concerns. Out of this encounter, and under the farsighted imagination of bishops such as Joseph Blomjous of Mwanza, Tanzania, emerged the formation of regional bishops' conferences throughout the continent (such as the Association of Member Episcopal Conferences in Eastern Africa—AMECEA) and the pan-African Symposium of Episcopal Conferences of Africa and Madagascar—SECAM).

After the Council, these hierarchical bodies directly or indirectly fostered a re-examination and re-appreciation of the values in African Religion and spirituality that had been ostracized by missionary catechesis. For instance, within SECAM, emerging and noticeable African theologians embarked on an unprecedented theological journey. They began to address much more seriously and openly ecclesiastical and theological issues specific to Africa without feeling any of the sense of betrayal of the African church's unity with Rome which any such discussion would previously have inevitably implied (see Hastings 1991:310–18).

However, perhaps the most important consequence of Vatican II for African Catholicism was the convocation in 1994 of the Special Assembly of the Synod of Bishops for Africa or African Synod, almost three decades after the closing of the Council. Spearheaded by SECAM, the desire among most African theologians and bishops had been for an "African Council" with the power of decision and legislation for the African church, not a synod with only an advisory mandate. This was not granted by the Roman church authorities: the assembly took place in Rome and for all intents and purposes it was highly controlled by Vatican officials. Yet, shortcomings aside, the synod deliberated on almost all of the issues that SECAM had been grappling with for the preceding decade: "theological and biblical stimulation, inculturation, Small Christian Communities, ecumenism (Islam and traditional religions), justice and peace (refugees, relations with national governments . . .), and social communications" (see Hastings 1991:312). The synod gave the church on the continent some of the self-confidence it sorely needed. To some extent, the African church became aware of its unique position within the universal church, even in terms of demography.

The Council produced another positive development for the African church. After 1965, African prelates began to be given policy and decision-making positions in the Roman Curia that could impact the universal church. We have in mind the Beninois Cardinal Bernadin Gantin and the Nigerian

Cardinal Francis Arinze. In 1984 Cardinal Gantin became prefect of the influential Congregation of Bishops, and in 1993 he took over as Dean of the College of Cardinals. Also in 1984 Cardinal Arinze became the new president of the Secretariat for Non-Christians. They are no longer in these positions, but they made a difference. As Aylward Shorter wrote about Cardinal Arinze, "The advent of an African President has naturally led to a new emphasis on traditional religion . . ." (Hastings 1991:186). To be sure, African Religion has not yet been accorded the recognition many African theologians think it deserves in the "community of religions," but its influence on Christianity and Islam can now no longer be denied or ignored.

Assessing in 1991 the effects of Vatican II on Africa, Bishop Patrick Kalilombe (see Hastings 1991:317) observed that for a long time after the Council, the "African Church seemed simply to follow the Western responses to the conciliar programme. Only later, especially beginning with the 1970s, and thanks to the growing influence of SECAM, has there begun to emerge a specifically African response to Vatican II."

It is possible and necessary to distinguish various trends in the developing "African response" to the principles of the Council, but all of them imply an effort at inculturation. Kalilombe mentions areas of concern that our research identified to be the concern of the majority of Christians in Africa: ecclesiology, ecumenism, and the role of the church in the contemporary social, economic and political situation of the continent. How the church in Africa should be constituted and organized, taking into account these realities, was the underlying question. In this matter Rwanda, before and after the 1994 genocide, is an illustration—though extreme—of the significance of the question.

Questions cannot be limited only to such cases; they can and must be addressed to the continental church as a whole, and in every area of life. How should the African church train its pastoral agents in view of its pastoral needs? This question, in particular, gains even more significance today when there is a tendency in Catholic Christianity toward centralism, implying less consideration of local realities and needs. One notices this in the area of seminary training, where insistence is once again on a uniformity of academic curricula under a Thomistic philosophy reminiscent of medieval times and the prescription of the Council of Trent of 1545–1563. As a result, explorations of possibilities for lay and, especially, women's, ministries are quite restricted in the African church. This in turn restricts the chances for ecumenism and interreligious dialogue, at least on the formal level, because of the predominating exclusivist ecclesiological models.

In the social issues of education, health, and, to a lesser degree, disaster relief, the church has been very deeply involved. The research showed that people appreciate this and want the church to continue with it. But the question can still be asked as to how far these efforts contain an African content and approach. This is not an idle question, as some may think, arguing that relief needs no cultural content. To argue thus is, however, a mistake importance of "cultural content" in social action is obvious, especi perceptions of education and medicine are concerned. But the question is not irrelevant in situations of ministry to refugees, hunger victims, or children orphaned because of the HIV/AIDS catastrophe. How may these people be helped while preserving the cultural roots that determine their identity and, to some extent, human dignity?

9

The Church in Mission

The Cultural Dynamics of Encounter

If cultural and religious interaction was already an issue in the historical
experience of Israel and the early Christian communities, it became much
more so with the spread of the Christian message beyond Jerusalem and
Palestine. But why did this expansion take place? Numerous New Testament
writings seek to explain theologically the missionary impulse that became
an important aspect of the Christian movement. In fact, we should more correctly say that they try to "justify" the church's constitution or essence as an
instrument of proclaiming Christ's message throughout the world. The
Gospels are a very good case in point.

THE ORIGINAL MISSIONARY IMPULSE

Biblical scholars have characterized several passages in the Gospels as referring to the "mission of the disciples" or the "sending of the disciples." These
descriptions introduce passages mentioning or intimating the thrust to spread
the Gospel message. Some very clear passages are Mark 6:8–13, Matthew
10:1, 5–14, and Luke 9:1–6. Luke 10:1–6 speaks further of Jesus sending
forth a large contingent of his disciples (the number "seventy-two" is spec-
ified, but is probably just symbolic). They were to act on his behalf, to teach,
heal, and cast away evil spirits from among their hearers in the same way
that he himself was doing.

If Jesus' message was intended from the beginning to be as widely inclusive as this, why is Jesus, according to Matthew 10:15–16, very explicit and
unambiguous in instructing the disciples *not* to preach in non-Jewish regions!
Donald Akenson (2000:57) is probably right in his assessment that this statement must have been difficult for Matthew to record. Matthew was in all
likelihood a Jew writing for a Jewish community, and he and his community
must have agreed with the restriction. The question is, how could he have
recorded this initial prohibition in the face of the Christian community's realization—as we understand from St. Paul's letters—that Jesus desired his teachings to spread to non-Jews? We can only conclude that the order must have
been genuinely from Jesus. Matthew decided to include it in his Gospel
because, as Akenson suggests, "the commandment was apparently so well
known in Christian traditions of the last quarter of the first century that it
could not be erased, though it clashed with the church's actual practice."

Jesus and the earliest Christians considered themselves completely Jewish in religious matters. The early Christian community, apart from preaching the risen Christ as the only teacher and center of its faith and eating together in his memory, continued to worship in the temple and to observe Mosaic Law, just as Jesus had done.

Twenty or so years later, the practice of the church had already effectively overtaken and transcended this narrow view of the Christian mission. Jesus' disciples soon accepted the position that mission applied "beyond all Israel to 'all nations'" (Brox 1996:5; see also Schnelle 1998:223–28). This is why the same Gospel according to Matthew, borrowing from Mark 16:15 and 20, attributes to the post-resurrection Jesus one of the most explicit beyond-Israel mission-centered utterances in all the New Testament. The passage known as "the Great Commission" in Matthew 28:19–20 should be seen as chronologically retrospective, an attempt to justify the missionary thrust of the church several decades after the death of Jesus. But more than any of the other texts in the New Testament, this particular text has historically been used by Christians to motivate, confirm and explain their missionary activity throughout the world.

MISSION IN MODERN TIMES

The missionary self-understanding of the church begins at its very beginning, in New Testament times. Jesus' immediate followers interpreted the meaning and intention of his actions in missionary terms. The church's missionary thrust has continued to this day.

The concrete forms of this missionary self-understanding have, of course, changed with the times and circumstances, and often in very drastic ways. It is enough to consider even in a cursory way the history of Christianity during any period to see this. Moreover, as many people will be aware, the motivations for and methods of mission have varied, and have not always been consistent with the effort to proclaim only the implications of the salvific work of the life of Christ. On the contrary, the missionary endeavor has sometimes been motivated by ethnocentrism, and the desire for wealth, power, and prestige.

Still, it is possible to distill even from this murky process of the church's geographical expansion the honorable spiritual dimension of proclaiming the Gospel as a message and action of liberation. It was undoubtedly through the agency of the Holy Spirit that this insight was never completely lost. The various Christian denominations are consequently always anxious to show in their theology and pastoral ministry that the foundational reason for doing mission is the mandate, understood as a consequence of Jesus' life and teaching, to proclaim his message of liberation throughout the world. It is enough to highlight only a few recent developments to exemplify this understanding.

In Catholic Christianity, the Council of Trent was aggressively defensive and inward-looking. It was intent on fighting Protestantism and keeping safe what it saw as the purity of the teaching of the Roman Catholic Church.

The Second Vatican Council, however, was convened by Pope John XXIII for a different purpose, and took place in changed times. These were times when the church was a little bit more relaxed about itself. The purpose of Vatican II, according to the vision of Pope John, was to listen to what other church communities, and indeed the whole world, had to tell and teach the Catholic Church. For Pope John, it was not to be a defensive assembly but, above all, a council that would set in motion a learning process, a reading of the "signs of the times," a transformation or, in his own expression, "*aggiornamento.*"

Vatican II showed an extraordinary openness to the world outside itself. Among other things, it emphasized without equivocation that, without a missionary thrust, the church cannot be Christ's church. The purpose and goal of the church, according to the Council, is to make Christ and his message of, and invitation to, total human liberation known everywhere in the world so as to establish God's Reign, whose outlines Jesus painted by his life and teaching. Vatican II acknowledges that the church is at the service of this Reign, and under it. It must listen to the prompting of God's Spirit and do all that it can to make this Reign of God a visible reality. After the Council, this point was underlined by numerous other documents at different levels of Catholic Christianity.

As for Protestant and other Christian churches, the World Council of Churches has always also laid great stress on the missionary nature of the church. Its theological position is likewise that the missionary responsibility of the Christian church draws from the clear intention of Jesus Christ himself. According to this ecumenical body, the Christian vocation is to make known, in word and deed, for humankind the meaning of Jesus' ministry, death, and resurrection contained in the scriptures. In other words, it consists in making concrete to the world God's vision for the world revealed through Jesus.

Despite their differences over specific points of doctrine relating to the perception of God, grace, sacraments, structures of the church, discipline within the churches, and so on, and despite differences over particularities of formulation and expression of teaching and its practice, all major Christian churches agree in principle that the missionary vocation is essential. This missionary fervor was played out concretely in Africa where various Christian denominations congregated at the end of the nineteenth and the beginning of the twentieth centuries, each with its own version of Jesus' message and church structures.

Contemporary scholarship has spent much time and effort trying to clarify the significance of the missionary vocation for the church and the theology underlying it. For instance, David Bosch in his book *Transforming Mission* (1991) issues an important warning with regard to the church's mission responsibility. He (1991:389–93) cautions that when Christians talk about the church's missionary responsibility, they should always bear in mind that they do so only in a very imprecise and analogical way. In its fundamental sense, he says, Christian mission does not belong first of all to the church but to God. This is because, in the first place, the message that the church proclaims is not its own but God's. Second, it is God who gives the church, as well as individuals in it, the power to proclaim the message of Jesus' life. Finally, the transformation that the message is supposed to bring about in the hearers is the work of the Spirit of God. Without God's assistance, the missionary-messenger proclaims inadequately and even in vain.

The principle of Christian mission must follow that of the early disciples' confession of faith in Jesus, which from the very beginning constituted the criterion of the genuineness of discipleship and the authenticity of their proclamation. Confronted with suspicion, doubt, derision, and even opposition and persecution, they could only declare that they spoke of what they had seen and heard from Jesus. And they felt that their actions were the evidence of their faithfulness to the message—and their best defense (Acts 4:9–10, 18–20).

Whatever failures Christian mission has experienced over the centuries can therefore often be attributed to shortcomings in following the example the early disciples set. The trouble has been that historically a gap has too often existed between what is proclaimed in words and what is lived concretely by those proclaiming the message, namely the church. The recipients of mission invariably notice this discrepancy and inconsistency, and the confusion that ensues in their mind has always been detrimental to the goal of mission, conversion.

It is not that this problem is unknown to the church: it openly confesses it in its own teaching. The church is aware that even though it has been entrusted a holy responsibility by God, it often fails to measure up, composed, as it is, of fallible human beings. Continual self-transformation by the church to be ever more faithful to the gospel message—*aggiornamento*—is, and will remain, an integral aspect of the mission of the church both inward (*ad intra*) and outward (*ad gentes*).

In practice, this means that, lest it turn Jesus completely into its own fallible image, the church must always remember that there is in its ministry the real and ever-present danger of proclaiming a less than perfect Gospel message, one that is tailored to its own liking. Indeed, the church must confess that, more often than not, in this historical instance or the other, it has regrettably done so. This is why Christian leaders such as Pope John Paul II have taken the extraordinary step of candidly asking for pardon for some of the historical sins of the church.

QUESTIONS FOR MISSION TODAY

What is mission and what does it entail? The full answer to this question comes only from a faith approach. The first disciples of Jesus, including and especially St. Paul, engaged in missionary activity because they felt that this is what the Lord had called them to do. They were impelled by Christ's Spirit and were ready to suffer anything, even to give up their lives, because of this spiritual conviction. If there was no other way out, death was preferable to abandoning their belief.

Today likewise, Christians engage in missionary activity in an authentic way only if they have come to know and believe, through their religious history and traditions, that this is the intention of Christ. But once this principle has been accepted as impossible to compromise, once the "why" question of mission has been answered on the basis of faith, what then? Then there emerges the practical and extremely difficult "how" question, pertaining to what we can call the "economy" or "modalities" of mission. This can become—as it has been from the beginning of the church—a very controversial question indeed. How mission? How does the church go about the task of proclaiming the message of Christ in different places and circumstances and in different ages and cultures, so that it is in each case experienced by a given people as good news, fresh and inviting, an announcement of God's Reign?

Here lies the crux of the matter. To the imperfect community that the church is and realizes itself to be, the task of making concrete Christ's sacred message of human freedom is an awesome charge. It admits neither of a single nor once-and-for-all answer. The problem is that the church is not "church" until and unless it is "made flesh." That is to say, the church cannot be realized as such until it becomes part of a particular people, and is immersed in a particular language and way of doing things.

This is the way God chose to realize God's own plan in the world. God became a human being. Through Jesus, the Godhead immersed itself in the history and life of the people of Israel, using their language, land, and even religion "in order to show through what he did for them what he intended to do for the whole human race" (John Paul II 1995: no. 60). Theology has described this method in terms of "incarnation," embodying or becoming flesh. The incarnation of God in Jesus Christ is paradigmatic for God's relationship and dealing with humanity and cannot be superseded or annulled.

In the evangelization process the church brings to different places the Gospel already incarnated, already very much a culture. It travels and works "in cultural clothing," so to speak, a cultural reality encountering people in new places. The horizon of encounter in the mission of evangelization is therefore fundamentally and irreducibly cultural. Deny, bypass, or explain away this fact and all efforts to understand the process become compromised from the start.

An inescapable level at which critical questions must be raised about the concrete practice of Christian mission in history must consequently be the cultural level. If we understand the call to mission to be the church's basic interpretation of its vocation and responsibility, then mission, in its universal scope, has to encompass all nations. It has to apply to the whole world and the entire universe. But what does this mean? In its simplest form, it means that Christ's liberating message, which is intended for all cultures, must be inclusive (which is the root meaning of "catholic," *katha holos*, in Greek). It must be truly cross-cultural or trans-cultural. Paradoxically, this means that mission is at the same time universal and local, timeless and situational.

In its concrete expression Christian mission will, indeed, be characterized by elements of race, gender or status, but its vocation is always to transcend

these and indicate a more profoundly human—yet still profoundly cultural—
way of life. This constitutes the Gospel challenge to culture as they encounter
each other: the church, continuing Jesus' intention in and for the world, cannot be bound exclusively to a nation, ideology, or genealogical lineage. This
is one side of the issue. The other side is that it cannot bypass them, either.

We might usefully borrow the excellent explanation of Christopher
Duraisingh (see Aagaard 1995:173) to clarify this point: "The saving work
of God in history is *doubly determined*," Duraisingh observes. "On the one
hand, it makes a people out of no people; it affirms identities; it names and
brings out distinct and authentic selfhood of peoples." Again, this is one side
of the coin. The other is that "at the same time, such a making of a people
with their distinct identity is always for a shared life and meaning. Each of
the twin correlates is equally important; it is freedom and fellowship, liberation and solidarity, identities and community."

At the time of Jesus, the Jews, it seems, were prone to making one mistake regarding this. They thought that being Abraham's physical descendants
sufficed for them to be children of God. They wanted to believe that it was
enough to be a physical descendant of the patriarch to gain divine privileges
and favors. What they failed to understand was that, for Abraham, election
was a responsibility in history: he was being called to an active trust in and
obedience to a God who would create history anew: "I will make you a great
nation" on condition that you consecrate yourselves anew to me. As the wisdom and prophetic traditions in the Old Testament gradually made clear,
Abraham's election by God was not meant for him and his descendants
alone, but for all of the human race. So Abraham and Israel were instruments of God, to show that God's care is present and real for all peoples.

With different degrees of clarity, the evangelists desire to make it clear
that Jesus was at pains to disillusion the Jews of this false pretension. He
wanted them to realize that in order to become a child of God, there is a
more stringent demand than an accident of birth. A person has to make a
decision to live according to God's will. It is in following what God wants
for the world—that is, adopting and fostering attitudes and structures of
universal love—which makes all people children of Abraham and children
of God in the inner, spiritual and primary sense. God is in those aspects of
every culture that foster this universal love.

From this perspective, the church's mandate to go and make disciples of
all nations implies necessarily that it cannot do so in spite of "the nations."
It can only "do mission" with them and because of them. The church cannot evangelize in spite of the various cultures of humanity but because of,
through, with, and by means of them. It is generally acknowledged today
that while the proclamation of the Gospel must transform cultures, it cannot do so satisfactorily unless it is "at home" with them, "taking them on
board," as it were, and becoming part of them. This is what the event of the
incarnation implies.

There is a fundamental mystical relationship at play here between a people and the Gospel, a relationship that is deeply theological. The Gospel car-

ried by the church influences and transforms the people and culture in which it is proclaimed. At the same time it is itself enriched by them. Being genuinely at home among a people and in a culture is a necessary condition for the authenticity of the Gospel wherever it is preached. It is also the precondition for its full understanding. Failing this, the profession of the Christian faith remains only a veneer, sooner or later to wear out. At the end of the day, this level of evangelization, or of mission, risks leaving the culture and people concerned the way they were before the encounter, substantially unchanged.

THE PRACTICE OF MISSION

Considering the history of the practice of mission in the world's southern hemisphere, especially in Africa in the last century, there is evidence of serious failures of balance in the encounter we are discussing. It is generally agreed that the Gospel has hardly taken deep root here because it was not allowed to become sufficiently immersed in the humus of Africa, in the cultures it was trying to evangelize.

Following the missionary impulse inherent in the church since its early beginnings, missionaries from Europe and later from North America, came in a concerted way to various parts of Africa toward the end of the nineteenth century, aiming to proclaim Christ's name and his liberating message (Baur 1994:103–371). Unfortunately, the vast majority of the early evangelizers were antagonistic to the "marriage" between the Gospel and the various cultures they encountered. Nevertheless, there was sufficient internal bonding between the two to make the Christian faith attractive to a large section of the continent's population. Today, conversion is apparently growing faster in Africa than anywhere else in the world, as official statistics by the churches confirm. What does this imply in terms of Christian mission?

The good news for Christianity in Africa has led some analysts to predict that the future of Christianity lies in this continent. Nevertheless, there are problems accompanying this phenomenal numerical growth which the church in Africa cannot afford to ignore. The issues at stake are basically the same as those the early church faced at Jerusalem and, a little later, when Paul and his collaborators carried the Gospel from Jerusalem to Antioch. As is the case today, there were differences of cultural outlooks among the very first Christians too, something that threatened to cause a serious rupture within the community.

Brox (1996:5–6) explains that the most "fundamental" and perhaps most serious difference had to do with the relationship between the Christian community and Judaism, especially in matters of language, Temple worship and the law. There were some among the Jews, for example, who felt closer to Palestine because they spoke Aramaic and considered themselves more "indigenous" to the land. There were others, however, who had lived abroad in Egypt, Greece, Asia Minor or Rome, and spoke Greek. Because of this they attended different synagogues and perhaps felt differently about the land, the Temple at Jerusalem, the law, and so on. These differences and divisions repeated themselves in the early Christian community at Jerusalem itself because, being a major city, its members were drawn from groups all over the empire.

In Acts the two main groups of believers at Jerusalem are called "Hebrews" and "Hellenists." Some material problems between them forced the apostles to allow the Hellenists to install their own leaders in order to maintain harmonious relationships in the community (Acts 6:1–5). Even more problematically, there were also differences in points of belief and its practice. The Hellenists in the Jerusalem Christian community tended to de-emphasize the importance of the Temple in Christian worship in ways that obviously "went beyond the limits of what synagogue discipline could tolerate . . . ," as Brox (1996:6) notes. "The [Temple] authorities intervened and drove these Christians from the city as Jewish heretics." Stephen was killed in the fracas, and Paul (at the time known as Saul) would have been involved in his execution or at least witness to it.

The problems further escalated, involving the difference between Paul's practice of accepting converts outside the Hebrews and Hellenists, from among the Romans and other societies in the Roman Empire. These were the Gentiles, properly so called by the Jews "of the circumcision." Chidester (2000:32–33) suggests that the struggle between the Hebrews and Hellenists shows that the Christian community in Jerusalem "had not [yet] seriously confronted the crucial question that Paul had found within the Diaspora: could Jews acknowledge uncircumcised men as brothers in the family of God?" When the question came from the ministry of Paul among the "uncircumcised," it brought with it many others as more and more people originally not bound by this Mosaic Law became baptized.

Most of the issues were predominantly of a practical nature: could Jewish and non-Jewish Christians share meals, homes and scriptures together without necessarily sharing the demands of the Law of Moses, at the core of which was circumcision? As can be expected, the Jewish Christian community at Jerusalem was of the opinion that Gentile converts too had to accept and practice Mosaic Law before they could become full members of the Christian community.

Paul represented the theological thinking and existential reality of the Gentile converts. He insisted that for Gentile Christians the Law of Moses was not necessary. According to him, faith in Jesus transcends Mosaic Law; it surpasses cultural and other differences (Gal. 3:26–28). Consequently, particular requirements, such as those the dominant group in Jerusalem community was intent on keeping, could not be binding on non-Jews. Paul was convinced that such requirements would demand the Gentiles shoulder an unnecessary, unbearable burden. He brought this case to the apostles in Jerusalem, who ruled in his favor (Acts 15:1–35). But that was not the end of the story.

Hardly had the ink dried on the letter written to the Pauline communities by the Jerusalem apostolic council than Peter caused a major scandal in

Antioch where, as we are told by Acts, the followers of Jesus were first called Christians. For fear of the Hebrews, he avoided associating with the non-circumcised Christians there, something he seemed previously to have done freely. Paul described Peter's behavior in this respect "to his face" in the letter to the Galatians as hypocritical and unbecoming (2:1–14).

It appears from various sections of the same letter that there was another, perhaps more serious headache for Paul around the same time. Jewish Christians, described as "certain people from James" (Gal. 2:12)—suggesting that they originated from Jerusalem, where James was the recognized leader—came to Galatia, insisting in their teaching that non-Jewish Christians should both be circumcised and obey the Mosaic cult. Against these "Judaizers" Paul insists very strongly that the Galatians are free to be who they are, creative in their faith: "What Christ has done is to set us free," he insists. "Stand firm, then, and refuse to be tied again to the yoke of slavery" (Gal. 5:1). The slavery Paul is talking about here most probably refers to the Galatians being forced to be bound by an alien law, and to modes of worship that do not speak to their cultural and experiential environment.

The controversy between Jerusalem and Antioch, between the Jewish and Gentile Christians, is always the problem, in the evangelization process, between the center and the periphery. The center in this case means the evangelizers and their culture, and the periphery are those to whom the Gospel of Christ is brought anew in the environment of a different culture. It is the (natural) problem of the center pulling inwards toward itself to homogenize everyone, and the periphery resisting this process to preserve its own identity.

This problem applies in different degrees to all cases of cultural contact—whether religious or secular—because it touches so much on the issue of identity, whether of individuals or groups. As a rule, all human beings and all societies simplistically tend to consider their own culture and worldview the model to which all others should, and in cases of conquest, must conform. There is therefore always conflict when cultures meet. The conflict may not be very obvious, and is often not openly violent in physical ways, but some form of psychological and moral violence usually takes place. For life to go on with a measure of normalcy, it has to be resolved somehow.

In the case when the Gospel message that has already taken on one cultural expression encounters and tries to situate itself in a new and different culture (in the process of primary evangelization), the problem may be formulated briefly with Jerome Crowe (1997: vii) as follows: "What happens when the gospel is carried from one world to another and a Christian community is born in a new culture? How do the dynamics of the gospel reshape the culture in which that mustard seed is planted? How does that culture in its turn enrich the church with new ways of self-expression and a deep grasp of its own identity?" Since the time Paul felt called to make known the name of Jesus as God's supreme self-revelation to the non-Jewish geo-cultural, social, and religious areas of his period, this has remained an issue to be constantly rethought. New questions have to be posed and answers have to be attempted with every new move of evangelization.

For the church in contemporary Africa, the issue has long been clear. To put it bluntly, the question is this: How may the message of the Gospel, culturally nurtured in Europe and North America, be able to inform and reshape African culture? And how can it do so without turning African Christians into Europeans or Americans, thus alienating them from themselves? Conversely, how may African traditional perceptions on life and God contribute to and enrich the (Euro-American) expression of Christianity and church that were received in Africa? And how can it do so without interfering with the identity of the church as a carrier of the Gospel of Christ?

All of this raises further questions for reflection that are of the deepest importance for the existence of the church and Christian mission and ministry in Africa. What, for instance, exactly happened when the Gospel message was carried from Europe to Africa? What *should* have happened? How must the church approach the evangelization of Africa now and in the near future given the concrete circumstances of the multiplicity of cultures and religious orientations in the different parts of this vast continent?

The implications for a mature, non-alienating encounter between the Gospel and Africa are extensive. The core issue is that both the African identity and the Gospel identity—as much of this identity as is preserved in the culture that introduced the Gospel to Africa—must be preserved. Neither may be diminished or destroyed if the encounter and the subsequent relationship between them are to be truly the liberating work of God; else, the encounter would be alien to the spirit of the Gospel and therefore theologically unacceptable.

What must always be borne in mind is that both the African identity and the gospel identity possess within them an irreducible divine character because both enjoy divine origin. Both exist because God has willed them to exist. For this reason, neither has reason to "apologize" to the other. Were this to happen, it would be extremely illogical because both are divine in terms of their positive inner values. They are therefore essentially identical, even though they may express themselves differently.

Furthermore, neither has precedence over the other, neither is more worthwhile in relation to the positive values that constitute the essence of their divine character. This fact is crucially important. Positive African traditional religious particularities and identities on the one hand, and their counterparts in the Christian gospel on the other, need to be understood as elements of one another as they encounter one another. They have to be allowed to interpenetrate one another and become one. This is because they constitute one order of reality in the divine scheme of things. Thus intermingled, they exist to support, nurture, and complement one another in the never-ending human quest for the face of God.

In practical terms, what then is the task at hand as the gospel in Western cultural clothing encounters African culture, and vice versa? In view of the divine character that is contained in both realities, what needs to happen in the ongoing relationship between them? And finally, what shape must the gospel message and the church assume in Africa as they challenge and nurture African culture and are in turn challenged and nurtured by it? Answers to these and related issues are far from easy. They form the subject of the ongoing life and identity-formation of the church here.

THE SHAPE OF THE ENCOUNTER

Still, it is possible to start addressing these questions by summarizing the answers in a general way.

A fruitful encounter between missionary Christianity and African culture must consist of the ongoing process of correlating and integrating two resources. The discourse must take into account God-inspired values inherent in African religious consciousness. These must be correlated with values revealed in and through the Christian historical consciousness as both are understood at a particular moment in time. This means that all values must always be left open to development with changing circumstances. This is so as to understand what they mean and what purpose they have for human life. The only goal of the gospel-culture encounter is to help the African people and the African church to come ever closer to God. More concretely, the goal is to help all African Christians and, indeed, all African peoples, to lead an integrated spirituality.

This is liberation, which means that no aspect of life at the physical, psychological, spiritual, institutional or moral level alienates the person. It also means that there is no great separation between the political, economic, and social spheres of existence, but that all of them are well integrated within the individual person and the social body. The process should lead to a point where African Christians can—as is now common to say—live their faith as "truly African and truly Christian," without a split personality from divided loyalty.

This is the desirable, basic dynamic of a gospel-culture relationship. It implies nothing of the idea of evolution, as though African culture was passing from the reality of one identity to another, as was previously erroneously presumed in most mission theologies. There is no question in this encounter of transcending African religiosity toward another kind of religiosity, even if that other religiosity is Christianity. Rather, what is implied in true Christian conversion is a dynamic of "confluence, growth, and [mutual] fulfillment" (Beller 2000:31). This is to say that the Word in the gospel encounters the Word in a culture. The revelation of God in the Christian scriptures meets the God who is already present in the values of a culture and in the history of a people. The two bond together, transforming and fulfilling each other in the process. And in the same process, people's perceptions and self-understanding on the one hand, and of God in their midst on the other, are changed.

Again there is no suggestion here of "christianizing culture" in the sense of replacing one set of images, symbols, and metaphors with another set, even if, once again, this other set is "Christian." The sense of gospel-culture encounter and true conversion is much more subtle, but closer to the meaning and purpose of true evangelization as championed by Paul and the Letter to the Hebrews. The encounter is meant to enable the gospel to claim what belongs to God in a culture, and to enable the culture in its turn to see itself in its true light as God's word, when indeed it is; or as an aberration from God's word when it is that. When this happens, African Christians are not alienated from their African identity. They are made instead to feel and see themselves more radically as African, finding God in their African-ness.

Here lies the principal problem with the European-American missionary methods of evangelization in Africa. They have as a rule rendered it difficult, if not in many cases impossible, for the process of African cultural-religious self-consciousness and identity to re-route itself through Christianity to rediscover itself. Similarly, they have not facilitated the process of the gospel message to discover itself through African culture. As a result, an integrated life of faith has for a long time eluded African Christians.

Although in theory everyone agrees that it does not make sense to force African Christians to live their faith in a manner alien to them, disregarding their own religious heritage, this counsel has in practice been very difficult to implement. Theological justifications for this failure can in every case be said to be rationalizations of psychological and, often, ethnocentric attitudes. All of them are not much different from those of the Judaizing "people from James" of the first-century church with whom Paul had to contend.

INCULTURATION AND ITS IMPLICATIONS

An integration of the gospel and culture in Christian life that will arrest the dualism and constant oscillation from one set of values to another contradictory one is what the contact between faith and culture entails. It begins to happen when the gospel discovers itself in a culture, accepting the elements that reveal the face of God already present, and rejecting those that do not. This is inculturation. The World Council of Churches has described it as a process founded on and motivated by "the mystery of incarnation":

> The Word was made flesh. Here flesh means the fully concrete, human and created reality that Jesus was. Inculturation, therefore, becomes another way of describing Christian mission. If proclamation sees mission in the perspective of the Word to be proclaimed, inculturation sees mission in the perspective of the flesh, or concrete embodiment, which the Word assumes in a particular individual, community, institution or culture. (See Kinnamon/Cope 1997:376)

Understood in this way, the process of inculturation does not involve mere "concordism" (Croatto 1995). Inculturation is not the effort to find "correspondences" between African and Christian religiosity. It is a much more radical process than simply replacing African religious practices with Christian ones. This often occurs, but it is "adaptation" on the superficial level; it causes and maintains the dualistic mentality that we have alluded to. True inculturation is a deep experience in the life of the individual and the community that occurs when there is a constant search for identification between gospel and culture, and when there is mutual correction and adjustment between them.

Let me illustrate this point by summarizing the insights of the Latin American theologian Diego Irarrázaval in his book *Inculturation: New Dawn of the Church in Latin America* (2000). According to Irarrázaval (2000:5), together with a theology of liberation, in Latin America a theology of inculturation is needed, one which involves the effort to decipher the work of God's Spirit among the people of God as a whole. This latter involves a theological interpretation of how people suffer, survive, resist oppression, celebrate, work, engage in dialogue, perceive their differences and cultivate their identities. As Irarrázaval sees it, inculturation "encompasses all aspects of life in faith: ethics and solidarity among persons in need, healing with popular wisdom, faith experiences of the youth, initiatives by women in grassroots religion, programs of inculturated catechesis, options for the poor in religious life and lay movements, paraliturgies and rituals of the people."

Irarrázaval sees the process of inculturation leading to authentic liberation even as liberation becomes the goal of inculturation. Theologically, Irarrázaval finds both of these to be grounded in the incarnation, the paschal mystery and Pentecost, all of which constitute the foundations of the Christian faith. They challenge all human potentialities and offer humanity new horizons of integral growth.

The insight that Irarrázaval brings is that mission as the activity of the Christian community in and outside the community must take into consideration the elements of culture and the work of the Spirit in culture. If the primary purpose of mission is evangelization, and the aim of evangelization is neither "to share a culture" nor "to evangelize culture" but to share the good news, mission can only mean the "discovery" or "re-discovery" of the Spirit within culture.

THE FUNCTION OF INCULTURATION

We need to emphasize that in Africa this discovery takes place when Africans who become Christians see themselves affirmed as Africans in and by the Gospel message. What this means in practice is that a degree of inculturation has taken place when African Christians do not feel guilty about expressing the truth about the God of Jesus Christ using the symbols and images immediately available to their heart, intellect and understanding. Conversely, inculturation has taken place when African Christians do not feel internally alienated when they use Christian symbols previously unknown to them to express newly appreciated truths, because these have now become part of their spiritual sensitivities. Both have merged completely to form one, integrated religious outlook in the individual and the Christian community.

Regardless of the many modalities of mission that are bound to come up in the history of the church, the goal of the church's mission remains to incarnate the word of God in particular places, among given peoples, at particular times, through the generous sharing of the evangelizer's life of faith. Pope Paul VI in *Evangelii Nuntiandi* (1975: nn.18–19) identifies the processes of evangelization and inculturation in their deepest meaning and implication by saying that if evangelization means anything, it must mean bringing the Good News into all the strata of human life and, through its influence, transforming humanity from within and making it new.

Radical inculturation implies signification, the dynamic of the production of social meaning, feelings and attitudes. It brings about and celebrates a perspective and a worldview, a way of looking at things and a way of living life. It aims at making Jesus and his life and teaching concrete among a people, so that God's intention and power, which Jesus represents, are to the highest extent possible appropriated in the manner of a particular locality. And if we believe in the work of God through the Holy Spirit, we must accept that God's presence and power do indeed form part of and belong in every locality.

This fact is not disputed by most missiologists today. Donal Dorr (2000:91) probably speaks for all of them when he writes, "The Spirit is at work among peoples, traditions, and in cultures long before the good news of Jesus reaches them." He adds, "This work of the Spirit becomes embodied to a greater or lesser extent in people's cultures and ways of life. So when a formal process of evangelization begins to take place the first task of the evangelizers is to recognize and celebrate this prior work of the Spirit."

The process of radical inculturation, signifying authentic evangelization, involves two axes: understanding and transformation. The former can take place only through the linguistic forms and worldview of the people encountering the Gospel. The latter comes as a consequence of the former and, through the power of God, changes minds, hearts and behavior. Both axes form one long Christian pilgrimage in responsibility: the truly evangelized must "own" or "take over" the Gospel and its message.

For any community, the appropriation of the gospel involves the task of continual interpretation or translation. Where the scriptures are concerned, this task "must give priority to those modalities of discourse that are most originary within the language of a community of faith . . . , those expressions by which the members of the community first interpret their experience for themselves and for others" (Ricoeur 1981:90). In *Evangelii Nuntiandi* (n. 63), Pope Paul says the same thing in almost the same words. "Evangelization loses much of its force and effectiveness," he warns, "if it does not take into consideration the actual people to whom it is addressed, [if] it does not use their language, their signs, their symbols, if it does not answer the questions they ask, and if it does not have an impact on their concrete life."

It is possible to understand this process at the level intended only if we do not lose sight of the fact that the God who showed his power and glory in the history of the Jews as interpreted by the writers of the scriptures is the very same God whose power and glory are preserved in different ways by various African communities' moral traditions. At the core of it all, God's demands contained in the two traditions are similar. Both the Bible and African religious oral, ritual, and moral traditions are more or less imperfect expressions of the unfathomable mystery of God. Yet they are a "true" or even "authentic" expression of it, each in its own way and to its own degree. There is often an expanded vision of the divine reality if and when they converge. This is the foundation upon which genuine inculturation must stand. When they are liberated from their negative, anti-life elements through the process of questioning, Christianity and culture draw closer together. The process of inculturation may then be described as "radical."

From time to time people in Africa and elsewhere have claimed that Christianity can never be at home in Africa because it is a foreign spiritual and cultural import. Lamin Sanneh and Kwame Bediako have given this issue much thought. They believe that Christianity possesses inner qualities that make it transcultural, giving it the potential of becoming as much a part of Africa as anywhere else. According to Sanneh, the most important of these is Christianity's ability to be "translated."

In its deepest meaning, the "translatability" of faith in Christ is what Paul realized earlier than the other disciples. He was convinced that the message of Christ's Gospel could be expressed in the Jewish culture just as well as in the Gentile cultures. Paul's theological missionary insight was that, while no culture or cultural system could claim to be the exclusive norm of God's truth (Sanneh 1990:30), every culture could claim it to a certain degree. None could be considered beyond the Gospel's pale. Consequently, the "boundaries of the proclamation" had to be enlarged.

The early church realized this. It began to understand that the Hebrew scriptures and the Jewish culture in which Christianity was born were merely "surrogate," not the message itself. This realization gave the early disciples the confidence to slowly go beyond Jerusalem and proclaim the Gospel in places where Greek and Roman cultures were predominant (Sanneh 1990:31–32).

The translatability of the Gospel message implies what Sanneh (1990:31) describes as a "bold, fundamental assertion." In terms of evangelization, "the recipient culture is the authentic destination of God's salvific promise and, as a consequence, has an honored place under the 'kindness of God,' with the attendant safeguards against cultural absolutism." According him, "Ultimately this gives the gospel a pluralistic character without imposing on it a uniformizing destiny." From a cultural perspective, Sanneh writes, "access to Jesus as Savior, Redeemer, and Judge was to be through the specificity of cultural self-understanding, and that cultural specificity is the ground of divine self-disclosure, with Jesus as the divine outpouring on the human scale."

But this has consequences. As Sanneh (1990:32) spells out, "Through the locus of cultural identity the Savior and Redeemer would emerge as recognizably one of us, though that would also bring the sword of discernment into our affairs." The gospel message becomes a two-edged sword. "The fullness of life that the Savior brings will place in a redeeming light the sin of human self-sufficiency."

The translatability of the Gospel message means its transculturality. As seen by Sanneh and Bediako, this becomes also its universality. This is not a merely theoretical assertion. Bediako (1995:109) sees it as a commitment, as a practical pastoral engagement. One of its implications is the need to translate the scriptures into various languages. Bediako argues that translating the scriptures into any language does not change the sacred character contained in their original revelation. Borrowing a phrase from Andrew Walls, he notes that on the contrary it only shows that this revelation is "culturally infinitely translatable."

Bediako (1995:110) points out that this exercise demonstrates that "behind the Christian doctrine of the substantial equality of the Scriptures in all languages, there lies the even profounder doctrine of the Incarnation, by which the fullest divine communication has reached beyond the forms of human words into the human form itself. 'The Word became flesh and dwelt among us.'" What does this mean in terms of the relationship between Gospel and culture? Bediako is convinced that from the point of view of the incarnation, "Translatability . . . may be said to be in-built into the nature of the Christian religion and capable of subverting any cultural possessiveness of the Faith in the process of its transmission."

INCULTURATION AS CONVERSION

"Subverting Western cultural possessiveness" of the Gospel and faith is crucial for the process of evangelization in Africa. For historical reasons, the West has officially engaged in this syndrome of cultural possessiveness. Paradoxically, this has been belied by the profound meaning and implications of biblical translations into the vernaculars the missionaries to Africa have so admirably fostered. It is imperative in the new millennium that the work of inculturation in Africa must involve the process of subverting any particular cultural possessiveness of the faith. But this is not a new phenomenon; it is part of the very nature of the growth of the Christian religion anywhere.

Jesus tried to make the Hebrew scriptures a transforming agent among the Jews rather than merely a façade by asking the people of his time to live beyond the letter of the Mosaic Law and according to its spirit. But this was seen by the Jews and Romans as subversion. Jesus' first disciples were similarly perceived and charged when, after Pentecost, they began to proclaim a new way of living, following the example of Jesus. This happened although both Jesus and his early disciples were operating within the same Jewish cultural and religious structures. The uproar of subversion must have been much louder when Paul and his Gentile converts insisted that they could not legitimately be bound by the letter of the Law of Moses in order to follow Jesus Christ. The tone of the controversy is already indicated in the Acts of the Apostles, but we can easily imagine that it must have been more complex and more chaotic than is portrayed there.

As the church moved into even wider and more varied cultural regions of the world in the post-apostolic period, things became even more complicated. The proliferation of heresies about the understanding or the intellectual, emotional and ritual translatability of notions about God, Jesus Christ, the Holy Spirit, Mary, the church, the human person, and human destiny into local languages and philosophical perspectives testifies to it. For, whatever else they are or are seen to be, heresies and the resultant schisms are often struggles against the cultural or philosophical "possessiveness" of the faith as it is transmitted to a different culture and way of thinking.

True heresy comes about as a result of a person's strong conviction in his or her truth against the truth or truths of the establishment, usually called orthodoxy. As a conviction of rightness and truthfulness, heresy is not seen as "heresy" by the one who holds it. On the contrary, he or she sees the establishment's "orthodoxy" as heretical, and desires with all his or her heart and strength to rescue the establishment from what he or she perceives to be its error. A heresy questions the methods of transmission and the meaning of the message of the gospel as it moves from culture to culture, or even within the same culture between different social strata and philosophical outlooks. To cite Jones (1924:13), the concern and emphasis of orthodoxy have throughout the ages been to preserve and transmit theories of truth, the acceptance of which has "come to be considered essential to salvation." Heresies, however, have usually evolved from a different starting-point. They "have been more concerned with life, with experience, with maintaining a continuous revelation of the Spirit here and now. They have inclined to shift the emphasis from heaven to earth."

Questions arising from new spiritual perspectives, new intellectual and social environments, and new ways of living life challenge established translations and existing meanings of the Gospel message. In a word, they challenge orthodoxy. To change or even modify the established view may not be easily accepted because the new answers that may be proposed often do not form part of the cultural-faith-philosophical-intellectual package that has up to that point shaped the dominant religious outlook. Nevertheless, dissenting questions remain a challenge to the verbal and practical expression of the gospel even after orthodoxy has categorized them as heretical. Frequently, they can bring about change in unexpected places.

The radical change that took place in Paul is what the New Testament theologically calls conversion. For people who proclaim the Gospel in an environment different from their own, inculturation requires nothing less in intellectual and attitudinal approach than conversion. The missionary must be prepared to "turn around," to see things in a different light, that is, in a manner they have not seen them before. They have to confirm in the other persons their own identity even as they also learn from it.

INCULTURATION AND IDENTITY

There is nothing unusual in a missionary proclaiming the Gospel for the first time in a new environment being at first a "Judaizer," someone who harbors a certain cultural possessiveness of the gospel and promotes her own cultural understanding of it. There are very few exceptions to this. Standing in a determined time and space, it is to be expected that most people's vision will be limited to what is immediately accepted and acceptable to them. The missionary's task of proclaiming the gospel will initially be defined by contemporary dominant factors familiar to her and her place of origin.

What goes against the spirit of the Gospel is not this initial attitude but rather the inability of the missionary to recognize the translatability of the Gospel or to remove obstacles from the process. Most frequently, this happens by denying culture its privileged place in the process of God's self-revelation, as when certain cultures are indiscriminately seen as pagan, which is to say "unclean." In the Acts of the Apostles (10: 9–16), St. Peter is depicted as confessing that such attitudes are wrong and unacceptable to the Christian faith. What God has created God has thereby made clean: no human being should call it unclean.

The moral of St. Peter's story applies to any missionary contact with cultures different from their own. The missionary must realize that "God does not show favoritism but accepts people from every nation who fear him and do what is right" (Acts 10:34–35). Nevertheless, a violent blow was in the past dealt to the cultural identity of the African person. Most approaches of evangelization sought to eliminate the reality of African culture altogether. But what about today, we must ask? Has the situation changed? How do we see the urgency of inculturation in Africa as we begin the twenty-first century?

We are touching here on the subject of an ongoing discussion about the relationship between culture and identity. The problem is much more complex than it ever was in the past because of new developments in the technological and commercial world. Underlying the current debate is the question whether we can any longer even speak of culture as a basis of personal and social identity in the modern world. When we say "culture," the issue is increasingly raised, what do we mean exactly? Is it possible today to justify the existence of distinctive cultures as foundations of personal and social identities in the same way that we might have done only a century ago (see Wijsen/Tanner 2002:4–36)?

What has complicated the issue has been the rise and spread of the phenomenon called globalization, a situation where, through the development of science and technology, the whole world has been brought closer together than ever before. The major agent of this development has been information technology in the form of instant communication via the mass media, particularly of the electronic kind—radio, television and the computer. Through easy and fast travel, there has also been extensive contact among peoples, religions, ideas, and cultures. There has developed, as well, an intensification of commercial exchanges between nations and regions that could not have been imagined even a century ago.

One well-known analyst of this process, Anthony Giddens (1990:64), defines globalization in functional terms simply as "the intensification of worldwide social relations which link distant localities in such a way that local happenings are shaped by events occurring many miles away and vice versa." Economics, politics, and other significant activities in life can no longer be considered merely local, but inevitably have worldwide implications.

Globalization and postmodernity affect cultural configurations and identities among peoples to the extent that some academics now assert that cultures in Tylor's (1871) and Geertz's (1973) classical anthropological models of clearly defined, internally integrated, consistent, and unique meaning-generating symbol systems do not exist. Today it is argued increasingly that people factually experience themselves as belonging not to one particular identity, but to multiple identities. Frans Wijsen (2001) agrees with this point of view and applies it to the discussion on inculturation. Given that modern and postmodern societies do not form a cultural "patchwork quilt or mosaic of separate pieces with hard, well-defined edges but a cultural mix or cocktail," as Wijsen argues, in what culture, he wonders, do we inculturate Christianity?

Wijsen (2001:221) proposes that the cultural reality we face in today's world calls for a new language that might better express the dynamic involved in it. Following the inspiration of Bishop Joseph Blomjous, he suggests "interculturation" rather than inculturation as the term to generate reflection to fulfill that role. "Interculturation expresses the idea that the process of inculturation is not simply the interaction between gospel on the one hand and culture on the other, as if they represent two monolithic meaning systems, but between multiple cultural orientations." He means that an already culture-embedded Gospel must confront not a single culture, but cultures no longer able to be clearly distinguished from one another.

The discussion on evangelization in the context of globalization and the reality of the contemporary multiplicity of cultures and personal and social identities is very complex and will continue, with various positions being taken by different scholars. While we must agree with social thinkers who point to the reality of multiple cultures and identities everywhere today, it is still an exaggeration to claim that this spells the death knell of distinctive cultures in the world. Perhaps this exaggeration arises as a reaction to the equally extreme and unrealistic classicist mentality that saw cultures as monolithic, un-changing entities. Even in the nineteenth century this view was a caricature of culture. Cultures have always been in contact, influencing, changing, and shaping one another. But this is much more the case today when, because of globalization, international cultural contact is so pervasive and so strong that no culture can remain in isolation, shielded from the impact of all others.

The following picture of the contemporary and future global cultural situation may be sketched. Cultures that are emerging as a result of globalization and whose outward characteristics may appear to be the same everywhere nevertheless possess certain inner "principles of action" that are particular and local. Just because these principles are not easily observed does not mean that they do not exist. In terms of inculturation, their depth and closeness to the human heart make them more significant than behavior and social attitudes that are easily apparent. The Gospel needs to engage in dialogue with these inner principles of action to be able to bring about radical change or conversion.

the cmuntvl circls

Touching on the question of globalization in another context, Jonathan Scott Lee cites Spanish sociologist Manuel Castells on the fluidity of culture today. Castells has coined the phrase "real virtuality" to argue that "human beings caught up in the culture of the information age are necessarily in constant flux." He explains that today, because of the pervasive cultural instability throughout the world, the "very nature of the human personality is in the process of being transformed, . . . we are becoming 'flexible personalities, able to engage endlessly in the reconstruction of the self, rather than to define the self through adaptation to what were once conventional social roles, which are no longer viable and which have thus ceased to make sense.' 'Nowadays . . . people produce forms of sociability, rather than follow models of behaviour'" (see Lee 2001:214–15).

It is not possible to argue with Castells on his main thesis: the fluidity of contemporary culture and the consequent ongoing construction of social behavior. But it is the pace of this fluidity and construction that is new, not the reality of change. But change, even change in the modern world, is founded on what already exists. New forms of sociability engendered by what Lee calls "the web of informational capitalism" must be seen to base themselves on certain axial "models of behaviour," even if over time they influence and change them. In every locality, the new expressions of sociability are an extension, modification or reformulation of deep currents of modes of behavior.

Giddens (1990:64–65) points out that local happenings shaped by events far away do not necessarily take the same pattern as the originating factors, the shaping events. Increasingly, they take a different route. Giddens gives as an example the nationalistic feelings out there in the world today. While globalization may in some aspects have diminished sentiments of nationalism, he says, it may at the same time have caused and reinforced them in other aspects. He remarks, "At the same time as social relations become laterally stretched and part of the same process [of globalization], we see the strengthening of pressures for local autonomy and regional cultural identity" (Giddens 1990:65). Why this happens is still a subject of continuing debate, but its importance for the process of evangelization and inculturation (as for global politics) cannot be overemphasized.

Simone Weil (1952:41) recognized this truth. Writing more than fifty years ago, Weil pointed out that to thrive as a human person, the human soul needs to be rooted in a particular community, participating naturally in it in a multiplicity of ways: by birth, geography, language, profession, and so on. Such participation does not normally exclude the influence of other kinds of factors. Yet it is important to bear in mind that "a given environment should not receive an outside influence as something additional to itself, but as a stimulant intensifying its own particular way of life. It should draw nourishment from outside contributions only after having digested them, and human beings who compose it should receive such contributions only from its hands."

Weil (1952:41) is quite clear that if outside influences are to bring about positive change, they should serve to confirm a person's or a society's own root identity. "When a really talented painter walks into a picture gallery," she writes, "his own originality is thereby confirmed. The same thing should apply to the various communities throughout the world and the different social environments."

While admitting that "being rooted" remains a difficult notion to define precisely, Weil says the search for it by individuals and peoples is not fortuitous. Rooted-ness is a possible and necessary experience. It refers to the deepest level in the human mind and soul. When these elicit certain perceptions, sensations, and impressions—that is, certain shared meanings—as a result of exposure to certain patterns of thought and behavior, and when they are influenced and shaped by a certain predominant environment, it is legitimate to speak of the possibility of cultural identity. This is so even if, as in the current situation of globalization, visible, audible, tangible, and concrete experiences may seem homogenous across the globe (see Harris 1999:19, Dillistone 1986:11).

Thomas H. Groome (2003:xix) notes on evidence from social scientists, and in substantial agreement with Simone Weil, "We need a sense of identity to live humanly; without it, we can literally feel lost." Explaining, he writes: "From the Latin *identitas*, meaning 'the same, repeatedly,' identity is that which holds together a continuous sense of our human 'being' as a person or a community. Read 'being' here as both noun and verb; identity is who we are and how we live. And though our personhood should ever be maturing into new horizons, we need continuity with what went before. In the imagery of the poet William B. Yeats, identity is 'the center that holds'; otherwise, 'things fall apart.'"

INCULTURATION AND IMAGINATION

There is some danger in talking about inculturation in the way we have been doing so far. We have been looking at the process of inculturation in a *post factum* kind of way, and analyzing it in order to make some sense of it. In doing so, the impression might be created that this analysis contains the foundations of the process. This would be inaccurate. Paul's complaint to the church of Jerusalem against coercing non-Jewish neophytes to be circumcised before baptism did not emerge from his own fancy. It was born of experience on the ground. What Paul did was to recognize the experience of his Gentile converts as legitimate. To his credit, he had the courage of the prophet to articulate it, and to demand against all odds that, as an inspiration God's Spirit at work in culture, it must be followed in the pastoral practice of the church.

When we talk about the process of inculturation, we must always keep in mind that it is first of all and fundamentally an intuitive process of finding one's faith and religious identity in the context of one's cultural world. At the very least, it is not as logical as it is often made out to be. As we have seen, faced with so much choice in political, economic and cultural values, a person or a whole people can acquire imperceptibly various sub-identities, and they can identify themselves differently at different times.

The encounter between Gospel and culture as a search for religious identity takes place at a level that is much more implicit and intuitive than this.
Here the Gospel as proclaimed in the particular circumstances forces the culture to re-discover itself in its values, language, symbols, and metaphors and
to compare and weigh them against it. A spontaneous "decision" on the level
of life-conduct rather than mere reflection is made. So we cannot speak of a
"choice" in the usual sense of the word here. It is much more accurate to
speak of an orientation toward new values, a reconfirmation of older values
against the new, or a unique combination of both. Without undue alarm at
the word's connotation, the latter result may be called "syncretism."

Although the syncretistic process—like much social change—is not easy
to observe, its consequences in Christian life are. In Africa, they are quite
visible in attitudes and practices that the church has often officially frowned
upon. Attitudes of veneration toward the ancestors and other spiritual powers, for example, remain substantially unchanged among African Christians,
despite concerted pastoral efforts in the Christian churches. The same goes
for some belief and ritual practices relating to marriage and death.

For the sake of convenience and clarity, scholars have referred to the
process I have just sketched as "popular" inculturation, distinguishing it
from the "official" kind, which is more reflexive, methodical, and planned.
The latter is usually initiated from above and its emphasis is on orthodoxy,
the right teaching to hold intellectually. Popular inculturation is rather "from
below" and expresses itself intuitively as living a Christian life in an African
way. Its emphasis is on life, not primarily teaching. Its main thrust is to deal
with the contradictions between the gospel as presented and the existing culture within the person and the community as they live life.

INCULTURATION IS ALWAYS WITH US

Whether recognized as such or not, this process in both its manifestations
has been part and parcel of the church's journey of evangelization from the
beginning. Evangelization and inculturation can hardly be separated because
of the nature of human communication. Communication makes inculturation inevitable. A person receives and understands a new idea on the basis
of his or her own experience. The proclamation of the Gospel among a people is the new idea, and the culture is the present experience. As in every
other encounter, these merge, willy-nilly and for better or for worse, in
inevitable forms of syncretism. Cultural construction may thus be looked at
as a series of examples of syncretism.

The official guardians of orthodoxy may regard certain aspects of syncretism as good, indifferent or definitely bad. Before they can make this judgment, however, syncretism has already taken place. Sometimes the desired
outcome may be deliberately guided, but this is only another level of the
process. It does not, and cannot, completely replace the spontaneous kind.
Indeed, the major characteristic of spontaneous syncretism, which involves
a "personal" way of receiving and accepting the message, is always present
even when syncretism is guided.

Pope John Paul II (1990: n. 52) touches upon this point. "As she carries out her missionary activity," he writes, "the Church encounters different cultures and becomes involved in the process of inculturation. The need for such involvement has marked the Church's pilgrimage throughout her history. . . ." Even though inculturation is not a new experience in and for the church, the pope considers it to be of particular urgency, calling for particular attention in the circumstances of the contemporary world. This urgency arises on account of the rapid changes that are taking place all over the world among peoples and cultures, making new and intense demands on the Gospel and the church as a set of cultural perspectives interacting and relating with other sets of cultural perspectives.

Successful inculturation as communication should methodologically be a conversation in which there is mutual, respectful sharing of views and convictions. According to a statement of the World Council of Churches, each partner in the conversation speaks and listens in turn. Both of these are active roles: "Speaking requires deciding how to communicate so that the other might better understand; listening requires patient and attentive engagement both to the speaker and to our own memory and knowledge" (see Scherer/Bevans 1999:191).

The foundations of the faith have already been laid in Africa. As the Letter to the Hebrews advises, there is no need to lay them all over again. What the African church needs now is to grow into them in maturity. This is possible only by taking seriously and accepting the process of inculturation. For those who must guide it, it is important to be conscious of its dynamic so that they not hinder the work of the Spirit of God.

This leads us to the need to investigate the scriptures and some Christian traditions on this process, even briefly. As in many other aspects of the Christian faith, they provide us with the most authoritative—or paradigmatic—examples of both the method and the nature of inculturation.

10

Ways of Imagining and Imaging the Holy

Every major religion possesses its own sacred narrative(s) of one kind or another. Some are written and handed down as a text, but others are oral, passed down through the generations as stories; some are brief, indicating only the main points of belief, but others are more comprehensive. The purpose of each of them, however, is the same: all the different elements in the sacred narrative are designed to show the relationship between God and the world, and specifically humanity. They are intended to indicate attitudes or behavior that is, or is not, expected on either side of the relationship.

Surrounding these narratives, especially the written kind, are usually traditions that develop as a way of interpreting them, to explain the proper or real meanings of various aspects of the text. The latter gain importance next only to the text. The older the tradition and chronologically nearer to the date of the original text, the more significance and respect they gain.

The Bible serves Christians as both a source of understanding God's will for the world and a criterion for obeying it. Consequently, it is a map for their ethical lives. It guides them in the knowledge not only of what is holy (that is, God), but also toward what is good (that is, ethics). It offers guidance to the question not only of what should I believe, but also how should I live to become god-like, holy. In contemporary language, we would call the Bible the Christian community's "constitution" without which the community's laws would have no foundation. Without it there would be no basis to hope for a future with God.

Although different Christian denominations place different emphases on the significance of the Bible in their day-to-day lives, they all agree that it holds an important place in their belief system and organizational structure.

CHRISTIAN NARRATIVES OF REVELATION AND INCULTURATION

There are at least two important questions about inculturation that must be faced when Christians make the assertion that the Bible is the word or revelation of God. Both are contained in the question: What does it mean to say that God's definitive, foundational, or paradigmatic revelation is contained in the Bible?

In one sense, the question is rather semantic. It refers to what the notions of "definitive," "foundational," or "paradigmatic" imply in this context. On the face of it, it would seem easy to explain this, but in actual fact it is not. These notions have in the course of history accumulated dogmatic and attitudinal nuances that make Christian attitudes to the Bible very complex. In the interests of reading the Bible correctly and beneficially in Africa, it is important to address these nuances and clarify their meaning.

The second sense of the question is even more critical to the process of inculturation. If indeed the Bible contains "Revelation" (now with a capital R), which is necessary and foundational for Christians everywhere, how should the African church handle it in reference to Africa's own cultural and religious experience? Is there also revelation in or through African history, culture and religion? If so, what significance does African religiosity have in relation to the "definitive" nature of biblical Revelation? In other words, if the one suffices, why do we need the other? Both of these issues refer to the problem of God's presence in both contexts. They also refer to the question of translatability: how can the message of the Bible be translated, that is, contextualized, into the African situation on the one hand and, on the other, how is African religiosity present and assumed in biblical revelation?

We shall discuss below the sense in which the Bible and some of the interpretations that have flown from it may be considered paradigmatic for Christian belief and practice everywhere throughout the ages. The task at this stage of the discussion is to try to see how the Bible imagines and images the holy in the concrete history of the Old and New Testaments. How did Israel in the Old Testament and Jesus and the early Christians perceive the relationship between humanity and God? Is it possible to detect beneath the faith a natural development of the blending of various cultural beliefs and attitudes—or novel developments in reaction against them—that we would characterize as inculturation? Given the circumstances of Africa, is it possible to find beneath the Gospel-culture contact a similar process of conception and perception, though with different nuances?

Let us illustrate some of the main points for each period and relate them to the situation in Africa. We may categorize revelation in the Judaeo-Christian traditions as calling for three kinds of ethical response: in the Old Testament we witness a morality based heavily on law; in the New Testament it is based almost exclusively on inner conviction and commitment; and in the subsequent periods of Christianity law and conviction are somehow combined and are expected to function together, whereby observing the law points to inner commitment.

In the African religious traditions, the Old Testament emphasis on legal purity has its counterpart in the taboo mentality of many African societies; the New Testament emphasis on conviction and commitment is expressed in the relationship imperative—the imperative of communion, participation and sharing in the social group; and the combination of law and conviction of subsequent, post-New Testament theology finds expression in the close relationship in African religiosity between taboo and social communion where breaking a taboo spells the automatic rupture of fundamental communion.

The Old Testament appropriately places the event of the covenant, the sealing, so to speak, of God's relationship with Israel, in the context of the

Exodus. The covenant is seen as a series of laws and regulations to keep: ". . . You shall be my special possession, dearer to me than any other people, though all the earth is mine. You shall be to me a kingdom of priests, a holy nation. This is what you must tell the Israelites" (Ex. 19:5–6). The response of the people to God through Moses binds them to these laws and regulations: "Everything the Lord has said, we will do" (Ex. 19:8). To break these laws means to dent or fracture the covenant with God, and it has consequences for the people; fidelity to the covenant will be rewarded while infidelity will be punished.

The entire law, the prophets and the writings constituting the Old Testament point to how to live to attain holiness. The almost exclusive significance of the law in the religious orientation of Israel remains prominent, even though it begins to be modified by demands of the change of heart of the (later) prophets. But even in the New Testament we encounter the tendency to put the law before attitudes of the heart. We see Jesus in the gospels and Paul in his letters fighting against this.

In African Religion, taboos play an almost automatic role in terms of holiness or the quality of being human (*ubuntu*). Holiness, in terms of African Religion, is not to be seen directly in the sense of preserving a covenant between God and the community, as is the case with the Old Testament understanding of the term. In African Religion it is rather to be understood in relation to preserving the unity of and communion in the social group in which the holy is made manifest. Fidelity to taboos is the normal way of preserving communion and therefore guarding and promoting personal and communal wholeness, *ubuntu* (see Mbiti 1969:141, Magesa 1997:64–71, Gaggawala 1999:27–32).

Despite this slight difference in specific outlook, Old Testament and African religious moral perceptions coincide at a most central point in that they are both legal moralities: the covenant in the case of the Old Testament, and communion in the case of African Religion, are preserved or suffer in so far as, respectively, laws and taboos are observed or broken. In a word, to be holy or good is to observe the law.

While not doing away with the law at all, the New Testament generally introduces a new, radical element in this moral perception by bringing up and emphasizing the issue of motivation in observing the law. Rejecting the conception of the law as an automatic path to holiness, the New Testament demands that observing the law must be an expression of what is in the heart, and must in turn change the heart.

The transition from external, legal morality to an interior conversion is not explicit in African Religion, but this is not to say that it is altogether absent. We find it in what we can call the maximal moral expectations society has of any of its members. You are required not only to avoid breaking taboos, for example, but you are also expected to take steps, to go out of your way to do what is good. More profoundly than the former, this is what makes an authentic *muntu* and shows before the community the most desired qualifications of personhood. The expectation does not constitute a law, and not fulfilling it does not necessarily lead to a breach of communion, but it does lower the level of its intensity and as such is a serious ethical consideration within the African religious world.

In introducing Christianity into Africa, this link between the New Testament demand for interior change (*metanoia*) and the demands of African religious maximal morality was missed. Since a greater part of the Decalogue is negative, and the Decalogue constituted one of the primary elements of instruction in the Christian churches, the legal moral mentality was unintentionally strengthened among African converts, to the detriment of their own maximal morality. The first part of the Decalogue, however, has historically engaged the spirituality of African Christians much more on account of its positive (maximal) note. This is the element in African spirituality whose spirit African and Africanist moral theologians are striving to recover.

QUEST FOR PERSONAL VOICE/AGENCY

Fernando F. Segovia (2000:146) has noted how, since the late 1960s, it has become necessary in (cultural) scholarship to "insist on such governing principles as honoring the plurality of perspectives, relishing the varieties of intellectual experience, and acknowledging the location and uncertainty of knowledge." These, he observes, constitute some of the essential parameters of any knowledge. In agreement with F. Inglis, whom he cites, Segovia says that these parameters are acknowledged most clearly and honestly if scholarship is understood as biography or autobiography: "Biography and autobiography bring about an ideal combination of observer and observed, subject and object, the way of the world and the way of seeing the world, as far as the human subject is thrust thereby as an actor into the world and the world is read in and through the life of this human actor."

Personal voice is the "destiny" or "fate" of the theologian today; there is no substitute for personal engagement in doing theology. Theological detachment is not possible. For theologians to begin to make the needed "synthesis" between African Religion and Christianity, they need to be not only theoretically committed, but also, and equally, practically engaged in both realities.

Commitment and engagement are of the very nature of theology as science. Timothy E. O'Connell explains that theology acts as "a sort of bridge between revelation and culture." It acts as an interpreter between the two. But interpretation is inherently also translation. So to theology inherently belongs the task of translation. O'Connell (1990:6) explains that if it is to be true to its character and objective of translation, to be truthful and to be heard "the challenge of theology . . . is to speak both from deep faith and from broad cultural sensitivity." Commitment to and engagement in the gospel of Jesus Christ in the context of the surrounding culture does not constitute a new approach to a Christian synthesis; rather it constitutes a return to the original, necessary process.

Bénézet Bujo engages himself deeply in his works in this quest for a personal voice—what Tinyiko S. Maluleke (in Kanyandago 2002:165) calls the "rediscovery of the agency of Africans." He has for a long time struggled with the issue of personal agency from the point of view of Catholic moral theology (see Bujo 1998a, 1998b, and 1999). In his most recent contribution to the debate, *Foundations of an African Ethic: Beyond the Universal Claims of Western Morality* (2001), he articulates a framework for an African ethic that arises from Africa's own cultural specificity.

The model Bujo makes explicit is indigenous to Africa, which means that it does not depend for its existence or validation on other external models. But this does not mean that it is ethnocentric, self-sufficient, or closed in upon itself. It does not mean that it is *a priori* or in principle unwilling to listen, relate to and benefit from other models. On the contrary, Bujo is at pains to show that the very essence as well as substance of this African approach to morality, which is also part of its uniqueness, is precisely its willingness in principle to relate with other models. This will enable it to develop itself for the sake of maintaining individual and community life in its fullness. Bujo argues that openness characterizes African moral procedure and distinguishes it from other traditions coming from outside Black Africa.

Let us then pause for a moment to consider the model as Bujo articulates it. Since he explains the framework in great detail, I will here highlight what he shows to be the most pivotal aspects of its main constitutive points, the most relevant hinges for the process of inculturation as a deliberate project in the contemporary church.

THE AFRICAN PALAVER

The framework is based firmly on a specifically African anthropology, the African view of the human person as an authentic living person in the world. Simply put, the moral or ethical question is: What is it that makes the human person or the person human? In other words, who is the human person?

From the African point of view, according to Bujo, the "decisive issue" that determines the human person is "relatedness" and "fellowship" considered in the context of specific, communally desirable and acceptable forms of living and behavior which strengthen community. These forms of living and behavior are not to be understood as *a priori* givens to which all members of the community are to adhere. Instead, he says, they are experiential, arising from the experience of living, and are validated according to whether they amplify the life of the community and the individuals within it.

The determining principle here is the life of the community together with its constituent parts. Community is constructed upon the existential experience of being known: "I am known, therefore we are," *Cognatus sum, ergo sumus*. Being known in the sense of "the concrete and unbroken interaction among all members of the community" is the essence of relatedness and fellowship. As such, it is not a favor that the individual owes to community or vice versa. Rather it is seen in African moral anthropology as the key of human existence. It is the essence of the structure of community itself, so much so "that refusal to accept it must lead to the death, not only of the individual but even of the community itself" (Bujo 2001:5, also Magesa 1997:64–71).

But how are we to understand community? This is a decisive factor in this framework. Consequently, Bujo takes as his secondary endeavor in *Foundations* to demonstrate the difference between Western discourse and communitarian ethics and African palaver ethics. He points out that in African anthropology communalism "occupies an intermediary position" between the two (Bujo 2001:71).

Community in Africa, quite different from what it implies in communitarian notions and discourses of the West, involves very intimately all the aspects of the person living with other people (kith and kin and beyond) here on earth. But it also involves the dead members of the group and whoever might be born in it in the near or distant future. It takes into consideration the universe with which the community interacts, whether that universe can be seen with the naked eye or felt in the community's spiritual sensibilities. Constant fellowship among all of these realities is the foundational element of the "palaver"—the African communitarian discourse—and the palaver constitutes the process of ethical consciousness.

The constitutive elements of this process are the power of the word, spoken or unspoken, the word as dramatized in dance or mime or symbolized in art; the "word" understood as action or "behavior"—in the constant presence of the community in its trinitarian dimensions of the living, the dead, and those not yet born. The sole purpose of the African palaver aims at creating, strengthening or restoring relationships for the sake of "the fullness" of life of the community through fellowship among all three dimensions of the community.

As such, the palaver is always a communitarian affair. It may take many forms and can happen at various levels of the community. For instance, there can be a palaver of healing between a patient and the medicine person, a palaver of family members about a perceived or potential positive or negative development affecting them, one of the clan for a certain enterprise or goal, or, supremely, a palaver (*indaba* in Zulu) of members of a tribe in matters that relate to the tribe's welfare. But in all its forms and at all of its levels the African palaver is dialogical, anamnestic, and in principle always intended to be therapeutic. It is at the higher levels of the clan and the tribe where these three characteristics are most evident.

The African palaver is dialogical because it is structured to involve in conversation and fellowship all the members of the community in very intricate ways. Ethical behavior is consequently never determined for the individual or the community except on the basis of "dialogue," that is, in palaver. As we mentioned, a fundamental aspect of the process is anamnesis. In the palaver, ancestral precedents are recalled in various ways, not, however, as cut-and-dried principles, but as guidelines for the existential situation. What is important in the palaver process with regard to anamnesis is that the fundamental intention of the ancestors for their own honor, for the well-being of the living and the not yet born, and for the survival of the universe must be preserved intact. Ethical action and behavior lie in this harmony between all dimensions of the palaver's partners. The palaver process needs to be therapeutic, but even when on occasion it is not, its trinitarian aspect is always present.

The palaver model Bujo articulates for moral theology is the same as that which Eugene E. Uzukwu had argued out five years earlier for ecclesiology in *A Listening Church: Autonomy and Communion in African Churches* (1996). To be sure, Uzukwu does not use the expression "palaver," but he outlines in the book a model of church based on communication, communion among the living, the dead and the not yet born. The traditional Catholic expressions of the "church militant," "church penitent" and "church triumphant" to depict the wholeness of the ecclesial community may slightly be inappropriate when applied to the African situation because they could evoke conflicting rather than communitarian sentiments. Still, apart from the fact that the Catholic expressions fail to make explicit reference to the future membership of the community by birth or through baptism, they express the same deep intention for ecclesial union as the African notion of palaver.

Consequently, from the African point of view, Cardinal Joseph Ratzinger correctly refutes the idea that Christian faith finds "its starting-point in the atomized individual." According to him, the human being *per se* is only such in "the totality of humanity, of history, and of the cosmos." The "single and entire human being," he affirms, "is marked most profoundly by the fact that one belongs to the totality of humanity" (see Bujo 2001:4). To be a real church community, all of the three dimensions of the church just mentioned must be in constant relationship with one another. Only in this way can the church enhance the fullness of life in the human community on earth, which is the Kingdom or Reign of God. In one word, being church is a question of solidarity.

Barring a certain trend in Placide Tempels's pioneering book, *Bantu Philosophy*, which tends to reduce the African understanding of the individual in community to the Western idea of "being" rather than "existential participation," his depiction of African anthropology is sound. Tempels makes clear that the individual in Africa cannot stand alone and remain human. To be human the individual must be linked in an active way with all three elements of reality of the past-present (the ancestral world), the present (the world here and now), and the future-present (the potential world). In Tempels's words (see Bujo 2001:86), "Every human person, every individual is as it were one link in a chain of vital forces: a living link both exercising and receiving influence, a link that establishes the bond with previous generations and with the forces that support his own existence. The individual is necessarily an individual adhering to the clan."

No economic, political, social or religious "norms" can have a harmonizing impact among Africans apart from this communal context. Outside of this view and goal they will only be disruptive of society and spirituality. The history of Christianity in Africa has shown this beyond any doubt. This is why the palaver model for Christian ethics, church government, sacraments and, indeed, the whole approach to the Christian faith in Africa is of such critical importance. The palaver is Africa's own voice, its personal agency in these matters of Christian belief. Africa recognizes itself and its own identity in the community of cultures worldwide in the palaver model. Bujo (2001:168) is right in considering the African palaver a "providential instrument" for approaching and appropriating the word of God. When it is taken seriously, it will then be possible to see "a Christianity incarnated in Africa." This will also "mean growth, and hence enrichment, for the entire Church of Jesus Christ."

THE BIBLE AS PARADIGM

We can now ask the question: Why must we consider the Bible to be paradigmatic or foundational for all Christian beliefs and lifestyles for every Christian community of every epoch? How is it that no community can survive as a Christian community without recourse to the Bible as a reference point? Perhaps the question is most easily answered with another: Without reference to the Bible, to the witness of faith by those who were the pillars of the movement, those who are "our ancestors in the faith," to what else would any Christian community go to find the most basic and authentic sources and interpretation of its belief and behavior?

The most authentic link between the church and the Christ the apostles knew is, above all else, the Bible. But statements like this create at least as many problems as they solve. It is necessary in saying this to take into account the problematic character of the experiences the New Testament recounts, given their polycentric approaches. These bring with them many difficulties of interpretation and understanding. Second, biblical or even New Testament experiences of life and belief cannot be applied literally and directly to contemporary times; after all they could not be interchanged in the various churches even then.

Further, throughout history the Bible has been interpreted and explained differently by various communities in various circumstances. The Catholic Church calls what it officially accepts of these interpretations and explanations "tradition," and gives it strong authority in its belief system, next to the Bible itself. Most Protestant churches would not place such strong emphasis on tradition, emphasizing in their teaching, as I have said, the sole authority of the Bible, almost in a literalistic sense. Nevertheless, in every church's practice, precedence plays a crucial role, in the sense that every church observes its own (sacred) tradition. In great part, religious groups and churches are both creators and creatures of tradition. All the elements that together factually (that is, historically) or putatively (that is, through myth or legend) link them to their foundations constitute it.

For Catholic Christianity, the Second Vatican Council dealt head on with the question of how the Bible and tradition are paradigmatic for the Christian in its *Dogmatic Constitution on Divine Revelation (Dei Verbum)*. The document relates the two elements by asserting that "Sacred tradition and sacred Scripture . . . are bound closely together, and communicate with one another. For both of them, flowing from the same divine well spring, come together in some fashion to form one thing, and move towards the same goal." United as they are in their source and goal, which is God, the document says that they are even more so in the way they function in the church. "Sacred Scripture is the speech of God as it is put down in writing under the breath of the Holy Spirit. And Tradition transmits in its entirety the Word of God which has been entrusted to the apostles by Christ the Lord and the Holy Spirit" (*Dei Verbum*, n. 9).

This second assertion of the document, that "Tradition transmits in its entirety the Word of God" is not as self-evident if taken historically as the document makes it sound. *Dei Verbum* is obviously referring to "Tradition" as interpreted by the hierarchy for the "universal Church." But we have seen that since New Testament times different local churches always held different traditions, both in the sense of understanding the life and work of Jesus, and of living out the gospel he preached. And even hierarchically, different interpretations of the gospel and Christian life which are difficult to reconcile have appeared in the history of the church. But they were all advanced as authoritative. An example of this is the dogma of papal infallibility (see Küng 1971).

In view of this, what is the task? It is to try to understand why and how, precisely, the Bible and some core tenets or Christian truths drawn from it over the centuries constitute the basic and "inerrant" foundation for the Christian way of life. How is the Bible the word of God that claims the Christian's total allegiance and commitment?

According to *Dei Verbum* again, "The divinely revealed realities which are contained and presented in the text of sacred Scripture have been written down under the inspiration of the Holy Spirit" (n. 11). In a sense, therefore, the Bible has dual authorship: it is the word of God in human expression. As *Dei Verbum* expresses it in the same paragraph, "To compose the sacred books, God chose certain men who, all the while he employed them in this task, made full use of their powers and faculties so that, though he acted in them and by them, it was as true authors that they consigned to writing whatever he wanted written, and no more."

From this it becomes clear that although the Bible is the definitive revelation of God, composed under the inspiration of God's Spirit, it does not do away with the fact that it is a situated form of revelation. God made use of people who, in writing the different segments of the Bible, "made full use of their powers and faculties so that . . . it was as true authors that they consigned to writing whatever . . . [God] wanted written. . . ." Therefore, every bit of the Bible belongs to a place and a time. Each is a manifestation of Jewish and early Christian understanding and interpretation of God and his power, given the circumstances of each writer, compiler, editor, and so on. It also demonstrates their inadequacy and poverty as they try to grapple with and grasp the impenetrable divine reality and its presence and activity among the people (see Legrand 2000).

Yet, it is precisely this particularity of the Bible as a local product in Israel's historical consciousness and in the history of the Christian community in first-century Palestine that gives it its privileged, special, or paradigmatic character as both a normative and uniting force. Israel's experience of God as Creator and the New Testament communities' experience of Jesus as God's Son are normative in the sense that no other experience could be accepted as having such divine force. The experiences recorded in the Bible are a reference point for humanity to be on the right way, the shortcomings in expressions there notwithstanding. The biblical experiences are uniting because the Bible unites our own experience of faith to these foundational experiences. There is a dynamism here which is never static; it is active and expanding spirally. It involves the believing community's search for meaning, inspired by the experiences of its ancestors in faith. What divine light did the ancestors see in certain events? What divine light do we see in similar events at a different time? These are the core and defining questions.

When liberation theologians from Latin America proposed the hermeneutic circle as a way of understanding the responsibilities that Christian life entails, they were expressing this task in the best way possible. Among their main points was that the existing social, political and economic—the entire human—situation of a locality should constantly be reviewed and assessed in the light of the scriptures to see where and in which way their meanings concur or diverge. In this assessment, as many elements as possible of a given question should be brought into the picture, and since it is impossible to consider all of them at once, the end of one round of the process should spell the beginning of the other, and so on.

However, the assertion that the Bible is paradigmatic or foundational does not and should not be taken to imply absolute exclusivity in the sense that the Bible is the sole experience of the self-revelation of God. This caveat is as important for inculturation as it is for Christian faith as a whole. God cannot be bound, and the Christian belief is that the Spirit of God acts wherever she wills. While the Bible is normative for revelation it does not preempt all other experiences of revelation.

God's self-manifestation is not something that other people and other religious traditions entirely lack. It must be seen in the context of the flow of similar, much larger and varied events that constitute the history of all humanity (see Haught 1987:885). From this perspective, the Bible is again paradigmatic not because it relates events that cannot be found anywhere else in human history; rather, it is so because it pinpoints better than anything else in Israel's history and Jesus' life the prototype and archetype of human history and the meaning of life, a meaning pertaining to God's activity in the world that is not as clearly found elsewhere. The Bible is in this sense an instrument of general universal revelation.

The Bible serves as a model for approaching the task of understanding the divine mystery, a mystery which is always active in human history. We have to emphasize again and again that what is essential is to realize that the reality of revelation and the task of interpreting it are never finished but are on-going, and that the Bible shows why and how this is so. The distinction that is at times made in theology between revelation as action and event, and revelation as knowledge or doctrine becomes useful here.

God's self-revelation to the world is first of all an event before it becomes knowledge. Divine "speech" is action and is primarily experienced as such. To become knowledge or doctrine it must be interpreted, and the forms of this knowledge will to some extent depend on the interpreter. Again, this is of crucial importance for the Christian community's understanding of itself. But it must be made clear, first of all, that because of the dynamic of revelation as action, it is ambiguous to speak of it as a "deposit" in the strict sense of that expression. The better and more accurate notion is that of discernment, by which we recognize and take account of the relationship that exists between God's action and human responsibility. The goal for humanity today is the same as it was in Israel and Jesus' time: it is to search for God. More accurately phrased, it is to let God find humanity. And the ways by which God condescends to find us are never fixed.

What does all this mean for inculturation in Africa? We may draw a few conclusions.

Biblical revelation and the experience of God in African Religion need to illuminate, strengthen, and encourage each other in this final purpose of letting God find us in our humanity. Christ achieved this "integration" supremely in his person, but every other person, every community, and every culture must make the journey to "meet God" or to "be met by God" steeped, as Jesus truly was, in their own socio-cultural environment. The question for African Christians is therefore how to read their history so that they can discover God actively guiding them and waiting for them there. The task is certainly not to adopt anyone else's history as their own. The African vision of God, and how we try to express and experience God, must be supplied by our "own" history. The Bible does not come to supplant it; it comes to help interpret it, and to "verify" it.

The Bible as the paradigm of Christian revelation means that the experience of God by Africans in their own history cannot be widely divergent from the interpretation and meaning of the good and the holy the Bible provides in the formative historical experience of Israel for the Old Testament, and that of the Christian communities for the New. Inculturation says that the two do somehow have to converge. We need to underline again and again that this congruence will not necessarily be in terms of symbols and language, but in terms of basic insight about the meaning of ways of living, relating and behaving. Denise and John Carmody (1991) have coined the expressive phrase "a way to the center" for this search. It is a way to the God who is waiting for us not only in the center of our persons, but in the center of our community, of our culture, and ultimately of all humanity.

Christian revelation is wider than biblical revelation, although in Catholicism some positions might lead one to think differently. For example, Vatican II's *Dignitatis Humanae* (n. 1) says that the "one true religion subsists in the catholic apostolic church." And *Dei Verbum* (n. 4) declares that ". . . we now await no further new public revelation" other than the "Christian dispensation" which constitutes the "definitive covenant." Statements like these are controversial. But they must be understood, especially in ecumenical circles, as statements of conviction that other faiths and religions can also make, and indeed have made, in defining themselves (see Pope/Heffling 2002). When they are read in the context of other major documents of the Council that are more centrifugal—particularly *The Decree on the Church's Missionary Activity (Ad Gentes)*, *The Dogmatic Constitution on the Church (Lumen Gentium)*, and *The Pastoral Constitution on the Church in the Modern World (Gaudium et Spes)*—it becomes increasingly clear that Catholic Christianity does not intrinsically deny the primary universal character of God's self-revelation.

In fact, the Council's document *Nostra Aetate* (n. 1) does explain that creation is the primary mode of divine revelation. It makes clear that God's "providence," "manifestations of goodness," and "saving designs" embrace all peoples of all races. According to this document, this truth is evidenced by the fundamental questions of existence that all people of every culture throughout the world ask about the nature, meaning and purpose of life; about morality, suffering and happiness; and about death and what lies beyond life in the world.

The same document (n. 2) goes on to explain that all religions "bound up with cultural advancement" have historically "struggled" to answer these questions with more or less "refined concepts" and more or less "developed language." By this the Council is saying in effect that culture, in its particularity and universality, is the matrix of all divine revelation. Divine revelation is impossible except by way of culture, known symbols, understood signs and expressed (or spoken) language. It is at the center of culture that God waits to meet us. As far as revelation is concerned, culture is "holy ground."

Faced with a centripetal expression such as that found in *Dei Verbum*, modern theologians counsel that the church must see and interpret such expressions in context. Catholic scripture scholar Daniel Harrington (1990: RG 30), for example, suggests that Vatican II must be seen not as a conclusion, but as a beginning of a long process of understanding not only the significance of scripture itself, but also its implications in Christian relationships with other Christians and religions. This is the challenge that lies before us in making the church more biblical.

A more biblical church is one that sees in the Bible not a narrow, confining and constricting bind, but a liberating work of the Spirit of God to create a church according to what it is saying to the contemporary Christian communities. The churches that emerge as a result will not be the same in every way. This is a normal consequence of the nature of the human person and communities. If they are authentically Christian, however, different persons and communities will be in communion with each other and with the scriptures. The development of doctrine in the post sub-apostolic and patristic church exemplifies this struggle. It is the history of struggle for balance between diversity and unity, with an eye to its necessary risks.

LIFE AS *THE* SACRED "TEXT" OF REVELATION

At the practical level of things, there are therefore three elements basic to the Christian faith. Deny any one of them and everything about Christianity crumbles. The first element is self-evident: there can be no Christianity without Jesus. This is easy to understand, for the whole of the Christian movement derives from the life and teaching of Jesus Christ. The second element is much less obvious, but just as basic: there can be no Christianity without the Bible, because belief in Jesus derives from the Bible. The third element comes as a consequence of this: any Christian church must be founded on and sustained by the message of Christ through the agency of the Bible.

The relationship among and between these elements is a necessary one. From the viewpoint of the Christian faith, the life and teaching of Jesus in the New Testament, and the understanding of God in the Old constitute the Bible. Although some Christian churches in Africa would seem to place more emphasis on the Old Testament because of its literal proximity with their followers' religious experience, they realize that the whole Bible is ultimately the story about the God of Jesus. Together the story and its subject constitute the foundation and the reason for the church's existence. And the church is of course the home in which the Christian finds—through the biblical story—nourishment for the spirit from Christ himself.

God, Jesus, the Bible and the church form an intricate unity in the Christian faith experience. But these three foundations of the Christian faith are meant for all of humanity. They are manifested in human history. Christian faith is endangered if they are not understood in the context of history.

In various practical ways, the AICs accept this and try to live it out in their organization by being ready to situate them in their particular environment. However, in some of the mainline churches, many Christians seem to experience a psychological barrier to accepting the historicity of Jesus, the Bible, and the church. While they profess Jesus to be God incarnate, yet a human historical figure, one like us in all things but sin (see Phil. 2:6–11), they can hardly bring themselves to conceive of him as such. They reason in their minds that, although he was human like us, he really was not completely human since he was also God. But this is a serious error, a fundamental contradiction of which they are seldom aware. Reasoning like this denies belief in the humanity of Jesus. It is a contemporary version of the ancient heresy of "docetism"; it considers Jesus to have had merely the appearance of a human being and not the reality.

What they in this way do with Jesus, they also do with the Bible in a way that is perhaps much worse. The very, very human development of the Bible is seldom acknowledged here, and almost never clearly articulated and taught. On the contrary, it is passed over in silence. If and when it is mentioned at all, it is with extreme embarrassment.

Despite the advances in biblical studies, doubts beset many Christians about the historical development of the Bible. Did it really develop from an original oral tradition—or more correctly—from many varied ethnic or clan stories of origin, growth and identity? Is it really a human interpretation of divine action in the world? In other words, is it God's Word in human words? Were different sections of it written and rewritten, copied and recopied, sometimes with mistakes, embellishments and even deliberate additions? Will the Bible retain its authority as the word of God if we acknowledge this? Were the books of the Bible standardized for the church only much later during the Common Era, and even then with certain books carrying different weight of authority for different regions? Does the fact that up to the present time some Christian denominations reject the canonicity of certain books that others accept lessen the authority of the Bible as the word of God?

In both the mainline and African Initiated Churches, many seem to be more comfortable with the idea of the Bible coming ready-made from heaven. However psychologically comfortable and appealing this idea may be, it is not Christian reality. The reality of the Bible is that it evolved from historical processes, where God shows himself to humanity through human events which become the mediators of his transcendence (Haight 1990/2001: 61–67). Any other perception of the Bible leads to its "idolization," examples of which we see rejected in the experience of the early Christians: the Sabbath is for humankind and not humankind for the Sabbath (Mk. 2:27). That the Bible becomes for Christians the foundational revelation of God is its uniqueness.

It is tempting to think that, apart from Jesus and the Bible, the historicity of the church would be clear and would pose little difficulty to anyone's faith. But this is not the case either: the church as a historical process—especially in its structures—is sometimes distorted or denied by well-meaning assertions to the effect that in its teaching and organization the church has been the same from the very beginning, and will forever remain so. With claims like these the church is petrified and turned into anything other than a living entity, which the church is. The liberating power of the God of history within it is thereby obliterated or strangled.

We do not find a static church in the New Testament or since. If we wanted to be very precise, we must acknowledge that we do not now have and never did have "a church" in the conventional, monolithic picture that some Christians would paint. What we have had throughout history are churches, dynamic, adapting and adaptable, faltering and picking themselves up again, and running, ever running, toward Christ their ideal. We have had in different local churches different shapes of runners and different paces and tempos, but all going toward the same goal. The early churches, as we have shown, were united in their motivation and goal, but they most certainly were not uniform in structure or specific theological outlooks.

What is true of the church's original times is true also of the centuries that followed, up to our own day. Only as the centuries go by the variations become much greater with the much greater geographical and cultural expansion of the church. Therefore, a conception of church that turns it into a static structure of discipline, and not the evolving magnet of conviction and free commitment that we see in the first decades of its existence cannot be sustained by the evidence at hand.

In many of the AICs the dynamic nature of the church may not be acknowledged in theory. Their teaching—where this is manifestly and consistently articulated—may indeed at times convey a picture of the church as a static militaristic and disciplinarian structure. However, in practice, most AICs are extremely flexible and amenable to change. Some would say that they are too fluid, lacking a sense of appreciable permanency. This can be put down to the fact that many of them have not developed a doctrine which distinguishes between "orthodoxy" and "heresy" within the particular church, as the early church eventually had to do.

Thus, although there is still a wide leeway of tolerance in belief and action in AICs, some of them are changing from their exclusive early dependence on charismatic leadership and are forming permanent structures of government. Their young leaders are being instructed in mainline theological schools. We are yet to see the consequence of all this in terms of the initial and present dynamic and evolving character of these churches.

In Catholic Christianity, Small Christian Communities (SCCs) have the potential to re-create and relive in our day Jesus, the Bible and the church as dynamic and vital realities (Radoli 1993). In Africa, at least, members of these communities want a Jesus they can adore, all right; but they relate even more to a Jesus who knows their problems of poverty and suffering, and who can help them out of these situations. In their meetings, this is what occupies them. Their prayers are more explicit in this regard: they address needs they experience every day and offer thanksgiving for favors received from God. Their prayers are rarely directed purely for divine glorification.

This aspect of prayer and worship is certainly not missing, but it is seen as an aspect of the other two. God is glorified when God answers the prayers of those who ask for help and, on account of the gratitude God receives, grants the supplicants even more good things. Christian worship from this perspective is constituted by the people's awe and joy of Jesus' response in the people's experience of life, seen in his activity among the members of the SCCs. This is why practical results in answer to prayer are expected.

Psalm 95 confronts Christians with the demand: "If today you hear his voice, harden not your hearts." The question out there for every generation of believers is how and in what way Christians can hear the voice of God. The answer seems to be that they can do so only through attending attentively to the daily experience of their life, through the guidance of the Bible and the church's ever developing (and hopefully deepening) understanding of it. A community's existential response at each point in time has historically been the most authentic way of interpreting the divine voice in this ongoing process.

11

African Constructive Imagination

Review of Literature

For some time now, Africanist theologians, scholars and thinkers have exhibited in their writings imaginative ideas in the service of inculturation on the continent. The purpose of this chapter is to briefly review and present some of these ideas, since they have shaped and continue to shape the understanding and orientation of the process, principally on the official level of the church. But their influence also flows up from the grassroots members of the church through their everyday practice of the faith, in spite of what the official church teaches, and down to them by way of catechesis, sermons and homilies, and church regulations and rules.

For the sake of clarity, I have grouped these works according to themes. These are arbitrary; many of the ideas intertwine and interrelate.

THEOLOGY IN A NEW KEY

Towards an African Narrative Theology (1996) is a contribution by Joseph Healey and Donald Sybertz about the on-going African journey of rooting the Gospel in local African societies and cultures. The authors present African proverbs, sayings, riddles, stories, myths, plays, songs, cultural symbols and real life experiences as guides in constructing an African theology and pastoral theology of inculturation.

Healey and Sybertz are convinced that in the encounter between culture and faith there should be mutual enrichment and ongoing dialogue; the cultural values and grassroots experiences of the local African expression of Christianity must enrich the world church at the same time as the experience and insights of world Christianity must challenge and enrich African cultures and local churches. This can happen when, for example, African proverbs, sayings, and beliefs are taken seriously as sources of divine wisdom.

Healey and Sybertz argue that the proper attitude in the dialogue between African culture and Christian faith should be that of humility. We must remember that God has always had witnesses everywhere in the world. The different gifts of the local African churches are like separate streams that come together and flow into the great river of the world church. A Kiswahili proverb says, "A river is enlarged by its tributaries": there are different threads of culture, literature, arts and symbols which contribute to the emergence of a genuine African church. New paradigms of African theology will arise through the development of a genuine African theological method-ology that uses African categories reflecting African experiences.

Zablon Nthamburi's book, *The African Church at the Crossroads: Strategy for Indigenisation* (1991) portrays the Christian church in Africa as a growing force that needs to be properly guided to maturity. Nthamburi is convinced that the Gospel has enriched the human values contained in tra-ditional African culture to such an extent that even the tidal wave of cul-tural globalization has not been able to undermine them. For him, the central question is how a Christian theology might reflect the traditional ethos of the African people and at the same time remain faithful to the revelation of Jesus Christ.

Nthamburi argues that when all is said and done, African Christian the-ology must be seen as a theology of liberation, rising out of reflection on the existence of the African people and their religious and practical experiences. Theology must bring hope, freedom and reconciliation where apathy, frus-tration, repression and oppression dominate. To have a liberating spirit, Nthamburi points out, African theology must not accept the facile and arti-ficial separation between the spiritual and the material, the religious and the profane, the eternal and the temporal spheres of human life. This is foreign to African spirituality. Instead, it must be concerned with wholeness in com-munity. Among other things, it must seek liberation from the domination of Western theology that stifles it.

There is a need to restore African religiosity in order to build a truly indigenous theology. Nthamburi counsels that the church in Africa does not need to inherit the burden of foreign customs, rites, and practices such as those of an impractical priestly caste. The law of celibacy causes, in his view, a serious disproportion between white missionaries and potential African priests for whom marriage is not a choice but a requirement of the corpo-rate community.

In another book, *The Pilgrimage of the African Church. Towards the Twenty-First Century* (2000), Nthamburi aims to suggest practical steps to be taken to prepare the church to face the twenty-first century. He argues that if Christianity is to claim the total allegiance of the African person, as it should, it must address itself to all of the dimensions of human life. The temptation to impose an artificial separation between the profane and the sacred must be resisted. African religiosity views the whole of human exis-tence as being subject to the sovereignty of God. It is important for evange-lizers to understand this tenet of traditional African spirituality if their work is not to be a source of confusion and alienation.

Second, there are several critical issues of life that Christianity in Africa needs to address. One is the issue of marriage. According to Nthamburi, this remains one of the major unresolved pastoral problems in the continent since the introduction of Christianity. When the church condemns polygyny as incompatible with the Gospel, it effectively excludes many people from its sacramental life. This shows pastoral insensitivity to those Christians who find themselves in polygamous situations for various grave cultural reasons, such as barrenness. Change in this and similar outlooks takes patience.

Further, the church will have to move away from the position of seeing only ordained men and women involved in ministry, according to Nthamburi. Christian ministry must involve the laity as well so that they might exercise the Christian calling and discipleship acquired through baptism. It is necessary to train in theology those of the laity who are able so that they will work hand in hand with the clergy to reflect professionally on the demands of the Gospel. Small Christian Communities can be the means through which the church can strengthen the ministries of the local church as well as encourage local leadership.

The Challenge of Black Theology in South Africa (1974), edited by Basil Moore, is a collection of essays seeking to reinterpret what Christianity means to the black personality in the context of then-apartheid South Africa. The study raises the question of how to understand the central realities of the Christian faith in a South Africa where a white-dominated Dutch Reformed Church provided the most powerful theological supports for the oppression of the black population.

Could black people in South Africa maintain their dignity as children of God when they were made to believe that salvation does not come through Christ alone, but by accepting the white way of living? How could they view God as a loving Father when they were told that everything they had and were was unworthy of God? Of course, all of this made Africans internalize a sense of inferiority, which was compounded by two other factors in religious symbolism.

First, the church's tendency in language and symbols to equate "black" and "evil" impressed on the African psyche that these two concepts were synonymous. Second, a theology that gave prominence to the "nobility" of servitude among an already enslaved and marginalized people had disastrous consequences. It seemed to sanction in the name of God the social structure of masters and servants, making worse the already bruised psychological situation of the blacks, by law at the lowest end of the social ladder. Black theology in South Africa developed in revolt against the physical and spiritual enslavement of black people and so against the loss of their sense of human dignity and worth.

Akin J. Omoyajowo notes in "An African Expression of Christianity" in the book just mentioned that the phenomena of African Initiated Churches (AICs) arose as a consequence of the Holy Spirit calling on Africans to give Christianity an African expression. This is why these churches have sought to establish a Christianity devoid of European accretions and in harmony with Africa's cultural heritage. Concretely, they have tried to evolve their own forms of liturgy and hymnody proper to the worship of God.

That women attain leadership positions in AICs impresses Omoyajowo because it avoids the discrimination toward women apparent in the missionary churches of the West. Moreover, AICs take the mission of evangelization very seriously by organizing frequent open-air evangelist campaigns. Their membership continues to grow. For Omoyajowo, the effectiveness of these churches shows that God can speak to Africans in their own lan and in their own traditional and cultural setting. This is a challenge

the churches that continue to hold the notion that unless Christianity is practiced in the Western way, it is heretical or idolatrous.

THE URGENCY OF THE PROCESS

John Mary Waliggo, Arij A. Roest Crollius and their colleagues contributed
to a volume of essays called *Inculturation: Its Meaning and Urgency* (1986).
The major point the book makes is that Christianity as such can be said to
exist only when it touches people and their lives in their physical environment, as they are in their own cultural context. As such, inculturation is not
just one aspect of the missionary activity of the church; it ought to be the
chief concern of evangelization.

Waliggo emphasizes in his essay the fundamental meaning of inculturation as an honest and serious attempt to make Christ and his message of salvation understood by people of a given culture, locality and time. This can
only be done through the insertion of the Christian message into the very
thought patterns of each people, in the conviction that Christ and his good
news are dynamic and a challenge to all. The central goal of evangelization
and inculturation in Africa is to enable the message of Christ to enter into
the very blood of Africans, to make it respond to their aspirations and anx-
ieties, and to make them recover their identity and dignity as Africans. These
tasks cannot be separated. Churches must embark on the task of studying
the cultures, traditional religions, worldviews and aspirations of the people
they come into contact with, and use whatever is good and noble in them to
present and consolidate the Christian faith.

This is why, writes Roest Crollius, there has to be dialogue between
Christianity and African culture. This will enable them to challenge each
other, giving each other new meaning. Considered in this way, the purpose
of inculturation is not primarily to salvage a traditional culture but rather to
render possible the process of cultural change in the light of the gospel, so that
that culture may become the worthy habitat of God's pilgrim people.

All contributors to this volume underline the fact that inculturation does
not limit itself to liturgical rites and ceremonies, art, music, sacraments, vestments, and other visible elements alone. It extends to life in its entirety. Since
this process has happened since the beginning of Christianity, the history of
the church is the strongest argument for inculturation. But lest this appear
to be limited to one process—the popular, intuitive one—Nkeramihigo is at
pains to show that inculturation is also the deliberate, organized and conscious effort of a society, touched by the phenomenon of cultural encounter,
to develop a satisfactory and appropriate response for its future by taking
into account changed circumstances.

Nkeramihigo makes the observation that Christianity is not inculturated
to the degree that people accept it, but to the degree that it accepts and integrates them into the liberating power of Christ. To inculturate Christianity
there must be a christology which calls culture to the liberty that God
promises and gives to the world in Christ. This means that newly christian-

ized countries should become familiar with their traditional culture as well as with the tradition through which the Christian message was proclaimed to them. But the two traditions must both stand before the judgment of Christ. The consequence of their encounter must be something "more Christlike." John Mutiso Mbinda similarly explains inculturation as the effort made by a local church to proclaim Christ and the values he stood for as found in the scriptures embodied in expressions and symbols taken from the life experiences of the local people. To achieve this, the local church must create suitable catechetical materials based on local life experiences: Christ must no longer be presented as a foreigner because he is not limited to a particular culture. Christ is transcultural. In practical terms in Africa, according to Mbinda, inculturation must lead to a church that is led by local people, that meets and answers local needs and problems. It must lead to a church that is self-ministering, self-propagating and self-supporting. It must also lead to the creation of an African theology, philosophy, formation programs, expression in worship, and church discipline.

Overall, this book marks a shift from a theoretical philosophical approach of inculturation to a more descriptive one, sympathetic to the findings of cultural anthropology, sociology and ethnology.

Waliggo, above, discusses the sources of inculturation, but it is Emmanuel Martey in his *African Theology: Inculturation and Liberation* (1993) who offers a more extensive list that includes the Bible, Christian tradition and theological heritage, African Traditional Religion, culture and philosophy, African anthropology and other social sciences, and African Initiated Churches. He argues that inculturation has had little impact on the concrete lives of Africans because it has not made adequate use of some of these sources.

METHODS AND STRATEGIES OF INCULTURATION

Peter Schineller's book, *Handbook in Inculturation* (1990), is a primer for church leaders on inculturation and highlights the meaning and scope of the process. Schineller (1990:6) borrows from Robert Schreiter the definition of inculturation as "the incarnation of Christian life and of the Christian message in a particular cultural context" so that the total experience of living the faith "not only finds expression through elements proper to the culture in question but becomes a principle that animates, directs and unites the culture, transforming and remaking it so as to bring out a 'new creation.'"

This definition is based on and draws from the mystery of Christ's life as noted in John 1:14, "The word became flesh and dwelt among us." It is in this sense that inculturation encompasses all areas of Christian life. For pastoral agents, this demands their own insertion into the way of life of the people just as Jesus, by his incarnation, became truly and completely human. This goal can be aided by an ecclesiology that emphasizes SCCs, an ecclesiology in which all members of the church are actively involved and which "sees the church as composed of primarily small groups of committed Christians, lay and clergy, in co-operation and collaboration inserted in and examining their particular situation to find the revelation of the Gospel in the situation" (Schineller 1990:51). Such ecclesiology facilitates the transformation of the communities concerned and the church as a whole, whose foundation the SCCs are.

The same line of thought as Schineller's is found in an anthology of papers edited by Anthony Gittins and published under the title *Life and Death Matters: The Practice of Inculturation in Africa* (2000). It comprises an extended definition of the process, with nine case studies illustrating the nature of the process.

Gittins's contribution explains the gist of the whole book. It argues that the agents of inculturation are the Holy Spirit and the local community; that the Gospel must be absorbed into people's lives; and that in genuine evangelization, the bearer as much as the recipients of the Gospel will be transformed by the encounter. Inculturation can never become the uncritical acceptance of a culture, any more than it can become the cosmetic adaptation of foreign forms of worship and spirituality. It must, however, be to some degree a "revelation" of a hitherto unknown or unimagined part of Christ, an unveiling of an astonishing new facet of God's infinitely multi-faceted splendor, a gift to the whole church and the whole world, a work of the Spirit in our time.

For proper understanding, adaptation and practice of inculturation in contemporary Africa, Gittins suggests studying several approaches that are already practiced in various places. He enumerates them as "prescriptive inculturation," "dynamic equivalence," "creative assimilation," "organic progression," and the "synthetic method."

The "prescriptive" or "magisterial approach" is a top-down, legal method on issues that do or do not already have precedence. Its main goal is to maintain unity, even though this unity is often superficial, without deep roots in the community.

"Dynamic equivalence," on the other hand, while accepting as a starting point the established doctrinal, liturgical, canonical, and pastoral forms of the church, tries to express them in other vernaculars and cultural forms. The emphasis here is the adoption of a form of translation that can express in other vernaculars and in other cultural forms the essential message conveyed in the originals. For translation to be meaningful, according to Gittins, this approach implies a careful search that presupposes knowledge of both the Roman liturgy and its cultural context on the one hand, and the target community's culture on the other. In spite of such limitations as the lack of equivalent words and precise nuances in the local vernacular, and the frequent opposition from the guardians of orthodoxy, the strength of this approach lies in the involvement of the local communities, who are enabled to discuss, experiment, and modify their language for meaningful communication of the Gospel of Christ.

Nevertheless, the approach poses some serious questions regarding the very suitability of such translation. For instance, is it necessary or appropriate to "translate" bread and wine, liturgical vestments or even liturgical ministries into a thousand different cultures? Besides, in what way can gratitude and thanksgiving, sorrow and repentance, joy and excitement be translated from one context to another, when people use different verbal and material symbols to express these emotions?

"Creative assimilation" accepts cultural practices that are not already part of the church's tradition. It endorses them as part of the faith practice of a particular people based on the conviction that the spark of divine creativity animates every culture and that God can be encountered and worshiped in myriad ways, many of which have not yet been realized by Christians brought up in the Western tradition.

"Organic progression" allows for some novelty in the process of inculturation, either by supplementation or by continuance—the former adding to, and the later extending or elaborating on previous liturgical and other forms. As stated in Vatican II's *Constitution on the Sacred Liturgy (Sacrosanctum Concilitum, n. 23)*, "care must be taken that any new forms adopted should in some way grow organically from forms already existing." Local churches may find in this approach both opportunity and justification for a greater promotion of official inculturation.

Gittins and his colleagues agree that the process of inculturation in contemporary Africa can succeed most efficiently by adopting the "synthetic approach." This is an all-embracing method which deliberately refrains from privileging any single method, and seeks to apply all of these methods to as wide an area as possible of human experience and Christian life of a locality.

A HOME-GROWN PRODUCT

Aylward Shorter in his *Christianity and the African Imagination after the African Synod* (1995) does in a sense accept Martey's point above and argues that for the mystery of Christ to become credible in contemporary Africa, it must appeal to the African religious imagination and must avoid the cultural-religious ambiguity in which the continent today finds itself. Just as the early missionaries did, the contemporary church must continue to promote African culture by giving its vernaculars literacy and using them in church activities and in Bible translation.

For Shorter, African art, which is rooted in traditions (such as oral literature, creative literature, and carvings), is an important aspect of the African imagination that must be cultivated. The church has a duty to encourage artistic expression in its most meaningful and sublime forms for the sake of providing apparatus for liturgical celebration (its ritual function), stimulating Christians toward prayer and adoration (its devotional function), teaching through images and artistic expressions (its catechetical function), and promoting a religious view of the world (its transforming function, which in turn means the salvation of art itself). But to what extent, Shorter wonders, does Christianity make use of this basic source of evangelization in its dialogue with African culture?

In Shorter's view, particular attention should be paid to surviving customs and traditions, for they constitute the African heritage. Thus he thinks that "threshold" or informal dialogue may in the end be a more productive approach to inculturation than formal or "conference" dialogue. In the former, Christians experience more directly the way people of other traditions live their own culture and religion. In this way, "deep speaks to deep"; an encounter takes place within hearts and consciences, not merely within the intellect.

The encounter resulting in inculturation must also take the form of "dialogue of generations." Oral tradition can best be expressed by people who are themselves participant-practitioners of the oral culture and whose dialogue with the tradition is spontaneous, unstudied and unforced. Through the representatives of the older generations who are the repositories of oral tradition, people committed to inculturation can make direct contact with that tradition. According to Shorter, SCCs can become part of the dynamic of the tradition, helping to carry it forward and ensure its survival in a Christian form. The basic religious expression to be adopted by African Christianity must be traditional imagery and symbolism because this is the grammar of African religious experience. As Shorter sees it, it is the most relevant language of the African Christian faith community.

Shorter's conviction is that real inculturation in Africa will result in "a new creation." This demands that people must be found in Africa who can reinterpret their oral culture creatively. While acknowledging that this is already being done in part through art and liturgical music, he insists that it also needs to take place in textual composition, choreographic dance, gestures and postures, and costumes and decorations. Priests should be trained not only to use their own talents in developing these things; they need to learn to discover and utilize the talents of the people they lead. Christians who are able to do so must be encouraged to study their culture thoroughly if the African religious imagination is to mutually challenge and be challenged adequately by the Gospel of Christ.

In Shorter's view, African Christians want a simpler and more congenial church, not one in which they feel estranged by Western forms and structures. They want a greater measure of participation, of community experience, and of communion with the church's leaders. They want Christian faith and practice to root them in their own culture, give them security, identity and social harmony as well as a sense of purpose and direction. They want a faith that speaks to them in their own social and cultural situation. Popular religiosity in Africa centers on the world of created nature as a "window" on the world of spirits, humanity and humanization, transmission of life, values of family and community and reciprocity between living and dead. Shorter concludes that African Christianity's future depends on incorporating this religiosity and making it its own.

Using the Maasai people of Kenya and Tanzania as a specific case study, Eugene Hillman in *Toward an African Christianity* (1993) explains how, often with missionaries as accomplices, the colonialists stripped Africans of their symbolic systems by terming them primitive and pagan. Westernization was made *the* way of human advancement, and people came to believe that "progress" consists not in affirming their own identities as people, but by imitating foreign ways. An example is the use of foreign names in baptism, presuming that they alone are "Christian," that is, able to inspire a Christian lifestyle. Fortunately, Vatican II and the World Council of Churches eventually introduced into Christianity a new, radical missionary and pastoral approach based on the modern discovery that the teachings of Jesus are translatable into the various multicultural conditions of humankind.

Hillman calls the church today to dialogue with the cultures and religious values of the different peoples constituting the human family. It is evident to him that African traditions are still alive, however "christianized" and "modernized" the African communities may be said to be. For example, in marriage ceremonies, mourning rites, and the practice of medicine, both Western Christian and African traditional practices can be found functioning side by side. As Hillman sees it, this makes the challenge of inculturation in Africa unavoidable. And so the question is: How and to what extent could the Maasai and, by extension, African Religion serve as the local Christian community's basic religious system, transformed by faith in Christ?

It is not enough, according to Hillman, to present Christianity in their language, understood in a merely semantic or literally sense. A more comprehensive "language" in the anthropological sense of symbol systems must be assumed and used. This language consists of indigenous cultural symbols, signs, myths, rites, images, customs and gestures, aspirations, ways of praying, loving, and looking at life. What God has done in Jesus and ordered to be communicated to all peoples in their respective historical periods and cultural contexts must be creatively reinterpreted and articulated through locally intelligible symbols already operative in the existing culture of each people. And this must be continued by successive generations.

Hillman suggests that successful inculturation can only be achieved through a full-time engagement by experts designed in cross-cultural ministries to awaken missionaries and pastors to a positive appreciation of the cultural worlds of the people to whom they have been sent. People should be helped to be open to change and to be ready to integrate positive innovations into their societal life. Like Gittins, Shorter, and Schineller, Hillman is also convinced that for this to be achieved, careful research as well as serious reflection, open discussion, and flexibility are all required. Inculturation as a way of making the Gospel incarnate in different cultures means the full acceptance of people where they are, in their own time and place, in everything except sin.

If many Christians in Africa are intuitively or articulately opposed to the overly Westernized form of Christianity that attempts to undermine African culture, they are not criticizing Christianity itself but the methods by which it was introduced and maintained. They identify in it elements that are merely of Western culture and not essential to the faith. Specifically, they think that Christian missionaries should reconsider their proscription against the baptism of polygamists and their wives as well as, in some ethnic groups, bride wealth as an element of legitimate marriage. The same applies also to African naming systems, which should be given the emphasis in the church they deserve.

These are points that Erasto Muga makes in an earlier study about the interaction in the colonial period and after independence between East Africans and the European missionaries. Entitled *African Response to Western Christian Religion: A Sociological Analysis of African Separatist Religious and Political Movements in East Africa* (1975), the book argues that Christianity should involve itself in politics and in the institutions that govern the society. The church has a duty that it must guard with all its strength, namely to pass judgment under God on the actions of society, and particularly the government. On the other hand, the church must cooperate with and help the government to fight against ignorance, disease, and poverty.

In his *Christianity and the Rites of Passage: The Prospects of Inculturation* (1992) Charles O. Onuh takes as his main thesis that the incarnation of Jesus—the definitive divine intervention in human history and the apex of God's self-communication to humanity—transcends cultural and geographical boundaries. It makes Jesus Christ part of all humanity. The incarnation principle dictates, in Onuh's view, that Christianity is expected to become part of the various cultures that constitute the whole of the human family. Pope Paul VI clarifies this point in his encyclical *Evangelii Nuntandi* that, although the Gospel is certainly not identical with culture, the kingdom, which the Gospel proclaims, is lived by men and women who are profoundly linked to a culture. The task of building up the kingdom cannot avoid borrowing the elements of human cultures.

How can Christians be helped to recover their unique identity as African Christians, rather than live a dualistic life with one foot in the world of Western Christianity and the other in their traditional world? This is the central question Onuh sees confronting the church in Africa today. He lists some practical steps to be taken. The church must have as its first goal to feed the deep spiritual quest of the people, to take hold of them and lead them away from any kind of superstition or false worship. This is why the celebrations of the sacraments must be clearly expressed in symbols real to them, something that can happen only when a catechesis is developed that will express and integrate faith in the thought patterns and cultural framework of the people. Cultural awareness should be created in the minds of Christians by establishing cultural commissions in all dioceses at parish, town and village levels under a regional coordinating body.

CRITIQUING AFRICAN RELIGION CONSTRUCTIVELY

As we have seen above, Aylward Shorter points out that the dynamic and dialectic of inculturation bring about a "new creation." The encounter between Western Christianity and African religiosity does not result in a choice of either the one or the other, but a kind of intricate synthesis of values. This means that not only Christianity but also African religiosity must face a rigorous and honest critique under the authority of the Gospel.

In *African Traditional Religion and the Christian Faith* (1985), Cornelius Olowola attempts to provide a constructive critical approach to African Religion. Taking as his starting point the continual revival of traditional religiosity that poses a challenge to Christianity in Africa, he focuses attention on analyzing the principal elements of African cosmology, namely, God, the spirits, and sacrifices. He proposes the following principles as fundamental, that:

- This world was brought into being by the source of all beings, the Supreme Being.
- The Supreme Being brought into being other divinities and spirits to act as his functionaries in the orderly maintenance of the world.
- Death does not spell the end to human life but opens the gate to the hereafter; hence prominence is given to belief in the continuation of life after death.
- Divinities and spirits, together with the ancestral spirits, dwell in the supersensible world, but are interested in what goes on in the human world.
- There are mysterious powers or forces in the world and their presence often makes human beings fearful.
- If men and women are to enjoy peace, they must live according to the directives laid down by the Supreme Being and his agents.

Olowola notes that Christian theology must take into serious account some of these principles of African Religion: the belief in a Supreme Being and in the existence of spirits, for example, is in conformity with biblical teaching. There are, however, recognizable defects in African Religion when viewed from a Christian perspective. For Olowola, the African emphasis on spirits runs the danger of breaking the law of God, who alone should be worshiped. Furthermore, African sacrificial systems cannot be adequate for the salvation of the human person after the sacrifice of Jesus on the cross.

PEACE AND RECONCILIATION

Inculturation cannot avoid social issues, and African thinkers have recognized this. *From Violence to Peace in Africa: A Challenge for African Christianity* (1999), a collection of essays edited by Mary N. Getui and Peter Kanyandago, addresses two closely related issues: the rampant violence in Africa and the search for reconciliation and peace.

In his article "Violence in Africa: A Search for Causes and Remedies," Kanyandago argues that Christian churches need to review their evangelization methods and rethink their theologies so that they are not oppressive to Africa. This leads to the need to redefine a certain understanding of inculturation that sees culture as a vehicle of expressing the Gospel instead of seeing the Gospel as already contained in culture. Kanyandago insists that rethinking inculturation in this way must go together with a critique of Western ecclesiologies, which have so far conceived the church using Western cultural images exclusively.

Carroll Houle in his essay "Empowering the Victims" makes the case for the necessity of de-compartmentalizing reality from the dichotomous categories of religious and political, and economic and aesthetic, which have been foisted onto Africa by modernity. He argues that the African world-view is that life, relationships, participation and community are holistic real-ities, blending the spiritual and the material organically. To Africans, peace implies a good relationship with the living, God, the dead and the not yet born, the sharing of the essential means of life. He is convinced that this African understanding and praxis of peace and reconciliation is closer to that of the Gospels than is the case in the West. According to him, the New Testament declaration of peace and reconciliation as personified and fulfilled in Jesus Christ adds immensely to the corresponding African understanding.

Another study on the same topic is *Peace and Reconciliation in Africa* (1983) by David W. Shenk. The reflections in this book emerge out of his experience in East Africa—in particular, Tanzania, where he was born and raised, and Somalia and Kenya, where he lived and worked as an adult. The book examines the ways in which African peoples have struggled to culti-vate peace and reconciliation in their traditional life as well as in the midst of their contemporary experiences. In other words, the book is an attempt to examine justice and reconciliation themes in Africa's pre-Christian her-itage, and to describe and interpret the Gospel of peace as it is experienced and expressed by many Christians in Africa today.

Shenk believes that the African peoples' positive response to the Christian Gospel must have been because God's providence had prepared them to hear and believe it through the gift of their traditional religious heritage. Their belief in one transcendent God and the hereafter, the myths of the sad sep-aration between God and humanity, and the understanding of the person and his place in the universe all pointed to the truths of the Gospel of Jesus Christ. Nevertheless, in spite of the similarities between the Gospel and tra-ditional African culture, it is necessary to avoid the temptation to strictly equate them. Thus, even though the concept of covenant is similar in both Christianity and African Religion, there are apparent incompatibilities which make each distinct from the other: for instance, according to Shenk, the role of the living dead in many traditional understandings of covenant is incom-patible with the biblical theocentric perception.

The transcultural nature of the church places the African church in a unique and significant position in the modern process of national formation in Africa, in Shenk's opinion. Often, when it seemed that multi-ethnic rival-ries might destroy national unity, the church has stepped in to affirm the unity of the people. But the church must recognize that it has also contributed to a serious fracturing of traditional community structures, to the extent that among some people the traditional mechanisms for communicating values have almost totally collapsed. The church has in many ways been unkind to and devastatingly destructive of traditional culture. It has been guilty of rob-bing people of their sense of dignity and worth. Rather than bring healing, the church has often contributed to the disease of brokenness and alienation.

In *Church and Politics in East Africa* (1974), Henry Okullu similarly seeks to show the reasons for the necessity of Christian involvement in economic development and political growth toward democracy, and the fight against tribalism and corruption as part of its mandate on earth.

ECUMENISM AND INTERRELIGIOUS DIALOGUE

Horst Burke contributed a paper on ecumenical dialogue in a collection called *Christian and Islamic Contributions towards Establishing Independent States in Africa South of the Sahara* (1979) in which he argues that the sectarian developments, some of which have grown into popular movements in various parts of Africa, are part of a search for an African identity within Christianity. These splinter groups contain a clear indication of those aspects of the African heritage that were denied a place in the European-oriented missionary churches. They are of particular interest for ecumenical dialogue because they try to recover something of the spirit of biblical and early Christian life. They include the re-awakening of certain charismatic phenomena, the presence of spirits in the form of extraordinary effects, and the conviction that salvation and healing go hand in hand.

Burke insists that dialogue between the churches of Africa and the churches elsewhere in the world must be encouraged because each needs the experience and the particular contribution of the other. But above and beyond all other particulars involved in ecumenical dialogue, the most important thing is that the church must be seen and experienced as one great world-wide community.

A similar theme marks the thoughts contained in *Variations in Christian Theology in Africa* (1986), a collection of papers presented at a symposium convened by the Olaus Perti Foundation of Uppsala University and edited by J. S. Pobee and Carl Hallencreutz. In his contribution, Pobee makes the point that African Christian theology must be contextual because the point is to get people to communicate the good news of Jesus Christ in terms of the realities of the situation in which the church lives and operates. Nevertheless, he warns that the expression "contextuality" must be used with care. It must not be turned into a crusade or a program or law. It is rather simply an instrument of the Gospel.

What is needed is an ever more careful delineation of the components of context and contexuality. Pobee cites Kofi A. Busia to the effect that the need for contextuality cannot be allowed to sever any particular church from what the church has accumulated throughout its long history, "her great hymns, her liturgy and above all her Bible." If the African church belongs to the universal church, then its theological education should reflect this belonging. The best method in theological education is dialogue. True contextuality happens where and when the identity and integrity of the people and their circumstances are recognized, respected and engaged in genuine dialogue with the eternal non-negotiable Gospel of Jesus Christ.

In another essay in the book, "African Symbolism and the Interpretation of Christianity," Pobee describes symbol first as representation; it witnesses to the presence and the power of the represented entity. Second, a symbol relates to the consciousness of the addressees; therefore a symbol is culture-bound. Third, in the use of symbols it is difficult to distinguish between the language of belief and non-belief; that is why there is sometimes a negative attitude to African symbols, appearing to some as synonymous with darkness and the kingdom of Satan. But they are in reality indispensable agents of change as a person moves from one worldview to another and from traditional religion to Christianity.

Byang H. Kato, reflecting on the same theme, defines contextuality or contextualization as an effort to express, for the sake of relevance, the never changing word of God in the ever changing modes of human existence. In *Biblical Christianity in Africa* (1985), he notes that contextualization can take place in liturgy, dress, language, church structures, and any other form of the expression of the truth of the Gospel. The content of God's teaching should remain what it is. If there are any inappropriate cultural beliefs or practices mingled with Christianity, they must be purged. The church must always express the unchanging biblical faith.

Because he feels that "Christianity is truly an African religion," Kato criticizes many theologians for spending their time defending African traditional religions and practices that he considers incompatible with biblical teaching, giving indigenous initiation rites as an example. Thus he thinks that the term "African theology" means too many different things to too many different people and contains the inherent danger of syncretism; it would be more appropriate to use the term "Christian theology" and then define its context. Theologians would therefore describe their work as, for example, Christian reflections from Africa on marriage, the world of the spirits, and so on. For Kato, biblical Christianity is in the end the only true form of Christianity.

Tite Tienou also calls attention to a continuing theological malaise within African evangelical Christianity, factors that contribute to it, its consequences, and possible directions for dealing with the problem in the future. In *The Theological Task of the Church in Africa* (1982), he observes that all African Christians privately feel the burden of having to bear at least two cultural loads, the modern and the traditional. They find themselves in two worlds and the center can no longer hold. This, he says, has implications for evangelical Christian living and theologizing. Under modern education and other influences, Africans have learned to think of their customs as pagan; but there are really no substitutes for the cultural elements they have been asked to discard. The situation leads to a crisis of faith. To help Christians out of it, we must study African culture in order to see the elements that are compatible or incompatible with the Gospel message.

Even if African religiosity did not, and perhaps could not, produce that which the Gospel now offers to the African people, according to Tienou, it did, however, tutor the Africans so that they could find in the Gospel that which their religiosity originally pointed to. This is why some beliefs, practices, and traditional religious leadership can be used for the enrichment of Christian life. To develop an authentic African Christian theology, Tienou, like most other African and Africanist theologians, calls for the investigation of African myths, beliefs, and religious practices so that they may be brought into dialogue with existing forms of theology.

OFFICIAL CHURCH PERSPECTIVES

Besides the imagination of African and Africanist theologians, has any reflection emerged from the official church? Have there been any imaginative initiatives there on inculturation?

We will summarize the reflections of one conference of bishops from East Africa—namely, the Tanzania Episcopal Conference (TEC)—in their pastoral letters. Although it is a summary, this review is a complete survey of the issues regarding inculturation that were addressed by the bishops in their response to the problems that have faced the church in Tanzania in the last thirty years.*

In 1972, TEC issued a pastoral letter entitled *Peace and Mutual Understanding*. The purpose of the letter was to underline the importance of communion between peoples and nations, between religion and development, and between individual rights and social justice for this young nation. For the bishops, it was crucial that if peace was to be maintained in the country some basic principles had to be spelled out and adhered to. There could be no understanding between peoples and nations, the bishops wrote, if the humanity of each person was not valued, loved, and respected. But understanding requires people to speak the truth without fear; otherwise it is impossible to recognize and remove the reasons that cause hatred and wars among peoples and nations.

In a 1981 letter addressed to his diocese, Bishop Yakob Komba of Songea, southern Tanzania, addressed the question of corruption at a time when economic sabotage was rampant. The structure and the style of this letter, called *Our God Is Not the God of Corruption*, are different from the bishops' usual pastoral letters. It is more a study of corruption than, as is usually the case with other letters, merely an affirmation of biblical truths and church doctrine. It takes an inductive, not a deductive or prescriptive approach to analyzing the problem.

Several interesting points emerge from this letter. The reference it makes to the wisdom of the ancestors indicates that the bishop was convinced that a solution to the problem of corruption could be found in the local culture. His reference to the Koran, though brief, shows his interest in interreligious dialogue: other religions cannot be ignored in seeking answers to ethical issues. This is perhaps the only pastoral letter that makes an explicitly positive reference to Islam.

On June 7, 1992, TEC issued another letter under the title *Authentic Human Development*. Clarifying the role of the church in society and its responsibility for contributing freely to authentic human development, the

---

* Except in the one instance indicated, all of these documents were originally issued in Swahili, the lingua franca of the country. It is to the Swahili editions that we have had access. The translation into English, including that of the documents' titles, is therefore mine.

letter disclaims knowledge of answers to technological questions. But it believes that the church can and must propose certain fundamental principles necessary for development that is person-centered, development that recognizes that human beings are made in the image of God and that they possess a body and a soul. For the Christian, the foundation and the basis of true development is Christ, in whom all things have been reconciled. The authentic meaning of development can be understood only through reference to Christ, the total human being.

The year 1993 in Tanzania was a year of civil discontent, rooted in massive socio-economic changes. First, there was the sudden change of policy: from three decades of experimenting with socialism under President Nyerere to a drastic form of laissez-faire capitalism. The new policy package included the devaluation of the currency, liberalizing trade, and establishing multiparty politics. As a consequence the country was beset as never before by huge unemployment, financial scams, favoritism, increased corruption, and interreligious tensions between Christians and Muslims. Against this background the bishops issued three different messages in quick succession.

The *Pastoral Messages of the Catholic Bishops of Tanzania* (1993) essentially condemned attacks on the Christian faith by members of other faiths, notably Islam. It deplores the government's silence and inaction against those who were fomenting interreligious strife, and noted the danger to which that attitude could lead. Respect for the sacred "is the spiritual foundation for respect for authority, the humanity, and values of other religions" (p. 4). Everything else leads to anarchy. The government's responsibility is to protect the right of religious freedom. All religions must be allowed to enjoy it without prejudice or segregation, provided they do not break the law. The message calls all the bishops, priests, religious, and the laity to remain firm in their faith and to make sure that peace and justice prevail in the country.

In *The Truth Will Set You Free*, issued only two months later, the bishops encouraged the faithful to persevere in prayer because things were happening in the country that were distorting the truth of faith, morality, politics, and economics. The message also maintained the bishops' stand against religious extremism and fundamentalism. In the midst of tension, it said, the church must invite the faithful and all people of good will to listen to the Christ of love and peace who speaks to society through the church. The message calls for truth, uprightness, patriotism, and self-sacrifice in politics. In the economic field, it called for better conditions for farmers, equal distribution of resources, and preferential consideration of the poor.

The third message of 1993 bore the title *Clear Conscience: The Direction of Our Nation*. The aim of the message was to help people recognize the political situation in the country and to examine the problems and causes facing the nation. How can citizens recognize, protect, and defend their rights?

According to the bishops, the things that had taken the wrong turn in the nation's policies included frequent breaches of the country's constitution, favoritism for the rich, and the deliberate disregard of the people's views concerning the plunder of the nation's natural resources and wealth by internal and external forces. There was also a false understanding about the relationship between politics and religion. The tendency to interpret and judge other peoples' religion and the tendency to see material things instead of the human person as the purpose of development also contributed to the conflict. The message deplored a freedom of speech devoid of truth and morality; it called on all the faithful to take steps to prevent this.

Archbishop (now Cardinal) Polycarp Pengo's *The Archdiocese of Dar es Salaam on the Vigil of the Synod of Bishops for Africa*, issued in the same year, tackled head-on some fundamental pastoral questions, including the shortage of priests, conflicts between Moslems and Christians in the archdiocese, and the tension within the Catholic Church between "official" Catholicism and popular charismatic movements—particularly Fr. Felician Nkwera's *Wanamaombi*. On the issue of the charismatic movements the cardinal wrote that true faith "comes to us only through the teachings of the Catholic Church." That is the case "because for Catholics, the Church is Mother and Teacher *(Mater et Magistra)*. It is only this mother and teacher who gives us leaders to guide the Catholic faith and to teach on her behalf" (p. 23).

In view of the fact that one of the themes to be discussed at the April-May 1994 Synod of Bishops for Africa in Rome was inculturation, the bishops decided that it would form the substance of their message for the Lenten season of 1994, *Faith and Inculturation*. The message defined inculturation as "an invitation to live our faith fully in the context and culture of Tanzania" (p. 6). Although it took into serious account the good taboos, feelings for the sanctity of life, unity and solidarity of clans, hospitality, respect for elders, and the songs, stories, sayings, and other elements of cultural heritage, it nevertheless curiously insisted that those who receive the Catholic faith have to accept its entire system, including all tenets of her discipline, many of which are of Western European origin.

Some Guidelines from the Catholic Bishops of Tanzania for the National Elections of October 1995 was issued in 1994 in both English and Swahili. It reiterated the basic principles upon which the nation was built: human dignity, justice, peace, equality, freedom, respect for all, unity, wisdom, patriotism, self-confidence, and self-reliance. The letter then elaborated each of those principles in the context of a multiparty democracy.

In his Apostolic Exhortation *Ecclesia in Africa* to the African Synod, Pope John Paul II asked all African bishops, priests, religious and laity to direct their efforts into "making everything new in Christ." To clarify this task the bishops in 1996 wrote *To Make Everything New in Christ: A Lenten Message for 1996* in which they invited the laity, as they had in 1994, to spend more time listening to the word of God, receiving the sacraments, living a life of prayer, performing acts of charity, and repenting, especially during the time of Lent.

Lastly, the bishops' document *1998: The Year of the Holy Spirit and Inculturation* was less a pastoral letter than a program of action that stressed once again the work of the Holy Spirit in the process of localizing the church.

CONCLUSION

All of the analyses and reflections about inculturation in Africa—those summarized above and most others besides—seem to share a common theme, that it is necessary to take local circumstances, cultures and forms of religiosity seriously in the process of "implanting" Christianity. All identify some of the sources for directing the process, including the actual local practices of Christianity by ordinary faithful, traditional belief systems, and new Christian movements. But they also need to take into account directives from the leaders of the church; this is important because, as is clear in the case of Tanzania, they are usually reactions and responses to existing perplexing local socio-religious issues. They provide a glimpse of the gap that usually exists between official church teaching and ordinary Christian practice. We note a general agreement that approaches localizing the faith, and the church must always be brought under the critique of Gospel values. Everything remains imperfect until it is brought to perfection in Jesus Christ.

Part Three

A LOOK TO THE FUTURE

The experience of inculturation as an implicit ecclesial process involves the presence of numerous factors and influences. These exist in the past and present time frames of a community as virtually silent realities, imperceptibly conditioning popular religiosity or spirituality. Because of this, and consequently its obliqueness, Clemens Sedmak (2002:77) is right when he points out that popular inculturation can often be "inconsistent, unjustifiable, or even dangerous." On the other hand, inculturation as an explicit project—when the process is taken up consciously to articulate in a systematic and scientific way its nature, meaning, and status—involves the same dimensions, but to a conscious degree. The latter's purpose is to be as transparent as possible and to suggest concrete orientations and practical models or faces the church might take in the future and why. Taking into account political, economic and social conditions, it constructs a sketch of the local church as a desirable possibility or an ideal. Even though, on account of human fallibility, it cannot eliminate all inconsistencies, rationalizations and danger, it gives more allowance than the implicit theology of inculturation does "to stand back and take a look." In other words, professional or academic inculturation is as a rule more critical of its own methods and conclusions than popular inculturation—or at least it should be.

Sedmak (see 2002:77) cites Karl Popper, who uses philosophy to illustrate that every individual has a philosophy of life, "whether or not we are aware of this fact." But since subconscious philosophies impact our lives for good or evil, it becomes important to improve them consciously through reasoned criticism. "This is the only apology for the continued existence of philosophy which I am able to offer," he concludes. Similarly, it is the only reason for the continued existence of academic theology and planned inculturation that we are able to see.

At the professional or academic level, theology is restricted to certain individuals in the church, that is, trained theologians and church officials. Here the process is at its most articulate and coherent (which is not necessarily to say correct or definitive) level. However, beyond mere description and analysis of how people in a certain locality live their faith, inculturation theology now can and must propose for discussion, evaluation, and possible implementation "the shape of the Church to come," as Karl Rahner titled a book dealing with this issue (Rahner 1983).

This final part of our discussion proposes to embark on this task for the church in Africa. The picture will not be comprehensive—no single book or author can do that—but it intends to show as clearly as possible the main outlines of the shape the church must take based on the criteria of inculturation that we described in Part One, and the historical processes we offered as examples in Part Two.

12

Practical Models of the Church

Someone once remarked that "correct ideas don't fall from the skies"; they are the result of experience, observation, hypotheses, syntheses, and so on. In other words, they are the result of observing creation and its hidden mysteries. This is as true of strictly scientific discovery—at which humanity seems to be doing very well now—as it is for theological innovation.

Clemens Sedmak (2002:2) explains the qualities of a good theologian of inculturation, qualities that could describe equally well a good physicist, psychologist or psycho-analyst, archaeologist or even a tourist who wants to gain understanding from his or her travels. It is all a matter "of being sensitive to concerns and of asking the right questions," Sedmak observes: "A good theologian . . . is a person who is close to people, who has a creative imagination and the gift of listening, who shows a commitment to hard work, who accepts the risk of making a mistake, who is a person of self-renewal." According to him, a good theologian considers his task as ongoing, never finished. Being a theologian is a reflection not only of one's knowledge about things to do with God but even more so of one's personality face to face with God as God acts in the world.

This has been called doing theology "from below" or "from the bottom." In technical terms it is referred to as "inductive" theology, in which nothing of God's creation, nothing that is real, nothing that concerns the life of humanity and the universe is alien. I think that this is depicted very well in the episode in Acts 10 that describes Peter's arrogant attitude toward non-Jewish people and his conversion toward realizing their true worth in God's sight. The episode ends, "What God has made clean, you are not to call profane" (v. 15). And later, enlightened, Peter explains to the Roman soldier Cornelius, "You know that it is unlawful for a Jewish man to associate with, or visit, a Gentile, but God has shown me that I should not call any person profane or unclean" (v. 28).

Cornelius had earlier received practically the same message about Peter, the Jew (Acts 10:30–33). What theologians have to watch for and incorporate in their programs are those realities in culture that lead people to God. As Peter put it, "In truth, I see that God shows no partiality. Rather, in every nation whoever fears him and acts uprightly is acceptable to him" (vv. 34–35). How the "fear of God" is concretely manifested at any given place and time must be discovered inductively. There are rarely any other ready-made laws or answers that the deductive method might suggest. Laws and regulations, particularly when these are universal—or grand stories—are important only as guidelines, beacons or limits, not destinations. This is the whole point of inculturation theology and the inculturation process as a program of action.

SOURCES AND RESOURCES FOR "PLANNED" INCULTURATION

Religious rites and rituals, social customs and behavior (ethos), art (painting and sculpture) and literature and drama, prevailing local political and economic conditions, and of course scripture and Christian tradition are all sources and resources for planned inculturation. Sedmak (2002) speaks of the task of using these sources as "reappropriating our traditions" where we "remember" (in the sense of making present the values in these sources) values that bring us closer to God by building up communities of understanding, love, and peace.

We will have more to say about some of the specific roles of these sources for inculturation later on, but here I would like to concentrate on the importance of anthropology and sociology in the process. With regard to spreading the good news of Jesus to those who have not yet heard it, Paul asks: "But how can they call on him in whom they have not believed? And how can they believe in him of whom they have not heard? And how can they hear without someone to preach? And how can people preach unless they are sent?" (Rom. 10:14–15). We could ask in our turn: But how can anyone discover the values of a despised culture? And how can one respect a culture unless one learns (about) it? And how can one learn a culture unless one immerses oneself in it?

Anthropology and the sociology of religion can play the role of a messenger and help us understand and respect the values of a culture (even our own) and reappropriate our traditions. It must be borne in mind, however, that "reappropriating our traditions" does not imply the total acceptance of them. The process is not an ideological one of total justification, refusing to be questioned and insisting that "for better or for worse, mine is best." Rather, reappropriation in this sense is an exercise in discernment and critical judgment when faced with new situations, experiences and understanding. It is true that a culture that refuses to grow ultimately dies. But growth means change: not the destruction of everything in the old reality but its transformation, hopefully to a higher level of existence.

The three levels of understanding a scriptural text can also be applied to understanding, appreciating, and applying the values of a cultural text: the meaning *within* any cultural text (that is, how a society may be living these values now), the meaning *behind* the cultural text (that is, the real or fictive reasons that brought these values about), and the meaning *in front of* the cultural text (that is, why and how these values may be reappraised and either accepted or rejected) bring people closer to God and create community. By way of example, let me consider briefly how a few cultural texts might evolve as they encounter the explicit Christian message. These are the understanding of community, the significance of naming, and levirate relationships.

Community and Personal Freedom

It has been established through many studies that the notion of community plays a determining role in the life of the African person. Apart from their community, African people are not fully persons. A person's personality and individuality are guaranteed only insofar as the individual is integrated into the community on the one hand, and the community serves and strengthens the individual on the other. So, the individual does everything in view of assuring the whole community's health and survival. Individuals may not be conscious of this as they work for their family, discipline it, and make sure no taboos are broken; or when they refrain from emotions that might disturb the community and which are usually associated with witchcraft. Yet the concern is nevertheless present, and resurfaces as a conscious reality immediately when something goes wrong in the community.

The imperative of building relationships and community is instilled in the individual from birth to death. Even after death, when the deceased person's belongings are distributed to different members of the family and clan (often according to prescribed rules), the purpose is to emphasize the reality of community. In death, if the person is revered as an ancestor, he or she bears the burden of assuring the health of the living and of the unborn by guaranteeing the living community's survival through plentiful offspring (Magesa 1997:35–114).

Living in small, often feuding, ethnic groups in the long past, Africans (much as the Jews before the time of the kings or other groups throughout the world) needed this kind of social "organization," if we may call it that. Their political, economic, and social survival could be assured only through communities that were tightly knit. Myths and legends developed explaining the origins of the community and its members' responsibilities to one another. Totems and taboos evolved to make sure that transgressions against the unity of the ethnic group were minimized. To acknowledge the wonder that is our universe, as well as other unexplainable phenomena that are always part and parcel of existence, there developed in Africa the cult of the ancestors, which is the foundation of African religiosity.

The question for inculturation is how the message of Jesus Christ finds itself reflected, or better, rediscovers itself in this life-text, and whether and how it can amplify and perfect it. This African text of community is part of the divine being itself, which Christ came to fulfill. We therefore cannot here speak quite accurately about the African understanding of community as a "seed" of or "preparation" for the Gospel, but rather its "context." If I may use New Testament metaphors, the message of Jesus becomes the yeast in the dough or the seed in the ground that grows into a big tree. The dough and the ground are, of course, the African understanding of community.

If the central point of Jesus' message was to establish a new community— a "new Israel"—and given that this manifested itself in the early Christian movement, which later became the church, this new community must be found in and emerge from within the African understanding of community and community life. The principles of mutual respect, sharing, solidarity, justice, and peace are shared principles; they only become clarified in the scriptures. In this sense, as Bujo explains, the centrality of Jesus also emerges from within the African text. For African Christianity Jesus is Ancestor or Proto-Ancestor, the "vital proto-force . . . from whom the existential strength and life of the [other] ancestors flow." To follow him is to walk toward the "vital creativity," which is the fulfillment of human life (Bujo 1988:23–24).

But if the message of Jesus is to act as the yeast in the dough, it must expand the vision of the African text. It must critique it and lead it toward even greater vital creativity. In the question of community, the Christian message expands the boundaries of community beyond the limits of African solidarity. "For all of you who were baptized into Christ have clothed yourselves with Christ. There is neither Jew nor Greek, there is neither slave nor free person, there is not male and female; for you are all one in Christ Jesus" (Gal. 3:27–28). As such we share ancestors in the church: Abraham is ancestor just as much as the Africans Sts. Charles Lwanga, Bakhita, and Blessed Anwarite are ancestors to all other Christians throughout the world.

The Gospel also makes explicit the absolute value of the individual person. Created in the image and likeness of God and imbued with divine breath, a person has value in and for him- or herself. One's value and dignity as a human person are not given by nor do they flow from one's community. They originate from God's own self. Similarly, strictly speaking, a person does not draw salvation from the church, but from God through the church. This means that a person enjoys a higher level of freedom under the influence of the Gospel than under the African understanding of person alone. But one must be careful: this is not to say that community as the African ethnic group or the church are therefore not important. The contrary is truer: the individual must use this freedom wisely, for it is precisely in freedom that the possibility of wrongdoing rests. People cannot begin to grow toward the full stature of their dignity as the image of God unless it leads them to community (see 1 Jn. 3:11–5:12, Js. 2:14–26) and, in our case, the church. Christian theology makes this clear in the doctrine of the Trinity, the conception of God as Perfect Community. This is the functional purpose of the doctrine of the Trinity.

Naming and Communion in the Trinity

Naming is one of the rituals in African tradition that underline the importance of humanity as community. Among the many important functions of this ritual—such as designating the "personality, status, function or destiny of the bearer" (Nyamiti 1988:42, also Magesa 1997:89–94)—we must emphasize its function of solidifying the vital force of the community. Naming unites the vital forces of the ancestors and the living through the child, thereby strengthening the life of the three dimensions of the

African community: the ancestors' names are perpetuated and therefore they are assured of their status as ancestors; the living community's life is prolonged by the addition of another member; and the young person being named will have children of his or her own to continue the community's circle of life.

The meaning behind this text is one of assuring the solidarity of community. Yet in this ritual we find elements of the Trinity as the Perfect Community. Tanzanian theologian Charles Nyamiti (1988:41–73) explains the link between the African tradition of naming and the doctrine of the Trinity. Even though his thought is extremely deductive and suffers from a dependence on medieval (especially Thomistic) speculative and abstract categories of thought and vocabulary, his attempt to marry African tradition and Western Christian thought is nevertheless admirable and serious. Taking naming in African tradition as an analogue, Nyamiti explains the dynamic relationship that exists in the three persons of the blessed Trinity.

First, he ascribes to the second person of the Trinity two levels of names: an "immanent" or "interior" name and an "exterior" name. I present here the gist of what he describes as the "naming process in the Immanent Trinity," of which, as he argues, its external names, such as Son, Wisdom, Logos are manifestations (Nyamiti 1988:48).

According to Nyamiti, God the Son, the Logos in the Trinity, gets his name from God the Father because it is the Father who begets the Son: in God, naming is the same as begetting and begetting is the same as naming. By begetting and naming the Son, the Father shares his being and personality with him. Thus, "naming in God is the actual production of personality." The Son is a person "because he is named by the Father." This means that the Father with love calls the Son into being, and the Son comes into being as a spontaneous love-response to the Father. But, "the Father's address to his Son, and this latter's 'Yes' to that address, imply the production of the Holy Spirit, since the divine Spirit is the product or expression of the mutual love between the Father and the Son" (Nyamiti 1988:51). Nyamiti concludes from this that the relationship of the Father to the Son is similar to that of ancestor to descendant, and that of the Spirit to these two is similar to the expression of their "life": "the personality of the Spirit—as distinct from the personalities of the other two Persons—consists in being the infinite Breath or Life issuing from the Father and the Son" (Nyamiti 1988:57). In this sense—faithful to the formulation of the Nicene-Constantinopolitan Creed— the Spirit is named, and therefore generated or begotten, from the Father *and* the Son.

There is no need to pursue Nyamiti's argument any further. The point he wishes to make has been made despite the many differences between the naming process in African tradition and communion in the Trinity, differences that the theological use of the analogy must be keen to note at every stage; it remains true that elements of the revelation of the Trinity are not altogether absent from African culture.

Polygamy, Levirate Unions, Human Dignity, and Respect for Life

Considering the African traditional form of marriage, in which a man can marry more than one wife, Bénézet Bujo has rightly warned that it would be a mistake to routinely regard it as "unjust and derogatory to human dignity." Not infrequently, he points out, polygamy served positive purposes in society. In its ideal form, given the prevailing social environment of traditional Africa, it protected women from prostitution. It also assured the stability of marriage in cases, such as barrenness, which would in Africa today lead to the break-up of the marriage bond. Further, in the same social environment, polygamy made sure that women's needs in such a union were catered to, thus assuring their dignity (Bujo 2001:133–34).

The same thing can be said of levirate unions where a male relative "inherited" the wife of a deceased man. This arrangement had two purposes. One was to preserve family ties: the ethical perspective was that the bonds of marriage should not be broken even in death. Thus, although bearing children by a brother-in-law or another relative, the widow remained legally the wife of her deceased husband, and she continued to bear children for him. Another purpose was to protect the woman's human rights materially and socially: even after the death of her husband, the widow has the right to be cared for by the extended family and clan of her deceased husband because, again, the bond of marriage once established could not be broken, neither could its responsibilities be easily escaped (Magesa 1997:140).

Looking at the present socio-economic situation in Africa, however, some pertinent questions must be posed about this tradition. These touch on concerns that not only women, but a wide range of the population all over the continent, have. Some articulate these concerns more clearly than others, but the usefulness of polygamy in the changed socio-economic environment of Africa today, as well as its ability to protect traditional values, are increasingly questionable. First of all, the traditional ideal is rarely observed by men today. But even where it is, argues Bujo (2001:134), "one must still ask whether it is compatible in modern Africa with the dignity of women." Christians, he says, must ask an even deeper question: Is this tradition compatible with Christ's message of the equality and dignity of all people before God? So, "what does inculturation mean here?" he asks.

One can approach this question on at least two levels. On one level, Constance Shishanya (see Getui/Holter/Zinkuratire 2001:147–51), for example, proposes that on the question of the dignity of women, it is necessary to critique, or "re-read" aspects of the Bible so as to "liberate" it. She rereads the Hagar narratives in Genesis 16:1–16 and 21:9–21 in the context of the Abaluhya culture of western Kenya. The treatment of Hagar, which these biblical narratives seem to sanction, is clearly unjust. In the first narrative, she is handed over to Abraham and "used" almost as an instrument of procreation in his search for a *male* child. Then she is mistreated by Sarah, abandoned by Abraham, and forced to flee into the desert. But she is instructed by God's messenger to return to this abusive relationship. In the second narrative, her son by Abraham, Ishmael, suffers with her the same fate of banishment. Where can she go as a single mother in a culture where single motherhood is not acceptable?

Sishanya shows that this is the situation that Abaluhya women have had to endure in their traditional society for centuries. The attitude is reinforced in women's psyches because, as she says, Abaluhya Christians (and Africans in general) tend to identify more with the characters and ideals of the Old than the New Testament. In order to bring home the value and dignity of women as human beings, such texts cannot be literally defended as presenting God's revelation; rather, they have to be interpreted in the context of contemporary understanding and social development. We can be led to a new interpretation by emphasizing Hagar's final liberty which, as Shishanya (see Getui/Holter/Zinkuratire 2001:151) puts it, shows that in the final analysis God does not favor social domination. Such an interpretation will also lead to a theology that, according to Anne Nasimiyu Wasike (see Getui/Holter/ Zinkuratire 2001:180), "affirms restoration in Christ Jesus, one that supports our uniqueness as persons—male and female, made in the image and likeness of God." The task before the Christian, and indeed, the human community, as Nasimiyu Wasike sees it, is to dismantle all the barriers that prevent people, especially women, from moving toward this goal.

The other level is of a more practical and logical nature. If an important aim of polygamy and levirate unions is to promote the life and life-force of the individual, family, and community, can it be argued convincingly today that they are fulfilling this purpose? We have in mind here the HIV/AIDS pandemic which in Africa is transmitted mainly through heterosexual contact. Leviratic unions and modern-day polygamy, in which the covenant element has been watered down, are some of the chief ways by which this infection and disease are spreading. But AIDS kills, and is second only to malaria in its destruction of human life in Africa. Surely it is not logical to continue to claim that such unions promote life? On this logical level alone, they have to be rejected now as agents, not of life, but of death.

Contact between African religiosity and the Christian message demands that we imagine other ways of being and living as we think about practical models of being church in the contemporary world. As an essential element of inculturation as a program we must imagine a new spirituality if we are to remain faithful to the call of Jesus Christ to protect the fullness of life in the world.

WHAT IS SPIRITUALITY?

Unfortunately, the Catholic tradition (and indeed the entire Western Christian tradition) tends to identify specific acts of spiritual life with the whole spirituality. So, it would characterize attendance at Mass and the reception of the other sacraments, prayer, meditation, making retreats, performing acts of charity, and so on as "spiritual life." The question, however, is: this is spiritual life in contradistinction to what? Are acts that are different from these in a person's life not part of his or her spirituality? Is habitual drunkenness, anger, sloth, lust, and so on, not part of a person's spiritual life, albeit in a negative way? To identify only the former as spirituality is reductionist.

(The same tendency toward reductionism takes place when people confuse a specific sexual orientation—say, heterosexuality or homosexuality—or certain sexual acts—such as rape, sodomy or child-abuse—with the whole of a person's sexuality. Sexuality is the entire created nature and cultural nurture that identify a person as male or female. These include physical appearance and hormones, but also mood, emotions, and those myriad things that culture socializes a man or woman to be and do. In this sense, specific sexual orientations and acts are expressions of a person's sexuality; they do not constitute his or her sexuality in its entirety. In other words, they cannot completely and totally define a person.)

As Gregory Baum made clear more than three decades ago, it is not possible to divide the actions of a person neatly into "natural" and "supernatural." Just as sin is present in all that human beings are and do, so is divine grace. "To suggest that man's secular life is not supernatural would be a Pelagian error," Baum warns. "To suggest that the interpersonal relationships through which men come to be and keep on creating the human community are purely this-worldly, humanistic, or natural events would go counter to the entire teaching of the Gospel," he writes, and adds: "Human existence is so deeply wounded and threatened by sin that the passage from fear to trust, from hostility to love, from ignorance to self-knowledge, from passivity to creativity, from self-centredness to concern for others are never purely natural events, determined by the human resources available to men; they are always co-determined by divine grace, they are always supernatural" (Baum 1970:134).

This is what François Kabasele Lumbala has also articulated in specific reference to Africa. The African worldview, he asserts, denies such divisions within human nature and the universe. In this view the human person is the universe in microcosm and the universe is a macro expression of the human person. It is in the human person that all reality, visible and invisible, touches. According to Lumbala (1998:3, 7), "the human person already forms part of the 'sacred'; he or she is even the figure of the divine." He or she is an "arch-symbol" of the divine reality, its "signifying" entity. Briefly put, "the human is in the sacred and the sacred in the human." Consequently, with the body we can give glory to or curse God (compare Jas. 3:3–12, especially verses 9–10, with reference to the power of the tongue).

We must therefore expand the notion of spirituality to include everything that a person is and does: body, mind, will, and emotions. The question for spirituality is: Do these, or the use of these faculties in given circumstances, lead a person toward or away from communion with God? Now, it seems quite clear from this question that we must look at spirituality in two ways: one positive, leading to God (or grace) and the other negative, leading away from God (or sin). But they are both equally spiritual aspects, because both concern a person's relationship with God. Both have to do with a person's final destiny.

Again, there are many factors that influence our spiritual habits and deci-sions, one of the most important and conscious of which is religion. But since any religion's aim is moral, that is, to guide its adherents toward the inte-gration of body, mind, will, and emotions so that they can be at the service of the Divine (however the Divine is conceived to be), religion's emphasis will be on the maximization of what it defines as the "good" aspects of our spirituality and the minimization of the "bad." It will be on those actions that seem to be more obviously oriented toward grace—such as prayer and so on—than those that are a little less obviously so. (Perhaps this is why in many organized religions the vocabulary of "spirituality" or "spiritual life" has come to be restricted to those acts religion sees as "religious.")

It is generally recognized now that African Religion or religiosity holds the more comprehensive view of spirituality, counting the whole of human life, both positive and negative behavior, as bearing upon a person's and a society's relationship with God. Personal and social acts are seen within this total context, and are confirmed, adjusted, or changed according to the way they strengthen or weaken the life-force of those concerned. For African Religion, blessings of whatever nature and degree are signs of goodness and right living, that is, of "spiritual" growth or grace. Similarly, calamities of whatever nature and degree are perceived as signs of badness and wrongful behavior, that is, of "spiritual" degeneration or sin. In the final analysis, African spirituality is concerned with which human behavior is good and right, and what actions help lead to either divine-ancestral blessing or censure.

The late Indian Jesuit theologian Anthony de Mello has left us a treasury of wisdom in his writings. I compare de Mello's numerous stories and say-ings to the fables of the ancient Greek Aesop, all of which were intended to offer practical wisdom for living. In regard to the present-day church in Africa, there is a little conversation in de Mello between a spiritual guide and his student that bears repeating:

> *The master was asked, "What is spirituality?" He said, "Spirituality is that which succeeds in bringing one to inner transformation." "But if I apply the traditional methods handed down by the masters, is that not spirituality?" "It is not spirituality if it does not perform its func-tion for you. A blanket is no longer a blanket if it does not keep you warm." "So spirituality does change?"*
>
> *"People change and needs change. So what was spirituality once is spirituality no more. What generally goes under the name of spiritu-ality is merely the record of past methods."*

Don't cut the person to fit the coat. (de Mello 1982:11, italics in original)

The significance of this story's moral cannot be overemphasized: Spirituality is never definitively defined "for us" by its form or source; if it does not per-form its function for the person for whom it is intended, it is not spiritual-ity no matter what kind of action it involves, who originated the action, or what it did for them then. In the midst of change, people, perceptions, an⌐

needs likewise change. So what was "spirituality" in a different age, for different people, at a different time or place may not necessarily be spirituality today or for us. It certainly is not spirituality if it does not help to bring us closer to an ever deeper understanding of our own inner selves, our relationship with one another, and with God.

This must be applied not only to religion in general but also directly to specific religious actions, such as liturgical forms and prayers. In his small but truly groundbreaking volume, *Towards an Indigenous Church*, Bolaji Idowu cites the case of Nigeria. He characterizes the liturgical forms in the Protestant churches there almost forty years ago as "spiritually undernourishing" to the worshipers. As he saw it, these forms of worship, which ought to have been the "Means of Grace" for the believers did not satisfy the requirements of the true meaning of Christian worship. An authentic Christian liturgy, explains Idowu (1973:26), should be a Christian community's indigenous way of expressing itself before God so as to find communion with God. "It is," he insists, "a means by which the human soul finds a link with the Living Spirit Who is God." But this link can hardly be established if the liturgy is not spiritually suitable, Idowu argues, that is, if it ignores the "soul" of the worshipers that is found in their material and nonmaterial culture—in their language, emotions, psyche, dress, body language, social context, and so on.

At a conference on worship in Africa held in Blantyre, Malawi, in 1992, Jonah Katoneene expressed the same sentiment by insisting on the "political" character of Christian worship in contemporary Africa. Because the word usually evokes party politics, Katoneene explained that he meant "the politicisation of Christian worshippers so that they understand the political agenda of God among his own people." The Christian God is "a God who is inherently a political God, a social God, and an economic God. Therefore, the kind of worship we hold in our churches must respond to the day-to-day cries of our people" (*JoT* 1993:7). It must not, as he puts it, be "suspended in the air." According to Silas Ncozana speaking at the same conference, Christian worship "should not lack cultural grounding in our life realities but rather should reflect the lives and needs of African people" of all walks of life (*JoT* 1993:8). This means in principle that no area of human experience can be said to be alien to worship.

Idowu avers that at the time of his writing, this consideration was to be found neither in the mainline Protestant churches, nor in what he almost ridicules as the "go-as-you-please" worship services of the Evangelical churches. The latter, he says, gave the impression of being more of a "concert" than worship. But the Catholic Church, which he praises as being perhaps more adaptable in other respects than its Protestant counterparts, also failed in this area on account of its rigid formalism. In Idowu's opinion, "A predominantly 'objective' liturgy," which he sees as characteristic of the Catholic Church, "is unsuitable in most of Nigeria because it is in the nature of Nigerians to participate actively and vocally in worship and feel that they are really involved in it. What gets them in the Roman Catholic ritual is the fact that it strongly appeals to them as a European system of incantation and magic. Disillusion them about this and the whole thing would look to them as little more than a gorgeous pantomime" (Idowu 1973:29).

Is what Idowu describes about the Christian churches' liturgical malaise still true today, a little less than four decades later? A visit to any mission-instituted church, urban or rural, in any part of East Africa at least, would show that what he describes is still often true in various churches. There have been changes (Chitando 2000:296–310) but it cannot be denied that too many of the official liturgical prayers and songs in many mainline Protestant churches in Africa still have a distinctly European flavor of text and melody; many of them are merely translations of the European originals. Moreover, these are largely literal translations, not what linguists refer to as "dynamic equivalents." Nevertheless, even when the latter effort is made, it remains true that "using Western melodies to accompany African translations of Western hymns . . . [is] like speaking disjunct English with the stresses and syllable breaks in all the wrong places" (*JoT* 1993:34). Where the Evangelical churches and especially the Pentecostals are concerned, the case may be said to be worse: they have imported almost wholly American-type "concert" services. They distinguish themselves, like their American mentors, by the quantity and quality of their electronic equipment and sound systems.

In the main, the Catholic Church has likewise found it hard to relinquish its uniform objectivism. In the research conducted in Kenya, Tanzania, and Uganda reported in Part One, most of these complaints were noted. People felt that worship services were too formal and dull, without sufficient participation by the worshipers. In fact, this was one of the reasons people who still considered themselves Catholics, nevertheless frequented Protestant or AIC worship services.

Ncozana attributes the situation prevalent in the African mainline churches to the continuing predominance of Western church power in Africa: from theological training to architecture, and from style of preaching to liturgical dress. What kind of long-term spiritual nourishment do these provide African Christians, he wonders? The challenge for ritual worship in Africa is, as he sees it, to "transform" Western forms of worship that are not in tune with the African ritual search for the divine so that Africans can rediscover their identity and "and bring out sharply the Africanness of the church" (see *JoT* 1993:9).

In order to create an environment for worship from the heart, there is no option for Africa but to regain its identity: the language of worship must make sense to the people. It must be one that arises out of their worldview and their contemporary situation. But, above all, as the Blantyre conference concluded, it must be a positive kind of language, "helping us to see ourselves reflected in God not as dark aberrations that need enlightening but as God's created people." This kind of language of worship "will allow us to depart worship knowing that we have celebrated our lives, our humanity":

From this . . . sense of self-identity we can then cultivate our capacity for self-determination, whereby we can build the ability to overcome hurdles that are political, social, and economic. Self-determination produces empowered individuals and communities that can help lead our people to a new day of liberation. This is why attaining our own identity as African Christians and reinforcing that identity liturgically is so important. (*JoT* 1993:16).

With expressions such as "self-identity," "self-determination," "self-knowledge," and so on, we should not understand self-centeredness, either personal or cultural. From a theological point of view, these are a summons by God for the human person or the community to come to know God through what God has given them and made them to be. This summons, as Baum tells us, is present in the dynamics that constitute who we are as individuals and as a people, our history and culture. Our response to this summons, Baum insists, "evoked by the power of the divine call," cannot be but a response to divine revelation. Therefore, "entry into self-knowledge *is* divine revelation" (Baum 1970:157; see also Lumbala 1998:4). It is an act of constant conversion, of knowing ourselves as God knows us.

The point being made here is that it is very difficult to begin to integrate life with the divine will—which liturgy is supposed to lead toward—if the community lives on "borrowed" material, mental, and linguistic categories of good and bad, or right and wrong, indifferent to or unconvinced of these things' worth or usefulness in their personal or social life. In other words, if the symbols we use in liturgy do not, or cannot lead us to self-identity and knowledge as we have explained them above, they are spiritually without value. For example, if the ring is seen culturally as merely a modern ornament, it will not act as a sign of unity between a woman and man in marriage, or a sign of commitment to Christ in the religious life. Moreover, if people have been socialized that it is rude to be totally silent and serious of face—and polite to joyfully sing and clap—in the presence of a great person, silent and pious meditation before the Blessed Sacrament will not seem a respectful attitude of worship. Further, whereas covering the head with a veil may be a sign of modesty for women as they enter a sacred building, wearing a hat for men may mean just the opposite—ultimate pride. The examples can be multiplied without end, and we will look at some major ones below. But we always need to keep in mind the cultural relevancy of language, symbols, and signs—the sources of revelation—as we think about spirituality. It is in these that the power of ritual lies.

THE POWER OF RITUAL CELEBRATION

The power of the Christian liturgy rests in the fact that it makes present and effective, under the veil of sacred times and places, and sacred signs and symbols, the mysteries of human salvation brought about by the life, death and resurrection of Jesus Christ. But ritual celebration and its significance are not restricted to Christianity; they are a feature of all cultures and all human beings throughout the world. Ritual action gathers life together, as it were, for those participating in it. Its symbols are intended to lead participants to dimensions of reality deeper than the merely visible. But it does this through a process of "veiling" and "unveiling." It unveils the mysteries of existence without allowing human beings to completely grasp them. In this sense it veils them. It explores the Promised Land, but never allows us to set foot there. "Humans are made in this way," declares Lumbala (1998:4), "always searching beyond themselves."

Rituals differ from culture to culture in structure and form. Some are simple and almost informal and others are complex and formalized. Nevertheless, the aims and purpose of ritual celebration among peoples the world over are similar: to get in touch with humanity's human condition and to link it in a special and intense way with spiritual powers.

Accordingly, in less formalized and stratified cultures, ritual celebration usually takes place when there is evident need, either to petition the Divine and/or other divine powers or to thank them for favors needed or received. Such celebrations would therefore take place during times of either blessing or affliction—harvest time, birth, marriage, initiation, death, accession to leadership positions, war, and other significant stages in the life of the individual and the community. This is the case with traditional African rituals. But the encounter between Christianity and African religiosity presents both with the question of how to integrate them without losing the specific values each brings to the equation. This is what we now wish to address by stressing the African values we think should enrich Christianity in Africa.

Ritual and Cosmic Unity

One of the most important contributions that African religiosity can offer to African Christianity is its acute consciousness of the unity between humanity and the visible and invisible universe, especially during worship. This awareness arises out of the realization that all morality, grace as well as sin, is acted out in the universe and has consequences throughout it. In Christianity as it is now, the predominant consciousness may be the presence of, or the desire for the presence of, God during worship, but it rarely makes the connection between this presence and the actual condition of the world. In African religiosity, this connection is very clear; in fact, it is the sole reason for worship, to make the connection and unity ever firmer. Without it worship does not take place. Consequently, worship in African religiosity implies the "real" presence of God, either in person, or (more often) through the ancestors and other spiritual powers.

This affects the manner and style of worshiping, the language and symbols used. If the presence of God and the ancestors is real, and if they are perceived to be personal beings to the worshipers—known and respected by them—then the language of worship is bound to be conversational, intimate, and uninhibited. It will be unencumbered by undue formalism or outdated language. The spiritual beings will be addressed as parents, brothers and sisters, peace-givers, and healers, and God as the Elder of the elders. The need of the moment will determine the language used, whether it is penitent, petitioning or thankful, respectful or rude. Evil powers need not be respected; they must be cast away, and politeness is not necessary or required. (Christianity has remnants of this in its rites of exorcism.)

The signs, symbols, and body postures used will also vary according to the worship event and the need or needs intended. But the awareness of cosmic unity gives natural things a central importance in African worship as they visibly and intelligibly connect the worshipers as well as the worship activity itself to the vital powers of the universe. Thus certain trees or their branches, certain animals, stones or buildings, water or oil, or even certain colors of the dust (sand) will feature prominently in various rituals. Each has its own specific ritual message or intention, usually drawn from a foundational story. In worship, the message intended by such symbols and signs is generally known and appreciated by all since these emerge from and belong to the whole community. In a different cultural setting, they would make no sense at all, or perhaps they would take on a different meaning than the one intended here. And thus they would be misunderstood. In other words, to be meaningful, ritual signs and symbols and body postures cannot be arbitrarily imposed; they must be "worn like clothing and dwelt in by the person who performs them" (Lumbala 1998:4–5).

In his *Worship as Body Language*, Elochukwu E. Uzukwu shows that in Africa the human body is the ritual "*primal symbol.*" As the instrument of communication among human beings and between them and the divine powers, the body is the central instrument of the unity of the cosmos. Ritual symbols, signs, and gestures converge in the gestures of the body and derive their meaning from them. What are interpreted as the most significant aspects of the body and of bodily functions for promoting life will in Africa be highly significant for ritual as well. One may mention, as examples, all aspects of sexuality, bodily gestures and movement, human voice, spittle, hair, and so on (Lumbala 1998:3). Explains Uzukwu (1997:10): "In gestures (verbal and nonverbal) the self reveals itself . . . as one complex reality—visible yet invisible; corporeal-incorporeal; part of, but also the center of, a complex universe of interaction. The rhythm of interaction in this universe is discovered, re-created, and expressed bodily by humans."

Promoting gestures in ritual that encourage the expression of and passion for interaction of all the vital powers in the universe should be the central concern of African Christianity at this time. The need for cosmic unity is the reason ritual exists: positively, to associate the human with the powers of good or, negatively, to ward off undesirable influences of the powers of evil. As I have indicated, the implications of this for prayer, music, sacraments, art, sacred space, posture, and all else in Christian liturgy are all-encompassing. Of all aspects of planned inculturation in Africa today, inculturating gestures in ritual should be the most daring. Inculturation of the liturgy is the only way to vindicate the maturity of African theology and to encourage its further development. This is how close theology and liturgy are connected in the life of the church.

Consequently, we make bold practical suggestions in the pages that follow. This is not to say, however, that they are without firm foundation. They are founded on the research results we have cited in the first part of this book, on the personal observation and experience of many Christians—both experts and ordinary—and on serious scholarship.

(Joyful) Noises and Movements

Noises and bodily movements, or music and dance, were part and parcel of Old Testament (Temple) worship. This is perhaps most clearly illustrated in 2 Samuel 6:5 concerning the transfer of the Ark of the Covenant from the northern kingdom of Judah to Jerusalem. David and "thirty thousand" men accompanied it on this trip, making merry "before the LORD with all their strength, with singing and with citharas, harps, tambourines, sistrums and cymbals." It can also be seen in the first verses of Psalm 92. But Psalm 150, called the grand finale of the psalter, is no less clear. It does nothing but urge the worshipers to use their musical instruments to shout and dance in praise of the Lord God:

> Praise the LORD in his sanctuary,
> praise him in the firmament of his strength.
> Praise him for his mighty deeds,
> praise him for his sovereign majesty.
> Praise him with the blast of the trumpet,
> praise him with lyre and harp.
> Praise him with timbrel and dance,
> praise him with strings and pipe.
> Praise him with sounding cymbals,
> praise him with clanging cymbals.
> Let everything that has breath
> praise the LORD! Alleluia.

In the New Testament, we glimpse the significance of song and dance in Christian life and worship in the instruction that Paul gives to the Ephesians (5:19): He commands the Christians to greet one another in song, in "psalms and hymns and spiritual songs, singing and playing to the Lord in your hearts." This is the general observation that we can make for every epoch of the Christian liturgy, that liturgy sees the Christian community "at sacred play." Like any other drama, it often involves music and dance when occasioned to foster the expression of deep human emotion.

Our interest here is the African church at sacred play, so there is no need to go into the details of how this has taken shape in other cultures at other times. Nevertheless, it is worth noting that the forms and instruments of liturgical worship, from the Old Testament on, have arisen from what the relevant culture had to offer. If anything is incontestable in liturgical history it is this. One wonders how it could be otherwise.

It would be ridiculous to imagine that Christians would invent musical instruments unknown in the prevailing culture to be used only in worship. It would be equally absurd to assert that Christian dance forms would be totally different from any other: the human body is capable of limited movements. It is true that instruments, sounds, and body movements can be adjusted for purposes of worship, and their meaning modified or even changed. This has been the case throughout the world. But this is not the same as saying that they are completely different instruments and movements. There is a bit more leeway with words to construct meaning in speech or song, but often the same rules apply or can be used to achieve the desired result.

The drum. Church music in many Christian denominations in Africa has been enriched over the years by the introduction of musical instruments such as the organ, piano, keyboard, guitar, and others. This is a blessing and is in line with the principle of cross-cultural fertilization. What was negative in the early days of missionary work was the condemnation of African instruments as unworthy for use in Christian worship and their complete replacement. In the established churches, where worship styles are modeled on those of the metropolises, the tendency to replace African instruments such as gongs, rattles, hand-pianos, and fiddles may still be noticed, even though they are not explicitly condemned.

In traditional African musicology, pride of place must go to the drum, the emotional impact of which few other instruments can equal (Nketia 1958:63). But the drum is not only an accompaniment; in many cases it enjoys an independent existence in a way that the organ and other instruments do not. The drum is often a symbol of authority in Africa and as such calls for a kind of respect in ways that gongs and rattles, for example, never did. The drum thus not only accompanied songs, but summoned meetings, relayed messages, and even summoned and announced the presence of spiritual powers. Some of these functions have, of course, been superseded by new scientific media which many Africans, especially the youth, have embraced. Nevertheless, the use of the drum as symbolic of (thunderous) divine power and its effect on the African psyche and emotions have as a whole not been superseded. In fact, in the African context, the drum reveals divine power.

Citing G. Niangoran-bouah with approval, Uzukwu (1997:12) compares the unique place of the drum in Africa to its place in the Bible and Koran: in African rituals it not only evoked and conveyed the foundational story ("primordial word") of the group, it often stood as the foundational story. More than in the Bible and Koran, playing the ritual drum in Africa elicited bodily movements and gestures as well as mental states that made the cosmic unity immediately palpable to the hearts and minds of the worshipers. It connects people to the earth and to the spiritual beings.

For this reason it is often used in the AICs in the rite of exorcism. In charismatic movements in the Catholic Church a degree of exorcism takes place that is just as dramatic as its traditional African counterpart (though

I suspect many in this movement would deny the validity of this comparison). There is no reason why the use of the drum should not be customary in such situations. Indeed, among the African rural populations, it remains the best instrument for recalling the foundational story of the Christ-event—the birth, ministry, death and resurrection of Jesus. It must also be given a prominent place in the celebration of the sacraments, especially the Eucharist, as the central sign of the remembrance (*memoria*) of the creation and ongoing re-creation of the Christian community. Here, dance, which the playing of the drum oftentimes urges, comes into play.

Song and dance. In his book, *The Spirit of the Liturgy*, Cardinal Joseph Ratzinger (2000:198–199) is categorical: "Dancing is not a form of expression for the Christian liturgy." It has pagan and heretical origins and implications, he argues, and its earliest advocates in the Christian era thought that it could take the place of the Cross since they really did not believe in the reality of the passion of Jesus Christ. "The cultic dances of the different religions," the cardinal emphasizes, "have different purposes—incantation, imitative magic, mystical ecstasy—none of which is compatible with the essential purpose of the liturgy of the 'reasonable sacrifice.'" He thinks that the purpose of dancing is to make the liturgy "attractive," the goal of which is to elicit applause.

Obviously, I cannot defend "inculturation" as it happens in other regions of the world, but few African worshipers would feel themselves fairly described in the cardinal's remarks. Dancing in the context of authentic African worship is not a spectacle, a display, a show, an act of entertainment; it is an integral part of worship in which all worshipers participate. There is certainly no "applause" after the dancing has run its course because it is harmonious and consistent with the whole act of worship. Ratzinger speaks approvingly of the "rhythmically ordered procession" of the Zairian liturgy and describes it as "very much in keeping with the dignity of the occasion." Yet, although this rite is a step toward an inculturated eucharistic liturgy in Africa (see Chapter 13), it is weakest precisely in this respect: it has been doctored too much to look respectable to an aesthetic, "a beauty," that is fundamentally not African.

Bujo (2001:39–40) is right:

Within the framework of the idea of *memoria*, dance is no mere choreography in which human beings reveal their ability and talent. Rather, it is a language that intends to communicate the deeper dimensions of the total reality of life. To see a kind of folkloristic beauty in African dance is to fail to grasp the depth of transcendental experience which is expressed by the person dancing. This is because the human being in Africa dances his own life. In fact, all existential events are danced: birth, marriage, and death, but also the new moon, political events, and so on. The various genres of dance express various hidden religious dimensions. For example, the dance can tell about pain and suffering, about joy and sadness, about love and thankfulness. It is always a cantatory, narrative *poiesis*, which makes the message from beyond the grave a present reality in solidarity with the entire fellowship.

Solomon Mbabi-Katana (see *JoT* 1993:34) makes the same point:

> Africans have always relied upon music to express their feelings and emotion. To the traditional African, music is not a luxury but a way of life. It is through music that Africans achieve communication with past life. It is through music that the medicine man heals the sick and dying. It is through music that mourning for the dead is most effectively accomplished. Funeral and succession ceremonies are dominated by music. Music plays a dominant role in infancy and puberty rites. Ceremonies such as weddings in traditional African settings are dominated by music whose texts are meaningful and have a lasting effect on the wedded couple.

Mbabi-Katana refers here to "traditional Africa," but what he says applies also to contemporary Africa. The love for music by African youth is remarkable. The ceremonies that Mbabi-Katana mentions, weddings, baptisms, even casual social gatherings are never quite complete without music—only oftentimes now it is music without useful instruction, contrary to tradition. But if you are in pastoral ministry anywhere in East Africa, for example— as I have been for almost three decades—you will not fail to notice that huge blaring radio-cassette players accompany bridal parties, together with dancing and ululation to the music, as far as the church door. As required by mainline church etiquette and aesthetics, things become quiet and somber— "dignified"?—in the church building itself. But the music is turned on again as soon as the service inside the church building is over.

It can be said with Ncozana in this regard that body language accompanying music can sometimes convey the spirit of worship better than can any other kind of expression. Again, the AICs have succeeded in this much better than the mainline churches; its members are not negatively self-conscious when they use this form of worship (see *JoT* 1993:10). The members of these churches march in the streets to the accompaniment of music and dance, inviting any and all to join in. But the music and dancing continue in the church building. They are used in exorcism and healing, both of which form a big part of AIC worship services.

It will be up to African musicians and liturgists to work out for the church what kind of music and dance are appropriate to which ritual. They will need the help and participation of rural folk from the different ethnic groups to gain an insight into the symbolism and functions of the various dances and the musical instruments used in them. What do the body movements and gestures mean when used in a certain context? They may be appropriate in one context but not in another. Catholic churches all over the continent today have "liturgical dance" during eucharistic celebrations. Unfortunately, however, this kind of dance is not integrated in the entire liturgy, but is appended to the Mass during the entrance, offertory, and final processions. As such, it often functions as a distraction, especially when it is performed by children.

Integrating African dance into the liturgy, if properly done, will not turn worship into the "concert" that Idowu decries in the Pentecostal churches. By definition a concert is a spectator performance, requiring performers and spectators or listeners. In African dance ritual there are no performers and watchers. All are performers. There are leaders, to be sure, but leadership in this sense does not imply monopolizing the performance. The leaders help everyone be integrated into the action of worship. In the African view of things, everyone present is an equal participant in the worship event.

It is here, by the way, that the new liturgical songs fall short of African expectations in worship, at least in the Catholic Church. Big strides have been made in composing songs to African melody and rhythm inspired by scriptural and other faith themes after the Council. Their effect on the hearts and minds of Christians as pedagogical instruments has been remarkable. But the idea of a choir that sings and the rest listens undercuts the sense of communal participation in worship, which is further undercut by the use of the organ, piano, and so on. In communal worship, the drum is not an instrument for listening, but for participation in dance. This fact needs to be carefully considered by liturgical musicians, and it brings us to a consideration of liturgical space.

Sacred Space and Time

Sacred space. One may be allowed to ask hypothetical but relevant questions concerning the architecture of the churches, cathedrals, and basilicas that the missionaries brought with them and spread all over the continent. What form would spaces of worship have taken had they arisen from within the worship experience of Africa itself? Would our church buildings be "designed with arched windows, a high tower with a bell, as in England or France or any other part of the western world?" (see *JoT* 1993:39). Would we have the altars where they are now? Would the benches or chairs be arranged in the same way, or would they be there at all? These questions are important because they apply to many other things that missionary Christianity brought with it as part of "proper" Christian worship. But they imply a certain theology, ecclesiology, and aesthetic.

The case for "synchronizing" liturgical space and African symbol systems was made by Andrew Muwowo at the Blantyre conference. Muwowo (see *JoT* 1993:39) advocates designing and constructing buildings for worship that bear "some African significance." For him this implies rotund structures because he thinks that this is the artistic tradition of Africa: "round huts, stools, and circular dance formation." Rotund structures would certainly facilitate the physical setting for worship on account of their familiarity. I think, though, that what is more important is how the space within the structure is used. Chairs or benches should be arranged so that there is plenty of space in the building for people to move around freely. Current arrangements confine worshipers and are not conducive to body movement other than swaying.

In this matter of sacred space, even the bigger AICs, which can afford chairs and benches, imitate the Western churches and overlook the need for free space. The smaller AICs, which worship in the open air or cannot afford chairs in their buildings, are much more inspirational. There is much more movement and communal participation in their liturgical action.

Given the mood for worship that the missionary church bequeathed to Africa, in which piety meant somberness, African ritual dance may appear somewhat chaotic. But we must recall in this case again what de Mello says about spirituality: if such movement helps to connect people with God, if it aids them in the task of inner transformation, it must be considered a positive element and not be curtailed. The appropriateness of something like this can be judged only within the culture; that kind of judgment cannot legitimately and validly be imposed from the aesthetics of another culture.

Sacred time. This is another element of communal worship about which African Christianity has not been allowed sufficient say. But its importance cannot be overemphasized. Much, though not all of it is practical in nature. It would be ridiculous, for example, liturgically to celebrate the harvest season during the time of planting, or to use symbols of death when one wants to celebrate life. The commemorative, recalling, or making-present aspect of the sacred events that sacred time suggests gains its fullest impact when it is synchronized as much as possible with "real" time in terms of seasons, and so on. In the *Constitution on the Sacred Liturgy (Sacrosanctum Concilium*, n. 102), Vatican II explains that in the course of the year the church has established a calendar in which "she unfolds the whole mystery of Christ from the incarnation and nativity to the ascension, to Pentecost and the expectation of the blessed hope of the coming of the Lord." This includes Sunday, the Lord's Day, and days commemorating martyrs and other saints whose lives of perfection the church puts forward as examples for the faithful to follow.

Except for Sunday, which the Council in this Constitution (n. 106) characterizes as "the original feast day" (and whose observance can be traced back to the earliest Christian practices), the Constitution (n. 107) does not close the door on necessary adaptations of the liturgical year. It only cautions that care must be taken so that the "specific character" of "the traditional customs and discipline of the sacred seasons shall be preserved or restored" in order to "nourish the piety of the faithful who celebrate the mysteries of the Christian redemption and, above all, the paschal mystery." This may be done by the "competent territorial ecclesiastical authority" with regard to "sacraments, sacramentals, processions, liturgical language, sacred music and the arts" (*SC*, n. 39). In case there is a need for even "more radical" adjustment:

- The local ecclesiastical authorities have to study which new local cultural and geographical values and elements must be taken into account in divine worship;
- The local church may be allowed to experiment with innovations to determine their suitability for Christian worship in the long run;
- It is recommended that local experts be involved in the study and formulation of the innovations that may be deemed necessary for the church in question (SC, n. 40).

For the Catholic Church, the renewal of the liturgy took place in several areas in the years following the Council, although events show that this is not an exercise that can completely have come to an end. The recent controversial ICEL (International Commission on English in the Liturgy) issue is a case in point: How do the English-speaking regions of the world translate scriptural readings or liturgical prayers originally written in Latin so that they make sense to modern English speakers? The question, as we have already noted, applies in various ways to Africa as well (and we shall touch upon it once again below). But here let us briefly consider the global question of the liturgical year.

Five seasons form the liturgical year in the Catholic Church: Advent, Christmas, Lent, Easter, and Ordinary Time. Their dating is complex and, as Monica K. Hellwig points out (see Glazier/Hellwig 1994:516), draws from a variety of sources, many of which were pagan. On account of the predominance of Roman religion when Christianity was being developed, some of its feasts were simply taken over and "Christianized." Many others, to do with the saints and particular devotions, also developed as Christianity spread throughout Europe, particularly during patristic and medieval times. They usually developed in a local church and were eventually taken over by the whole church.

However, each of the seasons of the liturgical year emphasizes a fundamental mystery in the economy of salvation: anticipating the birth of the Lord during Advent; celebrating his presence among us during Christmas; recalling his suffering and death for our sake during Lent; reliving his resurrection and ascension during Easter; and commemorating the significance of the entire covenant relationship between God and us during Ordinary Time. No one can say that any one of these mysteries of faith should not be commemorated in the Catholic Church. But given varying chronological, geographical, and climactic conditions, local churches are entitled to investigate *when* in their region they should be celebrated so as to make maximum sense and impact.

One recalls in connection with this that, until the end of the second century, the church in the West and East celebrated Easter on different dates, with the latter looking at the crucifixion as Easter. Victor I's (189–198 C.E.) attempt to force through a uniform Roman date for all the churches failed. It is also worth recalling that Christmas, celebrated in the West on December

25, is observed in the East on January 6; at any rate, it does not depict the exact birthday of Jesus. As Hellwig (see Glazier/Hellwig 1994:516) again notes, the dating of the Nativity does have "some connection with the winter solstice, pagan worship of the unconquered sun, and pagan winter festivals."

These examples give an idea of just what it takes to achieve radical inculturation in different localities. I will not presume to say which dates need what adjustments in the Roman liturgical year. I merely want to suggest, however, that African liturgists need to revisit the liturgical calendar and determine for the ecclesiastical authorities its relevance for the seasons of equatorial and tropical Africa, most of whose languages, for example, do not even have a word for snow in their vocabulary. Where "sacral time" is concerned, Uzukwu (1997:228) is correct when he notes that perhaps "the unique contribution of Africans to religious practice is the experience of the transcendent in the ordinary, of ancestral time in durational time, the one not destroying but revealing the other." The temporal periods and material symbols that are used to express this experience in Africa need to be recaptured in the inculturation process.

Cardinal Ratzinger (2000:103–105), however, firmly disputes this. He concedes that cosmic symbolism is extremely important in Christian worship, and that the symbolism now official in the church pertains to the northern hemisphere. He admits that in the southern hemisphere things are just the opposite. For him, "This raises the question of 'inculturation' with great urgency." But he rejects the possibility of change or adjustment: we cannot conform the historical events of the mystery of Christ to cosmic requirements. Because Christianity is not a "cosmic" but a "historical" religion, history has priority.

Given the conditions of inculturation I have tried to spell out in Part Two, as well as some of the changes that have been officially authorized by the Catholic Church—not to mention other, apparently non-cosmic, churches—I find it hard to understand arguments that do not seem to appreciate the locality of "the different other" and definitively subordinate identity and meaning to a sort of frozen history.

Gestures

We have previously observed that, however flexible and maneuverable it may be, the human body is ultimately limited in the forms of gestures and movements it can perform. Typical among ritual gestures in all religions apart from dance, though with certain minor variations from place to place, include: sitting, standing, squatting, kneeling, and lying down. Others are bowing, raising hands, waving, holding the palms of the hands together, shaking the whole or part of the body, shedding tears silently, gazing or looking intently, and so on. Still others include kissing, licking, holding hands, and even sexual activity. We will consider silent gestures in this section. Verbal gestures, such as shouting, wailing, grunting, laughing, and so on, will be discussed below under the category of ritual word.

If these are common ritual gestures, what distinguishes them can be summarized in this question: *When* in liturgy are they used and *to signify what*? In other words, how are they ritualized, to represent what meaning, and to achieve what attitude among the worshipers? It can easily be appreciated that whatever meaning a silent gesture is supposed to attain is completely a cultural construct; in the case of liturgy it is a cultural-religious one. The meaning of any one gesture is never a given, nor is the inner way of thinking and social behavior the gesture is expected to bring about. Thus kissing, or the striking of one's breast, or holding hands, or using the left or right hand to handle and pass things on, can and do signify different things to different peoples, and even to the same peoples in different circumstances. They might even signify nothing at all and so to the uninitiated remain mere curiosities, hocus-pocus. One might think that something as fundamental as the sexual act would mean the same thing to all peoples in all situations. But that is not the case. It would appear, in fact, that the more basic something is—say, sexual activity, or eating, or drinking—the more numerous are the meanings attached to it depending on when it is brought into ritual play.

In the religious ritual context, all gestures are given an ethical significance which confers a sacred character on them. This is why they are ritualized, that is, made repetitive and maintained for a long time. And even though over time the manner they are used or their significance or both may evolve, a religiosity or organized religion will usually maintain that such evolution or change has not taken place.

The need for inculturation of ritual gesture can be illustrated by a couple of examples that contrast Western missionary ritual practice introduced into African Catholicism and African ritual expectations. On the face of it, they may appear trivial, but that just may be the point. If we can be so wide of the mark in small things, I hate to imagine what confusion and harm can be done among a people where more significant gestures are concerned. I take the gestures of kissing and the striking of the breast. I choose these for two reasons: (a) because they are widely in use in the liturgy of the mass in Africa, and (b) because on their own they can be described as "neutral," in the sense that they are not judged as either "civilized" or "uncivilized." These two gestures are given different meanings in different cultures; that's all. And since their meaning may vary among other peoples within the East Africa region, I will also discuss them in the context of one ethnic group, the Wakwaya-Wajita around Lake Victoria in northwestern Tanzania. Many other ethnic groups will identify themselves with this as well.

Kissing. Several times during the celebration of the Mass in the Catholic Church, the rubrics direct that the priest kiss the altar or the book of the Gospels. Shortly after reciting the Lord's Prayer, before communion, the faithful are invited to share a sign of peace. In the West this can be given as a kiss, normally among people of the opposite sex who know one another well. A kiss in Western culture is a sign of affection and even veneration, as when a person kisses a picture of a saint or a parent. A kiss is usually given and received on the cheek or on the lips. In the latter case, when it is prolonged, it has amorous significance, connoting romantic love. All these types of kissing may be and are performed in public in the Western world without any kind of social disapproval or sanction.

Not so in many aspects in traditional—and to a great extent, even in modern—Africa. Among the Wakwaya-Wajita kissing is not a gesture that is culturally indigenous. It is performed as an "imported" gesture and carries with it an amorous connotation when people of the opposite sex engage in it. As a rule it is considered indecent to kiss in public and is consequently proscribed even for married couples. Among the Wakwaya-Wajita, it would be socially unacceptable to kiss someone with whom the rules of avoidance apply: for example, between son- and mother-in-law or father- and daughter-in-law, between mother and son or brother and sister. For this ethnic group the only time kissing is unambiguous is when a mother kisses her baby.

So, what does kissing in the eucharistic liturgy as required (or suggested) by the Roman Catholic rubrics signify to a congregation of the Wakwaya-Wajita? At the very least, it is an empty gesture, without meaning, since the things kissed are inanimate. It does not enhance the devotion of either the African priest or of his assembly. This is sad, because other cultural gestures are available to them that would express very well devotion, affection or reverence. Notice, for instance, what people do when they are left free to venerate the crucifix as they wish on Good Friday. There is indeed some kissing of Christ's image, but among the Wakwaya-Wajita the most common gestures are touching, in the form of cupping the image with both hands while kneeling and bowing deeply. The older people tend to lick Christ's image, perhaps thinking that this is what kissing is.

In the missal for Africa, if I may now generalize, the rubric of kissing the altar or the Bible should be rescinded. It will not be hard to find other appropriate gestures to replace it. One would be bowing deeply before the altar or the Bible or the crucifix; another would be touching them with the palms of both one's hands extended downward; a third would be just to go around the altar or hold the Bible up high for a while. I suspect that there would be little difficulty in finding a common gesture relevant to a large region, even for the whole continent south of the Sahara.

Striking the breast. The problem here is similar to the above. Repentance, sorrow, and apology (*mea culpa*) in the West may be expressed by the gesture of striking one's breast several times with one's fist. At the beginning of the canon of the Mass, the rubrics indicate this for the prayer of repentance. Although present in the culture of the Wakwaya-Wajita, the gesture expresses anything but remorse for wrongdoing, and rather the contrary. To strike one's breast is meant as a challenge and is often used to dare someone to "cross the line," as it were, and face the consequences. As such it is most inappropriate for repentance. For the Wakwaya-Wajita, crossing one's hands over one's chest while slightly bowed serves this purpose best. There is no reason why this or a similar gesture should not be used to indicate guilt and penitence.

Of course, we are not trying to say by these examples that the Wakwaya-Wajita should not borrow gestures from other cultures. We are simply stating again what we have repeatedly affirmed in this study. Cultural cross-fertilization takes place most meaningfully and bears transforming fruit only when it is not imposed. It must grow organically from the experience of the people themselves.

RITUAL WORDS AND ACTIONS

Not all gestures and actions in the liturgy are accompanied by words. However, many are, simply because a gesture or action may be misunderstood if it is not explained. The function of the word in ritual is therefore to explain and clarify, to vindicate a gesture or action. When the same word or words accompany certain gestures or actions and are, as it were, attached to them, they become ritual words. A good example in Catholic Christianity is the sign of the cross, or the ritual blessing in the name of the Trinity, or the canon prayers of the Mass. Here specific words are attached to specific actions, almost to the extent that, if the words are not said in the exact prescribed way, the gesture is rendered invalid or ineffective. The reverse is also true: if the gesture or action is not performed in the prescribed manner, the words become meaningless, mere words without the power intended by them. We find this across all Christian denominations and even across religions and faiths.

Preaching. At initiations in Komo, Mali, the people sing a song about the power of the word as follows:

> The word is everything
> It cuts, flays.
> It models, modulates.
> It perturbs, maddens. It heals or kills.
> It amplifies or lowers according to its force.
> It excites or calms souls. (See Uzukwu 1997:271)

In Christianity the word as explanation is used most extensively in the homily or preaching. Even though the words used in preaching are not the same at every liturgical occasion, Christian leaders use the homily to explain the scriptures to the assembly. When this is not the immediate object of the homily, scriptural references are nevertheless often employed to drive home whatever point the homily is trying to make, usually a concretely moral, ethical one. So, it is legitimate to characterize the homily as a ritual word. In the Catholic Church, Vatican II, faithful to the practice of the early church, emphasized that the homily should be an integral part of the eucharistic liturgy (for example, see *Sacrosanctum Concilium*, n. 35, 52).

In the view of Vatican II, preaching is therefore a ministry which should be taken most seriously, and for which ministers should be carefully prepared (for example, see *Lumen Gentium*, nn. 25, 28; *Christus Dominus*, n. 12; and *Presbyterorum Ordinis*, n. 4). A document of the Congregation for the Clergy (1999:20) on the vocation of the priest in the Catholic Church emphasizes this point, saying:

Elegant and accurate language, comprehensible to contemporary men and women of all social backgrounds, is always useful for preaching. Banal and commonplace language should be eschewed. While preachers must speak from an authentic vision of the faith, a vocabulary must be employed which is comprehensible in all quarters and must avoid specialized jargon. . . . Preachers should know their objectives and have a good understanding of the existential and cultural reality of their congregations. Theories and abstract generalizations must always be avoided. Hence every preacher should know his own flock well and use an attractive style which, rather than wounding people, strikes the conscience.

As the principal way of announcing the good news of Jesus Christ, preaching is a means of grace and as proclamation cannot be separated from the church. It is in fact the "mother" of the church; it gave birth to it in accordance with the will of Christ to his disciples, whom he directed to go, proclaim, and baptize. "Proclamation" refers directly to announcing the story of Jesus Christ, as all the Gospels show, and this is the most fundamental purpose of Christian preaching. But understandably, it has also taken different forms in the history of the church.

Early in the sub-apostolic period, preaching was influenced by the apologetics made necessary by the thriving Gnostic movements. This is already quite clear in the epistles, but especially so in the writings of the Fathers. In medieval times preaching was dominated by an overly intellectual flavor, sometimes far removed from the practical demand of the Gospel. During and after the Protestant Reformation, preaching in the Catholic Church once again became defensive, and confined itself to justifying pronouncements by the hierarchy. It had indeed become, as noted liturgist Joseph Jungmann characterized it, "the vulgarization of theological tracts" (see Hilkert 1990:997). Since Vatican II the struggle in the Catholic Church has been to return to preaching as proclaiming the good news of Christ.

From the African perspective, preaching as ritual word must be seen to derive from three sources: (a) from the fact that it flows from and is related to the Bible—that is, it is power in itself; (b) from the fact that it is uttered by an elder (whoever the preacher is) who represents the people—that is, it has power because it derives from the angst of the community; and (c) from the fact that it is a ritual word uttered during and accompanying ritual "cosmic" action (worship)—that is, it has power because of its function to gather together the whole universe—the spirits, humanity (including the unborn), and the rest of creation—in an intense period of recognizing mutual dependence.

In the African context, preaching is always a solemn action. Because the requirements of a life pleasing to God are explained here, the homily must always be a moral injunction, either in praise of a communal life well led, or against a communal life that has been offensive to God. In either case, instruction is involved. Even though the word preached is uttered by a human being, it is perceived as coming from God. The preacher does not speak in his or her own name but in the name of God (or, in many AICs, the ancestors) to the assembly or, as we shall see below, in the name of the assembly to God (or the ancestors or spirits). Skill in preaching may differ in different persons, but the basic belief remains that the preacher is an "envoy" or "mouthpiece" of God. Hence the respect that anyone (trained or untrained) who preaches the word of God enjoys in African Christianity.

Analyzing 299 AIC sermons in Malawi, Hilary B. P. Mijoga (2001) arrives at a conclusion contrary to what many African theologians have made, perhaps without adequate practical research. He found that sermons in the AICs do not exhibit exceptional attention to elements of African culture any more than does preaching in the mainline Christian churches. He argues, for example, that the AICs' use of African practices, such as telling stories, citing proverbs, or singing songs in the sermon, occur no more frequently than in established churches.

From his analysis, Mijoga asserts that, if preaching were the criterion, AICs cannot be said to be "vanguards of African culture." He points out that even the moral themes addressed replicate those encountered in the mainline churches—themes like "adultery, stealing, drunkenness, pride, jealousy, lying, unbelief, witchcraft, in that order" (Mijoga 2001:143–68, at p. 161). If Mijoga is right in his contention, this is because these preachers try to identify as much as possible what they say with the Bible as the "word of God," so as to draw authority from it. Indeed, the sermons that Mijoga quotes throughout the book seem to indicate this. For this reason, interpretation of the scriptural text(s) is minimal and application to the issue(s) at hand almost literal.

Nevertheless, the African assemblies as listeners—whether in the AICs or in the mainline churches—bring with them characteristic African attitudes. They receive the ritual word in the sermon or homily as the power of God, which is why they rarely question what the preacher says even if they may disagree with it. Questioning the authority of the preacher is equated to questioning the authority of God in the Bible. The task for inculturation in all Christian churches as far as preaching is concerned then seems to be the same. To drive the message of the Gospel home, preachers must learn to employ styles of oratory that carry with them a characteristically African flavor, including, as Mijoga mentions, story telling, use of proverbs and riddles, and illustrative songs.

On account of human sin, the power of the word of the preacher is liable to be misused. This is offset by the second attitude I have mentioned, that the power of the word of the preacher as elder simultaneously rests also in the angst of the people he or she represents and on behalf of whom he or she speaks. The vertical dimension of the homily as divine word is balanced by its horizontal, lateral dimension as human anguish or joy. The preacher, from the African perspective, must first of all be a listener.

While the African assembly may be loath to question what is said in the homily for fear of questioning God's authority, African preachers are well aware that unless they bring out the communal angst in such as a way that the assembly recognizes itself in the sermon, they risk losing members. On account of the training of its priests in Western speculative philosophy and theology, which has so far paid little attention to actual social experience, the Catholic Church is particularly vulnerable to this phenomenon. One of the reasons that some Catholics prefer to worship in other churches is precisely because they do not see their "joy and hope, grief and anguish" (*Gaudium et Spes*, n. 1) in the sermon.

Moral reality is of course the same all over the world. There is nothing in adultery, lying, stealing, murder, and drunkenness, for example, which *per se* can be said to be characteristic solely of a certain group of people. Still, the perceptions of these moral realities and their gravity in cultural systems differ. The task of the homily is to be aware of these perceptions, not to bless them, but to bring them ever closer to the expectations of the Gospel. In the African social-cultural context, the more existential the approach to these issues, the more effective the homily. For example, a theoretical treatise on the evil of polygamy would not be as effective to the ears of most Africans as would a story about how a particular individual acts against the instructions of the Gospel by being polygamous. On this issue a sermon about Matthew 19:1–12 from the Abale A Yesu Church that was recorded by Mijoga (2001:42–42) said:

> Brethren, God blessed and ordered man and woman to leave their parents and become one body. God didn't tell us to have as many wives and husbands as we want. I came across a certain man in Nkhotakota who told me that he had twelve wives. When I heard this, I didn't believe him so I arranged to pay him a visit one day despite the tight schedule I had. . . . At long last the day came and I paid him a visit. When I reached his village, I asked a young boy who was playing around if at all he knew this man and he told me that he was a son to the man I was looking for. He took me to a big house which at first I thought was a rest house. But I was shocked to learn that it was actually the house built by this man for his twelve wives. Looking at his wives, they were all beautiful ladies and I asked many questions in my heart saying: Is this not exploitation of women? Why is he having so many wives for himself? . . .
>
> Brothers and sisters, God wants us to get wives, but not to have more than one.

Mijoga's analysis of the content of AIC sermons is surprising because it shows that, although God, Christ and the Holy Spirit feature in many of them, ancestors and other spirits do not. Yet in the daily experience of most African Christians' spirituality, they are the realities that dominate. Perhaps in failing to address them in official rituals and in preaching, Christian spirituality received from the West fails the Africans. The question is therefore how these realities will be reintegrated into the African Christian worldview. In so doing the ritual for the African worshiper would become the focal point where all reality meets and where the community would refurbish its vital power in all of its aspects. The sermon is particularly privileged because it can audibly call the assembly together for this purpose.

Prayers. Writing a foreword to Ecclesiasticus around 132 B.C.E., Sirach's grandson warned readers about the difficulties of translating from one language to another:

> You are now invited to read it [the translation] in a spirit of attentive good will, with indulgence for any apparent failure on our part, despite earnest efforts, in the interpretation of particular passages. For words spoken originally in Hebrew are not as effective when they are translated into another language. That is true not only of this book but of the law itself, the prophets and the rest of the books, which differ no little when they are read in the original.

More than a century before the birth of Jesus, people were already very much aware of the shortcomings that translations inevitably cause. Yet, with practically no exception, official liturgical prayers in the Catholic Church in Africa are translations of translations. This must be the single most serious criticism against them. As translations from English of prayers originally composed and written in Latin, the prayers for the celebration of the Eucharist and other sacraments rarely capture either the style or the spirit of African praying.

For one thing, as an oral culture, African prayers during sacrifices and offerings, or during rites of passage or exorcism, or during séances were spontaneous. This enabled them to address the need for prayer directly, taking into account all, or at least the major, elements surrounding the occasion. No one, however, can insist totally on this characteristic of African prayer today in the highly formalized liturgical structures of the Christian churches. Even the more informal liturgical assemblies of the AICs use many formal and standardized forms of prayer, although they still enjoy a higher degree of spontaneous praying than, for instance, in the Catholic Church.

Nevertheless, it is necessary to point out the serious shortcomings of translated prayers and to insist on the importance of locally composed prayers if they are to take into account the imagery of the place and the gestures of the people concerned. How can the body gesture correctly accompany the word of prayer if they mean two different things? If shaking the head from side to side means yes in one culture and no in another, the "Amen" in prayer should be accompanied by whichever is appropriate to the local culture.

This is obviously important, but even more so is the sense of the prayer itself. Is it addressing matters the worshipers can relate to? For instance, when reference is made in prayer to Jesus' self- "sacrifice" on the cross, this is translated from the Latin *sacrificium*. It is translated into Swahili as *sadaka* in all the prayer books. Does it have the same meaning in all three cases? I cannot speak of the equivalence of the English to the Latin, but in Swahili the meaning intended by the notion of sacrifice in relation to the cross is really *kafara*, and not *sadaka*. The former term conveys the sense of bloody ntion on the cross. Why then has it not been used? In the African mind *kajara* denotes a messiness that does not conform with the Western (non-biblical) sanitized connotation of the reality. In this sense, the Swahili speaker misses out on many aspects of the spirituality of the notion.

Again, in the interests of spiritual cross-fertilization, not all prayers received from the West can or should be jettisoned. However, most must be. Local prayers need to emerge from local situations so that they are suited to the language and mentality of the place. As Uzukwu (1997: 265–321 and *passim*) and Lumbala (1998 *passim*) amply demonstrate, there is no lack of creativity in this area (see Chapter 13 below).

Participation in ritual action. Etymologically the word *leitourgia* (Greek for liturgy) originally held a secular meaning. It meant any service performed for the sake of others, for the common good. Later, however, it acquired an exclusively religious sense and came to be applied—as in the Greek Old Testament—to any act of public worship led by the community's ministers. Despite this development, the sense that liturgy was an action "for the sake of others," for the common good, never completely disappeared.

Although for various reasons the word liturgy was replaced in Catholic Christianity for a long time by such terms as divine or ecclesiastical office or sacred rites it was revived in the eighteenth century to denote the church's worship activity. This meaning, together with its inherent sense of being a communal act for the sake of others, was indirectly endorsed by Vatican II. The *Constitution on the Sacred Liturgy (Sacrosanctum Concilium)* describes the liturgy as an occasion where all the faithful manifest Christ in themselves and to others (n. 2), insisting (n. 7) that in the eucharistic celebration Christ is not only present in the minister, the eucharistic species, and the word preached but also in the whole community gathered together in worship and prayer.

The *Constitution* makes numerous precise rules about how and when the faithful are to participate in the common liturgical action. The spirit of these regulations is perhaps best summed up in numbers 26–31 of the *Constitution*. This section of the document casts liturgical activity in a hierarchical form, with the bishop and priests holding primary responsibility. But the document is equally clear that liturgy manifests the church as "the sacrament of unity" where everyone needs to be active. Thus, "In liturgical celebrations each person, minister, or layman who has an office to perform, should carry out all and only those parts which pertain to his office by the nature of the rite and the norms of the liturgy" (n. 28).

This is in the interests of good order, which is necessary in every public gathering and celebration. What every local church needs to look into and adjust, however, are what the document calls "the nature of the rite and the norms of the liturgy." In the experience of the Catholic Church in Africa because the nature of the liturgy and the norms of liturgical rites have been predetermined by Rome, the participation of the faithful in the liturgy has been curtailed according to the African mentality. Idowu has noted this, as we saw above. Consequently, attendance at Mass has been compared to going to a theater where the priest performs (acts) and the faithful watch.

The analogy is far from facetious. In Europe and America, it is not infrequent to hear people saying to the priest after the eucharistic liturgy, "I enjoyed *your* Mass, Father" in the same breath as "I enjoyed *your* homily, Father." This unfortunate view of the eucharistic celebration is to be found in Africa as well.

In Chapter 13 we shall offer examples of new rites that are sensitive to the African social psyche of participation. They have originated from and have been suggested for use in Africa. They are certainly not without guiding norms and are attentive to the nature of the different rites. It is only that the perception of the nature and rites of the different liturgical celebrations is essentially African. It involves much more physical movement such as dance and vocal participation (such as communal singing, prayers, and prayer responses).

SACRED IMAGES

Images, like myths, are a form of symbolic language: one picture or image can speak volumes, as the saying goes. This is true. Sculptures, paintings, pictures, and other images are important pedagogical and spiritual tools. In one form or another they are found in all cultures. Archaeology shows that they were one of the principal means of primitive human communication. Most were used to depict moral, ethical, or sacred themes.

Looking at art, one misses the point if one always insists on trying to get the "literal" meaning of a sculpture, picture or painting. Often, these are not exact representations or replicas of reality. The whole point of the icon, as Cardinal Ratzinger (2000:133) rightly points out,

> is to lead us beyond what can be apprehended at the merely material level, to awaken new senses in us, and to teach us a new kind of seeing, which perceives the Invisible in the visible. The sacredness of the image consists precisely in the fact that it comes from an interior vision and thus leads us to such an interior vision. It must be a fruit of contemplation, of an encounter in faith with the new reality of the risen Christ, and so it leads us in turn into an interior gazing, an encounter in prayer with the Lord.

Even when they are exact representations, as in photographs, one can—and in contemplation and prayer must—always read something more in them from the posture, the angle from which the photograph was taken, or from the expression of the subject or object's features. The three levels of meaning in reading sacred literature—the levels behind, within, and in front of the text—can be applied with equal validity to sacred images.

Western Christianity's sacred images, introduced into Africa during the missionary era, have played havoc with the African Christian psyche because they were presented as and almost taken for the reality they were supposed to represent. In looking for the literal, superficial meaning of these white,

Western images, the African Christian came away with the sense that the sacred could not be anything but white, with white features: that black was fit only for the depiction of the devil. But the deeper meaning behind them—the understanding of divine nature they were trying to portray—instilled in the African the same debilitating feeling of cultural, racial, and spiritual inadequacy. It is a feeling that has been difficult to change in many of the faithful.

What is needed, according to Jon Michael Spencer (see *JoT* 1993:18), is "a kind of therapy of history" and "reconciliation of history." These are deliberate efforts designed to remove the African sense of inferiority on account of skin color, and at the same time to remove the Euro-American sense of superiority for the same reason. As Spencer puts it, when Africans can "come to love and worship a Jesus who is portrayed as black, and do so without any sense of hesitation or repulsion, then we will have grown to cultivate our capacity to appreciate and love fully our blackness and our Africanness."

Cultural perceptions dictate artistic depictions. In matters sacred, cultural perceptions are compounded by human imagination about the infiniteness of sacred reality, be they God, saints, or spirits. It is for this reason that Judaism and early Christianity did not favor images of sacred reality in their places of worship; they argued that any depiction of it in art is ultimately a potentially dangerous reduction of it. Some Protestant churches—nineteenth-century Calvinism and Pietism in particular—held a similar view. They are right in that no image can capture the tremendous majesty of God or the nature of spirit existence. However, in another sense they are wrong, in that human religiosity craves divine and spiritual imaging so as to make some sense of them, in order that, as the Seventh Ecumenical Council of Nicea put it in 787, the indefinable can become definable (see O'Grady 2001:14). The life of prayer and devotion in many religions can be inspired by works of art. This is therefore why a variety of depictions are preferable; each may be able to capture an aspect of the human perception of the sacred and therefore enrich one another.

Among others, Ron O'Grady (2001) has assembled images that celebrate the richness and variety of Christian art from various continents through the ages. Important to note are not only variations by culture, but also the variations by theme; geographic, historical, and social environment; place of origin; and intended recipient and purpose of the art object material(s) used, to say nothing of the social and psychological background of the artist. In light of this book, it was rather amusing to read in some Western newspapers that people were complaining of something so trivial as the pope presiding at a mass in Papua New Guinea at which a bare-breasted woman read the epistle. Apart from the fact that breasts are not an erotic symbol in some cultures, contrary to what Gerard Warner in the Scottish *Spectator* (December 14, 2002) imagined, sexual parts of the human body and of other beings, as well as the sexual act itself, have been used all over the world to express aspects of the sacred. Christians speak proudly of the church as the "bride" of Christ. To all but the most prudish this is a sexual expression. Moreover, Western art (sculpture, painting, and literature) is full of examples of the nude human body as an expression of some aspect of the holy.

New Zealand's Colin McCahon's *Crucifixion* (see O'Grady 2001:131) depicts the crucified Jesus totally nude.

In an enlightening essay entitled, "'. . . and Foolishness to the Gentiles': Images of Christ from Africa and Asia," Volker Küster (1995:112) shows that Third World representations of Christ are moving from mere accommodation to true inculturation. At the stage of accommodation, "western Christian motifs were for the most part directly transformed into traditional iconography." Today local motifs and the Gospel message interpenetrate and interpret each other, yielding not only iconographical originality, but also what Küster (1995:97), in substantial agreement with Umberto Eco, calls a "sense-creating role to the individual receiver." This releases the possibility, or indeed probability, of a multiplicity of meanings or "polysemy" in the process of interpretation of an article of art. To be able to interpret this new art fairly, it is necessary to be as familiar as possible with the context of the artist. But it is also necessary to reread the scriptures with an eye to the context from which the work of art emerges. This means that inculturated art interprets scripture in a new way at the same time that scripture legitimizes an article of art as *Christian* art. Theology and art interpenetrate and interpret each other. Reminiscent of African theology, therefore

> the focus of African art is the human being. This applies to prehistoric rock paintings as well as to masks and sculptures or jewellery and ornaments. Nature is only depicted if it has a function for humankind or if it refers to it symbolically. The artist knows that he is embedded in the big stream of life which through the ancestors goes back to God himself and through the descendants is flowing into the future. Life always means life within the community, there is no such thing as an autonomous artist. Art is related to the community and thus to tradition, which is why a value-conservative tendency is inherent in African art. Like the African religions with which it is very strongly interwoven, art has a life-supporting function. (Küster 1995:100; see also Magesa 1997:64–71, 77–82)

Accordingly, in analyzing four African depictions of Christ's crucifixion, Küster (1995:108) notes that the predominant motif is not the suffering Christ (*Christus patiens*) but the victorious Christ (*Christus victor*) who triumphs over death and brings life. Even in the depiction arising from the then-apartheid South Africa, human suffering is shown as participating in the suffering of Christ, not for itself but for the sake of overcoming it "in the resurrection." At any rate, all four depictions are completely different in outward appearance from the images of the crucifixion that the African Catholic Church has inherited from Western missionaries. (See p. 98 for the images. In addition to Küster 1995, it is interesting for the sake of comparison with Asian artists to read also Küster 1999 and 2001).

It is legitimate and necessary to ask whether the sacral artistic images brought into Africa really express African perceptions and spirituality. Are they in accord with developing African theology? Moreover, do they affirm the identity of the African people in their own eyes as beloved of God? The answer to all of these questions seems to be no. With proper catechesis, they must be substituted with African ones more in tune with these aspects of African Christianity. If not, African Christians will continue to live with sacred art in the same harmful situation of double-consciousness already experienced in theology, unable to identify God's saving power in their own history. But this means also, in practical terms, that African Christian artists must be encouraged and supported by the church.

I have already said something about architecture. It ought to be both symbolic and practical with regard, for example, to space for movement and bodily expression, as in dance, But one wonders with Lumbala and other African theologians whether such things as masks, trees of life, ancestral huts, and so on might not be usefully used in church to signify to worshipers the ancestral and cosmic union discussed earlier. However, I will not be surprised if such direct connection with Africa's past is rejected out of hand and termed "pagan" despite the spiritual-emotional attraction it has. It is a sign of Africa's cultural alienation that no protest is ever voiced about such symbols as the golden chalices, tabernacles, monstrances, or smoking thuribles. Lumbala (1998:44) is right: We should not let those who wish to ridicule or minimize the influence of our ancestors succeed.

It is not possible to conclude a discussion of the symbolism of images in the church in the twenty-first century without saying something about the significance of literature and film, especially for the younger generations. If traditional Africa respected the power of the word, often spoken in person to the audience intended, today the written and electronic media are playing that role.

Fortunately, we are witnessing in Africa at the beginning of this new century a rapidly increasing number of Christian radio and television stations. Care must be taken, however, that they be held accountable to the high professional standards expected of any similar institution, and do not exist only to serve the ego of the bishop. In the few instances when this has sadly been the case, their effectiveness has been confined only to the "converted" few. There have also been few significant African film productions with specifically Christian themes. If film makers in Nigeria, for example, have succeeded in mass marketing videos based on such traditional themes as witchcraft or polygamy, it should also be possible for African Christian film makers to market films about how Africans understand God, Jesus, the Blessed Virgin Mary, the ancestors, and so on. The electronic media can be a very effective means of inculturation.

Although Africa has produced a Nobel laureate for literature, Wole Soyinka, literary works exploring Christian concerns are nowhere to be seen in Africa. Africa's literary luminaries—among them, Chinua Achebe, Cyprian Enkwensi, Ngugi wa Thiong'o—have been able to establish indisputably that there is an African literature. They touch on Christianity, often in a critical way in their work, but they do not write Christian novels per se. It is in the interest of inculturation in Africa to promote this aspect of art as well.

THE SEVEN SACRAMENTS

There has always been the danger in the history of the Christian sacraments of turning the sign or symbol into what the symbol points to, of making the signifier into the signified. It is like thinking that the road sign to a destination is the destination itself. Everyone knows that this is ludicrous but, where the sacraments are concerned, it is always a temptation. This is why Christian sacramental symbols are often frozen and rarely open to adjustment and change, even when they no longer signify what they were originally intended to. This issue is very important when symbols are used across cultures. I have already pointed out that symbols do not mean the same thing in every culture. Colors, for example, have different meanings in different places, so that white can symbolize death in one place but resurrection and joy in another. The same holds true for different kinds of oil, food and drink, plants, and so on.

In many cases, the choice of which symbol to use as a sacramental sign was originally really a matter of convenience, of what was available. It was a time- and circumstance-determined choice. To make such signs inflexibly integral parts of any sacrament is to miss the point of the sacrament; it is to confuse the symbol with the reality intended by the symbol, the *meaning* behind the symbol. But how convenience can easily harden into stubborn requirement is well illustrated in de Mello's rather humorous story, "The Guru's Cat" (1982:63):

> When the guru sat down to worship each evening the ashram cat would get in the way and distract the worshipers. So he ordered that the cat be tied during evening worship.
>
> After the guru died the cat continued to be tied during evening worship. And when the cat expired, another cat was brought to the ashram so that it could be duly tied during evening worship.
>
> Centuries later learned treatises were written by the guru's scholarly disciples on the liturgical significance of tying up a cat while worship is performed.

The actual forms that the liturgy of some of the sacraments, especially the sacraments of initiation, might take will be discussed below in the chapter dealing with African initiatives in creating inculturated rites (Chapter 13). At the moment, I would just like to note some symbols that have been suggested by theologians (for example, Lumbala 1998, Uzukwu 1997, and Bujo 2001) as appropriate for celebrating sacraments in the African context.

Baptism, Confirmation, and Eucharist

Baptism, confirmation, and the Eucharist are referred to in theology as sacraments of initiation, and indeed they correspond very closely to the traditional African practice of initiation as a rite of passage. The African initiate was instructed in the ways of the community in a serious and sustained way, was physically marked by its symbol(s)—sometimes indelibly, as in circumcision or scarification—and at a feast was ceremoniously integrated into it as a full member to participate fully in its life (see Magesa 1997:94–104). The ritual made liberal use of many symbols. White kaolin or red ochre painted over the body symbolized the liminal or threshold period; bathing signified cleansing after the seclusion period; anointing with oil denoted strength, beauty and readiness to marry (i.e., adulthood); and feasting with the community meant integration or full incorporation into the group. All of this was done to connect the initiates to both the visible and the invisible worlds whose vital forces were understood to interpenetrate for the sake of the human person. Sponsorship of the initiate throughout the process by an adult member (or members) of the community was taken very seriously.

Of course, we no longer live in completely traditional Africa. So it is not practical to advocate uncritical transposition of these symbols into the Catholic rituals of sacramental initiation. But it is similarly unwise to completely reject them, especially the meaning they advanced to the initiate and the community. Lumbala (1998:9–18) gives several examples of how some of the most meaningful of these symbols might be integrated in a Christian context without implying mere adaptation, parallelism or concordism. The symbols themselves should present little problem if they are explained and contextualized in modern African settings. Even though they might present a problem in odd cases (see Uzukwu 1997:231–32), this is part of the challenge of inculturation in Africa today.

Deep down African Christians, like their non-Christian brothers and sisters, are attracted to rites that reveal the interconnection of the vital forces, the "webs of interrelationships between spirits and humans," as Uzukwu describes them. Yet the actual rites and symbols that served this purpose have been so eroded by Christianity, Islam, modernity, and globalization that, as Uzukwu notes, many people inevitably feel ambivalent about them. Nevertheless, they seek the experience behind them through exorcists, charismatic groups, healing ministries, and in movements and groups that cater to this need. In my opinion, if allowed to operate unrestrained by Western-inspired cultural rejection, creative initiatives are already present in the African mainline churches that, as in the traditional setting, "will adequately cater to biological cycles and social crises" that form the human context not only for initiation but for the whole process of passing through life to death and beyond. This is the sanctification of life (Uzukwu 1997:233, 244–56).

Of course, real inculturation raises a number of questions that must be faced. For one, it necessitates a rethinking of infant baptism as a routine practice in Africa. Does it really square with the fundamental meaning of the African initiation process which intends to confirm the initiate into conscious adulthood? I am not unaware that this opens up a controversy begun in the second century C.E. This has continued not only in the Catholic Church but also, since the Protestant Reformation, among Christian churches (e.g., the Anabaptists). But the question is still debatable. The *Constitution on the Scared Liturgy* (*Sacrosanctum Concilium*, n. 67) itself hints at such when it decrees that "the roles of parents and godparents, and also their duties, should be brought out more clearly in the rite" of baptism for children. As recently as 1980 the Roman Congregation for the Doctrine of the Faith was concerned enough about the questions being asked about this practice to issue an instruction reaffirming it (CDF 1980).

Another question it raises concerns the duration of time for and manner of the Rite of Christian Initiation of Adults. Once again, this is not a new question. Following the Constantinian dispensation in the fourth century, many people chose to remain catechumens until the point of death because they feared the severe sanctions that accompanied a breach of their baptismal vows. However, the question now is increasingly whether the academic learning of doctrine alone is enough to qualify a person for baptism. The *Catechism of the Catholic Church* (CCC, n. 1229) offers some general guidelines:

> From the time of the apostles, becoming a Christian has been accomplished by a journey and initiation in several stages. This journey can be covered rapidly or slowly, but certain essential elements will always have to be present: proclamation of the Word, acceptance of the Gospel entailing conversion, profession of faith, Baptism itself, the outpouring of the Holy Spirit, and admission to Eucharistic communion.

This journey, I suggest, is what needs to be looked at in Africa in terms of such realities as the ages of the catechumens, the seasons to celebrate these sacraments so as to bring out the meaning of baptism as incorporation, and confirmation as affirmation of identity within the Christian community.

As for the Eucharist, Bujo (2001:159) asks the African church to think again whether bread and wine as the matter of the Eucharist are "an appropriate expression of hospitality shared with Christ and with all believers." When church leaders insist on them as a dogmatic issue, as they have done since the introduction of Catholicism on the continent, the situation concerning African identity becomes extremely serious. "Africans are left with the unpleasant feeling that God ultimately does not accept them completely," he laments, "since he is not willing to identify himself with the fruits of their own soil and fields. What then does 'incarnation' mean? Does not the rejection of the African fruits amount to discrimination?" As Lumbala (1998:19–20) notes, "On the table of the disciples at Emmaus, Jesus did not take out his own sandwich or picnic lunch. He took what the disciples had with them. He ate it in a new way that proclaimed his death and resurrection."

And Bujo (2001:159) perceives another motivation behind this imposition, even if it is rationalized by theological arguments: "One cannot resist the impression that bread and wine imported from abroad also serve commercial interests, that is, that this is an economic exploitation of black people." The solution, according to Bujo, is to be found in dialogue: "We need a palaver, and the magisterium ought not to intervene *ab extra*, but rather charge the local churches with the task of examining this issue in depth, involving all the members of the church—including the laity."

In my opinion, convincing arguments have long been advanced by scholars and pastors concerning why local staples should be used as species for the celebration of the Eucharist. I do not feel it necessary to repeat them here. But as Lumbala (1998:50–57) explains, the use of African staples has consistently been denied on the basis of three arguments: (a) that Jesus himself used bread and wine at the institution of the Eucharist, (b) that church tradition has always maintained this practice, and (c) that the unity of the church would be jeopardized were other elements allowed. (These arguments are generally also advanced when other important questions in the church are raised, such as the discipline of celibacy and the ban on the ordination of women.)

Important though they are, the strength of these arguments is limited, especially in the light of present-day scholarship. The Latin Church insists on using *wheat* bread and *grape* wine in the celebration of the Eucharist based on what it considers the historical action of Jesus; but it is far from certain that Jesus used wheat bread (could it have been barley, as in Jn. 6:9, 13, the use of which appears to have been quite common?). But even then, as Uzukwu has rightly argued (see Lumbala 1998:55),

> The unique transformation of the Jewish ritual by Jesus does not lie in the domain of the elements. He ate and drank like any other Jew . . . products of the land. . . . Jesus used the food items of his culture because he was establishing the Eucharist in the context of a meal. . . . This means that the question of the use of wheat or barley bread and grape-wine, is not a dogmatic but a disciplinary issue. . . . We have to celebrate the Eucharist memorial with food and drink but this food and drink do not necessarily have to be wheat bread and grape-wine.

Second, it is inaccurate, to say the least, to assert that wheat bread and grape wine are the only elements that have been used for celebrating a valid Eucharist all over the world at all times. There have been documented occasions when wine derived from sources other than grapes has been used validly in the Eucharist; and even the one exception (but there are many)—even when granted by church authorities—would destroy the validity of this claim. The "unity" argument is perhaps the weakest. As we have noted, it was once used with regard to the liturgical use of Latin. The unity of the Church did not crumble with the introduction of the vernacular. What was demolished was uniformity. On the contrary, using local species for the Eucharist might in fact be at the service of ecumenism. But it is above all the symbolic significance of bread and wine in the African context that is at issue here.

Let me summarize briefly some of the most significant symbols that African Christianity could bring to the celebration of the sacraments of reconciliation, marriage, comfort to the sick, and installation to ministerial priesthood.

Reconciliation

The communal nature of African societies and the perceived communal effects of wrongdoing make it necessary to symbolize reconciliation as a communal act. Individual auricular confession as a sign of reconciliation is extremely ineffectual to the African mind. I am not unaware of the stages the sacrament has gone though in the history of Christianity, especially in the area of public confession. Some of these developments appear similar to what we propose here. But if reconciliation is to be meaningful in the African context, the church needs to learn from African practice. Public offenses (such as known adultery, murder, aggression, friction between families, and so on) require public rites of reconciliation. There is no reason why these rites should not be the same as or similar to those performed in the secular sphere—only given a new context. If you consider that in the African world-view these rites had a religious purpose anyway, then it shouldn't be too difficult to make the transition to the exclusively sacred realm.

Whether public or semi-public—rarely, if ever, completely private—reconciliation must always include the exchange of a material object as a gesture of pardon given and received. The object exchanged might be as large as a meal or as small as the leaf of a tree. With the different ethnic groups in Africa, the range is very wide, but relevant symbols and gestures do exist. And always, the community must somehow figure in any rite, because ultimately it is the community that is injured by sin committed by any of its members. Accordingly, there needs to be at least once a year a celebration of reconciliation that brings together the whole community. Here, everyone would renounce their sins (actual and possible ones, for "we are all potential witches," whether we know it or not), and cleanse individuals and the community for a new beginning.

Marriage

Marriage in Africa demands attention to detail. The details, properly performed at each stage of the long process of the undertaking, confirm and sanctify the marriage. The rights and responsibilities of all concerned—the boy and girl, their parents and other relatives, the clan, and the village(s)—must be fulfilled for the marriage to take effect. The engagement token, the consent of the parents, the bride wealth, the gifts to the aunt and uncle, and the consummation of marital sexual relations within a given time, among other things, need to be properly accomplished. Again, there will be a wide variety of ways to do this, not only among different ethnic groups, but also between rural and urban areas. The traditional requirement of the conception and birth of a child to seal the marriage is today debatable from the theological and human rights point of view. It remains true, however, that to enter a marriage with the stated intention of excluding the possibility of conception and birth of a child must invalidate any marriage covenant.

Comfort to the Sick

When celebrating any of the sacraments, the presence of the community or its representatives is itself an important symbol. From the African perspective, however, it becomes even more important and essential in the event of serious illness, when life-negating forces seem concentrated and palpable. These forces can only be countered by the life-affirming energies represented by the presence of relatives and friends who never leave the sick bed. "We are with you," is the clear message the sick person is continuously given and, if the illness is terminal, the individual dies with this assurance. All other symbols of solace gain meaning within this context. In this context, anointing with oil, laying on of hands, sharing food with or in the presence of the sick person remind that person of the union of vital forces throughout the universe, to which his or her own vital force will be joined at death. The sting of death is thus somehow diminished, or at least placed in proper view.

Installation to Ministerial Priesthood

Finally, ordination confers authority to preach the Gospel and to administer the sacraments of the church. The current official signs in the Catholic Church are inadequate to show the confering of authority clearly to the African Christian communities and I wonder why traditional African symbols cannot be used. To preach the Gospel, the preacher needs to be "drunk" with it. This could be shown, for example, by placing a gourd of water on the Bible and then drinking the water with a vow to fulfill this responsibility. In one place in Congo, as Lumbala (1998:92) reports, the book of the Gospels was placed on the ground, and the ordinands to the deaconate stepped over it to remind themselves "of the traditional gestures when a solemn oath is given and powers are transmitted." Stepping over the book of the Gospels means to soak this power into one's person.

Again, in the administration of the sacraments in Africa symbols and symbolic acts will vary widely from one part of the continent to another, and it might take time to settle on the appropriate ones for a given location. This discussion means to say only that this task can be done and that we should resist the "idolatry" of turning the signifier into the signified. The latter is infinitely greater and beyond containment in the sign. The sign may change to better express the signified without changing it.

OTHER SACRAMENTS IN LIFE

One clear instance where a symbol has hardened into an intractable prescription in the Catholic Church, for example, concerns the number of the sacraments. It is well known from biblical scholarship that the number seven is a symbol of perfection in Hebrew thought. There are several incidents in the scriptures that indicate this symbolism: the creation of the world in six and one days (Gen. 2:2–3), forgiveness seven times and more (Mt. 18:21–22,

Lk. 17:4), multiplication of the seven loaves (Mt. 15:32–39, Mk. 8:1–9), the notions of the sabbatical and jubilee year in Leviticus 25, and so on. This was clearly one of the reasons why the sacraments were fixed at this number early in the history of Christianity.

Does it mean, therefore, that there are no other signs of God's grace, no other sacraments, as significant as the seven? Do the seven exhaust the manifestation of God's action in the world for the salvation of the human race? Can, and might, other cultures possess symbols of life that are sacramental, that is, visible signs of God's grace? I realize, of course, that the classical definition of a sacrament, in addition to being a visible sign of God's grace, must be that it was instituted by Christ. But is this the case for all of the seven sacraments we now have? Can we trace *direct* institution by Christ for all of them? With the only clear exception of the Eucharist, the jury is still out.

Pivotal as the seven sacraments are, it would appear they do not, and cannot, exhaust the possibility of "sacramental signs of grace" the world over. They are sacraments of grace in the same way that the church is a sacrament of Christ: they include and witness to salvific grace just as the church includes and witnesses to the ministry of Christ—but without exhausting it. There are other visible signs of grace that draw from the spirit of the saving work of Christ. These could also be called sacraments. We can give only a few examples here in the context of Africa.

Violence leading to bloodshed goes against everything that Jesus stood for. At his birth the message given from on high was that there should be peace in the world. The Gospels stress this when they write about the appearances of Jesus after his resurrection: His greeting to his followers was at every occasion "Peace be with you." Before his ascension, peace was what he bequeathed to his apostles: "My peace I give you, my peace I leave with you." In the world, violence is perhaps one of the most virulent countersigns of the Gospel. An effective ritual to restore and maintain peace must surely be counted as a sacrament of God's grace. This is especially the case given that violence in the world is not transient, and that it emerges from the very roots of human sinfulness: hatred, pride, and greed.

There were just such effective rituals in many parts of Africa; one of the most prominent was that of forming "blood friendships" or "blood brotherhood." There were various forms of this, but one involved an exchange of a drop of blood, drawn from the bodies of representatives of one group and applied to the tongues of the representatives of the other group. This was a covenant: It meant that there could be no more bloody hostilities between or among the hitherto opposing groups. As far as historical anthropology can testify, this was usually adhered to. It produced among many groups what is called a "joking relationship," a relationship where tensions may indeed exist, but where they are not allowed to surface into open conflict. Joking relationships diffuse ethnic tensions before they explode into violence (see Magesa 1997:112–114). This is sacramental.

It is not possible to cite this example without thinking immediately about the tragedy that was Rwanda in those fateful days of April, 1994. As everyone knows, in the space of four weeks, more than 800,000 people lost their lives in a largely tribally orchestrated bloodbath. It is a moot question now, but one cannot help wondering whether, anticipating the hostilities, the above ritual between Hutu and Tutsi representatives could not have averted the genocide. Perhaps a more relevant question is which Christian sacrament—even now, after the massacre—might be capable of dealing with the magnitude of the situation. What form of sacramental reconciliation? Certainly not the sacrament of "penance" as it is at present constituted. The situation demands a more public and communal ritual involving all the members of the Rwandan communities, and a ritual like the one I am describing is capable of dealing much more credibly and effectively with the situation.

One more possibility pertains to political life. Goodness knows what Africans have had to suffer in the last forty or so years since their nations gained independence. It has been mostly an experience of tyranny and oppression by those in political power. The freedom and egalitarianism that the people hoped for have been elusive. In other words, the situation is one that Jesus decried: the rulers "lording it" over the subjects. But such was not always the case in traditional Africa. The installation of the Asantehene (paramount chief) of the Ashanti of Ghana was a ritual that made leadership the kind of sacred service that Jesus recommended. It united the leader and his followers in a covenant of harmony. In a previous study (see Magesa 1997:261–262) I noted how the people, through a representative, sent a message of instruction to the prospective Asantehene:

> Tell him [that] . . . we do not wish that he should disclose the origin of any person [since some are descended from slaves]. We do not wish that he should curse us. We do not wish greediness. We do not wish that his ears should be hard of hearing. We do not wish that he should call people fools. We do not wish that he should act out of his own head [without consultation]. . . . We do not wish that it should ever be that he should say "I have no time." We do not wish personal violence.

The ruler's acceptance of these terms must be accompanied by an act of sacrifice or offering to the ancestors (or God) that sealed the covenant. One is not unaware that at their inauguration new African leaders swear on the Bible or the Koran to uphold the constitution. But if their performance so far is any indication, it appears that this Christian- or Islamic-oriented oath is merely a formal act and given little weight. (Incidentally, this is a question to be looked into as well whenever offices in the church in Africa are concerned. When Jesus decried the Gentiles' use of power and authority, he was talking in the context of the Christian community. The leaders of the Christian community should not be that way. In the interests of inculturation, African church leaders need to examine themselves about what models of authority they employ. In many cases it has not been very edifying.)

The various rites of passage in African traditional moral practice provide further examples of rituals that can certainly be seen as avenues of grace—or sacraments—in the Christian sense. These are rituals of life to those who practice them. Therefore, to trivialize rituals of pregnancy, birth, general initiation, induction into elderhood, or mourning is, in the view of their practitioners, to trivialize life itself. It was a mistake for the mainline Christian churches to ignore or prohibit them.

13

Christian Initiatives
toward New Rites in Africa

Many rituals and rites in the mainline churches failed to satisfy the religiosity of their adherents in Africa. This had two consequences. As we saw in
Part One, one was that inspired leaders simply broke away to start their own
movements. They instituted or encouraged ways of worship with which they
felt at home. Another slower and less spectacular movement happened within
the mainline churches themselves, with theologians and liturgists gradually
creating rites and bishops submitting them to Rome for approval. The
response from Rome was and has often been disappointing. Currently, in
view of Roman systematic centralization after the centrifugal phenomenon
spearheaded by Vatican II, it is becoming more difficult for an initiative of
this kind even to be submitted to Rome: many bishops are either afraid or
embarrassed to do so. Enterprising liturgists have consequently grown dif-
fident about suggesting anything new. In this chapter, I wish to review both
processes very briefly because they have already been discussed extensively
in other studies.

AFRICAN INITIATED CHURCHES

Several times already we have referred to how AICs have pioneered a degree
of successful inculturation in their churches. We need to elaborate on their
success as well as to indicate where and how they have failed in this goal.

In most AICs, interest in new or renewed ways and forms of worship is not
theological and theoretical but pastoral and pragmatic. This was the case from
the very beginning. Few founders of these churches had formal theological
training. Most of them were charismatic people who had a passion for authenticity and the spiritual dignity of their followers at heart. We saw in Part One
how some of them declared that to plan their worship they did not need seminars or workshops to help them. They usually attribute the structural and
worship models of their churches to the inspiration of the Holy Spirit.

In a brief description published in 1990, and which is still valid today, I
classified AICs into three groups: neo-traditional or revivalist, neo-Judaic or
Hebraist, and neo-Christian (see Namwera/Shorter 1990:49–59; also ibid.
pp. 63–68 for a clarifying response by A. Bellagamba). Those in the first
group—as for instance *Dini ya Msambwa* (Kenya)—are integrationists. The
notion of syncretism can be applied to them very specifically. They borrow

only a few elements from Christian teachings to enhance their basically African worldview and values. They represent, according to some scholars, original initiatives in belief, which, they think, can hardly be called either "Christian" or "churches." But in my view, they may be referred to as churches for two reasons: First, their origin lies in the desire to free themselves from the overbearing domination of Western missionary Christianity and colonial (or, after independence, national) political administrations of African culture and aspirations. Second, unlike original African religiosity, which was amorphous, they are organized groups with a structure similar to the mainline churches.

As their collective designation suggests, the Hebraic or neo-Judaic AICs identify themselves very closely with Old Testament religiosity, laws, and customs. The names they give themselves and the type of official symbols they use (such as manner of dress) reveal their desire for this identity. Accordingly in Uganda we have the Bayudaya, the meaning of which is simply "The Israelites."

Finally, the third group that seceded from the mainline churches was encouraged by evangelical movements from North America, or was a result of original African Christian creative imagination, as Bellagamba shows (see Namwera/Shorter 1990:63–65) and are what scholars in general describe as African-initiated *Christian* Churches. An example of these is the Legio Maria Church.

AICs are characterized by a search for identity. Unfortunately, this sometimes leads to ethnocentrism, partly necessitated by accidents of geography and demography. They can also exhibit strong tendencies toward millenarianism or chiliasm—derived from a certain interpretation of Psalm 90:4, 2 Peter 3:8, and Revelation 20—with often tragic consequences. A recent example is Credonia Mwerinde's Movement for the Restoration of the Ten Commandments of God in Uganda. Many of its members perished in a fire deliberately set by the leaders when the end of the world did not come in 2000 as they had prophesied (see Magesa 2002:17–18). Others expect rewards here and now in the form of wealth, healing, and other forms of harmonious living with the forces of the universe. On the liturgical level, however, AICs are autonomous and are psychologically and structurally freer to be themselves and to innovate.

Bellagamba (see Namwera/Shorter 1990:66–67) lists three sources of this freedom: non-elitist leadership, poverty of means, and creativity of action. First, the founders and foundresses of many of these communities were not distinguished from the rest by their level of education or any mark of social status. They were not of the elite but were like everyone else in the community. They were completely integrated into the structure of society. They justified their charisms not on any social distinction, but only on the power of the Holy Spirit. Second, many of these churches did not and do not enjoy the luxury of extensive material possessions. They are thus spared the arrogance that usually comes with wealth. Rather, they trust in God to promote their work. Third, because the churches are autonomous, without a hierarchical chain of command, they can shape themselves according to the needs of their members. They have wider leeway to be innovative and creative with regard to cultural promptings.

One of their most significant initiatives was the use of vernacular languages in worship long before the mainline churches, the Roman Catholic Church in particular, would even think of it. But even in the Protestant churches, where use of the vernacular has its roots in the Reformation of the sixteenth century, most hymns and prayers were renditions in the local languages of their European counterparts: the melody and the theology remained European. With the exception of only a few AICs, such as the Legio Maria in western Kenya and northern Tanzania, most used new hymns and prayers rooted in Africa through forms and spirituality. This was largely a result of the founders and foundresses having had little Western academic or missionary theological education, which in this case must be seen as providential. Increasingly, younger AIC leaders are now being encouraged and helped by institutions affiliated with the World Council of Churches to study theology in Europe. Though well intentioned, the move is not without ambiguity. Will they be encouraged to develop a truly African theology? The danger is that they might end up internalizing the very same thing their predecessors rejected—that is, European theological views and logic to the exclusion of African spiritual values.

We must consider also the element of spontaneity in prayer. The fact that many of the founders and foundresses of AICs were either unschooled or just minimally so forced them not to depend on written prayers. Even though the Bible was central to many of them, they often used it in an oral way: it was not read in church as much as it was related orally. The proclamation "The Bible says" was followed not by a quotation but by a general explanation of scripture. The point of all this is that they were not restricted in their vision by any nation extrinsic to them of what was "correct" or "scientific." Scriptural interpretation was therefore "popular," done by the people, although now the faithful defer more and more to their leaders for this responsibility.

Exorcism and healing rituals in these churches attract Africans because they touch on the most important principle in the African worldview: casting away evil forces, which cause suffering and disharmony, and welcoming the forces which enhance life. The healing process integrates also a kind of confession and removal of guilt for wrongdoing. When you cleanse the soul, in a certain way you also heal the body, and vice versa. In many of the AICs the ancestors are at the center of this process. The refusal by most mainline churches to leave room for the recognition of the ancestors in their theology and liturgy creates a vacuum in the hearts and souls of African believers.

Finally, there is the question of marriage—not a negligible one for the AICs. Leadership requires maturity, and in the African worldview the status of being married is one of the conditions for it. The admiration that Africans accord to the celibate priesthood of the Catholic Church is ambiguous. It is essentially one of amazement—how can they do it? rather than one of approval—it is good that they do it. When the question of African ontology is taken seriously, married leaders fall right in place in the outlook, structures, and pastoral practice of the AICs.

EXPERIMENTATION IN THE CATHOLIC CHURCH

Uzukwu (1997) and Lumbala (1998) have discussed examples of innovative and creative liturgies in African Catholicism in great detail. It is not my purpose to repeat what they have already skillfully demonstrated. However, for the sake of a sense of what has been and is happening, I wish to note a few of the major attempts at formal liturgical rites that have been formulated in the categories of baptism-confirmation, the Eucharist, and religious consecration, and in the process indicate how they are more in tune with African fundamental spirituality than the classical Roman Catholic liturgies.

Baptism-Confirmation Liturgies

Because the central intention and purpose of baptism is the effective incorporation into the Christian clan of the persons being baptized as pure and responsible adults, the prayers, locations, and the timing of the ritual must speak to this purpose. From the African point of view, baptism is the sacrament of identity, of belonging, necessary to make one what and who one is in the community. The Ranzinni-Ouedraogo rite of the Mossi (Burkina-Faso) that Lumbala (1998:12–14; see also Uzukwu 1997:289–293) describes takes into account the structural elements of request and presentation, separation, instruction, symbolic identification, and incorporation necessary for an initiation. Lumbala discusses the ritual only in its last stages, what takes place during the baptism itself. But it can be considered within the framework of the entire initiation process.

Just as in the initiation process, the candidates for baptism-confirmation request their sponsors (their Christian community) to present them to "the head of the family" (the priest) for the privilege of baptism. The community must ascertain that they are ready (or of age). This is a serious responsibility that the community assumes. The language used, at least in Mossi, indicates this. Those who present the candidates to the priest attest to both the firm determination of the candidates to follow the teaching of the Gospel as well as the obligation that the community itself bears in presenting them for baptism:

And we have asked them, "You who see the effort that must be made, will you follow the path that they [who have been baptised before you] have taken? You have said that you will. But have you no concern that you will fall back and live as you did before?" They have said no, they will not return to their old ways.

And this is why we have taken this upon ourselves. Our heart is firm, because when someone counts on you, you must do everything in your power not to let them down. That is what has brought us here today, and that is why we ask permission of the head of the family [for the candidates to begin the process]. If you agree, then it is you who are the master of your work (see Lumbala 1998:12).

This constitutes the first step of the catechumenate, the journey toward baptism.

The second stage involves something like separation, and there should be occasions when this is (at least symbolically) evident—such as reserving a particular place for them in the worship area. The mysteries of the Christian faith are explained, with special emphasis on the practical demands of the faith in the catechumens' own context. Baptism itself with water is, of course, the traditional sign and symbol of Christian incorporation.

The process should not be difficult to implement. The Rite of Christian Initiation of Adults (RCIA), which came into effect after Vatican II, preserves almost all of the elements of the African initiation process in its general structure. Here is the form that baptism-confirmation should actually take:

- Acceptance into the catechumenate after discernment and decision (petition);
- A period of formation in Christian faith and values (seclusion);
- The rite admission into the Christian community through baptism itself (physical/moral impression); and
- Incorporation, when the newly baptized now must live and act as Christians (integration).

The examples Lumbala and Uzukwu provide argue that without compromising the central Christian tenets of love of God and neighbor, the administration of the sacraments of initiation can take up the structure and content of the African traditional initiation ceremonies.

Because of the central place Easter holds in Christian belief, it seems important that baptism and confirmation coincide with it. However, this means that the stages preceding the actual baptism and confirmation must coincide with the relevant local seasons in the different regions of Africa. Again, this should not be difficult to do because the proper times are already determined in the traditional initiation process.

Eucharistic Liturgies

Both Uzukwu and Lumbala mention the Ndzon-Melen Mass (Cameroon) and the Zairian Rite (Democratic Republic of Congo) that were initiated in the late 1960s as good examples of attempts to create African eucharistic liturgies. These rites have achieved official or semi-official local status, and the Zairian Rite was permitted by Rome under the name "The Roman Missal for the Dioceses of Zaire." But there are other initiatives throughout eastern, central and western Africa which the two authors discuss at length. These largely remain proposals on paper, and even local experimentation with them has been limited or forbidden altogether. At least this has been the case in eastern Africa.

In practically all of the initiatives, however, emphasis has been placed on participation by the assembly at all stages of the liturgy. The initiatives point to the value in African worship that the presider should not "monopolize the show," as it were, but facilitate it. The leader's major responsibility is to create an environment for the congregation so that its members individually and together can establish communication with the spiritual powers. (Incidentally, the *General Instruction of the Revised Roman Missal* [see n. 2–3] and the *Constitution on the Sacred Liturgy* [*Sacrosanctum Concilium*, see n. 19] both urge this, but in practice assembly participation is very limited in the typical Roman Catholic eucharistic liturgy in Africa.) In the proposed rituals communication consists not only of words, but also of postures, gestures, and other physical expressions.

Against this background several points from the new initiatives on eucharistic worship may be isolated for closer examination: the language of prayer, the place of the ancestors in this liturgy, and hospitality. In terms of traditional Western Roman Catholic theology, these are all sensitive issues; but they need to be rethought from the perspective of African spirituality. Therefore, I am not here making positive assertions; rather, I am posing exploratory questions.

Language. The question with the language issue is not merely the use of words (and gestures), but what sentiments certain notions evoke. Consider for example the offertory prayer for the second Sunday in Ordinary Time from the Roman Missal and an African offertory prayer. The first reads:

> Father,
> may we celebrate the Eucharist
> with reverence and love,
> for when we proclaim the death of the Lord
> you continue the work of his redemption,
> who is Lord for ever and ever.
> Amen.

The second, from the Meru people of Kenya (and suggested in 1973 as part of a Kenyan eucharistic prayer), reads:

> Owner of all things,
> We offer you this Cup in memory of your Son.
> We beg you for life,
> For healthy people with no disease,
> May they bear healthy children.
> And also women who suffer because they are barren,
> Open the way by which they may see children.
> Give the good life to our parents and kin
> Who are with you. (See Uzukwu 1997:313)

An analysis of the two prayers reveals certain differences very quickly. One cannot help noticing first of all the abstractness of the Roman prayer. Here the prayer speaks of "reverence" and "love," and proclaiming the Lord's work of "redemption." But what kind of redemption? And redemption from what and to what? All of these aspects of the petitioner seem to be taken for granted and are therefore not spelled out, even in the African situation. To the uninitiated, the prayer may even seem to be for God's benefit.

No such ambiguities bedevil the African prayer, particularly in the original Meru. It is clear from the beginning of the prayer that the benefits are intended for the supplicant, and things prayed for cannot be expressed more concretely. If we are doing now what we are doing, the prayer says, we are doing it so that you, God, will grant us the one thing that makes us what we are as human beings: life. And this life is sustained by physical health and fecundity. The supplicants pray for these things not only for themselves, but also for the invisible members of the community: those who are going to be born that they be "healthy," as well as the ancestors that they may enjoy "good life."

Because of the spontaneity of African prayer forms, the actual wording and the structure of such prayers may vary from time to time and from place to place, but the elements of concreteness and the concern for human life will always be there. For Africans the latter constitutes the reason for worship and all other concerns are seen to flow from it.

I do not wish to enter here into the debate about whether or not abstraction in conceptualization—as found in Western philosophical/theological-inspired prayer forms—enables prayer to be more universally applicable, and therefore have an advantage over and above the more concrete forms of prayer as found in the traditional African approach. That is certainly possible and deserves consideration. But the more fundamental questions are, first, whether universal application should supersede meaningfulness and understanding and, second, whether worship should be attuned to felt local rather than generalized universal needs.

While it is good and necessary for spiritual and theological development that horizons of experience and language always be broadened by contact with other realities, this can only happen fruitfully from the basis of directly lived experience. This kind of interaction alone is able to generate meaningful liturgical (or indeed any other) language.

Ancestors. In Christian spirituality, God alone is the object of worship. Catholic sacramental theology makes a clear distinction between latria (Greek *latreia*, service owed to the gods), dulia (*douleia*, respect due to a master), and hyperdulia (*hyper-douleia*). Latria in its highest degree, then, belongs to God, the Lord and creator of all existence. Deuteronomy 6:13 and Luke 4:8 provide the scriptural basis for it: "You shall worship the Lord your God, and him only shall you serve." Dulia is consequently not completely divorced from latria; it is a lesser degree of worship given by Catholics to the angels and saints whose heroic deeds and exemplary lives put them in close contact with God. They are thus in a very good position to intercede for us. Catholic devotion to them is usually also referred to as veneration. And because of the special relationship between the Blessed Virgin Mary and God through her motherhood of Jesus Christ, she is given a higher form of veneration—called hyperdulia—than that given to the angels and saints.

I mention this distinction in Catholic theology because it is very useful in our discussion about the place of the ancestors in liturgy. It is closer to the African religious worldview in worship than the Protestant approach. Taking inflexibly the injunctions of Deuteronomy and Luke that I have just quoted, Protestantism generally rejects any intermediaries and mediators between God and humanity other than Christ. In the view of Protestantism, the believer is able to go directly to God in prayer without the mediation of other beings, either human or spiritual. The cult of the saints does not therefore play a significant role, if any, in the Protestant spirituality of prayer.

In traditional African worship, God is rarely approached directly and immediately, but when need be through the intercession of the ancestors. This is analogical to the general African practice of approaching an elder or a very senior person through an intermediary. In normal circumstances one prays to the ancestors who are believed to be able to answer petitions and to accept libations and offerings through the power of God because they are very close to God. They therefore act on behalf of God. And because they are at the same time very close to the living, having shared their life, and therefore being very familiar with their problems, they are able to sympathize with their plight or to take part in their joys. In the letter to the Hebrews (4:14–5:10) this "privilege" is of course reserved supremely for Christ as High Priest. However, Catholic hagiology extends it to a lesser but important degree to the saints. *Mutatis mutandis* it can easily and usefully be applied to the ancestors in the African context, even if the African ancestors are indigenously perceived to have more power and more direct influence on the living than are the saints in Catholicism.

The importance official Catholic theology accords to Mary as mother of Christ and mother of God in hyperdulia is also consistent with African sociological perceptions and spirituality. In the African family the mother is as a rule the intercessor between the father and the children. Rarely is the father approached directly for favors; this is often done through the mother who is considered to be very potent in such matters. I would therefore think that, given the role of Mary in the scriptures and the African understanding of the mother's role in the family, Africans would not have any difficulty identifying with the sentiments (although not exactly the language) expressed in the Catholic prayer to Mary, the *Memorare*:

Remember, O most gracious Virgin Mary, that never was it known that anyone who fled to thy protection, implored thy help, or sought thy intercession was left unaided. Inspired with this confidence, I fly unto thee, O Virgin of virgins, my mother. To thee do I come, before thee I kneel, sinful and sorrowful. O Mother of the Word Incarnate, despise not my petitions, but in thy mercy hear and answer them. Amen.

Another thing that is practiced by official Catholicism but which would be frowned upon by mainline Protestantism (and incidentally also Islam) as idolatry is the veneration of the relics of the saints. This practice was sanctioned already by the Council of Nicea, reinforced by the Council of Trent, and alluded to by Vatican II in the *Dogmatic Constitution on the Church* (*Lumen Gentium*, n. 50). My point is merely that this practice is very close to the African veneration of the relics of the ancestors, some of which were kept in the houses, or at least very close to home. The African respect for graves was partly an expression of this, as were the dwellings (tabernacles) built for them in the family compound. If saints' relics are embedded in every altar, why can physical ancestral symbols of the clan or the ethnic group not be permitted in Catholic worship? Ancestral veneration is so much part and parcel of the piety of many Africans that to ignore it is to undercut one of the most important aspects of African spirituality.

Hospitality. This is not a trivial point. We are touching here on a long-standing, historically complicated and acrimonious ecumenical question regarding the theology of the Eucharist and intercommunion, as well as the validity of ministers and ministries among the Christian churches. Is the Eucharist a meal or a sacrifice? In what circumstances, if at all, is intercommunion among members of Christian churches theologically justified and justifiable? What is the minimum requirement for it? Is it possible on the official level of the churches to have a mutual recognition of ministers? These continue to exercise the minds of theologians and many church leaders. For Africa the question has been acute and scandalous even since the advent of Christianity in the nineteenth-century mission churches.

From the beginning, Christians of different denominations were forbidden to attend each other's worship services, and particularly to participate in intercommunion. The missionaries could not see the serious implications of this from the African viewpoint. To deliberately exclude anyone from festivity—be it a worship event, a meal, or any other community activity—implies far more than the fact of exclusion itself. It implies that the excluded person is tainted, evil, or an enemy. That is why it is very easy to persuade and convince African Christians of one denomination that members of other denominations with whom they were not permitted to share worship or communion were enemies. The sometimes deadly inter-Christian rivalries that have played themselves out in various parts of Africa, notably in nineteenth-century Uganda, and whose symptoms are not at all extinct, testify to this.

This situation in African Christianity will begin to change when the different ecumenical agreements—on the Eucharist, ministry, and grace—are implemented.

Essential Components of Eucharistic Liturgies

To African and Africanist liturgists fall the task of constructing a ritual or rituals that will be able to take into account all the sensitivities and emotions that African spirituality calls for. Nevertheless, it is possible to list some of the necessary ingredients for the structure:

- *Joyful or solemn/sorrowful gathering according to the nature of the occasion.* In terms of visible mood, all liturgies cannot be the same in Africa. The prayers, the gestures, and the symbols used will be different, and will indicate the occasion and purpose of the service. The music, especially, will announce the meaning and purpose of the occasion, so that from the beginning of the service the service demeanor is clear and it is not necessary to inquire into it.
- *Announcement of the theme/themes of the day (or purpose of gathering) by the presider of the assembly when necessary.* In regular Christian Sunday gatherings and other liturgies, the theme of the service may not be obvious to everyone. In these cases the presider of the worship service will announce it in language calculated to evoke the appropriate emotions.
- *Penitential and reconciliation rites (with some form of general exorcism when needed).* The importance of penitence in African religiosity cannot be overemphasized: as far as possible those who approach God and the ancestors in worship must be spiritually clean. In the Catholic Mass, the penitential rite must therefore be accorded more significance than it usually is. It must be seen as a serious rite of cleansing as we "approach the altar of God," the God who is our help and our salvation.
- *Prayers by the assembly and invocation of the ancestors (local, regional, and continental) and the saints.* This may become one of the longer parts of the liturgy not only in the interest of participation, but more especially in the interest of giving the service a personal or local character, with the ancestors being invoked to be present at the occasion. Whether these are local, regional, continental, or universal (as in the case of the saints), they will have been deliberately appealed to because of their perceived interest in helping the worshiping community. This part of the liturgy can only be ignored at the risk of seriously diminishing its relevance to and impact on the African worshiping community.
- *Presentation of and prayer over offerings.* In the Eucharist Christ himself is, of course, the sacrifice and offering to God. No animal or foodstuff can replace this. In fact, Catholic theology stresses that Jesus' self-sacrifice on the cross and symbolically at the altar replaces these. But this is not to say that the offerings given by the worshiping community do not have a place in the eucharistic service. It is not out of place, speaking theologically from the African perspective, to offer what we have to Christ as our proto-ancestor so that he can present our prayers and petitions to God. We can also do this through our human ancestors, not by actually sacrificing an animal to replace the Eucharist, but to recall the self-manifestation of God through Christ in the life and activities of our earthly ancestors.
- *Consecration.* When something is separated from ordinary human use and dedicated to God, we say that it is "consecrated" to God. In addition to the words of consecration over the specific matter of the Eucharist, therefore, it seems to me that the consecration of the people's offerings—the products of the "work of human hands"—clearly needs to be performed.
- *Proclamation of the scriptures (reading and homily).* We have already emphasized the importance of the word in the African worldview. The

word of scripture is paradigmatic in Christian tradition as the word which interacts with and transforms—and may be transformed by—the African story. This interaction is essential for both. The liturgy is impoverished, therefore, whenever the scripture is omitted.

- *Communion.* This aspect forms perhaps the most important aspect of the eucharistic liturgy. In "sharing in the feast," the worshipers demonstrate their communion not only with God and the ancestors, but also with one another. In the African view, the person who does not share in the feast denies this communion and poses the danger of disrupting the whole purpose of the liturgy. That is why eucharistic hospitality is an important issue in African theology.

- *Blessing and dismissal.* The blessing and dismissal mark not the end but the beginning of a spiritual journey, at a different level than before. After a worship service, people are sent away to re-create the order that the worship signified in word, song and gesture. The dismissal is an instruction: Go, be peaceful, love and serve the Lord and each other well, live what we have done here. These are not words to be said casually, but must be given with the gravity they deserve. Concretely, they are intended to raise the ethical conduct of believers, so that they continue to grow into the perfection expected by their Christian calling.

It will be seen that this structure does not necessarily exclude other elements of the customary eucharistic rites, such as the *Gloria*, the profession of the faith, praying the *Sanctus*, the Our Father, and the Lamb of God. The suggested African rites cited by Lumbala and Uzukwu show that they can be and are, in fact, included and integrated well without prejudice to any of the elements critical to African religiosity.

Liturgies of Solemn Consecration of Persons

Uzukwu and Lumbala give examples of liturgies about people being consecrated to the religious life, notably, women religious (Uzukwu 1997:298–302 and Lumbala 1998:96–99). I think, however, that the major elements of these liturgies can be applied to the ordination of priests in Africa. These elements consist of presentation and reception, covenant or pact, and commission. As Lumbala points out, all aspects of the Roman ritual for religious profession are incorporated here, but they are highlighted in ways that are relevant to Africa.

The presentation is done on behalf of the clan by the parents, the uncle or aunt, or a senior representative of the family or clan (the clan understood, of course, as the living members and the ancestors). As many members of the clan as possible will be encouraged to be present. After seeking the permission of the clan, the candidate for consecration or ordination is presented to the bishop together with some material goods as a sign of the continuing support by the clan for their child in his or her new life. The words of presentation should be chosen carefully to make clear the clan's free "offering" of one of theirs for the service of God. In the Democratic Republic of Congo

(DRC), the parents of a candidate joining the Sisters of Charity use the following words (see Lumbala 1998:97):

> May you only find soft earth beneath your feet. We who are your family, we have nothing against you, we let you leave, without rancor, may your way be white like the kaolin. Do not step on the scorpion or the snake. May you only find soft earth beneath your feet.

Or in Kasai province, the father similarly presents his daughter with this blessing (see Uzukwu 1997:300):

> My daughter, our Ancestors say, "the insect which is inside the bean can destroy it with ease." I gave life to you; I do not take it back from you. I am in accord with your desires. Go ahead and persevere. Let your route be as white as this chalk. "Do not step on any scorpion or any serpent so that you may march only on soft earth and tender herbs."

The bishop may want to assure himself of the purity of this intention on behalf of the assembled Christian community by asking whether any member of the clan has any serious objection to this "gift" they are about to make of their son or daughter to God and the community, and whether the words of the leader reflect the consensus of the clan. Upon receiving a positive answer the bishop receives the candidate with words of welcome and encouragement, and leads him or her to the altar. The gifts accompanying the candidate may be received by the representative of the bishop or the superior of the community the candidate is about to join. It would be good that a short explanation be made about the use to which they will be put, and about the responsibility of the Christian community, as the person's new clan, to take care of him or her from now on.

The dominant aspect of the liturgy of consecration is the covenant or pact the person makes with God, and indeed with the entire church. The blood pact ritual that has been used for some time now in the rites of religious profession in the DRC (see Lumbala 1998:97 and Uzukwu 1997:299) is one of the most striking—and is the one that makes most sense to many African ethnic groups. But there are other symbols that can be used, as long as they show concretely the seriousness of the commitment a person is making.

The traditional Christian vows of solemn dedication to the service of Christ and the gospel—poverty, chastity, and obedience—can be made at this stage. It is, however, unfortunate, from the African perspective, that the negative implications of these vows have usually been emphasized in the Christian liturgy, something which is very difficult for many Africans to appreciate. Why would any family or a clan give their son or daughter to a life of want, barrenness or sterility, and servitude? On the contrary, any family would consider it an honor to do so for a life of sharing, social and spiritual fecundity, and indiscriminate service. The latter, as Uzukwu notes, are appropriately the dominant metaphors in the new rites of consecration in the DRC.

Commissioning is done by the bishop on behalf of the Christian community, or by the superior on behalf of the congregation. Here the responsibilities facing the newly consecrated person are explained. A representative of the assembled community may also welcome the consecrated person and voice the church community's expectation of him or her.

CONCLUSION

It needs careful study and planning to construct these rites. It will also need "experimentation" on a small scale before they are made available for approval and general use. But the radical step and transition must be made to change the predominantly European rituals to predominantly African ones.

14

Some Pastoral Dimensions

Christianity's failure in Africa to touch deeper than a superficial degree the religiosity of the African person has been attributed almost universally by African and Africanist scholars to the failure or refusal of Western missionary Christianity in particular, and Western Christianity in general, to understand Christ's teaching and the scriptures as a whole in contexts other than the Euro-American one. In the African case, it has involved a refusal or failure to situate and understand the Gospel from the perspective of the African view of the world and life in the world. This attitude has been both pervasive and longstanding: officially it applies in some degree to almost all areas of theology and pastoral directives.

With regard to the liturgy, for example, we have seen that Idowu (1973: 26–49) complained as long as three decades ago that Nigerians do not find "spiritual suitability" and stimulus in any mainline Christian denominations—be they Anglican, Methodist, Evangelical, or Catholic. Referring to official Catholic documents, such as the encyclicals *Humanae Vitae* (1968) of Pope Paul VI, *Veritatis Splendor* (1993) of Pope John Paul II, and the monumental *Catechism of the Catholic Church* (1992) from the Congregation for the Doctrine of the Faith, Bujo (2001:73) laments similarly that their claim to universality has in actual fact "little to do with the world outside Europe and North America." Many African scholars share his view that even the new code of Canon Law issued in 1983, "which was supposed to make the fruits of the Second Vatican Council accessible and comprehensible in ecclesial praxis, simply failed to take heed of the concerns of the non-European churches. Not only judicial thinking, but its entire theological and ethical categories remain wholly Western." The situation compounds the anthropological pauperization of the continent:

This ethnocentrism affects all non-European churches, but applies in a particular way to Black Africa, since the black continent is receding into the background of consciousness, even in terms of the global community. If, however, it is true that an economy without a culture cannot exist, then Africa must resist a globalisation that seeks to level down all cultures, and thus perhaps all ethical insights too, into a kind of world ethos. What applies to the economy as a whole applies even more to the church, which must avoid a false absoluteness that denies ethical pluralism. (Bujo 2001:74)

This has also been the gist of this book's argument. But it becomes necessary at this point to spell out further issues touching the self-identity of the African church. I will do this by considering a few specific examples which impinge upon it: the process of government, the application of canon law, some urgent pastoral issues, and the question of maintaining unity in diversity.

SELF-IDENTITY OF THE AFRICAN CHURCH

Is there hope for the survival of the church in Africa if it does not develop an identity of its own? The Coptic Church in North Africa survived the onslaught and persecution of Islam—even if reduced to a relatively small core—and the Ethiopian Church has had a long history mainly because both churches were rooted in their localities. They had become part of the culture of the people, not an external intrusion. Once the church and the faith become cultural, it is very difficult, or perhaps impossible to eliminate them, short of annihilating the entire population of believers.

The second attempt at Christianizing Africa, or what Baur (1994) calls "the second encounter of Africa with the Gospel," from the sixteenth to the first half of the nineteenth century, did not leave much of itself in the vast southern region of the continent below the Sahara desert because of its association with the slave traders. As an official of the Propaganda Fide (the precursor of today's Roman Congregation for the Doctrine of the Faith) complained in 1833: "The greatest hindrance of the missions is the slave-trade, operated by the [Portuguese] Christians of Angola. It renders our religion odious to the Africans who keep in mind their chains instead of seeing the freedom brought to them by Jesus Christ" (see Baur 1994:95).

Other hindrances Baur mentions included the thorough Westernization of the African priests who trained in Portugal. The missionary methods and goals were also quite misplaced and contributed to the difficulties: (a) their approach was individualistic, not communal; (b) they concentrated on saving souls rather than establishing the church; and (c) they insisted on assimilating the African convert into the European religious culture.

Although these hindrances are still present during the "third encounter," the period with which this book is concerned, I cannot now imagine a situation where the Christian faith, or even the institutional church in some form, can be eliminated from the continent. Just as in Egypt and Ethiopia, Christianity is now rooted too deeply here for that eventuality to be realistically entertained. But these roots are still mainly in the form of popular Christianity. They also need to become part of official Christianity for Christianity in Africa to develop the more comprehensive and integral self-image that we have outlined in this part of the book.

Church Government

Africans in general admire the Catholic Church's system of installing its leaders. It is much less discordant and divisive than in other churches, where the choice of leaders is more democratic. For the faithful to fight among themselves and for churches to split across tribal or geographical lines over leadership controversies is known to happen from time to time in the latter in Africa, but hardly in the Catholic Church. Yet, this positive aspect, if not approached carefully, can work against the self-identity of the local church.

The essential leadership logic of the Catholic approach and structure is centralization. Centralization, however, means that the local church has no room to move on any major matter pertaining to its life. All direction comes from the center, from Rome, which may not promote the identity of the local church: various proposals for local liturgical rites have often not been approved by Rome, and translations of liturgical prayers in the vernacular have often been rejected. One hears in defense of this system that "the church is not a democracy," which is true. But if carried to excess it walks over very important theological points which are fundamental to the very meaning of the church itself.

The principle of the "sense of the faith" of the faithful—technically known as *sensus fidei* or *sensus fidelium*—constitutes one of the most important elements of the life of the church. Its complement is the principle of reception. Vatican II's *Dogmatic Constitution on the Church* (*Lumen Gentium*, n. 12), explains these principles. They are summarized in the *Catechism of the Catholic Church* (nn. 91–93):

> All the faithful share in understanding and handing on revealed truth. They have received the anointing of the Holy Spirit, who instructs them and guides them into all truth.
>
> The whole body of the faithful . . . cannot err in matters of belief. This characteristic is shown in the supernatural appreciation of faith (*sensus fidei*) on the part of the whole people, when, "from bishops to the last of the faithful," they manifest a universal consent in matters of faith and morals.
>
> By this appreciation of the faith, aroused and sustained by the Spirit of truth, the People of God, guided by the sacred teaching authority (*Magisterium*), . . . receives . . . the faith, once for all delivered to the saints. . . . The People unfailingly adheres to this faith, penetrates it more deeply with right judgment, and applies it more fully in daily life.

What is said in these paragraphs of the universal church, world bishops, and teaching authority can and must be applied first of all and in a most fundamental way to the local church and the local bishop. The "supernatural appreciation of the faith" does, in fact, most effectively take place here. Here is where the church is primarily to be found and concretely realized. Here is where the universal church emerges, in the sense that in the local church are contained all aspects of the universal church—faith, sacraments, and ministries—and not the other way around. Here is where the church must first of all "manifest universal consent in matters of faith and morals" and their practical requirements. This is what "reception" means, and it is by this process that the church, "the whole body of the faithful," is preserved in the truth.

When this expression of the faith is denied to the local church and is centralized from above—with appreciation of the faith not allowed to grow from below but being that of a supposedly universal nature—two consequences follow. First, the local church loses its identity. Second, and even more important, the people, as both the *Lumen Gentium* and the Catechism put it, can neither penetrate the faith deeply with right judgment nor apply it more fully in daily life.

Church Law

The need for law in the church, a standard or norm by which to measure and guide our lives as Christians—which is what the word "canon" in canon law implies—needs no justification. Norms are evident from the earliest times in the history of Christianity, as is evident in the *Didache* (c. 140) for the liturgy, the *Apostolic Tradition of Hippolytus* (c. 225), and the *Apostolic Constitutions* (fourth century) for election and ordination of bishops, presbyters, and various other matters.

Norms emerged with and were demanded by changing ecclesiastical circumstances and needs. Norms were formulated as supplements to or clarifications of the Gospel message, and were never intended to replace it. Obviously, they have constantly evolved and multiplied, and with the spread of the church to many places and cultures they became unwieldy. From very early on efforts were made to manage them. Most significant of these efforts for our purposes was Gratian's who in 1140 gave them the form to which current Catholic canon law is most indebted. Gratian followed the example of Peter Abelard's *Sic et Non* (1130), which tried to summarize the opinions of the Fathers on various theological issues.

The further centralization of the administrative structure of the church in Rome, and subsequent increasing legislative pronouncements by popes, councils, and individual bishops gave birth to Pope Benedict XV's *Codex Iuris Canonici*, the Code of Canon Law, which was promulgated in 1917. Essentially, law was now conceived as a kind of absolute formulation, abstract and independent of any concrete circumstances, to be applied in all circumstances. The new 1983 Code contains 1752 canons. It was promulgated by Pope John Paul II and intended to incorporate the insights of Vatican II, but it retained the essential outlook and form of the previous Code about the conception of law.

Nevertheless, it must be said that the Code of Canon Law does not contain the whole law of the Catholic Church: the pope and bishops can still legislate on particular issues not prescribed in the Code. Apart from necessary general prescriptions about the most fundamental aspects of the faith and Christian living, it is hardly possible to see how the life of the church worldwide can be micromanaged by regulations coming from a central place and still preserve the identity of the local church. That is why the code sometimes leaves room for local bishops or bishops' conferences to legislate on certain matters pertaining to a particular place. Without gainsaying the importance of universal law as guidance, one must, however, emphasize the importance of particular laws for particular areas and people. The pastoral aspect of the life of the church is touched in a special way by this issue.

It is neither possible nor desirable to illustrate this with too many examples from the code. Let one example with particular relevance to the African worldview suffice. Canon 227 talks about the Roman Catholic tradition of celibacy for clerics, saying that they "are obliged to observe perfect and perpetual continence . . . and therefore [perpetual] celibacy." The canon, drawing from the conciliar *Decree on the Ministry and Life of Priests* (*Presbyterorum Ordinis*, n. 16), calls celibacy a gift "for the sake of the kingdom of heaven," attempting to link the tradition with the New Testament (see Mt. 19:12). Both the canon and the document avoid, as F. Wulf (see Coriden/Green/Heintschel 1985:210) notes, "all untenable motives for celibacy—arising from notions of cultic purity or from subliminal depreciation of the body and of sexuality. . . ." The theology behind all this is an improvement from older church perspectives. Nevertheless, the discipline as it stands for the universal Catholic Church still presents a problem for Africa.

Lumbala (1998:106–108) shows that the discipline involves intrinsic and profound difficulties in Africa for the pastoral ministry of secular bishops and priests, among whose responsibilities is governing the people of God, the church. Not that sexual continence is foreign to Africa, he concedes, but this was in most cases required as a temporary, not a permanent state. At any rate, it was never required of persons who had responsibility over the people, who had to share completely in their life. These had to be married to fulfill their status as elders:

> An elder or a chief without a family is unthinkable in our cultures because he must be like the ancestors—a symbol of the transmission of life. Since the symbol unifies in itself the life visible and invisible, it is not enough that the priest exhibit only spiritual fatherhood (i.e., invisible life). In the concept of the church as family in Black Africa, priests and the bishops responsible to and for local Christian community must also be married and fathers of families. If the pastor is a person who has not transmitted life, he will be considered like a functionary who comes to a particular place for a certain period of time to perform a certain job. Even more, he will be considered as a kind of child, not as a full adult. It is enough to see how celibates are looked upon and treated in African traditions. No matter what their chronological age, they will never be able to sit in a meeting where the problems of life are treated. Marital experience is considered a requisite if a man is to exercise responsibility for guiding the human community.

Does this therefore mean that celibacy has no place in the church in Africa? This is not the case, as Lumbala further argues. Vowed religious of both sexes will continue to be celibate as witnesses for the Kingdom. But they should not have permanent governing responsibility in the church in Africa, such as bishops or parish priests. "They can only be animators of certain celebrations to which they are called in as visitors or when they are called upon to accomplish specific duties at a particular moment in a Christian community."

SOME PASTORAL QUESTIONS

During the second half of the twentieth century, questions arose which would involve the attention of the church in Africa more than ever before, and it seems they will continue to do so in the century we have just started. Some of these questions, such as the HIV/AIDS pandemic, are new and demand fresh and courageous thinking from the church. Others have been part of society for a long time; they only require being contextualized in new situations. All of them, however, relate in a fundamental way to the process of inculturation. They are part of "the joy and hope, the grief and anguish of the men [and women] of our time, especially of those who are poor or afflicted"—of which Vatican II's *Pastoral Constitution of the Church in the Modern World (Gaudium et Spes)* speaks in its opening paragraph—that are also, according to the same document, part and parcel of the life of the church.

Democracy, Justice, and Peace

Against claims that before colonialism most African societies lived either in total anarchy or complete autocracy, recent anthropological studies have shown evidence to the contrary. There existed both sophisticated forms of government and different levels of democratic governance in the various African societies. These levels differed depending on whether the particular society's political organization was based on diffused kinship, lineage or clan leadership groupings, or a centralized hierarchy of administrative authority.

Democracy in its primitive and pristine form as truly "government of the people, by the people, for the people" was more evident in the former than the latter. In the former, authority was truly authority by consensus, as among the Sang people of Namibia and Botswana. It was not so much an honor but a service, not to be too eagerly sought on account of the responsibilities it entailed. But there were mechanisms even in the truly hierarchical forms to curb extreme kinds of autocracy by the chief of the council of elders, as among the Ashanti of Ghana and the Nyoro of Uganda (see Magesa 1997:245–283).

In each of these systems, there was an intricate relationship between the rights and the responsibilities of the individual in society. To many observers, the responsibilities seemed to overshadow the rights, so that concern for the well-being of society as a whole appeared to take no account of the well-being of the individual person. In this sense justice seemed to be compromised. In the practical order of everyday life, this may have happened, as it does perhaps to a greater or lesser degree in all societies. Nevertheless, philosophically, it was expected that for society to thrive, every member had to be protected from harm, even if it came from "society." This is in fact what constituted the spirituality of African societies. They believed that it was especially on this harmony or peace within the social entity that the survival of all creation depended.

The slave trade movement and colonialism upset this philosophy of equilibrium profoundly, and undermined the practice of democracy and the vision of justice and peace that has previously been culturally envisioned in these societies. At independence, there were therefore few footprints for the new African rulers to follow with regard to these issues. Consequently, practically all post-independence governments became autocratic and brutal, respecting neither the human rights nor the social and economic development of the societies they were governing. It is important to acknowledge the role some prominent church leaders played as advocates of justice in this situation all over Africa. A few, like Bishop Janani Luwum of the Church of Uganda under the dictatorial regime of President Idi Amin, even gave up their lives in the process.

The structures that guard democracy and human rights are not yet securely established in Africa. There are two questions in the ongoing debate on this matter to which the Christian churches can make a contribution. One relates to the kind of democratic structures which would be relevant to Africa, and the other is how to go about constructing them. The churches' long experience with plurality, both conceptually (the church as one despite members' tribal and other differences) and practically (the church's unitive administrative machinery), is an asset in this discussion and process. Could the Christian churches, by their own life, offer theoretical and structural examples to society at large?

Of course, the churches themselves must be aware of their own very grave limitations. First of all, their lack of unity as Christian churches may belie much of the positive contribution they might wish to make to the debate. The animosity and lack of cooperation among them are sometimes glaring. Furthermore, as the 1994 genocide in "Christian" Rwanda showed, they have not been completely able to be a unifying factor among the different ethnic groups in Africa. This deprives the church of credibility in its witness to democracy, justice and peace. Moreover, some of the churches' lack of democratic structures and procedures in their own constitutions is a cause of lack of credibility as well. Even if the church, as God's instrument for human salvation, is not necessarily a democracy in the civil sense of the word and cannot structure its government that way, the hierarchical constitution must not be turned into an idol. It exists for and must always be put at the service of the faithful.

"Democracy, properly understood as respect for the dignity and rights of every human person and every group . . . is the clearest expression of the 'pastoral approach' of Jesus" (Magesa 2002:89). This calls for subsidiarity: let things be done at the level they can effectively be done without being usurped by a higher level of power. In the African clan model of church that theologians like John Mary Waliggo (1990) and E. E. Uzukwu (1996) advocate, even the chiefs (the popes and bishops, in this case) must listen to the community if they want to be faithful to the "Word," which is of its nature too big for them alone. They need to facilitate dialogue and participation.

Therefore, what Uzukwu (1996:130) describes as "the imported Roman and feudal autocracy which dominates the present ministerial practice of the Roman Catholic Church" does not have roots in African conduct. Nor, according to the Gospels, does it in Christian conduct. As the Gospels state, Christian leadership does not entail "lording it over them," but service. The "Son of Man did not come to be served but to serve . . ." (Mt. 20:28, Mk. 10:45); "Whoever humbles himself like this child is the greatest in the kingdom of heaven" (Mt. 18:4); "The greatest among you must be your servant" (Mt. 23:11, 20:27, Mk. 10:43); "the one who is least among all of you is the one who is the greatest" (Lk. 9:48; Mk. 10:44), and so on. This is the spirit of Christian leadership and church governance. On this matter as in many others the Gospels find expression in deep African expectations.

Poverty, Ignorance, and Disease

This is a subject about which much has been written in the context of Africa; discussion about it is as interminable as the solution is elusive.

Material poverty, lack of education, and disease were identified by the founding fathers of African independence as the enemy of African development, its "Axis of Evil." Many preventable diseases, illiteracy, and deficiency of necessities for a decent life still ravage the African continent. In all three areas, much more could have been done within Africa itself and by the international community to curtail their destructive effects in the decades since independence. That not much headway has been made in this struggle is an indictment both of African governments and of the political will of governments in the developed world which, while spending colossal amounts of resources on agents of death (such as armaments), are not willing to invest in developing human capital in Africa.

The Christian churches have participated in the battle against these forces since the beginning of evangelization in Africa. Establishing schools and hospitals was one of their main concerns. Christian missionaries may be faulted for some of their approaches to these issues, but it is clear that their effort helped in major areas of the development of the continent. Though perhaps indirectly and unintentionally, they certainly contributed to the success of the struggle for freedom. Freedom could not have happened had Africans not been educated, many of them in mission schools.

The pastoral questions for today, as Africa tries "to catch up" with the developed nations, involve the danger of materialism leading to secularism, misuse of the information revolution, and abandoning the spiritual in medicine and healing. The Christian churches can help Africa now look back to its own spiritual traditions. The central point of these traditions is the importance of the human person above everything else, and his and her holistic nature. The highest value cannot be consumerism but whether as many people as possible enjoy the necessities of life. Information alone cannot lead to enlightenment but the goal should be to use information to make life better for as many as possible. Finally, true healing of the person involves more than the curing of the body; it also means healing the soul. The two must take place simultaneously.

Sexual Ethics and HIV/AIDS

Human sexuality is the same everywhere. The moral issue is how peoples structure and use it—in the relationship between the genders, in marriage, and in sexual relations. Again, from the universal perspective, only general principles can be stated about this all important aspect of human life. The details are best left to the peoples involved, that is, to a particular culture. It is remarkable how, in contrast to the "holiness code" of Leviticus, little is said about sexuality and sex in the New Testament, particularly in the Gospels, either sociologically or ritually (in terms of ritual purity). By his words, attitude and actions, Jesus unmistakably emphasizes the dignity of the human person, and of women in particular; and he clearly underscores the unity of man and woman in marriage. St. Paul, on his part, also emphasizes the dignity of, and order in, marriage, and disapproves homosexual *acts*. Beyond these few basic points, however, the New Testament is silent. But the silence is eloquent: let cultures give direction to the structuring of human sexuality.

With various small differences from place to place, African culture structures sexuality and sexual activity around marriage and procreation. Normally, the use of human generative powers is permitted only within marriage and for the purpose of procreation. Any other use is subordinate and, apart from it is considered an aberration, often with negative consequences for the individuals concerned and for society at large.

This view of sexuality both protected and oppressed the woman in African society. Because the woman was seen to be the source of life, the utmost human and spiritual good, she was valued and respected. Her voice in things to do with life-elements such as cultivation, planting, and harvesting could not be ignored. Yet, she was oppressed in precisely the same areas; most often she was seen and valued only in these terms, that is, as a source of children and food and not fully as a human being in herself. For this reason, women were married off young, were socialized to accept polygamous unions, and their labor was exploited. Barrenness was invariably treated as a curse.

In this regard change has taken place in African external behavior, but the deepest convictions among many African men and women still rely on this principle. Some of the negative, anti-life aspects of the traditional approach to sexuality and sex are combining with the worst in the "modern" approach to complicate gender relations in Africa. The idea that women are instruments for men's sexual pleasure is widespread, so that even though traditional simultaneous polygamy is slightly on the decrease for economic and social reasons (such as the education of women), a new form of polygamy is on the rise. This is known in French-speaking Africa as *le deux-ième bureau* or "the second office," and is practiced throughout the urban areas of the continent. In this case a man has one official wife, but consorts with numerous mistresses whom he may or may not support financially. Some women get involved in these relationships willingly because it affords them "independence" from the ties of marriage along with the social and financial benefits of a relationship with a man, even if transient. But the situation can easily destroy family ties as well as degrade the human worth of the woman. In traditional polygamous unions all women in the union were considered truly wives, were entitled (at least in theory) to the same rights, and their children belonged to the clan, fostering the spiritual notion of ancestorship. In the developing system none of this necessarily applies, with incalculable detrimental effects on the social, moral, and spiritual fabric of society.

The most devastating consequence of this situation, however, has been the spread of the HIV/AIDS pandemic in Africa. The continent has the highest number of cases in the entire world of people infected by the virus and suffering and dying from the disease. The infection is almost entirely spread through heterosexual relations. This is different from other continents where a significant percentage of HIV/AIDS sufferers are homosexuals or drug addicts. It is not difficult to conclude from this that many of the heterosexual customs and much of the behavior in Africa are no longer instruments of life but of death. They need to be critiqued and rethought in terms of sexuality's purpose of enhancing life.

Bujo (2001:133–34) has already critiqued polygamy in the context of inculturation as being, among other things, "incompatible in modern Africa with the dignity of women." He argues correctly that in a changed culture, polygamy is no longer in the interest of life broadly conceived. His question is pertinent: "What does inculturation mean here?" To promote life, which is the ultimate goal of both the Gospel and African culture, polygamy must not be considered part of the picture of sexual relationships. This is so particularly in the midst of the AIDS epidemic. In contemporary African societies it is without doubt a contributing factor to the spread of HIV/AIDS.

This means that similar customary practices and rites that used to be agents of promoting life can no longer be seen as such and must be stopped. I am referring specifically to the levirate practice, cleansing rituals in which sexual relations take place and, in those rare occasions where it is still accepted, sexual hospitality. These practices are not only incompatible with the dignity of woman, they are agents of death. African cultural values in defense of life are upheld in transcending rather than in adhering to them.

One of the most vexing questions for the Catholic Church in the context of HIV/AIDS is the use of physical means (that is, condoms) as a help to prevent the spread of HIV/AIDS. The official teaching of the church has been consistent in rejecting their use to prevent procreation. It argues that every marriage act must be open to the transmission of life, and that only this openness makes possible the unitive aspect of marriage. This teaching was summarized after the Council by Pope Paul VI in his encyclical *Humanae Vitae* which maintains that condoms further promote "a contraceptive mentality" and are therefore morally intrinsically evil.

Unfortunately, the same reasoning is applied without modification to the use of condoms in the context of HIV/AIDS. The official Catholic Church argues that it is not allowed to use evil means (condoms) to achieve a good end (preventing of the spread of HIV/AIDS). But might not the argument be a little different here? Might it not be a case of preventing a greater evil (death by the epidemic)? Taking someone's life is always objectively evil, but when this happens in a situation of self-defense or in the process of defending someone else's life, or in a situation of justified war, then it is permissible to take a life. Obviously, any such argument must be carefully circumscribed. Still, might it not be a lesser evil to use condoms in a marriage situation where one partner is HIV-positive and the other is not? In Africa, the question is not academic.

SEARCHING FOR UNITY IN DIVERSITY

This section could very well have been titled "Maintaining Diversity in Unity." If inculturation as incarnation by definition accepts the identity of human groups and cultures—indeed of every human person as a unique creature of God—then diversity is a given and cannot be reduced to monism without injury to individuals or social groups. In this sense, diversity is a value that has to be maintained. But at the same time, it would be equally harmful to persons and human groups if diversity meant extreme separation in the sense of denying the existence and importance of reference points or benchmarks of human relationships and communion.

In the end this denial would nullify the purpose of the Christian faith, which is to gather all people in Christ irrespective of the legitimate differences that exist among them. It would also mean undercutting the very incarnation of Jesus Christ who, by being born among a particular people—the Jews—became human "like us in everything but sin," Jesus, in the Christian order of things, becomes therefore not only the archetype or paradigm of identity and diversity among humanity but also the point of its communion and unity. One of the tasks of the Christian community in the process of inculturation, and as a part of inculturation, in fact, is not to lose sight of the points that unite the church and that lead to the unity of humanity.

In this penultimate chapter of our work, let us discuss some concrete examples of developing African theological and pastoral perceptions. Rightly considered, they would clearly distinguish the African church as "truly African," as Pope Paul VI insisted in 1969 in Kampala, Uganda (Okure 1990:32–6). They would also mark it equally clearly "truly Christian," not tearing it apart from the universal communion of local churches.

There are some areas to which African theological thought has given considerable attention, and which are of capital importance both to African ecclesial identity and universal communion. They include the conception of the church, the perception or image and role of Jesus and Mary, and the nature of the spiritual world. Keeping both aspects of identity and unity in mind, let us in turn consider each one of these areas briefly.

The Church as Family of God

Since the end of the African Synod in 1994, what has been hailed as its most original important contribution was the synod's image of the church as "God's Family." In his post-synodal exhortation, *Ecclesia in Africa* (n. 63), Pope John Paul II singled out this point for special notice:

> Not only did the Synod speak of inculturation, but it also made use of it, taking the *Church* as *God's Family* as its guiding idea for the evangelisation of Africa. The Synod Fathers acknowledged it as an expression of the Church's nature particularly appropriate for Africa. For this image emphasizes care for others, solidarity, warmth in human relationships, acceptance, dialogue and trust. The new evangelisation will thus aim at *building up the Church as Family*, avoiding all ethnocentrism and excessive particularism, trying instead to encourage reconciliation and true communion between different ethnic groups, favoring solidarity and the sharing of personnel and resources among the particular Churches, without undue ethnic considerations. (italics in original)

Quoting the express wish of the synodal bishops, the pope then entrusted the work of developing this idea of church as family to the theologians and hoped that they would show "all the riches contained in this concept, showing its complementarity with other images of the Church."

Here, perhaps more than anywhere else in the document, the pope captures both the best characteristics of the African community as well as the real dangers it is and has always been exposed to. If the church is a community, as it is meant to be, it cannot but be made up of people who care for others in a concrete way. This in Africa is manifested in the reality of the family beyond the West's nuclear conception of it. Taking care of the poor, the sick, the orphans, the widows and the otherwise poor, as the Gospels instruct us, is in Africa the responsibility of any and all members of the family. It is, in fact, an expectation. Refusal to accept the responsibility incurs, beyond a feeling of guilt, the probability of disrupting the community with attendant suffering.

But all this, plus solidarity, warmth in human relationships, acceptance, dialogue, and trust necessitate a new perception and structure of church where they can be expressed concretely: "to bring glad tidings to the poor," "to proclaim liberty to captives and recovery of sight to the blind," "to let the oppressed go free," "to proclaim a year acceptable to the Lord." It will not be possible to do so in a perception of church that is more theoretical than real, an impalpable idea of church where these are conceived as "spiritual" rather than practical demands.

In the former conception concern, warmth, dialogue and trust seem like "extras," actions performed to score points with God. In the latter, they are the ordinary demands of living as a community, actions performed because the life and cohesion of both the individual and society require it. This does not mean, of course, that they are not spiritual acts, but that their spiritual quality emanates from their nature as loving acts, intimately joining together people in the community.

The structure of a large parish or even sub-parish with hundreds of members that meets only for Sunday liturgies is not amenable to the practice of the church as God's family. I have said that the idea of church as God's family was original from the Synod; but let me correct that impression somewhat. The expression was original and precise. The reality, however, had already been in practice in the Eastern African dioceses for two decades, since the early 1970s. The Association of Member Episcopal Conferences of Eastern Africa (AMECEA) mandated then that "Church life [in the region] must be based on communities in which everyday life and work takes place: those basic and manageable social groupings whose members can have real inter-personal relationship and feel a sense of communal belonging, both in living and working" (see Magesa 1993:5–6). The bishops were referring to their call to establish small Christian communities throughout the region. They emphasized that this was necessary for the church in the region to become a truly "local" church, to have its own identity; but these are also the essential structural elements for constructing the church as family.

The fact that this ideal of establishing viable SCCs as local churches does not diminish their importance and necessity for constructing the church as church of God; it makes them even more essential. Yet, we cannot afford to ignore some of the dangers inherent in this model of church in the African environment. Pope John Paul mentions them in his exhortation as "ethno-centrism" and "excessive particularism." In the tribal context, these may threaten to disrupt the internal unity of communities and the unity that exists between and among them. These are the dangers that must be fought against as Africa struggles to build a church which is not only local but possesses a family structure and spirit.

The family model of church will facilitate facing the issues that confront Christians even more sharply in the new millennium. Agatha Radoli (1993:x) enumerated the major ones for the African church:

- To shed off the earlier attitude of privilege inherited from the Western missionaries because this does not promote dialogue, ecumenism and the establishment of structures that respect human rights.
- To shift from the dependency situation it has maintained to the present time as this does not lead to maturity.
- To reshape its theology, liturgy, forms of ministry and church government according to the experiences and needs of the People of God in this region.
- To take its prophetic call more seriously so as to enlighten the people to the prevailing situation of change within the region.

- To use some of its material wealth for the millions of poor and suffering people of the region.
- To discern daily what the signs of the times in the region mean in terms of its mission.

Jesus: Brother-Ancestor-Healer in the Church as Family

Among other African theologians, Bujo (2001:154) declares that "a genuinely African model of church must necessarily have recourse to the idea of the ancestors." Practically all African theologians agree. It is remarkable that in 1967 in his *Message to the People of Africa* (*Africae Terrarum*, n. 10) Pope Paul VI himself spoke favorably of the African ancestral cult, "the bond with the ancestors, which finds expression in so many widespread forms of worship." Perhaps more than any other theologian to date, the Tanzanian theologian Charles Nyamiti has elaborated this theme. One may differ with some of his conclusions, but his basic orientation lies in African spiritual sensitivity and cannot be disputed. In an article specifically on ecclesiology, Nyamiti (1993:36–56) explains why and how Jesus Christ can be called an ancestor in the African sense of the term. And since in Christian theology the church is the concrete expression of the mystery of Christ among us, Nyamiti goes on to show very carefully why and how we can use an "ancestral ecclesiology to structure the church and experience it as such.

The characteristics of an African ancestor, he argues, can be applied to Christ. Both can be spoken of as sharing blood with their descendants, the African ancestors through generation and Christ through the incarnation. Furthermore, both are seen to be sacred, possessed of superhuman power, and mediators between the visible world of human experience and the invisible world of the spirits and God. Further, both can and do communicate with us in various ways, helping us to live an ethical life. Their life remains an example for us to follow. Christ's ancestorship to us, however, rooted as it is in the relationship of the Trinity (the Godhead), is far beyond all expectations of human ancestorship in its perfection. It "transcends all clanic, tribal, racial or sexual distinctions." Yet, analogically, it expresses the African idea of and relationship to the ancestors and vice versa.

As the extension of the mystery of Christ, ancestral ecclesiology must be seen to possess and express the same "elements related to Christ's ancestorship, such as universal kinship, beneficial mediation, exemplarity of conduct and frequent encounter with Him through regular devout prayer and ritual offerings, especially the Eucharist" (Nyamiti 1993:40). Underlying all of these characteristics, according to Nyamiti, is the foundational element of community and communion, in Christian terms the communion of saints in its tripartite dimension: the church militant, the church suffering, and the church triumphant. In my view, this corresponds to and should arise from the African conception of the living and yet-to-be-born, the spirits, and the ancestors.

From a Black African perspective, this means that Jesus founds a new clan fellowship and is himself its founding ancestor, who thus combines in himself the roles of ancestor and father of the tribe. Through his death and resurrection, however, he infinitely transcends . . . the African concept of ancestors. Jesus is not simply the primal or founding ancestor, but the proto-ancestor, and this means that he alone initiates the eschatological dimension of the living, the dead (i.e., the living-dead), and those not yet born. (Bujo 2001:155)

Nyamiti notes that this model of ancestral ecclesiology has several dimensions, which he calls "sub-models." Each of them has certain moral demands. Explaining these dimensions and their implications, Nyamiti (1993:53–54; see also Bujo 2001:143–60) says that the liberation dimension implies freedom from personal and structural sin; the sacramental dimension implies devout celebration together of the sacraments as a sign of Christian communion. Respect for authority is a demand of the institutional dimension, and meditation on the scriptures is a demand of proclamation. From the African perspective, healing and hospitality are also basic dimensions of the church. These emphasize integral healing of the person, social inclusiveness, and inter-religious dialogue. Every ecclesial and ecclesiastical dimension should have as its final view the creation of a church with an "African physiognomy," that is, the obligation of making African all areas of life in the church.

Mary: Queen/Mother of the Christian Community

On December 8, 1854, Pope Pius IX proclaimed in *Ineffabilis Deus* the doctrine of Mary's immaculate conception—that Mary was conceived without sin. Almost a century later, on November 1, 1950, in the *Munificentissimus Deus* Pope Pius XII declared as revealed teaching that Mary, "after her life on earth, was assumed, body and soul, to the glory of heaven." These two doctrines and the consequent practice of the Catholic Church in prayer and other devotions of looking at Mary as "mediatrix" between the Christian community and God have long been a source of much controversy in ecumenical circles.

While the Eastern Orthodox Church does not have much problem with this kind of mariology, Protestant churches object. Seeing Christ as the only redeemer, mediator and source of grace, they see the Catholic and Orthodox approach as dangerously close to placing Mary on the same level of Christ in the economy of human salvation. They thus see the danger of "mariolatry" (worship of Mary) in this approach, something they find hard to square up with the unique salvific role of Christ.

This problem goes back in various ways and intensity to the time of the Fathers. Recall the debate in the fifth century about Mary being the mother of Christ *(Christotokos)* or mother of God *(Theotokos)*. Nestorius, patriarch of Constantinople, and his followers, the Nestorians, said she was to be seen simply as mother of Christ; God cannot have a mother. Cyril, bishop of Alexandria, however, was vehemently opposed to this view and defended Mary as truly mother of God. This position won the day at the Council of Ephesus in 431.

Vatican II was very concerned about this enduring problem among Christians. Its position was that by being granted the grace to be mother of Christ and thus mother of God, God so exalted Mary that she is to Christians truly "Mother of divine grace." Christians can therefore approach her in prayer with the sure knowledge that she will intercede for them before her son. The Council advised Christians in the *Dogmatic Constitution on the Church* (*Lumen Gentium*, n. 58), to have a deep, permanent and sincere "filial love toward our mother and to the imitation of her virtues."

Apart from the various philosophical aspects of the theology of Ephesus, such as the definition on the hypostatic union of Jesus' human and divine natures in one person, Africans should not have any problem at all conceiving Mary as intercessor or mediatrix between humanity and God. On the practical level, not only the mother, but feminine nature as a whole, are conceived and valued precisely because of this quality of mediatorship. In the family and community, mothers are seen as especially endowed with this gift. One does not hesitate at all to approach one's mother for a favor one knows only the father can give.

This becomes even more obvious when the woman in question has a high profile in the community—a queen-mother, for example. By virtue of being mother of Christ and mother of God, Mary enjoys central devotion among African Christians as the mother of the clan. Through her, life has come to us in Jesus Christ. We can say that together with Christ, she is the founder of the Christian clan. If Christ is our brother-ancestor *par excellence*, Mary is our mother-ancestress *par excellence*. Such mariology can hardly be questioned in the African milieu.

The Activity of the Spirit and the Spirits

Pentecostalism and other spirit movements are today, as we know, worldwide phenomena within Christianity. In African Christianity, the modern Pentecostal churches and gatherings attract interest from people in all walks of life. People flock to them for healing or exorcism or wealth. But it is also obvious in the spirit-oriented AICs, which emphasize spiritual healing.

From the perspective of the African worldview, the spirits are part and parcel of the cosmos, and the human community has to deal with them in one way or the other. Good spirits are to be welcomed and cherished, and bad spirits must be cast out and driven away. In its extreme form, this belief leads to animism, which may lead to a neurotic view of reality. But considered properly, it is a way of looking at reality that cannot with integrity be condemned wholesale by Christian theology.

African Christian theology will see in the African belief in spirits the power of God acting mysteriously in the world. Examples of such action are abundant in the Old Testament. But they are not absent in the New Testament. They appear in the Gospel narratives about the birth of Jesus and his childhood (for example, Mt. 1:18–25, Lk. 1:26–38), his life and teaching (for example, Mk. 1:12–13, Lk. 4:1–13), and in the Acts of the Apostles (for example, Acts 10, 16:25–34). When people claim the privilege of certain apparitions, most Africans are more inclined to believe than to disbelieve.

Of course, much guidance is needed in all of this. But this is not to say that belief in the existence of spirits must be eliminated as contrary to Christian maturity or reason in the manner of rationalist philosophy. Belief in the existence of spirits does not necessarily contradict reason. On the contrary, it helps the contemporary age to accept a holistic view of life.

The Christian understanding of the Holy Spirit can grow into profound appreciation within this context. If the spirits are an integral part of human life, even more is the Holy Spirit. In Christian circles, her presence must then always be felt, permeating and animating everything and blowing wherever she wills. This leads inevitably to a greater appreciation of the presence among, and concern for, us of God the Father and of Jesus Christ his Son. It leads to a more practical theology and ecclesiology.

15

Concluding Remarks

We must go forward, not backward. . . . We must build our own faith. . . . For better or for worse we are living in the world of the . . . [twenty-first] century, and our lives must be lived amid the complexities which the accumulation of many generations have produced. We cannot bodily lift and take over for our spiritual uses the religious setting or the intellectual outlook of any former period. We can find inspiration, kindling power, leadership, eternal truth, immortal words, and the most dynamic Person of all the centuries when we go back to the . . . heights where the stream began, but we must work out our own Church, our own faith, our own body of thought, our own interpretation, our own social order, and if we are ever to have a kingdom of God it must be one we ourselves build by going forward with our faith and hope and love. (Jones 1924:23)

This metaphor of Rufus Jones is very telling as an illustration of the responsibility that faces all levels of the church with respect to inculturation; it draws out the implications of the process as well. We can be enriched by the passing stream, but because we are situated in a new time and space, we cannot touch the same water of the stream twice. The stream of life is ever flowing. Similarly, as Jones warns, "We cannot recover the pure Galilean religion any more than we can recover Eden. Earthly paradises and pure perfections that have been in earlier, simpler ages cannot be 'restored'" (Jones 1924:23).

Bolaji Idowu uses the same metaphor to make the same point. He compares the church "to a powerful living stream which flows into and through the nations." Its waters enrich the lands through which it passes with the silt it has collected throughout its journey. Even as it does so, however, the stream cannot help but adapt itself "to the shape and features of each locality, taking its colouring from the native soil, while in spite of all these structural adaptations and diversifications its *esse* and its *differentia* are not imperilled but maintained in consequence of the living, ever-replenishing, ever-revitalizing spring which is its source" (Idowu 1973:13).

AFRICA IN THE TWENTY-FIRST CENTURY

At the beginning of the twenty-first century, what are the shape and features of the African continent through which the stream of the Christian faith and the church flows? How may we envision the coloring it should take while enriching the continent with the good, fertile soil it has collected from other lands and continents throughout the centuries? For a start, we must first try to grasp the forces that are influencing the continent and therefore also the church here.

The existential situation in Africa appears to be determined by two powerful factors. There is, on the one hand, a search for identity or the desire for self-authenticity. On the other hand, there is an equally strong desire to keep pace with other members of the world community in terms of modernizing its political and economic institutions and social structures. This latter effort is usually referred to as the process of development. Both of these factors influence all levels of personal, private and public life. Indeed, it can be said that, in the long run, it perhaps determines them, at least to a certain extent. In concrete terms, this means that political decisions, economic planning, social policies and even religious orientations take place with these factors as theoretical or practical foundations, so that many of the authors of these decisions in personal or communal life openly claim to base themselves on, and to draw legitimacy from, these factors. It is true, at any rate, that different ways of approaching national and religious issues in the different African states can be traced back to one or the other or a combination of these factors.

Africa's struggle for identity and authenticity is mainly a cultural question, whereas that of development is essentially a technological one. Identity, as we have insisted, calls for the re-appropriation of cultural roots for the sake of an inner sense of direction, psychological security and social confidence. It is thus in itself a rather "theoretical" endeavor. But it is vitally important and its results are closely linked to the more overtly practical or pragmatic issue of development, whose purpose is to provide the material necessities and comforts of life which, although taken for granted in many other parts of the world, are hardly a reality for the majority in the region. Together, "identity" and "development" spell holistic human progress, not only "having" more but "being" more.

Neither issue (that is, identity or development) is new in the practical historical experience of Africa and its peoples, but each is made extremely urgent now by the prevailing world situation in which Africa must try to realize both of them. John Tomlinson (1999:2) has explained accurately that the world situation today is made up of personal, social and international interconnections that are very complex. The process involves a "rapidly developing and ever-densening network of interconnectedness and interdependencies." Together and in very intricate ways, this network affects Africa's struggle for identity and development in at least two very significant ways.

First, it makes the interaction between the searches for identity and development very uncertain and tricky, each seeming to stand in the way and consequently impede the realization of the other. Second, it renders very difficult Africa's linkage on anything like equal terms with other parts of the world, especially those enjoying a high degree of scientific and technological know-how and, therefore, cultural dominance. But technological culture today forms the "engine" or "motor," as it were, of contemporary global life. Without scientific know-how, what kind of partner can Africa become in the dialogue of nations? What kind of partnership between Africa and the rest of the world in any given area of human life emerges in this situation of technological, and therefore political, economic and social disenfranchisements?

I will discuss below the first issue with reference to the Christian church: namely, how can the church, with a minimum of complications, approach the question of identity and development in Africa as part of the process of "being at home" here? I will discuss this question by indicating some limitations to the institutional church's effort to insert itself in these current realities. These limitations, if taken seriously, will enhance the church's own identity while at the same time promoting desirable development for the continent. For the moment, however, let me consider how the process of globalization has forced contemporary Africa into a liminal condition, bringing the continent into a situation of transition, culturally and economically, with all the uncertainties and pain associated with this condition.

We might profitably use a historical analogy. Technologically and economically, the Industrial Revolution in the eighteenth and nineteenth centuries in Europe marked its transition from a feudal, agrarian society of the late Middle Ages to one characterized by the mechanized production of goods. Intellectually and culturally, the Enlightenment also marked this transition. "Central to Enlightenment thought were the use and the celebration of reason, the power by which man understands the universe and improves his own condition. The goals of rational man were considered to be knowledge, freedom and happiness" (NEB/4 1989:504). The Enlightenment and the Industrial Revolution gave impetus to each other to become the cultural and technological foundations of contemporary Europe.

But what interests us in these European phenomena are the human factors involved. The Industrial Revolution necessitated a degree of slavish labor and destruction of social relationships previously unknown in Europe. Community was gradually replaced by an individualistic outlook on life, an outlook concerned above all with material advancement. Spiritually, the transition was probably even more traumatic. The spiritual and emotional power that the church had previously held over people began to crumble before the assaults that the supremacy of reason and empirical knowledge made on society. Renaissance humanism emphasized the primacy of rationality, which Europe eventually came to accept as its guiding principle in practically all aspects of life.

In a way, these developments resemble what Africa has been experiencing for the last fifty years or so, during its own time of transition from a traditional to a modern outlook. It is important to mention one big difference between the two, however. The version of this transition in Africa is more rapid, much deeper and much more sweeping than what Europe experienced. The globalization process engulfing Africa is a much more encompassing phenomenon. The new realities of globalization make the continent unsure which way to go or how to get there. This leaves it open and vulnerable to many negative aspects of the process. For example, it has become literally a dumping ground for obsolete technologies from industrialized regions. Even worse, Africa has been turned into a place to dump poisonous substances and conduct dangerous experiments. The cultural sphere is no safer. Globalization pushes Africa, with financial and political pressure, to become an uncritical consumer of values that may appear attractive and irresistible on the surface, but are hardly useful in terms of its identity and its authentic and holistic development.

Historical events have left a lasting legacy on Africa, one that combines with globalization to make things worse. When this fact is denied, it merely exacerbates matters. If, however, it is accepted and faced with courage, Africa's prospects could be brighter. I have too often mentioned or alluded to the experiences of slavery and colonialism to repeat them here. What has not been as clearly appreciated until recently is the international systemic or institutionalized racism that complicates Africa's struggle for identity and development, as was proved by the United Nations-sponsored Conference on Racism, Racial Discrimination, Xenophobia and Intolerance held in Durban, South Africa, from 31 August to 8 September 2001.

SYSTEMIC RACISM

Richard Jenkins (1997:49, 83) suggests that racism is an ideology forming "an aspect of the social construction of ethnic differentiation." As he explains, it "exists in institutional arrangements and practices which have systematically detrimental outcomes or consequences for 'racial' categories. . . ." The consequence is what Albert Memmi (2000) has described as "ethnophobia," or, more broadly, "heterophobia." In the context of Africa, it refers to the dislike of the black race: Black people are seen not as the "others," human persons with equal dignity, but rather as the "rest of them," unequal to "us" in every way. Practically, it justifies feelings of superiority and privilege or, at an extreme but by no means rare end, hostility and aggression over them.

In this area, the circumstance of African-Americans in North America and the Aborigines in Australia can be seen as microcosms of what, macrocosmically, faces the nation-states of sub-Saharan Africa and Africa as a whole in the international community. Steve Martinot (2000), introducing Memmi's book on racism, discusses the African-American predicament: "For African Americans, white racism has produced a kind of double consciousness: 'the sense of always looking at one's self through the eyes of others.'" It involves, he argues, a feeling of absolute powerlessness among the African-Americans, "the feeling that one's consciousness and one's world are always spoken for, narrativized before the fact, and appropriated by the surrounding white society. For African-Americans, this translates into the inability to be non-black in an America that rejects Blacks, or the refusal to be non-American in an America that refuses Black Americans" (Martinot 2000:xvi).

The point here is not to dwell upon racism in the United States, but to explain the condition of the African continent in this matter. In view of

Martinot's observation, three distinct but related realities emerge in the prevailing African situation. Africa lacks the courage: first, to define itself; second, to transform its own experience of the world into an asset for its own advantage; and, third, to accept its own African-ness in a world that vastly rejects it.

Africa cannot, in its present state, take for granted what other regions of the world simply "assume," whether in the economic, political, cultural or social realms. For most other continents and regions, inclusion in the international socio-economic and political discourse on a more or less equal footing is not much of an issue. For Africa, however, it is an endless struggle. Accordingly, Africa's conflicts, its refugees, its diseases, and so on, do not attract as much international attention or resources to solve them. Unless they threaten to spread globally, they are often trivialized and referred to as "Africa's problems." One U.N. World Health Organization official was recently quoted as saying that if HIV/AIDS had devastated Europe the way it has Africa, many more resources in terms of finances and experts would have been committed to its prevention and/or cure.

Deep uncertainty about its place and role among the community of nations in the three areas I have mentioned above now places Africa in a liminal or transitional stage in its history. To go forward on a sure footing, it has to try to clarify to itself what form its identity will take and, based on that, what the direction of its development should be. While it is not possible to tell for sure at the present time the outcome or resolution of this process, it is to be expected that it will be a painful one before it settles down to some sort of acceptable order.

ASPECTS OF LIMINALITY OF THE CHURCH

Let us now turn to a brief discussion about the process of interaction between identity and development with reference to Christianity and the Christian church in Africa. As can be easily appreciated, it is a process greatly influenced by the conditions that I have just outlined. What in the Christian church today is called the "struggle" for, or process of, inculturation and contextualization, is similar to the search for identity and development in the wider society. With different ultimate motivations and perhaps using different means, both, but each in its proper sphere, tend to the same goal.

Globalized and globalizing Christianity have created for the African church the "problem" of inculturation in the acute form we find here. As we have shown throughout, inculturation is fundamental to the church because the church is by nature missionary and so, in a sense, the problem of inculturation is inevitable. Historically, however, this process was short-circuited in Africa, so that, as Appiah (2001:25) points out, "African peoples and cultures were denied the freedom to interact with the Christian message in such a way that would yield an African incarnation of Christianity." Appiah explains that "By the time Christian missionaries arrived in Africa the dichotomous consideration of peoples tended to apply to 'civilized Europeans' and 'primitive Africans,' 'Christian Europe' and 'heathen (pagan) Africa' etc. Europe was now the new Kingdom of God on earth, and the Christianizing motive accorded European conquerors the freedom to operate *sicut miles Christi* [like soldiers of Christ]." Pope Nicholas VI, for instance, instructed the king of Portugal in 1494, to "invade, conquer and submit to perpetual slavery" the people of Africa in the service of the Gospel (Appiah 2001:24).

The problem of inculturation in the essentialist sense is therefore much more complicated in Africa today than it should have been. It has now become, as Sékou Touré described it, an exercise in restoration or "rehabilitation" of the suppressed, sometimes unacknowledged values of African people's spiritualities (see Okolo 1994:47). Ironically enough, many indigenous religious leaders are themselves ambivalent about this, and it is the missionaries who, by and large, now wish to correct the situation. "'We have talked them into it, now we have to talk them out of it,' seems to be the sentiment of many missionaries when they see a catechesis, liturgy and a Christian lifestyle that are increasingly irrelevant to Africa" (Doornbos 1995:262). Inculturation is further complicated by the chasm described above between the level of industrialization in Africa and that in the developed regions of the world.

Considering the existentialist aspect of inculturation, the question is how and to what extent the church in Africa can and should engage itself in the political and economic issues that now face the continent. The question involves a search for a solution to the many practical issues that arise as a result of the state of relationships in the contemporary world. It brings to the fore some of the acute negative elements of this state that impact human life in Africa. We can mention only a few as illustrations: famine and hunger, ethnic conflict and genocide, consumerism, foreign debt, corruption and acts of terrorism in almost every African city. These are the factors that form the context of the life and ministry of the church today. How can it influence them in an ethical way and in the process not compromise African identity, on the one hand, and the need to develop, to be an adult, self-reliant member of the world community, on the other?

But there are "limitations" to the church's insertion in this task. I will speak of what the church *cannot* do, given its present constitutional makeup. I will also speak of what the church *should not* do, because it might compromise African identity and the Christian meaning of authentic development.

The first is perhaps the easiest problematic to explain. In general, the institutional church in Africa, on account of its existing structure, lacks a sufficient awareness of the processes of globalization and its practical consequences, both positive and negative. Individual Christians and certain Christian associations are, of course, very knowledgeable about the questions and issues involved for the church and for society in general, mainly because of their work in civil society. They would be ready and willing to share this knowledge within the church. But the institutional church as it now stands in Africa lacks avenues for this participation by the laity. The result is that many of these individuals and organizations are kept at the sidelines of the church's engagement in the contextualization process that is called for by globalization.

It is not that the church lacks the theoretical tools to enable this participation and engagement. To give only one example: the body of literature known as the Social Teaching of the Church, begun in modern times by Pope Leo XIII in 1891 with his encyclical *Rerum Novarum*, has not been static; it has constantly been updated at both the universal and, in some regions, very effectively at the local level as well. Pope John Paul II's work, for example, is remarkable in this area. Whereas he has built a reputation of being rather restorationist in dogmatic questions, he has been very progressive and quite even-handed in pointing out the effects of globalization on peoples and the environment and the need to engage the laity in dealing with them. But this body of ideas currently forms an integral part of neither catechetical nor on-going Christian formation in Africa, and consequently remains unknown and ineffective there.

It is rather ironical and difficult to explain the fact that as the church in Africa is today in the midst of the transition from a predominantly missionary-structured and -oriented church to an African-based one, it at the same time seems to be engulfed by a fortress-like mood. Its hierarchy is very defensive of traditions that, in the long run, can help consolidate neither African Christian identity nor authentic Christian development. This situation has to be faced because "the churches cannot constructively undertake important changes without a better understanding of the emerging situation, a rethinking of what we have to offer to this kind of a world, and how best to offer it" (Stackhouse 2000:15).

Therefore, while the church must, for the sake of contextualization, be constantly engaged in the dialogue of ideas and action with today's globalized world, it nevertheless needs to approach this relationship in the right way. I am referring to attitudes of mind which have been pervasive within the church in its relationship to the world, but which are no longer helpful. Let me list a few of the most conspicuous ones and explain each briefly. These are: dogmatism and duality, and triumphalism and exclusivity. Some of these have already been reflected in what we have discussed in this book as reasons behind the Christian church's failure to be at home in Africa.

A sense of identity for all partners in a conversation is, of course, necessary for any dialogue to be meaningful, but identity is not dogmatism. By its very definition, globalization means rapid change and a fluidity of ideas and realities. While the church must know where it stands on issues and be clear about its ethical position on fundamental moral questions, it can no longer bring predetermined answers to the conversation about them or how to resolve them. This is one of the points that have negatively affected the process of inculturation in Africa, because the church has not been open enough to the realities that deeply affect the continent. It has had too strong a sense of what I will call "duality," of being absolute about good and bad in the world. It has not realized seriously enough that, in many modern situations, such clear-cut divisions are not *a priori* possible. It takes time to arrive at a satisfactory answer to many issues and questions, and even then, indeed, the vision may still be blurred. In today's world, a blurred vision on many issues is often what, as people of faith, we have to work with.

Consequently, attitudes and practices of triumphalism and insularity, attitudes that reflect exclusivity, do not serve the cause of inculturation. The image that we have already alluded to and employed, first proposed by Eugene E. Uzukwu (1996) and developed by Bénézet Bujo (2001), cannot today be more appropriate for the African church in this regard: it has to be "a listening Church" with big ears. It has to be able to see everything, to listen to all and, in a joint endeavor with as many people and groups as possible, thereby decide what the Christian thing to do is.

Describing inculturation as a reality that puts the African church in a liminal condition, or a state of transition, does not mean that the tasks it implies and calls for will someday come to a complete close. On the contrary, inculturation in both its essentialist and existentialist forms is an ongoing process for the entire life of the church. Nevertheless, there must come a time when a particular local church must arrive at a clear perception of its identity precisely as particular and local; it must realize and know its role as part of a particular culture and as an agent of holistic development; and it must also be seen as a distinct entity in the community of other entities. When such a time comes, we can, at least in the sociological sense, say that the period of transition has passed. This is what we wish. We pray that the church on the African continent will become.

Bibliography

Aagaard, Anna Marie. 1995. "Pluralism, Ambiguity and Dialogue: Towards an Inter-cultural Hermeneutics for Mission and Ecumenism" in Anton Houtepen, ed. *The Living Tradition: Towards an Ecumenical Hermeneutics of the Christian Tradition* (Utrecht: IIMO).

Akenson, D. H. 2000. *Saint Saul: A Skeleton Key to the Historical Jesus* (Oxford: Oxford University Press).

Amaladoss, Michael. 1995. "Gospel and Culture in Cross-cultural Mission: Some Hermeneutical Reflections" in A. Houtepen, *Ecumenism and Hermeneutics* (Utrecht: IIMO), pp. 101–116.

Andreas, Brian. 1993. *Mostly True: Collected Stories & Drawings* (Decorah, Ia.: Story People).

Appiah, Simon Kofi. 2001. *Africanness, Inculturation, Ethics: In Search of the Subject of an Inculturated Christian Ethics* (Frankfurt am Main: Peter Lang).

Baum, Gregory. 1970. *Man Becoming: Man in Secular Experience* (New York: Herder and Herder).

Baur, John. 1994. *2000 Years of Christianity in Africa: An African History 62–1992* (Nairobi: Paulines Publications Africa).

Barrett, David B., ed. 1982. *World Christian Encyclopedia: A Comparative Survey of Churches and Religions in the Modern World, AD 1900–2000* (Oxford/New York: Oxford University Press).

Bediako, Kwame. 1992. *Theology and Identity: The Impact of Culture upon Christian Thought in the Second Century and Modern Africa* (Oxford: Regnum Books).

Bediako, Kwame. 1995. *Christianity in Africa: The Renewal of a Non-Western Religion* (Maryknoll, N.Y.: Orbis Books).

Beller, R. 2000. *Person and Community in Africa: A Pastoral Approach to the Spirituality of the Focolare Movement* (Nairobi: Tangaza College, M.A. Theology Thesis, mimeo).

Bergant, Dianne. 1982. *Job, Ecclesiastes* (Collegeville, Minn.: Liturgical Press).

Bernier, Paul. 1992. *Ministry in the Church: A Historical and Pastoral Approach* (Mystic, Conn.: Twenty-Third Publications).

Bettenson, Henry, ed. 1963. *Documents of the Christian Church* (London: Oxford University Press).

Blenkinsopp, Joseph. 1992. *The Pentateuch: An Introduction to the First Five Books of the Bible* (New York: Doubleday).

Boff, Clodovis and George W. Pixley. 1989. *The Bible, the Church, and the Poor* (Maryknoll, N.Y.: Orbis Books).

Borg, Marcus J. 1987 (1991 ed.). *Jesus—A New Vision: Spirit, Culture, and the Life of Discipleship* (San Francisco: HarperSanFrancisco).

Borg, Marcus J. and N. T. Wright. 1999 (2000 ed.). *The Meaning of Jesus: Two Visions* (London: SPCK; San Francisco: HarperSanFrancisco).

Bosch, David J. 1991. *Transforming Mission: Paradigm Shifts in Theology of Mission* (Maryknoll, N.Y.: Orbis Books).

Brown, Raymond E. 1977. *The Birth of the Messiah: A Commentary on the Infant Narratives in Matthew and Luke* (New York: Doubleday).

Brown, Raymond E. 1979. *The Community of the Beloved Disciple: The Life, Loves and Hates of an Individual Church in New Testament Times* (New York: Paulist Press).

Brown, Raymond E. 1984. *The Churches the Apostles Left Behind* (New York: Ramsey).

Brox, Norbert. 1996. *A Concise History of the Early Church* (New York: Continuum).

Bühlmann, Walbert. 1976. *The Coming of the Third Church* (Slough, England: St. Paul Publications; Maryknoll, N.Y.: Orbis Books).

Bühlmann, Walbert. 1982. *God's Chosen Peoples* (Maryknoll, N.Y.: Orbis Books).

Bujo, Bénézet. 1988. "Can Morality Be Christian in Africa?" in *African Christian Studies* 4:1, pp. 5–39.

Bujo, Bénézet. 1998a. *African Christian Morality at the Age of Inculturation* (Nairobi: Paulines Publications Africa).

Bujo, Bénézet. 1998b. *The Ethical Dimensions of Community: The African Model and the Dialogue between North and South* (Nairobi: Paulines Publications Africa).

Bujo, Bénézet. 1999. *African Theology in Its Social Context* (Nairobi: Paulines Publications; Maryknoll, N.Y.: Orbis Books).

Bujo, Bénézet. 2001. *Foundations of an African Ethic: Beyond the Universal Claims of Western Morality* (New York: Crossroad).

Bultmann, Rudolf. 1934. "The Study of the Synoptic Gospels" in Frederick C. Grant, ed. and trans., *Form Criticism: A New Method of New Testament Research* (Chicago/New York: Willet, Clark and Company).

Burke, Horst. 1979. "African Churches' Contribution to the Ecumenical Dialogue" in Institute for Foreign Cultural Relations, Stuttgart & Institute for Scientific Cooperation, Tübingen, *Christian and Islamic Contributions towards Establishing Independent States in Africa South of the Sahara: Papers and Proceedings of the Africa Colloquium* (Bonn-Bad, Godesberg, 2–4 May 1979).

Carmody, Denise L. and John T. Carmody. 1991. *Western Ways to the Center: An Introduction to the Religions of the West* (Belmont, Calif.: Wadsworth Publishing Company).

Catechism of the Catholic Church (CCC). Second edition. 1997 (Vatican: Libreria Editrice Vaticana).

Chidester, David. 2000. *Christianity: A Global History* (London: Penguin Books; San Francisco: HarperSanFrancisco).

Chitando, Ezra. 2000. "Songs of Praise: Gospel Music in an African Context" in *Exchange* 29:4, pp. 296–310.

Comfort, Philip Wesley. 1992. *The Origin of the Bible* (Wheaton, Ill.: Tyndale House).

Coriden, James A., Thomas J. Green and Donald E. Heintschel, eds. 1985. *The Code of Canon Law: A Text and Commentary* (New York/Mahwah: Paulist Press).

Cozzens, Donald B. 2002. *Sacred Silence: Denial and the Crisis in the Church* (Collegeville, Minn.: Liturgical Press).

Croatto, Severino. 1995. *Biblical Hermeneutics: Towards a Theory of Reading as the Production of Meaning* (Maryknoll, N.Y.: Orbis Books).

Crossan, John Dominic. 1991 (1992 ed.). *The Historical Jesus: The Life of a Mediterranean Jewish Peasant* (San Francisco: HarperSanFranciso).

Crossan, John Dominic. 1998. *The Birth of Christianity: Discovering What Happened in the Years Immediately after the Execution of Jesus* (New York: Harper San Francisco).

Crowe, Jerome. 1997. *From Jerusalem to Antioch: The Gospel Across Cultures* (Collegeville, Minn.: Liturgical Press).

Davies, Philip R. and David J. A. Clines, eds. 1998. *The World of Genesis: Persons, Places, Perspectives* (Sheffield: Sheffield Academic Press).

de Mello, Anthony. 1982. *The Song of the Bird* (Garden City, N.Y.: Image Books).

Dillistone, F.W. 1986. *The Power of Symbols in Religion and Culture* (New York: Crossroad/Herder & Herder, 1986; London: SCM Press).

Doornbos, Martin. 1995. "Church and State in Eastern Africa: Some Unsolved Questions" in H. B. Hansen and M. Twaddle, eds., *Religion and Politics in East Africa* (London: Currey), pp. 260–270.

Dorr, Donal. 2000. *Mission in Today's World* (Maryknoll, N.Y.: Orbis Books).

Dupuis, Jacques. 1997. *Toward a Christian Theology of Religious Pluralism* (Maryknoll, N.Y.: Orbis Books).

Ela, Jean-Marc. 1988. *My Faith as an African* (Maryknoll, N.Y.: Orbis Books).

Gaggawala, Paul O. 1999. *Fully Christian . . . Fully Human: A Model for the New Evangelization* (Boca Raton, Fla.: Jeremiah Press).

Gallagher, Michael Paul. 1998. *Clashing Symbols: An Introduction to Faith and Culture* (Mahwah, N.J.: Paulist Press).

Geertz, Clifford. 1973. *The Interpretation of Cultures* (New York: Basic Books).

Getui, Mary, N. Knut Holter and Victor Zinkuratire, eds. 2001. *Interpreting the Old Testament in Africa* (Nairobi: Acton Publishers).

Getui, Mary and Peter Kanyandago, eds. 1999. *From Violence to Peace in Africa: A Challenge for African Christianity* (Nairobi: Acton Publishers).

Getui, Mary, Tinyiko Maluleke and Justin Ukpong, eds. 2001. *Interpreting the New Testament in Africa* (Nairobi: Acton Publishers).

Giddens, Anthony. 1990. *The Consequences of Modernity* (Cambridge: Polity Press).

Gittins, Anthony J., ed. 2000. *Life and Death Matters: The Practice of Inculturation in Africa* (Nettetal, Germany: Steyler Verlag).

Glazier, Michael and Monica Hellwig, eds. 1994. *The Modern Catholic Encyclopedia* (Collegeville, Minn.: Liturgical Press).

Goergen, Donald J. 2001. "A Bibliography of African Christology" in *African Christian Studies* 17:4, pp. 93–97.

Goergen, Donald J. 2001. "The Quest for the Christ of Africa" in *African Christian Studies* 17:1, pp. 5–41.

Groome, Thomas H. 2003. *What Makes Us Catholic: Eight Gifts for Life* (San Francisco: HarperSanFrancisco).

Haight, Roger S. 1990 (2001 ed.). *Dynamics of Theology* (Maryknoll, N.Y.: Orbis Books).

Hall, Stuart G. 1991. *Doctrine and Practice in the Early Church* (Grand Rapids, Mich.: Eerdmans; London: SPCK).

Hannerz, Ulf. 1992. *Cultural Complexity: Studies in the Sociological Organization of Meaning* (New York: Columbia University Press).

Harland, Bryce. 1996. *Collision Course: America and East Asia in the Past and the Future* (Singapore: Institute of Southeast Asian Studies).

Harland, P. J. 1996. *The Value of Human Life: A Study of the Story of the Flood (Gen. 6–9)* (Leiden: Brill).

Harrington, Daniel J. 1981. *Interpreting the Old Testament: A Practical Guide* (Collegeville, Minn.: Liturgical Press).

Harrington, Daniel J. 1990. "The Bible in Catholic Life" in *The Catholic Study Bible: New American Bible* (New York: Oxford University Press), pp. RG 16–30.

Harris, Marvin. 1999. *Theories of Culture in Postmodern Times* (Walnut Creek, Calif.: Altamira Press).

Harvey, A. E. 1970. *Companion to the New Testament* (Oxford: Oxford University Press).

Hastings, Adrian, ed. 1991. *Modern Catholicism: Vatican II and After* (Oxford: Oxford University Press).

Haught, John F. 1987. "Revelation" in Joseph A. Komonchak et al., eds., *The New Dictionary of Theology* (Collegeville, Minn.: Liturgical Press), pp. 884–899.

Healey, Joseph and Donald Sybertz. 1996. *Towards an African Narrative Theology* (Nairobi: Paulines Publications Africa).

Heisey, Nancy R. 2000. *Origen the Egyptian: A Literary and Historical Consideration of the Egyptian Background in Origen's Writings on Martyrdom* (Nairobi: Paulines Publications Africa).

Hilkert, Mary Catherine. 1990. "Preaching, Theology of" in Peter E. Fink, ed., *The New Dictionary of Sacramental Worship* (Collegeville, Minn.: Liturgical Press), pp. 996–1003.

Hillman, Eugene. 1993. *Toward an African Christianity: Inculturation Applied* (Mahwah, N.J.: Paulist Press).

Ibekwe, Patrick. 1998. *Wit and Wisdom of Africa: Proverbs from Africa and the Caribbean* (Oxford: New Internationalist Publications).

Idowu, Bolaji. 1965 (1973 ed.). *Towards an Indigenous Church* (Ibadan: Olusey's Press).

Irarrázaval, Diego. 2000. *Inculturation: New Dawn of the Church in Latin America* (Maryknoll, N.Y.: Orbis Books).

Jenkins, Richard. 1997. *Rethinking Ethnicity: Arguments and Explorations* (London: Sage Publications).

John Paul II. 1982. "Letter to Cardinal Agostino Cassaroli, Secretary of State" in *L'Osservatore Romano*, 20 May 1982, pp. 7–8.

John Paul II. 1990. *Redemptoris Missio* in J. Michael Miller, ed., *The Encyclicals of John Paul II* (Huntington, Ind.: Our Sunday Visitor, 1996), pp. 493–570.

John Paul II. 1995. "Post-synodal Apostolic Exhortation (*Ecclesia in Africa*)" in African Faith & Justice Network. *The African Synod: Documents, Reflections, Perspectives* (Maryknoll, N.Y.: Orbis Books, 1996), pp. 233–286.

Jones, Rufus M. 1924. *The Church's Debt to Heretics* (London: James Clarke).

(A) Journal of Theomusicology. 1993. 7:2 (Fall) (Duke University Press), pp. vi–55 (abbrev. as *JoT*).

Jurgens, William A., ed., vol. I, 1970; vols. II and III, 1979. *The Faith of the Early Fathers* (Collegeville, Minn.: Liturgical Press).

Kanyandago, Peter, ed. 2002. *Marginalizing Africa: An International Perspective* (Nairobi: St. Paul Communications).

Kanyoro, Musimbi R. A. 1999. "Called to One Hope: The Gospel in Diverse Cultures," in J. A. Scherer and S. B. Bevans, eds. *New Directions in Mission and Evangelization 3* (Maryknoll, N.Y.: Orbis Books), pp. 134–145.

Kato, Byang H. 1985. *Biblical Christianity in Africa: A Collection of Papers and Addresses* (Achimota, Ghana: African Christian Press).

Kee, Alistair. 1982. *Constantine Versus Christ* (Valley Forge, Penn.: Trinity Press International; London: SCM).

Kinnamon, Michael and Brian E. Cope, eds. 1997. *The Ecumenical Movement: An Anthology of Key Texts and Voices* (Grand Rapids, Mich.: Eerdmans).

Kinoti, Hannah W. and John Mary Waliggo. 1997. *The Bible in African Christianity: Essays in Biblical Theology* (Nairobi: Acton Publishers).

Knitter, Paul F. 1985. *No Other Name? A Critical Survey of Christian Attitudes toward World Religions* (Maryknoll, N.Y.: Orbis Books).

Knitter, Paul F. 2002. *Introducing Theologies of Religions* (Maryknoll, N.Y.: Orbis Books).

Küng, Hans. 1971. *Infallible? An Inquiry* (Garden City, N.Y.: Doubleday).

Küng, Hans 1995. *Christianity: Essence, History, and Future* (New York: Continuum).

Küster, Volker. 1995. ". . . and Foolishness to the Gentiles: Images of Christ from Africa and Asia" in *Mission Studies* XII, 1:23, pp. 95–112.

Küster, Volker. 1999. "Accommodation or Contextualization? Ketut Lasia and Nyoman Darsane—Two Balinese Christian Artists" in *Mission Studies* XVI, 1:31, pp. 157–172.

Küster, Volker. 2001. "Renunciation of Inculturation as Aesthetic Resistance: The Indian Artist Solomon Raj Seen in a New Light" in *Exchange* 30:4, pp. 359–371.

Lee, Jonathan Scott. 2001. "The Testament of Julius Nyerere" in J. M. Bahemuka and J. L. Brockington, eds., *East Africa in Transition* (Nairobi: Acton Publishers).

Legrand, Lucien. 2000. *The Bible on Culture* (Maryknoll, N.Y.: Orbis Books).

Lumbala, F. Kabasele. 1998. *Celebrating Jesus Christ in Africa: Liturgy and Inculturation* (Maryknoll, N.Y.: Orbis Books).

Luttikhuizen, Gerard P., ed. 1999. *Paradise Interpreted: Representations of Biblical Paradise in Judaism and Christianity* (Leiden: Brill).

Magesa, Laurenti. 1993. "The Church in Eastern Africa: Retrospect and Prospect" in A. Radoli, ed., *How Local Is the Local Church? Small Christian Communities and Church in Eastern Africa—Symposium of Nine Papers* (Eldoret, Kenya: AMECEA Gaba Publications), pp. 3–35.

Magesa, Laurenti. 1997. *African Religion: The Moral Traditions of Abundant Life* (Maryknoll, N.Y.: Orbis Books).

Magesa, Laurenti. 2000. "Oliver Onwubiko: The Church as the Family of God (Ujamaa)—In the Light of 'Ecclesia in Africa.'" Book review in *Exchange* (29:4), pp. 374–76.

Magesa, Laurenti. 2002. *Christian Ethics in Africa* (Nairobi: Acton Publishers).

Maher, Michael. 1982. *Genesis* (Wilmington, Del.: Michael Glazier).

Martey, Emmanuel. 1993. *African Theology: Inculturation and Liberation* (Maryknoll, N.Y.: Orbis Books).

Martinez, Florentino Garcia and Gerard P. Luttikhuizen. 1998. *Interpretations of the Flood* (Leiden: Brill).

Martinot, Steve. 2000. "Introduction: The Double Consciousness," in A. Memmi, et al., *Racism* (Minneapolis: University of Minnesota Press), pp. xv–xxxiv.

Mbiti, John S. 1969. *African Religions and Philosophy* (London: Heinemann).

Mbiti, John S. 1975. *The Prayers of African Religion* (Maryknoll, N.Y.: Orbis Books).

Memmi, Albert et al. 2000. *Racism* (Minneapolis: University of Minnesota Press).

Mijoga, Hilary B. P. 2001. *Preaching and the Bible in African Churches* (Nairobi: Acton Publishers).

Moore, Basil, ed. 1974. *The Challenge of Black Theology in South Africa* (Philadelphia: John Knox Press).

Muga, Erasto. 1975. *African Response to Western Christian Religion: A Sociological Analysis of African Separatist Religious and Political Movements in East Africa* (Nairobi: East African Literature Bureau).

Mugambi, J. N. K. and Laurenti Magesa, eds. 1990. *The Church in African Christianity: Innovative Essays in Ecclesiology* (Nairobi: Initiatives).

Namwera, Leonard and Aylward Shorter et al. 1990. *Towards African Christian Liberation* (Nairobi: St. Paul Publications).

(The) New Encyclopedia Britannica (NEB/4). 1989 ed. (Chicago: The University of Chicago Press).

Neill, Thomas P. and Raymond H. Schmandt. 1957. *History of the Catholic Church* (Milwaukee: The Bruce Publishing Company).

Nketia, J. H. 1958. "The Contribution of African Culture to Christian Worship" in *The Church in Changing Africa: Report of the All Africa Church Conference* (New York: International Missionary Council), pp. 58–65.

Nthamburi, Zablon. 1991. *The African Church at the Crossroads: Strategy for Indigenisation* (Nairobi: Uzima Press).

Nthamburi, Zablon. 2000. *The Pilgrimage of the African Church: Towards the Twenty-First Century* (Nairobi: Uzima Press).

Nyamiti, Charles. 1988. "The Naming Ceremony in the Trinity: An African Onomastic Approach to the Trinity" in *African Christian Studies* 4:1, pp. 41–73.

Nyamiti, Charles. 1993. "An African Ancestral Ecclesiology: Its Relevance for African Local Churches" in A. Radoli, ed., *How Local Is the Local Church? Small Christian Communities and Church in Eastern Africa—Symposium of Nine Papers* (Eldoret, Kenya: AMECEA Gaba Publications), pp. 36–56.

O'Connell, Timothy E. 1990. *Principles for a Catholic Morality: Revised Edition* (New York: Harper Collins).

O'Grady, Ron, ed. 2001. *Christ for All People: Celebrating a World of Christian Art* (Maryknoll, N.Y.: Orbis Books; Geneva: World Council of Churches).

Okolo, Chukwudum, B. 1994. *The African Synod: Hope for the Continent's Liberation* (Eldoret, Kenya: AMECEA Gaba Publications).

Okullu, Henry. 1974. *Church and Politics in East Africa* (Nairobi: Uzima Press).

Okure, Theresa, Paul van Thiele, et al. 1990. *32 Articles Evaluating Inculturation of Christianity in Africa* (Eldoret, Kenya: AMECEA Gaba Publications).

Olowola, Cornelius. 1985. *African Traditional Religion and the Christian Faith* (Igbaja, Nigeria; ECWA Theological Seminary).

Onuh, Charles Ok. 1992. *Christianity and the Rites of Passage: The Prospects of Inculturation* (Frankfurt: Peter Lang).

Paul VI. 1975. *Evangelii Nuntiandi,* in Theresa Okure, Paul van Thiele, et al., eds. *32 Articles Evaluating Inculturation of Christianity in Africa* (Edoret: AMECEA Gaba Publications, 1990).

Pobee, John and F. Carl Hallencreutz, eds. 1986. *Variations in Christian Theology in Africa* (Nairobi: Uzima Press).

Pope, Stephen J. and Charles Hefling. 2002. *Sic et Non: Encountering Dominus Iesus* (Maryknoll, N.Y.: Orbis Books).

Porter, Roy. 2001. *The Enlightenment. Studies in European History* (New York: Palgrave Macmillan).

Quinn, Frederick. 2002. *African Saints: Saints, Martyrs, and Holy People from the Continent of Africa* (New York: Crossroad).

Radoli, Agatha, ed. 1993. *How Local Is the Local Church? Small Christian Communities and the Church in Eastern Africa* (Eldoret, Kenya: AMECEA Gaba Publications).

Rahner, Karl. 1983. *The Shape of the Church to Come,* trans. Edward Quinn (New York: Crossroad).

Ratzinger, Joseph Cardinal. 2000. *The Spirit of the Liturgy,* trans. John Saward (San Francisco: Ignatian Press).

Ricoeur, Paul. 1967. *The Symbolism of Evil* (Boston: Beacon Press).

Ricoeur, Paul. 1981. *Essays on Biblical Interpretation* (Minneapolis: Fortress Press; London: SPCK).

Sanneh, Lamin. 1990. *Translating the Message: The Missionary Impact on Culture* (Maryknoll, N.Y.: Orbis Books).

Scherer, J. A. and S. B. Bevans, eds. 1999. *New Directions in Mission and Evangelization 3* (Maryknoll, N.Y.: Orbis Books).

Schineller, Peter. 1990. *A Handbook of Inculturation* (New York: Paulist Press).

Schnelle, Udo. 1998. *The History and Theology of the New Testament Writings* (Minneapolis: Fortress Press; London: SCM Press).

Sedmak, Clemens. 2002. *Doing Local Theology: A Guide for Artisans of a New Humanity* (Maryknoll, N.Y.: Orbis Books).

Segovia, Fernando F. 2000. *Decolonizing Biblical Studies: A View from the Margins* (Maryknoll, N.Y.: Orbis Books).

Sen, Amartya. 2000. "Beyond Identity: Other People" in *The New Republic* (December 18), pp. 23–30.

Shenk, David W. 1983. *Peace and Reconciliation in Africa* (Nairobi: Uzima Press).

Shorter, Aylward. 1988. *Toward a Theology of Inculturation* (Maryknoll, N.Y.: Orbis Books).

Shorter, Aylward. 1995. *Christianity and the African Imagination after the African Synod: Resources for Inculturation* (Nairobi: Paulines Publications).

Sim, D. C. 1998. *The Gospel of Matthew and Christian Judaism: The History and Social Setting of the Matthean Community* (Edinburgh: T & T Clark).

Stackhouse, Max L. 2000. "General Introduction" in *God and Globalization: Religion and the Powers of the Common Life*, vol. 1, ed. Max L. Stackhouse and Peter J. Paris (Harrisburg, Penn.: Trinity Press).

Theissen, Gerd. 1987. *The Shadow of the Galilean: The Quest of the Historical Jesus in Narrative Form*. Trans. John Bowdon (Philadelphia: Fortress Press).

Tienou, Tite. 1982. *The Theological Task of the Church in Africa* (Achimota, Ghana: African Christian Press).

Tomlinson, John. 1999. *Globalization and Culture* (Chicago: University of Chicago Press).

Tracy, David. 1981. *The Analogical Imagination: Christian Theology and the Culture of Pluralism* (New York: Crossroad/Herder & Herder; London: SCM Press).

Tylor, Edward Burnett. 1871. *Primitive Culture: Researches into the Development of Mythology, Philosophy, Religion, Art, and Custom* (London: J. Murray).

Uzukwu, Eugene E. 1987. "African Personality and the Christian Liturgy" in *African Christian Studies*, 3:2 (June), pp. 61–74.

Uzukwu, Eugene E. 1996. *A Listening Church: Autonomy and Communion in African Churches* (Maryknoll, N.Y.: Orbis Books).

Uzukwu, Eugene E. 1997. *Worship as Body Language: Introduction to Christian Worship—An African Orientation* (Collegeville, Minn.: Liturgical Press).

van Seters, John. 1999. *The Pentateuch: A Social Science Commentary* (Sheffield: Sheffield Academic Press).

Vermez, Geza. 2001. *The Changing Faces of Jesus* (New York: Viking).

Waliggo, John Mary. 1990. "The African Clan as the True Model of the African Church," in J. N. K. Mugambi and L. Magesa, eds., *The Church in African Christianity: Innovative Essays in Ecclesiology* (Nairobi: Initiatives), pp.111–127.

Waliggo, John Mary, Arij A. Roest Crollius, et al. 1986. *Inculturation: Its Meaning and Urgency* (Nairobi: St. Paul Publications).

Walls, Andrew F. 2002. *The Cross-Cultural Process in Christian History* (Maryknoll, N.Y.: Orbis Books).

Weil, Simone. 1952. *The Need for Roots: Prelude to a Declaration of Duties towards Mankind* (London: Routledge & Kegan Paul).

Werblowsky, R. J. Zwi. 1997. *Magie, Mystik, Messianismus: Vergleichende Studien zur Religionsgeschicte des in Zusammenarbeit mit Hermann Simon und Andreas Nachama* (Hildesheim/New York: Olms).

Wijsen, Frans. 2001. "Intercultural Theology and the Mission of the Church" in *Exchange* 30:3, pp. 218–228.

Wijsen, Frans and Ralph Tanner. 2002. *I Am Just a Sukuma: Globalization and Identity in Northwest Tanzania (Church and Theology in Context 41)* (Amsterdam-New York: Editions Rodopi B. V.).

Zaehner, R.C., ed. 1997. *Encyclopedia of Living Faiths* (Oxford: Helicon).

Index